IN DEFIANCE OF OLIGARCHY

The Tory Party 1714–60

IN DEFIANCE OF OLIGARCHY

The Tory Party
1714–60

LINDA COLLEY

Fellow and Lecturer in History,
Christ's College, Cambridge

LIBRARY
BRYAN COLLEGE
DAYTON, TENN. 37321

CAMBRIDGE UNIVERSITY PRESS

CAMBRIDGE

LONDON   NEW YORK   NEW ROCHELLE
MELBOURNE   SYDNEY

84130

Published by the Press Syndicate of the University of Cambridge
The Pitt Building, Trumpington Street, Cambridge CB2 IRP
32 East 57th Street, New York, NY 10022, USA
296 Beaconsfield Parade, Middle Park, Melbourne 3206, Australia

© Cambridge University Press 1982

First published 1982

Printed in Great Britain by
Western Printing Services Ltd

Library of Congress catalogue card number: 81–10004

British Library Cataloguing in Publication Data
Colley, Linda
In defiance of oligarchy.
1. Tories, English – History – 18th century
I. Title
324.241′02   JN1129.T7
ISBN 0 521 23982 6

Contents

For my parents
and Toby

Preface

This book had its origin in a Cambridge University Ph.D. dissertation, 'The Tory Party 1727–60', completed in 1976. Since then, the work's scope and format have been changed more frequently and more radically even than has the domicile of its author. Girton College, Newnham College, King's College, and Christ's College have each in turn given me the shelter and finance necessary to complete this project. I am most grateful to them all. The Henry E. Huntington Library of San Marino, the British Academy, and the Twenty-Seven Foundation of the University of London have also contributed very generously to my work.

Reconstructing the history of a forgotten party in a neglected period of British history made manuscript-hunting more than usually essential, and the assistance I received from English and Welsh Record Offices more than usually welcome. I have to acknowledge the gracious permission of Her Majesty the Queen to consult the Georgian, Stuart and Bootle papers at Windsor Castle. I am also indebted to the Anson Trustees, the duke of Bedford, the Trustees of the Chatsworth Settlement, the marquess of Cholmondeley, the marquess of Northampton, Viscount De L'Isle, Sir J. G. Carew Pole, Sir Richard and Lady Elizabeth Hamilton, Miss A. Bagot, Mr Thomas Cottrell-Dormer, and Mrs Gwen Beachcroft for allowing me access to the manuscript collections in their care. As my endnotes demonstrate, the work of the History of Parliament Trust has proved invaluable, as have its transcripts of eighteenth-century documents, which Mr E. L. C. Mullins so often and so patiently made available to me.

It would be impossible for me to do justice to all the scholars and friends who have read and commented on earlier versions of this book. I have acknowledged individual contributions in the relevant endnotes and shall confine myself here to mentioning two outstanding debts. This topic was first suggested to me by Professor John Cannon, now of the University of Newcastle upon Tyne. His belated and somewhat dubious reward was to receive the penultimate draft of this book, which he criticised with the same blend of skill, wisdom, and caustic wit that he gave to my first undergraduate essays in eighteenth-century history. I can only hope that the finished product will repay some of his time and trouble. My research at Cambridge was supervised by Professor J. H. Plumb, now Master of Christ's College. That the premier biographer of Sir Robert Walpole should promote work on a bunch of dissonant tories is some indication of Jack Plumb's generosity and historical verve. He has never failed in his support, encouragement, and incisive advice and I am most grateful for all his help.

Jan Colley, Ruth Cigman, Doron Swade, John Lyon, and two friends who shall be nameless not only contributed more to this book than they might imagine, but also tolerated and sustained its author.

L.J.C.
Christ's College, Cambridge
1981

PART I

_____

The Problem of Tory Survival

The Nature of the Challenge

All's whiggery now,
But we old men are massed against the world.
W. B. Yeats, 'The Seven Sages',
The Winding Stair and other Poems (1933), 23.

Much greater ingenuity and a much higher imaginative endeavour have been brought into play upon the whigs, progressives and even revolutionaries of the past, than have been exercised upon the elucidation of tories and conservatives and reactionaries.
Herbert Butterfield, *The Whig Interpretation of History* (1931), 95.

As an explanation of why those tories who were excluded from political power between 1715 and 1760 have been deprived of scholarly attention since Keith Feiling's unsatisfactory 1938 study, *The Second Tory Party*, Yeats' poetry is more illuminating than Butterfield's prose. Chronicling mid-nineteenth-century British toryism is after all a growth industry. A historiographical world in which Michael Foot can take Lord Butler to task for impugning Benjamin Disraeli's integrity – and this under the title of 'The Tory as Hero' – may be confusing, but is clearly not uncaring.[1] Disraeli however had the wit to pass a Reform Act and write provocative novels; the martyrdom of his antagonist Robert Peel brought middle-class plaudits and Gladstonian liberalism in its wake. Mid-eighteenth-century tories by contrast have been neglected not because of their bias, not even because their fortitude in adversity was, in the end, unavailing, but rather because it has been assumed that even in their own time they were obsolete.

It was not just the nineteenth-century whig Lord Macaulay, drawing on the novels of an eighteenth-century whig Henry Fielding, who described the tory gentleman of Georgian times as a picturesque relic – 'boorish, stupid, unlettered...of good heart and no wit', a rural mammoth stranded in the age of Mammon – but also the judicious Sir William Holdsworth, writing in 1938.

At the beginning of George I's reign the majority of the landowners were Tories. The Whigs drew their support both from the more progressive commercial classes, and from men of sufficient independence of mind to be dissenters from the national church...The Whig aristocracy included a large part of the best intellect of the nation. It included men who were in touch with the most modern political, economic, and scientific ideas; men whose outlook was towards the ideas of the future, and not to the theological and royalist ideas of the past. And since England, from the sixteenth century onwards, has known no impassable class barriers, there was a constant tendency towards an intermixture of the more conservative landed and the more progressive mercantile classes. This made for the gradual permeation throughout the nation of the more modern ideas for which the Whigs stood.[2]

Even Daniel A. Baugh, writing in the 1970s, invites us to contemplate what would have happened to England in 1714 'if the Whig monopoly of government had not supervened'. The nation would have fallen into the hands of the tories – a party which Baugh identifies not with the landowners *tout court* but with that equally imprecise social category, the landed gentry, who, he tells us, 'implied anarchy in national politics'.

The bulk of the Tory gentry was at bottom independent and unruly, and Tory religious policy was dangerously divisive. Moreover, the party's turbulent allies in the City of London, the lesser merchants and tradesmen who...resented the power of the great financial institutions on which the government relied, were hardly a stable element in politics. It is therefore easy to imagine a continuation of the party strife that marked Queen Anne's reign if the Tory party had remained organised as a potential force in government.

Fortunately for England the tory party succumbed after 1714 to the brilliant politics of Robert Walpole, who bestowed on the nation one-party government, peace, stability, and an efficient executive. On these achievements were founded commercial expansion, the growth of empire, and the benign government of 'a small body of whig aristocrats'. 'They were not democrats', Baugh remarks, perhaps gratuitously, of this elite, 'but they paved the way for democracy through parliamentary means.'[3]

Such roseate history would not be worth opposing if it did not reproduce in distorted form one of the most brilliant, multi-faceted, and durable interpretations of England's development in the seventeenth and eighteenth centuries. In 1967 J. H. Plumb published his Ford Lectures of two years earlier, as *The Growth of Political Stability in England 1675–1725*. The impact of this work was deservedly immense, and its main theme was reinforced by Geoffrey Holmes' survey of high politics in the reign of Queen Anne and W. A. Speck's examination of the Augustan electorate.[4]

Plumb's aim was to elucidate the process whereby a turbulent seventeenth-century England, inured to 'conspiracy, plot and invasion', managed to acquire in the next century political stability – a condition he defined as 'the acceptance by society of its political institutions, and of those classes of men or officials who control them'. From the 1650s onwards England's executive – her revenue departments, her Treasury, her army and navy administration – grew in size and efficiency, but for three reasons this refinement of the 'core of government' did not immediately result in a strong centralised state. Between 1660 and 1688 England was perplexed by continuing conflict between her monarchs and her centrifugal landed gentry. After 1688 the patronage and employment supplied by executive growth only fostered rivalry between the whig and tory sections of the landed elite. And, Plumb argued, because the post-revolutionary tory party came increasingly to attract the independent lesser landed gentry outside Parliament, as well as the more vociferous critics of centralised government inside Parliament, political stability was bound to remain elusive for as long as the tory party had the chance of a share or – as in 1710–14 – a near monopoly of state employment.

Holmes and Speck, engaged like Plumb in smiting the a-party historical analysis of Robert Walcott, also used their books to supply cogent and extensive evidence of the vitality of whig and tory party alignments and ideology at Westminster in Anne's reign. Like Plumb, too, they stressed the growth and frequent independence of England's electorate. Between 1689 and 1714, largely because of the 1694 Triennial Act, the country experienced twelve general elections: 'scarcely a borough avoided a poll, and the majority were fought time and time again'. Electoral pressure, they argued, not only magnified the real and propaganda divisions between the two parties, but also unsettled successive administrations: 'until this electorate was reduced, subjected, or prevented from voting', wrote Plumb, 'there was no hope whatsoever that England would achieve political stability'.[5]

In describing so vividly the flux and tensions of late-seventeenth- and early-eighteenth-century politics and society, these historians all posed themselves the same explanatory problem. How was the infinite variety of late Stuart England, which such extensive and scholarly custom had proved unable to stale, transmogrified into the stability of the reigns of George I and George II? For few historians doubted that these reigns were stable (just as few undergraduates doubted that their stability also implied dullness). The years between 1714 and 1760, according to Basil Williams – that is, the years which witnessed two Jacobite invasions, the Excise Crisis, Britain's imperial take-off, the emergence of Methodism, the development of the novel form and the provincial newspaper, a crucial stage in urbanisation, entrepreneurial activity, and population growth, and the first real signs of nascent trade unionism – were 'an age of stability in politics, in religion, in literature, and in social observances'.[6]

Plumb's analysis of the causes of instability inevitably determined his account of the pre-conditions of England's reputed stability in the mid eighteenth century. The conflict between whig and tory had to give way to one-party government and to one-party *whig* government. A volatile, frequently exercised electorate had to be rendered docile by the Septennial Act of 1716 and by a decline in contested elections. The patronage made available by a growing and increasingly complex executive had to be confined to whig sympathisers, and to those rich and influential elements in society whom it would be dangerous to leave unappeased. The transition from instability to stability, Plumb claimed, was a rapid one; much of the credit was to be given to the ruthless endeavours of Robert Walpole; and essential to this process and his success was a tory *Götterdämmerung*. After 1715,

The Tory party was destroyed, destroyed by its incompetent leadership, by the cupidity of many of its supporters, by its own internal contradictions; weakened by its virtues and lashed by events, it proved no match for Walpole ...By 1725, Tories were outcasts...By 1733...Toryism as far as power politics at the centre was concerned had become quite irrelevant.[7]

There was of course a certain tension between Plumb's assertion that one of the foundations of Hanoverian England's stability was the 'sense of common identity' which prevailed among those who wielded political, economic, and social power, and the familiar assumption that in late Stuart and Augustan England the bulk of the landed class was tory. How was Walpole able both to proscribe tories from government and to put 'gentlemen back at the heart of English political society'? Plumb's solution was twofold. First, he claimed that most tory peers and premier landlords soon realised that their party's proscription was irreversible and consequently lost no time in defecting to the whigs. Second, he drew on the economic analysis of Sir John Habakkuk.

In two seminal articles Habakkuk had argued that between 1680 and 1740 the decline in agricultural prices attendant on an increase in production and a stable population, combined with high taxation on land during the Nine Years War and the War of Spanish Succession, forced many lesser landowners to sell out. Their estates were purchased, he claimed, not by *nouveaux riches* merchants and financiers who found the new London stock market a more attractive source of investment, but by landowners already possessed of substantial acreage. In true biblical fashion, those landowners who already had much, acquired more; those with very little, lost even that which they had. While Plumb pointed out that many mid-eighteenth-century tory M.P.s were in fact substantial landowners, several less subtle historians succumbed to the temptations of neat economic determinism. It was so convenient to assume that this decline in small landowners was the economic counterpart to the political decline of the tory party; that the increasing rigidity of the eighteenth-century land market which Habakkuk had postulated was the necessary libretto to the operatic extravaganza which was whig oligarchy and Walpolian success.[8]

It is this combination of supposed economic obsolescence and supposed political impotence which has made the proscribed tory party so unattractive to historians. From a twentieth-century liberal or socialist perspective, eighteenth-century rioters, criminals, shopkeepers, and (just occasionally) middle-class professionals are deserving of study because later centuries have conferred on these groups ideological significance and/or limited political power. Tory landed gentlemen by contrast are assumed to be not only too disreputable and ineffective to attract the afficionados of cabinet intrigue and economic progress, but also too classbound to warrant close attention from those historians who focus on the socially dispossessed.

The prime contention of this book is that such neglect is mistaken; that the tory parliamentary party retained ideological identity, a capacity for concerted political action, and considerable economic power during its proscription; and that consequently the current orthodoxies about pre-1715 political instability, about political stability between 1715 and 1760, and about the rapidity and novelty of political change after 1760 need to be substantially modified. What the rest of this chapter is intended to do is first, to argue that economic development in no way predicated tory political decline after 1715, and second, to advance a different chronology and suggest rather different causes for such growth in English political stability as occurred between the mid seventeenth and mid eighteenth centuries.

The eighteenth and nineteenth centuries certainly witnessed a drift of landed property in favour of the large landowner, but it is likely that this process accelerated only after 1750. As Christopher Clay, B. A. Holderness, and T. H. Hollingsworth have demonstrated, such consolidation in English and Welsh landed estates as did occur before 1750 varied with each county, and often owed more to demographic accident than to aristocratic calculation.[9] And there is no evidence that changes in eighteenth-century English landed society favoured whigs more than tories. Warwickshire and Northamptonshire – two counties where established families do seem to have increased their land-holdings between 1650 and 1750 – were dominated throughout by tory landlords.

A survey of the proscribed tory parliamentary party does throw up some examples of impoverished landowners – the resonantly named Sir Boteler Chernock, M.P. for Bedford, and Sir William Pole, who was ruined by successive contests at Honiton – but far more representative of their party were the Wodehouses, the Pophams, the Strangways, the Holtes, the Portmans, and the Trevanions, all entrenched county families with annual rentals of over £4000.[10]

Individual tory case-histories also confirm the continuing vitality of the eighteenth-century land market. John Rush, the son of a vinegar distiller, purchased his estate only three years before he was returned for Wallingford as a tory in 1741. Much of the unprecedented flux in landed property in Georgian Wiltshire was owing to the purchases of two tory dynasts. William Beckford used some of the profits of his West Indian sugar plantations to buy 4000 acres in the county in 1736; he was to buy another Wiltshire estate in 1762. Beckford's chief competitor was Henry Hoare, the great tory banker and one-time M.P. for Salisbury. Hoare and his father poured £46 000 of City-derived cash into purchasing the manor of Stourton in Wiltshire as well as estates in Dorset. Hoare's profession and his connections – his wife was the daughter of the tory Lord Masham, and he married his own daughters to the tory Lords Bruce and Orrery – stand as a reminder that socially cohesive as they indubitably were, tory M.P.s and peers were neither socially homogeneous nor tending towards impoverishment.[11]

The great majority of tory M.P.s (like the great majority of whig Members) were landed men, but, *pace* John Owen, tories could be made as well as born. Why otherwise would Charles Gray, the son of a whig glazier, and Samuel Savill, the son of a mercer, choose to stand as tory candidates for whig-dominated Colchester in 1741? Why did Philip Henry Warburton, the son of a Presbyterian minister, Edmund Lechmere, son of one whig M.P. and nephew to another, Isaac Whittington, the son of a haberdasher, Henry Pacey, the son of a yeoman, and a gaggle of merchants and industrialists – Ambrose Crowley, Sir Robert Ladbroke, Henry Marshall, Thomas Coster, Richard Fydell, Felix Calvert, Richard Lockwood, John Walter, and Thomas Best – all attach themselves to the tory party, if toryism was only the hereditary perquisite of country-gentry status? The reason usually given is that many of these M.P.s represented the great commercial cities, where an opposition and particularly a tory opposition stance paid electoral dividends. But once one acknowledges the electoral rapport between toryism and the centres of population and trade, it becomes rather difficult to interpret tory decline in terms of a rural-based party overtaken by economic diversification and social change.[12]

It is indeed arguable that for some tories, as for some nonconformists, political deprivation was an incentive to entrepreneurship and investment. Tory politicians would certainly have been more restive had not so many of them found distraction from and consolation for their proscription in intensive and profitable economic activity. By 1720 the development of the Strand and St Martin's Lane in London was bringing the tory earl of Salisbury £3263 *per annum* – more than a third of his estate income. The Grosvenors bribed their voters in Cheshire with the proceeds of their estate in Mayfair. The second Lord Foley derived £7000 a year from his Worcestershire ironworks and was reputed at his death in 1766 to have had £500 000 in the funds.[13] The fifth and sixth Lords Ward of Birmingham exploited their mines and their employees around that town, and lent one of their family names – Dudley – to the 'best thoroughfare and trading street' in Wolverhampton. Namier's archetypal tory M.P., Sir Roger Newdigate, combined a seat at Oxford University with canal-building and coal-mining in North Warwickshire. Sir John Hynde Cotton, fourth baronet, inherited from his father an estate in Cambridgeshire and an unequalled collection of royalist ephemera; from his father-in-law – yet another tory M.P., Humphry Parsons – an interest in the Red Lion Brewery, which he went on to manage, in Lower East Smithfield.[14] (The increasing confluence of mid-century tory M.P.s and metropolitan radicals was to be sustained by economic contacts and inter-marriage, as well as by the two groups' common alienation from the ministry. When James Sharp, a radical Common Councilman and a future ally of John Wilkes, bought himself into a London business in 1759, he did so with money lent by his cousin, the wife of the leading Somerset tory Thomas Prowse.) And tory benefit from economic diversification was not confined to the parliamentary party. Edward Cave, the tory entrepreneur who founded the hugely successful *Gentleman's Magazine*, also invested £750 in Lewis Paul's spinning machine in 1740 – a transaction facilitated by their common friend, Dr Samuel Johnson.[15]

Fewer tory than whig peers and M.P.s held Bank of England stock before 1760, but the number who did so rose steadily throughout this period – a sign both of increasing tory economic modernity and of increasing tory acquiescence in the Hanoverian state. At least sixteen tory M.P.s owned Bank stock in the 1727–34 Parliament, twenty-two in its successor, and thirty-three in the 1741–7 Parliament.[16] The private London banks met with no economic resistance from the tory parliamentary party or from its gentry and mercantile supporters. Indeed, one of the main reasons why the great tory banking houses of Hoare's and Child's were able to survive the financial upsets of the first and third

decades of the eighteenth century was that both put increasing emphasis
on attracting a landowning – especially a tory landowning – clientele.
The duke of Beaufort and Lords Bruce, Thanet, and Berkeley of Stratton
all kept accounts at Child's, as did county tories like Sir Walter Bagot,
Sir Thomas Sebright, and Sir Richard Warwick Bampfylde.[17] In the
same way, the tories' avowed distaste for the stock market was exorcised
by the suitably partisan origin of the South Sea Company, founded in
1711 by Robert Harley. In July 1720 Robert Walpole was to purchase
£2000 of South Sea stock; so also was the leading tory M.P., Sir
William Wyndham. 'When we come to Exchange Ally', a journalist
had written just one month earlier, 'We hear Whigs and Tories...like
People in a General Business, all their Animosities are laid aside.'[18] If
Bolingbroke and his nostalgic and disgruntled retinue were correct, and
Georgian England did succumb to the mores of the counting-house,
whig and tory must share the blame or credit.[19]

Whig political supremacy, then, was not dictated by economic change;
was the political subordination of the tory party after 1714 the necessary
price of political stability? England was obviously a far more stable state
in 1750 than she had been a hundred years earlier, but the enormity of
the contrast between the Pelhamite and Interregnum eras can be misleading. The events of 1649 and 1688 may have led the absolute princes
of Europe to regard England with self-congratulatory horror, but in the
sixteenth and early seventeenth centuries England had been, by European
standards, a remarkably stable nation.[20] In the 1560s the Scots enforced
the abdication of their Queen; the Netherlands revolted against Spanish
rule; the Swedish nobility deposed their King; France became embroiled
in civil war; and what of England? England had the Northern rebellion
– as messy and abortive as were most Tudor rebellions, and led, like
the rest, by men who avowed their fundamental loyalty to the Prince. As
for the supposedly recalcitrant gentry of early Stuart Parliaments,
modern scholarship has so absolved them from the charge of plotting a
concerted assault on royal authority, that one is occasionally brought to
wonder why it was that the Civil War ever occurred. Occur it did,
however; its short-term impact on the Crown, the Church and the
peerage was seismic; and its impact on the landed elite, the lower orders,
and English political theory was far more protracted.[21]

But, as Lawrence Stone has wisely remarked, it was largely because
it had been lulled into social complacency by pre-Civil War English
stability, that the nation's elite allowed itself to be edged into a disruptive
and internecine war in 1642. The mistake was not repeated. 'No doubt
there might have been a revolution in 1681, if the memories of 1642
had been less vivid', Betty Behrens has written. 'The lesson of 1642,

however, had been thoroughly learnt: Revolution meant social upheaval,
insecurity of life and property, and military despotism.' It is indeed
arguable that the landed Parliaments of the 1660s, 1670s, and early
1680s were so mesmerised by the spectre of social dislocation that the
Civil War had revealed to them that they sometimes ignored or tolerated
the threats to their authority posed by Charles II and James II.[22]

For it is in the decades after the Restoration that we see the social
pre-conditions of stable, landed political power being ensured. The first
Game Act, restricting the killing of game to men with landed qualifications, was passed in 1671. This marked the beginning of an exponential
increase in capital offences against property, especially landed property,
which was to disfigure English law until the 1830s. Having curtailed
the Crown's power to tax the landed elite, Parliament began to place
more emphasis on socially regressive taxation like the 1671 additional
excise on beer and ale. In 1757 Lord Chancellor Hardwicke, in a rare
moment of populism, was to refer to 'the bargain, which the nobility
and gentry made with the Crown soon after the Restoration, when they
purchased out their own burdens by the tenures and wardships by laying
an excise upon beer and ale to be consum'd by the common people; for
those liquors, when brewed in private houses, are not subjected to it'.[23]
At the same time as the canaille were being exposed to more rigorous
laws and taxes, socially aspiring plebs were losing some of their very
limited opportunities for higher education. It has been estimated that
students describing themselves as sons of plebeians made up over 50 per
cent of Oxford University's student body in the 1570s; even in 1660
about 150 students in this category were admitted to the University. By
1680 the comparable figure was only 100 and the decline continued
into the eighteenth century.[24]

And below the surface-turmoil of high-political and parliamentary
activity in the reigns of Charles II and James II, three of the crucial
components of Sir Robert Walpole's state system were gradually if un-
steadily evolving. Between 1673 and 1679 Lord Treasurer Danby
explored some of the ways in which the executive might use state
patronage to manage Parliament. The growth of the Treasury, the Navy
Office, the Pay Office, and the Customs and Excise departments increased both governmental efficiency and patronage fodder. One historian
has even claimed that 'most of the essential features of [the] "financial
revolution" – the notion of a National Bank...the securing of Treasury
supremacy and the institution of a modern system of debt management'
had been pioneered before the Glorious Revolution.[25]

The Revolution of 1688, a polite and economical affair in comparison
with the Civil War, was far more decisive in terms of high politics. The

tension between the Crown and the landed elite – the persistent if un-acknowledged *Leitmotif* of seventeenth-century English political conflict – was largely resolved. The struggle for primacy became internalised within the landed elite itself and this struggle was mediated by way of the whig and tory alignments. But despite its superficial extremism, whig and tory rivalry in the reigns of William III and Queen Anne was not at base a source of political instability; rather it was a stylised, often ruthless, conflict which took place within a social consensus; a manifestation of the confidence and fundamental political unison of England's landed elite.

There is nothing new about this seemingly bizarre analysis. 'Parties in the State', John Toland remarked coolly in 1717, 'are just of the like with Heresies in the Church: sometimes they make it better, and some-times they make it worse; but held within due Bounds, they always keep it from stagnation.'[26] From 1688 to at least 1708, party was held within due bounds. This was partly due to the stubbornness and craft of William and Anne – two monarchs of widely differing temperaments and abilities but alike in toughness. One reason why Walpole was able to become so powerful and therefore seem so indispensable to stable government in the 1720s and 1730s was that George I and George II exercised less royal initiative than did these two last Stuart sovereigns. Both William and Anne were insistent on their right to supervise and mediate between the contending parties, and this stern royal surveillance was a consider-able (and often forgotten) guarantee of political equilibrium. The fact that both monarchs favoured mixed administrations encouraged many (though not all) careerist politicians to moderate their partisan prejudices, and mixed administrations prevented that substantial high-political re-sentment which, as Robert Harley foresaw, would be the concomitant of prolonged one-party government.[27]

But, it will be objected, was not Augustan England's ruling elite rent asunder by issues of fundamental importance as well as by the struggle for power?[28] Arguably, no. The issues which divided whig and tory in Anne's reign were very far from cosmetic, indeed, they continued to be operative long after the Hanoverian Succession in 1714, but they were not as clear-cut, or felt to the same degree by all party sympathisers, as contemporary propaganda might suggest. There was, predictably, a great difference between the extremism of a whig or tory constituency activist, the vociferous prejudice of an ill-informed whig or tory back-bencher, and the more muted sentiments of those responsible whig and tory ministers who assisted the Queen in actually conducting policy.

Only thirty of all the M.P.s elected to Anne's five Parliaments were dissenters. Whig and tory Members might differ over how far the

Church of England was to be protected in her special status, and over how far, if at all, dissenters were to be tolerated, but their near-unanimous Anglicanism was crucial to stability. It ensured for instance that while the tories after 1710 had sound reasons to be nervous of a Hanoverian monarch, and while alarmist foreign observers predicted a civil war when Anne died, the tories in fact joined the whigs in quietly accepting and advancing the Hanoverian Succession in 1714, motivated in part by their aversion to the Catholicism of the rival Stuart claimant.[29]

Church versus Dissent remained – and was to remain under the Hanoverians – the most obvious way in which divisions in the constituencies mirrored and sustained those at Westminister. But in England as in the rest of Europe, religion's capacity for civil disruption was muted and contained in the eighteenth century. The Sacheverell affair is the showpiece of Anglican enthusiasm, yet one can still detect in it signs of a curious moderation. Dr Henry Sacheverell was, after all, given a parliamentary trial and he was also set at liberty. He was not branded, or mutilated, or flogged, or subjected to the prolonged, debilitating bouts of imprisonment which had been the lot of Anglican, dissenting, and Catholic zealots between 1630 and 1688. In March 1710 Sacheverell's London supporters staged a large and destructive riot: but it was a disciplined riot, which claimed only two lives. The Doctor's case was discussed in a barrage of pamphlets and broadsides which testified both to the scale of its notoriety and to a society sufficiently relaxed to dispense with strict censorship. And the very fact that it was the practice of Occasional Conformity which provoked some of the Doctor's fiercest polemics is a reminder that, by the Augustan era, the heroic age of Dissent was over.[30] At Westminster especially, it was the hypocrisy and whiggism of ambitious nonconformists, rather than Dissent itself, which was the main tory bugbear. In the 1714 debates on the Schism Bill (initiated by Lord Bolingbroke primarily to embarrass his ministerial rival, Lord Oxford), neither Bolingbroke's ally, Lord Bathurst, nor the High-Church M.P. for Oxford University, William Bromley, adopted a stance of *ecrasez l'infâme* on Dissent. Both were prepared to let nonconformist academies continue in their work of indoctrination, if the invariably whig dissenters would acquiesce in their own disfranchisement.[31]

From 1701 at least until the Battle of Malplaquet in 1709, the parties were agreed on the need for a war to contain France. They differed over more detailed questions of strategy, the extent to which Britain should co-operate with her continental allies, and the timing and terms of the peace. Here, as in religious affairs, party polarisation was often a corollary rather than a cause of party rivalry. The whigs' championship of 'No Peace without Spain' stemmed not only from the party's more ready acceptance of Britain's European responsibilities, but also from the partisan consideration that the Hanoverian heir took the same attitude. Similarly the tory insistence on the need for a speedy peace on terms advantageous to Britain if not to her allies derived not only from tory insularity, but also from an opposition party's appreciation that by 1710 the bulk of the electorate wanted an end to war. The earl of Nottingham was to leave the tory party over the Treaty of Utrecht, but even after his defection he remained resolute in defending the tories from whig accusations of unreasoning pacifism: 'Even till very lately they were as forward to prosecute the war as any whatsoever, for there is not an instance of any one Tory of any note who ever opposed, or gave his negative to the necessary supplies.'[32] Nottingham's observation is important, given the persistent belief that the war led to a rift in British society which partly corresponded to the division between whig and tory. 'The political sparks produced by the friction between the landed and the monied interests', W. A. Speck has remarked, '... generated heat so fierce that it threatened to melt the foundations of the political nation.'[33]

Yet as Colin Brooks has argued, if the 'conflict of interests' in Augustan society involved more than a partisan squabble over the London money market, one would have to prove that it had provincial and national ramifications. If the majority of squires were tory, and if they spent the War of Spanish Succession fulminating over the Land Tax, why was the Land Tax always paid? The answer is simple enough. The Land Tax was ratified by Parliament – the organ of the landed classes – so landed men of whatever party persuasion accepted the levy even if they grumbled at its misapplication. Gentry acquiescence was facilitated by the way the tax was administered. Although Land Tax Commissioners were sometimes appointed on a partisan basis, the Land Tax collectors, who did the bulk of the work, were a-party, local men, chosen for their 'stake in society'.[34]

Of course Jonathan Swift and Bolingbroke stigmatised the exaction and played on the squirearchy's fear of social dispossession, when they were writing to prepare the nation for a tory peace. But the real tory (and often whig) gentry objection to wartime taxation was not so much its incidence on land, as its inability to tap the new monied incomes. This emerges clearly from the tory response to Walpole's Excise Bill of 1733. P. G. M. Dickson has quoted a speech from that year by Joseph Danvers, M.P. for Bramber:

The Landed Gentlemen bore the greatest Share of the late War; by that they had been loaded with many heavy taxes: by that were all the Funds created out of which the Plumb Men of the City of London have made most of their estates, by which they are enabled to deck their Wives in velvet and rich Brocades, while poor Country Gentlemen are hardly able to afford their Wives a Gown of Lindsey Woolsey.

'Danvers and other squires', comments Dickson, 'must have felt that war finance, by depressing their class and elevating the monied interest, had made a mockery of the triumph of Liberty and Property in 1688.' Dickson omits to mention that Danvers was not a disgruntled tory squire, but a ministerialist M.P. What he and other government spokesmen were endeavouring to do in 1733 was to appropriate traditional tory arguments against heavy taxation on land, in order to support the Excise Bill. The tories' immunity to these arguments and opposition to the Excise scheme, which would have reduced the Land Tax, suggest that they recognised these polemics for what they were: propaganda and not accurate economic analysis.[35]

As for the monied men, it is of course true that the London money market prospered from and was crucial to Britain's war with Louis XIV. Between 1702 and 1713 31.4 per cent of English war expenditure was financed by public loans. Since this was a slightly higher percentage than was to be obtained for the 1739–48 war effort, one must suppose that her creditors at least believed in Augustan England's fundamental stability. Most of these major creditors were certainly whig. But having said this, one immediately has to make an important distinction. Was tory criticism of the Bank of England, of the New East India Company, and of the stock market primed by the party's aversion to this form of economic enterprise, or by partisan dislike of whigs and whig auxiliaries? Both the tory experience before 1688 and the tory experience between 1710 and 1714 suggest that the latter was the real irritant.[36]

In the 1680s the major government creditors in London – the Royal African Company, the Old East India Company, and individual financiers like Charles Duncombe – were all tory. Having lent extensively to Charles II and James II, Duncombe tried in 1689 to ingratiate himself with William III by lending him £20 000 at 6 per cent interest. His initiative was wasted. William gave his favour increasingly to the whigs, and that party earned his favour by inaugurating its own, more advanced, credit system. The Bank of England, masterminded by the Junto whig Charles Montagu in 1694, had only two London tories as Directors during William's reign, as against twenty-three London whigs. It was not surprising that aggrieved tories like Duncombe hated the Bank. Nor is it surprising that when Harley established his administration in 1710, and coupled tory self-interest once more to the London money market, many of these tory scruples evaporated. In May 1711 (partly to compensate for the tories' lack of success in the Bank of

England's internal elections in April), Harley set up the South Sea Company, in which tories hastened to invest. He went on to appease the Bank by using it as receiver in three of the four lottery loans floated in 1711 and 1712, thereby covering the revenue deficit and enabling Britain to emerge from the war financially sound. In 1717 and looking back to the reign of Anne, the tory M.P. and economist Archibald Hutcheson was to focus on the machinery of state finance as the major area of agreement between whig and tory: 'How much soever they may have differed in other Points of Politicks, they have in this perfectly agreed...and in their several Turns have spoken the same words.'[37]

But if post-revolutionary ideological and social tensions 'never remotely threatened to destroy the political system', did the Augustan tory party's inferior capacity for parliamentary cohesion and its persistent suspicion of the executive prejudice English governmental stability?[38] If the tory sector was as disruptive as has sometimes been suggested, it seems strange that in the period 1688–1714 – when the tories were almost always a majority in Parliament – England was nonetheless able to fight and win the largest and most expensive war Europe had ever known. And when in 1710 Robert Harley, the future earl of Oxford, became, against his will, first Minister of a predominantly tory administration, he scarcely demonstrated the incompatibility of tory dominance with effective government. Between 1710 and 1714 Oxford lost only one major division in the Commons. He endeavoured to bring Scotland to heel by a deft allocation of patronage, and intensified executive control by insisting in 1711 that all sales and purchases of army commissions must in future be sanctioned by the Crown. He established a productive relationship with the City and upstaged the whigs in using journalists as government auxiliaries. He negotiated a peace which can be criticised in detail, but which shaped British foreign policy for some thirty years, and he dealt with the social dislocation of food shortages and a returning soldiery without recourse to a Riot Act.[39]

Of course the tory party's large Country wing, inflated by the 1710 and still more by the 1713 election, complicated parliamentary management and, occasionally, executive efficiency. In March 1711 Harley's proposal for a heavy excise on leather foundered, as Plumb has noted, on the rock of concerted resistance by the 150 or so tory backbenchers who made up the October Club. But it is noticeable that this manoeuvre was regarded by many tory commentators as both exceptional and wrong. 'If they oppose the methods of raising the money without showing better', wrote one tory courtier, 'they would be reckon'd so ill a Parliament as not to be trusted another session.' Shortly after, when Harley cracked the whip and threatened to prorogue Parliament, the

Octobrists tamely submitted to a disguised Leather Tax.[40] And normally Country tories lacked the organisation, the parliamentary assiduity, and the talent to disrupt government in this way. Once the October Club had folded – as it had by 1712 – one wonders just how troublesome Oxford would have found his backbenchers, had they not received encouragement and direction from Oxford's rival, Viscount Bolingbroke – 'the eloquent spokesman of many inaudible persons', as Bagehot, with an eye to Disraeli's antics in 1846, was to style him.[41]

Only perhaps in one area did Country sentiments succeed in obstructing Oxford for any period of time. Winning eight of the ten general elections held between 1689 and 1713, tory M.P.s regarded the electorate with understandable complacency, and when in 1713 and again in 1714 Oxford contemplated repealing the 1694 Triennial Act, his eventual withdrawal may have been prompted by adverse party opinion.[42] But as the tories' electoral record demonstrates, Augustan England's so-called 'volatile' electorate was not in fact volatile at all: it was almost invariably tory. And while frequent elections might redound to the whigs' disadvantage, they did not of themselves necessarily lead to ministerial flux. Nor was a large electorate a completely novel phenomenon. J. H. Plumb's conservative estimate of 200 000 voters in 1689 and Geoffrey Holmes' more generous calculation of 340 000 voters by 1722 have yet to be reconciled with Derek Hirst's suggestion that, out of a smaller population, 300 000 men may have been able to claim enfranchisement in 1640. Why the pre-Civil War period should have witnessed electoral expansion is fairly clear. Not only had the Commons enfranchised new boroughs so as to increase its numerical strength, but the growing attractions of a seat in Parliament had also led to an increase in contested elections and to more men being encouraged or compelled by their social superiors to vote. An increased electorate, in other words, had come into being at the will of the landed elite. To a considerable degree it was to serve as the creature of that landed elite and continue to do so well into the nineteenth century.[43]

It is of course as unwise to generalise on either voter deference or voter independence for the seventeenth century as for the eighteenth and nineteenth centuries. Voting behaviour always varied in accordance with the individual voter, the landed structure of different counties, and the political climate in which a general election occurred. It is likely however that throughout the late seventeenth and the eighteenth century complete independence was enjoyed only by a minority of voters. As far as Queen Anne's reign was concerned, such a contention may seem perverse, given historians' emphasis on the comparative freedom of the freeholder vote, and on the political significance of what Holmes has

called the 'National Will'. Yet however electorally active the Augustan
era may now appear to be in comparison with the mid eighteenth
century, its more frequent contests and triennial elections only lent a
specious appearance of vitality to a distorted and narrow representative
system. And it is important to note that that system was contracting
before the Walpolian era, usually with the consent of both political
parties. In 1696 Parliament passed the Last Determinations Act, placing
a ceiling on borough electorates and encouraging poll books – an obvious
aid to landlord control. In 1711 another tory Parliament passed – with
little whig opposition – the Landed Qualification Act. Such legislation
only confirmed the pre-existing tendency for parliamentary seats to be
the adjunct of considerable wealth. This was increasingly the case in
Anne's reign, for it was that period (and the 1690s), *not* the post-
Septennial Act era, which saw the cost of parliamentary seats beginning
to escalate, and the tiny boroughs of Wiltshire, Devon, and Cornwall
beginning to succumb to affluent, absentee candidates in preference to
indigenous minor gentry or merchants.[44]

Geoffrey Holmes has drawn attention to the residual flexibility of
early-eighteenth-century England's ossifying electoral system. He points
out that in 1700 only four of the thirty-two provincial towns with 5000
or more inhabitants were denied representation. This is true, but it does
not mean – as he goes on to suggest – that England's towns were *fairly*
represented. In 1700 the rapidly expanding port of Liverpool had two
M.P.s elected by some 1000 freemen. They could be out-voted by the
four M.P.s returned by East and West Looe, declining Cornish villages
with a combined electorate of 100. The Looes and not Liverpool were
the more typical eighteenth-century borough constituency. Holmes argues
that this discrepancy between the concentration of voters (and still more
the concentration of population) and the allocation of seats was partly
alleviated by the county elections. Certainly so long as county contests
were fairly frequent – as they were up to 1734 – the freeholders of
unenfranchised Leeds, Birmingham, and Manchester might, if they were
lucky, be given some electoral outlet (though Lancashire's freeholders
voted only twice at general elections between 1701 and 1734 and Warwickshire's only once). But the 159 000 freeholders who returned
England's eighty county M.P.s in 1715 could (and did) have their
partisan choice reversed by the 3500 voters in England's smallest
boroughs, who between them returned 148 M.P.s.[45] And as Norma
Landau has shown for the 1713 and 1715 Kent contested elections, even
when a freeholder had an opportunity to vote and was immune to direct
landlord influence he could still be exposed to a variety of pressures,
chief of which were the parson and the partisan Justice of the Peace.

The proliferation of canvassing lists in the manuscript collections of Augustan gentry can, as Plumb suggests, bear witness to the independence of the freeholder vote; it can also bear witness to the close management to which freeholders were often subjected.[46]

It is similarly imprudent to interpret Augustan England's huge output of electoral propaganda as evidence of a free and politicised electorate, without considering for whom, in a semi-literate society, this propaganda was intended: for the voter or for his immediate and influential social superiors? 'Public opinion', J. A. Downie has written, 'was crucial to the security of the Oxford ministry.' This was true, but as he goes on to remark, 'The audience of the *Examiner* [Oxford's prime organ of propaganda] . . . was made up principally of landed gentry and provincial clergymen.' What we have here is both historiographical confusion and an Augustan truth. Of course political information in Anne's reign could penetrate to the lowest strata of English society; in the large towns especially it might even reach the illiterate. But it should be remembered that in 1700 only about 20 per cent of Englishmen lived in towns of any description, and how far handbills and newspapers reached and were read in the average isolated hamlet can only be conjectured. Of course the plebeian readers of Swift and Defoe in the 1710s, of Bolingbroke in the 1730s, and of Wilkes in the 1760s could evolve political opinions of their own. But the public opinion which impinged on the political centre, the public opinion with which politicians *in office* were normally concerned, was the opinion of the educated, the prosperous, and, most especially, the landed.[47]

A glance at the political chronology of the 1710 tory electoral landslide, presented by Holmes as the masterpiece of a volatile electorate, only reinforces the argument that however large, independent, and well-read the electorate, it could not on its own subvert a government. Throughout 1710 the Queen and Harley had worked to erode Godolphin's whig administration. In August Harley and other tory politicians replaced it. In September the major Junto whigs were evicted from the Cabinet. The general election in which the tories won 332 seats in England and Wales to the whigs' 181 was held one month later. Clearly the nation was still convulsed by the Sacheverell affair and war weariness was endemic. But it was also the case that, while the Crown and the new tory administration had been restrained in their electoral campaign, the Queen, by way of her pre-election ministerial appointments as well as by some purges in local government, had made it crystal clear to every ambitious J.P., clergyman, and landowner with electoral influence at his disposal which party was to have her favour in the immediate future.[48] The result of the 1722 general election suggests that in 1710 it was this latter factor, rather than public opinion in the widest sense, which had been crucial. In 1722 at least 129 English constituencies went to the polls – two more than in 1710. The whig administration had been discredited by the South Sea Bubble; the National Will was pro-tory or at least anti-whig; and, as Walpole's return with an increased majority demonstrated, it simply did not matter. Since the whig ministry could show that it still possessed royal favour, it could mobilise those influences which were inseparable from the unreformed system – influences which Walpole and Co. certainly systematised to an unprecedented degree, but which had proved their efficacy before 1715.[49]

Adopting Plumb's wider definition of political stability, 'the acceptance by society of its political institutions, and of those classes of men or officials who control them', it can surely be argued that, despite the superficial high-political turmoil at the end of Anne's reign, that state had already been achieved. Ever since the fifteenth century England had been unusually stable in her political and social arrangements. After the major aberration from that stability, the Civil War, the landed elite had consolidated its social, legal, and political authority. Post-1688 administrations had shown themselves able to employ executive pressures and perks to control a recalcitrant House of Commons. The Augustan electorate had indeed proved a lively and growing phenomenon, but it was rendered incapable of subverting the Crown's chosen Minister by a variety of local electoral patrons and coercive agents, and by the idiosyncrasies of the representative system. And beneath the political surface, more extensive factors were also operating in favour of durable national stability. In the late seventeenth century and the first half of the eighteenth, England experienced barely any growth in population. Prices, particularly food prices on which low-level social quiescence relied, were either stable or falling. Gilboy's cost of living index drops from 120 in 1710 to 97.7 in 1750.[50] The tory Treaty of Utrecht ensured Britain's European reputation and colonial expansion. Abroad, her main rivals and trading competitors – Holland, France, and Spain – had been seriously weakened. At home, Britain was already rich, and irrespective of the bias of her administration, all set to grow richer still. And for the first time since the 1650s, if not since the Armada, a sense of collective national achievement was available to offset socio-economic divisions.

The *élan* with which Stanhope, Sunderland, Walpole, and Pelham ousted their tory rivals after 1714 and exploited court, Treasury, and electoral patronage is therefore misleading. Because these Ministers – especially Walpole – were gifted, single-minded men, and because in the mid eighteenth century they presided over a stable nation, it is tempting to attribute that stability to their essentially partisan manoeuvres. This would be quite wrong. Given past domestic and foreign policy achievements – to which the tories had largely contributed – any competent administration attaining power in the early Hanoverian period was likely to enjoy stability. Indeed, it may be argued that, in two senses, the victorious whigs put this stability at risk. Since the Augustan electorate had always been contained, its further subjugation, via the Septennial Act and extended Treasury and patron control, was not a prerequisite of political stability in general, though it was crucial to the stabilising of power within the whig party in particular. And just as this electoral overkill was likely in the end to breed a much more radical grass-roots resentment, so the artificial suspension of two-party conflict was likely to implant potentially corrosive desperation at the heart of Britain's ruling elite.

In 1707 Robert Harley had recognised that the days when both whig and tory might be blended in a mixed administration were drawing to their close. What he anticipated would replace this uneasy arrangement was a self-regulating two-party *system:* 'like a door which turns both ways upon its hinges to let in each party as it grows triumphant'. In 1715 the door was slammed shut upon the tories and it remained jammed in that position for some forty-five years. For this one group of men the 'openness' which foreign observers identified as the distinctive feature of mid-eighteenth-century English society did not apply. The 'Opportunity State', as Macpherson called Georgian England, persisted in discriminating against tories and made thereby an unprecedented rift in the landed elite – the vital pre-condition of real political instability.[51]

It is seldom recognised how extensive tory proscription was. In most counties, especially before 1745, class unity on the Bench was endangered by the tories' enforced minority status in the Commissions of the Peace. In some counties, such as Somerset and Wiltshire, it was not until 1757, when the Militia Act necessitated their co-operation, that whig and tory began even to socialise together, much less regard themselves as an integrated ruling class. Proscription affected tories at the highest level of society. The third earl of Oxford was Herefordshire's prime magnate but, like every other mid-century tory peer, until the 1760s he was denied access to the Lord Lieutenantships and court perquisites which were the normal concomitants of his rank. In 1748 he had to write to a friend, confessing his inability to secure him patronage: 'The Proscription laid on my Family above 30 years ago does not seem to be yet taken off. Interest with the great people I never presumed or affected to have & my acquaintance with them is as small.' If a tory like Oxford could be spurned, proscription was bound to harass the weak. As soon as the whigs secured control of Norwich corporation in 1715, they made sure that its plumbing and street lighting contracts went only to whigs. Any publican in this city, as in whig-dominated Coventry, who persisted in voting tory was liable to have his licence revoked.[52]

Higher education and the professions only emphasise the tory dilemma. When the University of Cambridge elected a Vice-Chancellor in 1729, St John's tory Fellows ran Dr Lambert against the Master of Corpus Christi, Dr Mawson. Lambert won by one vote, but as one tory commentator noted, the whig candidate had his compensation: 'Dr Mawson stood in the Whig Interest, and got a bishopric; the Tories supported Dr Lambert, who got Nothing.' He was quite right. By dint of his subsequent ecclesiastical promotion and not because of his theological writings (which are sparse), Mawson is allotted two pages in the *Dictionary of National Biography*; Lambert, like the vast majority of mid-century tories, went undistinguished by the State, and gets none. And the effects of proscription were cumulative. Once Mawson had done his time in the poor diocese of Llandaff, he was rewarded for compliant voting in the Lords by advancement to the see of Chichester in 1740. This meant that he obtained sixty-five benefices as well as miscellaneous sinecures to throw in the way of suitably disposed Corpus graduates. The clerical aspirants of St John's College were likely to find advancement more difficult.[53]

Lord Chesterfield might assure a friend in 1756 that 'People will only trust their property to the care of the ablest lawyer, be he Whig or Tory, well or ill at Court', but this in fact was only partly true. Certainly many tory landowners set their younger sons to be attorneys, but they could not always guarantee them general employment. In 1739 the whig M.P. Colonel John Selwyn refused to employ the Gloucestershire attorney Charles Barrow because, although known to be efficient, he was also known to be an ardent tory. And while many tory lawyers achieved respectable careers, the top jobs and honours – including K.C.s – were almost invariably restricted to whigs. Hence the significance of Paul Lucas' data for the Inns of Court in the mid eighteenth century. In the 1710s Oxford men had made up 64 per cent of Lincoln's Inn admissions and Cambridge graduates only 31 per cent. By the mid 1750s only 38 per cent of Lincoln's Inn students were Oxonians, while the Cambridge contingent had risen to 48 per cent. Oxford University was predominantly tory; Cambridge University preponderantly whig. Many bright young tories had evidently decided that under the first two Hanoverians a legal career was not for them. The consequences of the tory gentry's partial withdrawal from the legal profession may have been extensive. For the Law, Lucas writes, the reign of George II was 'an era of great opportunity for the relatively lower orders'.[54] Such an opportunity for social mobility must have contributed to social harmony amongst Britain's middling classes; may it not also have prejudiced that sense of common landed identity which is supposed to have buttressed and lent stability to early Hanoverian Britain's ruling elite?

Under proscription many able tories must have had their career aspirations frustrated; many more stolid but economically powerful tory landowners must have been embittered. And whereas a disgruntled nineteenth-century tory landowner like Ralph Sneyd, whose lack of political success in life was due only to his own indolence, could play the stoic – 'one repeats some pregnant passage of Burke – & sighs – & grumbles – but does one's duty', in the mid eighteenth century disgruntled tories were usually deprived of those local and central duties which their rank and acreage would normally have commanded. With some of them, as we shall see, bitterness found expression in virulent parliamentary criticism; with others, in far more insidious flirtations with extra-parliamentary dissidence. The atomisation of the political elite, which John Brewer has cited as a crucial ingredient of the convulsions of the 1760s, was far more pronounced in the reigns of George III's grandfather and great-grandfather.[55]

This book examines the tory parliamentary party's response to its exclusion between 1714 and 1760. Its wider concern is to substantiate the core of the argument which I have been able only to outline in this introduction, and to re-evaluate various facets of mid-eighteenth-century British society by approaching them from a tory rather than from the customary whig perspective.

Since such stress had been laid on the bitterness of proscription, it may be wondered why after 1714 anyone should have chosen to remain in the tory camp. Some historians have in fact argued that tory frustration drove the party into Jacobitism. Had this been the case, there would have been little tory challenge to whig oligarchy and no creativity in that challenge – English Jacobitism invariably doing more for Sir Robert Walpole's career than ever it did for either Old or Young Pretender. A more influential group of writers would claim that there could be no tory response to proscription, because after 1714 the tory party swiftly ceased to exist. Chapters 2 and 3 are intended to answer both these lobbies, and to suggest why many contemporaries believed that a tory parliamentary stance was compatible with self-interest and a Hanoverian king. Chapter 4 advances the claim that not only did the bulk of tory politicians see themselves as a constitutional opposition party and act as a remarkably organised one, but they also preserved a distinct ideological entity. Both in its original form and in its post-1714 variants, the tory platform was electorally tenacious and popular beyond the scope of the electorate. Chapter 5 examines the tories' electoral base. Chapter 6 suggests that if J. H. Plumb is correct in detecting two political nations in early Georgian England – one high-level and contracting, the other excluded, but increasingly literate, mobile, and affluent – then the tories bridged the gap between them more effectively than did any other eighteenth-century Westminster group.[56]

The four chapters in the final section of the book provide a chrono-logical if sometimes impressionistic survey of tory high-political activity between 1714 and 1760. They make no claim to step-by-step high-political analysis. Too often such an approach conceals polemic under an appearance of exhaustive and colourless history; too often it succeeds only in exhausting the reader. In the case of the tories, limited and patchy evidence would anyway make such detail impracticable. I have chosen to place these chapters at the end of the book because I assume throughout them that the tories were, for their period, a remarkably unified party, that they nurtured political ambitions, and that these ambitions could at times have been realised under both George I and George II. Few readers will initially share my opinions; those I can persuade may need Parts I and II to convince them.

As should now be obvious, it is not only Hanoverian whig oligarchs which this book is intended to challenge. Approaching the eighteenth century by way of an alienated and dissentient body of men is bound to be a temptation to an unduly perverse and unbalanced assessment. I am sure that this temptation has not always been resisted. But any account of British society in this period must be able to contain the tory experience and render it comprehensible; most of the available histories do not.

The Tory Response to Proscription

Horace Walpole, who was even more adept than Lord Hervey at writing Old Corps whig propaganda in the guise of history, argued that the Hanoverian Succession left the tory party with three options: 'In truth, all sensible Tories I ever knew were either Jacobites or became Whigs; those that remained Tories remained fools.' His verdict is still current. Until recently it was assumed that talented and ambitious tories responded to proscription by defecting to the whigs, and so reduced their original party to a rump of fiercely independent country gentlemen analogous to the tory remnant of 1847. As the post-1714 tory residuum lacked a Disraeli and was incapable of efficient parliamentary opposition, it provided for the emergence of an opulent and immune whig supremacy; it also rendered the well-defined political parties and binary party conflict of the Augustan era obsolete. The whig ministers of the mid eighteenth century – Lord Stanhope, Sir Robert Walpole, Henry Pelham, and the duke of Newcastle – could be assailed only by whig dissidents – men whose opportunism was bound to corrode their party's sense of a collective identity, but who could usually be bought off by state employment if they proved too disruptive.[1]

This presentation of tory dissolution and its related insistence on the a-party nature of early Georgian politics have been challenged by Eveline Cruickshanks, Paul Fritz, and, more subtly, by J. C. D. Clark. The tories, it is now supposed, remained sufficiently careerist to want to regain state office. Since tory office-holding was incompatible with the maintenance of the Hanoverian dynasty, the party sought its salvation in the Pretender: 'up to 1745 the Tories were a predominantly Jacobite party, engaged in attempts to restore the Stuarts by a rising with foreign assistance'.[2] Recognising perhaps that it is actually rather difficult to demonstrate extensive tory ideological or practical commitment to the Pretender, Clark has retained this crypto-Jacobite identification while extricating himself from the need to prove it. He argues that, as some tory extremists did engage in Jacobite plotting after 1714, and as a Stuart restoration was the obvious solution to tory proscription, the party was bound to acquire a distinctive and treasonable identity, however innocent the majority of its M.P.s. The whigs (and one must include the first two Hanoverian monarchs in this category) were necessarily lent cohesion by their common suspicion of a disaffected toryism and by their justified apprehension of a Jacobite invasion based on the military and diplomatic supremacy of France. The fear or the actuality of Jacobitism thus becomes the vital preservative of the two-party division up to 1745 'and by implication for sometime thereafter'.[3]

These two interpretations of tory behaviour after 1714 share a common assumption: that George I and George II were bound invariably to concur in tory proscription and, as a partial consequence of this, that whig control in this period was impervious to constitutional challenge. If one accepts this premise then it may indeed be logical to consign the post-1714 tory party to parliamentary impotence or treasonable activity; if however one finds that the tories had cause to believe that they could salvage their position by legitimate political endeavour, then it becomes necessary to reassess the security and the stability of the whigs' supremacy.

I

As a whig pamphleteer was to remark in 1744, it was difficult to reconcile the tory party's reputation for either crypto-Jacobitism or parliamentary independence with the fact that its members had 'at times, at all Times that offered, shewn a ready Disposition to be good Courtiers'. Queen Anne's death was followed not by a tory resort to the Pretender but rather by the tories' competing with the whigs to pass loyal and lucrative legislation on behalf of her Hanoverian successor. On 12 August 1714 Horatio Walpole's motion that arrears be paid to those Hanoverian troops who had fought in the War of Spanish Succession was seconded by William Shippen – formerly one of the most prominent of the seventy-odd Jacobite tory M.P.s – who 'very ingenuously owned, he had opposed that payment in the late reign, but that he was for it now'.[4] The same month saw tory aristocratic careerists like Lord Anglesey scouring London for language tutors so that they could brush up their French and more easily impress an alien Court. Even the earl of Mar, who was to lead the 1715 rising in Scotland, was initially able to consider his employment prospects under Hanoverian rule with complacency and relish: 'Jacobitisme, which they used to brand the Tories with, is now I presum out of doors, and the King has better understanding than to make himself but King of one partie, and tho' the Whigs may get the better with him at first, other folks...may have their turn with him too.'[5]

A similar happy anticipation of state office informed the tory rush to

Court at George II's accession in July 1727. The second earl of Oxford's absence from St James' at this time (a diffidence attributable to filial piety rather than to legitimist scruple and overwhelmed by self-interest in 1731) was considered such a singular example of tory disinterestedness as to merit a commemorative ode:

> Whilst thick to Court transported Tories run...
> Expecting better, and secure from worse;
> Beyond their Principles now Passive grown,
> They lick the Spittle which the Whiggs have thrown.

Nor was this desire for royal recognition confined to the tory elite. In 1727 the example of unabashed toadying set by Lords Strafford, Gower, Bathurst, Lichfield, and Scarsdale was followed by the bulk of tory M.P.s. So too, after Sir Robert Walpole's resignation in February 1742, it was the tory parliamentary party as a whole, 'all except Shippen, & a very few more', which marched from its London headquarters at the Cocoa Tree coffee-house to the King's levee at St James', making thereby a coherent and remarkably dramatic appeal for state employment in the post-Walpolian political world.[6]

If the tories did regard the Hanoverian dynasty as illegitimate, they clearly felt no moral obligation to hold themselves aloof from its service. Ever since 1689 tory theorists and politicians had shown themselves capable of squaring their party's traditional adherence to passive obedience with practical acquiescence in the Glorious Revolution and in the dynastic modifications which that coup had entailed. The tory pamphleteering stance on the Act of Settlement had wavered after 1710, but this was largely due to the party's apprehension that its peace negotiations with France would incline the Hanoverian heir towards the whigs, not to belated tory qualms about James Stuart's divinely ordained right of succession. A similar insecurity had led Lords Oxford and Bolingbroke to dabble in Jacobite intrigue, and such tory–Jacobite activity as occurred after 1714 was just as pragmatically conceived.[7]

Jacobite agents tacitly recognised this fact by emptying their English propaganda of legitimist theory. In 1718 the earl of Mar, now acting as the Pretender's Secretary of State, sent George Flint some instructive advice on his new and pro-Stuart London weekly:

I think you had best personate one of those, called King George's Jacobites, I mean one who was resolved to have acquiesced in the settlement made... but that your seeing...how far George and his son are different from the fine characters given of them had made you bethink yourself of the wrong way you were in...You might go back as far as the Revolution, but, because many are now alive, who acted a part in that...I think you had best but touch that lightly, if at all.

This polemical line became the norm for the Jacobite press. *Mist's Weekly Journal* in the 1720s, its equally opaque and popular replacement *Fog's Weekly Journal*, and *The Mitre and the Crown*, inaugurated in 1749, attacked long Parliaments, electoral corruption, standing armies, and social injustice, but only rarely engaged in the mildest of Stuart apologetics.[8]

This neutral opposition format owed more to the decline of the Nonjurors than to government censorship. By 1710 all but one of the bishops who had been deprived of their sees for not taking the oaths to William and Mary had died. The influential nonjuring cleric and publicist Henry Dodwell, together with his followers, took the opportunity to rejoin the conforming Anglican Church, and only the movement's more uncompromising and less attractive wing remained to provide the Stuart dynasty with some genuinely committed literary advocates. In 1716 a posthumous publication by a Nonjuror of this type – George Hickes' *Constitution of the Catholic Church* – sparked off the Bangorian controversy and alienated many tory Anglican clergymen. Two years later the remaining Nonjurors split over a debate on the Prayer Book; their annual output of political pamphlets fell by half; and by 1720, Charles Leslie, the movement's most talented journalist and author of the pro-Stuart periodical the *Rehearsal*, had been reduced to acceptance of whig governmental subsidies.[9]

A few nonjuring Jacobite writers remained active – the eccentric Matthias Earbery is a picturesque example – but far more typical of Jacobite publicists after 1715 was John Matthews, a radical Londoner who rejected the consolations of nonjuring clerics before his execution, and whose 1719 pamphlet *Vox Populi, Vox Dei* urged popular activism on behalf of the Pretender: 'Sure you ought to fight with more resolution for liberty than your oppressors do for dominion. Count your Numbers.' In common with many mid-century Jacobite authors, Matthews also espoused contract theory, and this says something about the audience at which these writings were aimed. It was always James Stuart's hope that his cause might attract not only tory but also dissident whig support – hence in part the varied political arguments employed by his apologists. Such a strategy incurred certain risks. By adducing Lockeian and Country doctrines in support of a Jacobite restoration Stuart polemicists might (and did) attract the more *outré* whigs; they might also antagonise more conventional tory, Catholic, and nonjuring readers – very few early-eighteenth-century tories would have concurred in the doctrine of contract.[10] More important, by concentrating on denouncing the corruption of the whig regime Jacobites ran the risk of making the Pretender redundant. As the tory M.P. for Hastings, Archibald Hutcheson, told the earl of Sunderland in 1720: 'These New Jacobites are by no wise influenc'd by any Regard to the Pretended Hereditary Right, and act purely upon what they take to be Revolution Principles...They are certainly the Jacobites to be most apprehended; but surely, the easiest to be regain'd.' Since James was to be restored not because he was a Stuart but because he would implement Country reforms and end tory proscription, his appeal to the tories was liable to be undercut by a Hanoverian prince or a whig Minister who offered, or who seemed likely to offer, analogous concessions.[11]

II

The eclecticism of the Stuart appeal deprives us of an ideological litmus test with which to determine the Jacobite content of tory political argument. Nor can one gauge the extent of the party's disaffection from its behaviour in 1715. An extreme whig, Thomas Burnet, claimed that 165 tory gentlemen had joined in devising the projected English insurrection of 1715, each conspirator subscribing 'two thousand pound apiece to assist the Imposter if he would land'. Two tory sources point to a more modest confederation of about twenty-five tory peers, M.P.s, and clergymen, including Lord Lansdowne, the earl of Scarsdale, and Sir William Wyndham.[12] This cabal seems to have made some attempt to stockpile weapons, but its plans and military expertise were lost when the great tory general, the duke of Ormonde, took both himself and his papers across the Channel to escape the consequences of his impeachment. The plotters were even more dismayed by the death of their prime European ally, Louis XIV, especially when Bolingbroke, then in exile in France, sent over information that the new Regent would withhold French aid. 'We are left upon our own bottom', wrote Lansdowne to Wyndham in September, 'and the question is askt, if that will doe: Pray let us have your opinion...our Councils are a good deal broken and divided.' Clearly an unsupported rising in England would not do, and those tories who had been informed of the plot went to ground. Only nine English tory M.P.s were arrested for their involvement in the conspiracy. Two of these, John Anstis, M.P. for Launceston, and the Worcestershire Member, Sir John Pakington, were able to convince the Privy Council of their innocence. Of the remaining seven only the M.P. for Northumberland, Thomas Forster, took up arms for the Pretender.[13]

This skeletal account tells us very little. More to the point is whether one interprets Forster's subsequent remark that 'he look'd on the whole body of the Torys to be in it' as evidence of the wishful thinking which was to dog Jacobite intrigue, or of extensive tory underground support which failed to materialise in 1715 only because of the lack of a French expeditionary force. Certainly in Somerset there is evidence that Wyndham had secured promises of assistance from some of the county gentry in the event of an efficient invasion's being staged.[14] In Devon and Cornwall, however, two counties supposedly permeated with disaffection and certainly well endowed with tory gentry, there were few signs of active sedition. Sir Richard Vyvyan, formerly M.P. for Cornwall, was taken into custody with some other local tories, but according to the Member for Newport, Sir Nicholas Morice, these men were victims not of their own treason but of whig vindictiveness recently primed by the general election campaign: 'They have not entered into any association to ye prejudice of ye Government...they having sense & judgment enough to discern that one single step towards its overthrow would be ye utter ruin of themselves & estates, & consequently of their posterity.' If Morice's tory testimony is suspect, one can perhaps accept the assurances of Walter Moyle, writing from Cornwall, and those of Lord Carteret from Devon, that in neither country was there evidence of Jacobite associations amongst the tory gentry or of a mobilisation of tenants and employees in readiness for a rebellion.[15]

Some tories were neither fish nor fowl: sufficiently critical of the Hanoverian regime to be regarded as seditious by whigs and Jacobites alike, but failing to convert their disaffection into active treason. Sir William Blackett, M.P. for Newcastle upon Tyne, found himself in the farcical position of being 'pursued by Mr Forster and a great many Northumberland gentlemen, who were then in arms against King George...and that he was as much pursued by the King's forces, who suspected him to be in the rebell's intrest'. Blackett had supplied some of his colliers with arms; it was never established on which side he intended them to fight. What is certain is that in 1715 he solved his personal dilemma by fleeing to London to assure the King of his devotion and that in the 1718 Newcastle mayoral election he was able to display letters from Lord Stanhope testifying to his loyalty.[16]

Such ambiguous behaviour merited government suspicion; those tories who implemented their loyalty to Hanover in 1715 met with no better response. Sir William Pole, the M.P. for Honiton, who had been turned out of his court office in 1714, refused in 1715 to sacrifice 'Religion and Country' to his 'own spleen or resentment', and organised men and money for his country's defence. His endeavours met with incredulity and sometimes obstruction from Devon's whig authorities, as he complained: 'Won't they distinguish between a Hanover Tory and a Jacobite, and must I who have bin ever zealous for the Protestant Succession...be used as a Jacobite Tory?' Sir Thomas Cave, tory M.P.

for Leicestershire, provided horses and supplies for government troops. The letters in which he detailed these loyal arrangements were carefully intercepted by the county's whig postmaster.[17]

Loyal tories were exposed not only to genuine whig mistrust but also to calculated whig reinterpretation of their passive or active acquiescence in the Hanoverian regime. Tories who had stayed at home during the Jacobite invasion, argued Robert Walpole in 1716, 'differed from declared Rebells only in that they wanted courage to draw the Sword'. When tory peers and M.P.s joined in measures against the Young Pretender's invasion in 1745, Horatio Walpole was quite unimpressed: 'not only the Whigs, out of real zeal, but also the Tories, *for fear of being suspected*, joined in the associations, and a great many of them in the subscriptions'.[18]

Consciously or no, Eveline Cruickshanks utilises the same tactical double-think. 'Some historians', she writes, 'have regarded the bulk of the Tories as overwhelmingly well-affected to the House of Hanover. If they were, why did they not say so?' As she goes on to make clear, many did say so by participating in the flurry of Loyal Addresses sent up by the constituencies in the spring of 1744 at the prospect of a French-aided Jacobite invasion. Cruickshanks promptly reminds us that such Addresses were ritualistic gestures signifying nothing. Yet some tory M.P.s had hastened to deliver not only their own constituency's Address but any others in need of sponsorship.[19] Sir Robert Long – listed in 1743 as a potential Jacobite – delivered both Wiltshire's Address to the King and, on a different occasion, a subsidiary assurance of loyalty from the Bradford and Trowbridge clothiers. Sir Richard Grosvenor was jostled out of presenting Cheshire's Address by the county's whig Lord Lieutenant, so he, together with Sir Robert Bampfylde, who had been unable to deliver Exeter's Address, accompanied their tory colleague Thomas Prowse and Somerset's affirmation of loyalty to Court. Cruickshanks implies that such men were acting either *ex officio* or to deflect well-deserved governmental suspicion. Possibly so, but how were pro-Hanoverian tories to demonstrate their loyalty? How, indeed, could they evade the unfailing optimism of Stuart agents? In June 1745 Lord Sempill had the task of convincing the Pretender that those tories who had accepted state employment during the party's short-lived *rapprochement* with Henry Pelham were nonetheless committed to overthrowing their Hanoverian paymaster: 'The Tories who have places under the Government are as zealous as ever for your Majesty & as ready to concur in the deliverance of their Country as those who have no places, the only difficulty is to prove this disposition.' Indeed.[20]

Sempill does at least seem to have been honest and assiduous; Jacobite agents were rarely either. James Hamilton, who worked in London in the 1720s, combined, according to the Scottish and arguably biased Jacobite George Lockhart, the disadvantages of being Irish, illegitimate, vain, and socially presumptuous: 'men of first rank in England...were more cautious than to have any dealings with him...employing such mean rattle-headed persons gave a great discredit to the King's affairs'. Hardly better was Colonel Cecil, who served as the Pretender's premier English agent in the 1730s and who also served Walpole as a purveyor of Jacobite information. Cecil's bilateral loyalties seem to have been known to leading tories like Sir John Hynde Cotton, so the authenticity of the tory confidences he imparted to Rome must surely be suspect.[21]

The nonjuring antiquarian Thomas Carte exemplifies a rather different but not uncommon Jacobite infirmity. He was a man of absolute integrity, a close friend of Sir John Hynde Cotton and of the much less suspect tory M.P. for Cornwall, Sir John St Aubyn, and his reports to Rome have been used to buttress most accounts of the tory–Jacobite nexus. Yet as a fellow Nonjuror was to remark, though 'very great with many Tories', Carte was 'not perhaps so great as he pretends'.[22] His gullibility was such that in 1738, under the impression that Walpole was inclining towards the Stuarts, he discussed with that Minister the anatomy of English tory–Jacobitism. Having learnt of this indiscretion the Pretender had Carte excluded from real business. Yet we are to suppose, on the basis of the letters which the antiquarian continued to transmit, that cautious tory M.P.s confided to such a man information which, had it been discovered, could have hanged them. How much, one wonders, were Carte's outpourings the exaggerations of a rather peripheral scholar wanting to accentuate his importance and involvement in the outside political world?[23]

That Jacobite information was polluted at source is the commonplace not merely of whig historians; it was recognised by whig contemporaries. In 1720 one journalist drew attention to the ironic circularity whereby whiggish and inflated assessments of crypto-Jacobitism were passed on to Rome:

I would have the Jacobites consider, how they are deceived by their Enemies ...when they read Accounts of the strange Increase of Jacobitism, of the Partiality of the Justices of the Peace in their Favour, and of the great Influence of the Clergy in propagating Jacobite principles; when they are told, that such a County, or Town, swarms with Jacobites...These Accounts have been transmitted by them to their Friends Abroad, to prove, by the Confession of their Enemies, the strength of the Party at Home.[24]

Christopher Layer is a classic instance of a Jacobite swallowing this kind of ministerial line. In the early 1720s he compiled a list of Norfolk gentry which has recently been printed as a guide to that county's Jacobite bias. Yet as Layer admitted under interrogation, this was not *ab initio* a list of Jacobites at all: 'The Pretender asked him, what other Norfolk Gentlemen he knew? To which he answered, That he knew all the Tories. That the Pretender asked him, if he could recollect their Names ...and that accordingly he, Layer, drew up a fair List of the Tory Gentlemen of Norfolk.' William Pulteney, the government's manager at the parliamentary inquiry into the Layer and Atterbury plots in 1722–3 and a man unlikely at this stage to be biased in favour of tory innocence, had at least sufficient acumen to caution the Commons:

They think it a justice due to those gentlemen, to observe, that Layer has owned to the Committee, that, in order to magnify the number of the Pretender's friends, he did in several of the lists found among his papers, insert the name of persons, as well affected to the Pretender's service, without having the least authority from them for so doing; and his false assertion to the Pretender, that all the gentlemen in England, except those in places of profit and trust, were intirely devoted to his interest, shews, that he made no distinction between the innocent and the guilty.[25]

The often disreputable and occasionally comic-opera quality of Jacobite intrigue can be doubly deceptive in that it can lead historians into too bland and simplistic a negation of tory crypto-Jacobitism. In the first decade of proscription the novelty of the Hanoverian dynasty, the lack of a unified party leadership, and the talent of some of the Pretender's more opportunistic English advocates – most notably Bishop Atterbury and Sir William Wyndham – did allow Jacobitism to make some inroads into tory loyalties. Had it not been so, it seems unlikely that Atterbury and the Hertfordshire tory Charles Caesar could have accumulated the £10 000 they contributed towards the Swedish plot of 1716, or that a similar sum could have been promised (though not all, it would seem, collected) by the 1721–2 conspirators. So, too, the fact that tory–Jacobitism was becoming residual in the later 1720s was signalled by a falling-off of subscriptions in aid of the Stuarts and their cause. George Kelly, a Jacobite agent who had been imprisoned in the Tower after the Atterbury plot, had initially received over £120 a year from English and Welsh sympathisers, including the tory M.P. for Denbighshire, Watkin Williams Wynn. By May 1728 Atterbury's son-in-law was noting that subsidies such as these were coming to an end: 'Several of ye Benefactors are dead; several weary of such Incumbrances; & ye whole Club, (from whence greatest parts of ye Bounty came) is in a manner dissolved.'[26]

In the 1730s and 1740s the only English coterie known to have funded the Pretender was the Remitters, a society of tory and Catholic noblemen and gentry who were described by Lord Shelburne as forming 'quite a distinct party' from the tories in general, and whose donations were intended, and, it would seem, were only sufficient, for James' personal comfort. When Jacobite agents approached Sir Watkin Williams Wynn in 1743 and 1745, they found him subdued in his legitimist propensities and considerably meaner. He refused them money, arguing that he had no more than £200 in spare cash at his disposal. He was to donate exactly half this sum to the Denbighshire Association on behalf of George II in 1745.[27]

Wales provides another yardstick for both the initial extent of Jacobitism and its attrition in the 1720s. The near-seigneurial authority in Cardiganshire of Lewis Pryse, a Jacobite M.P. who had been expelled from the Commons in 1716 for not taking the oaths, and the analogous suzerainty of the Wynns in North Wales, permitted a certain amount of fund-raising and arms-collecting as well as minor treasonable demonstrations in these areas. Pryse died in 1720, and the dwindling of overt Welsh Jacobitism was facilitated by a prolonged minority in the powerful and Jacobite Mansel family of Glamorgan and the absence of an adult duke of Beaufort. The heir to this latter family, which had helped hold Wales for Charles I and had been Roman Catholic until 1667, spent much of the 1720s in a Grand Tour: he organised a ball in Paris 'for all the Pretender's friends at St Germains' and subsequently visited James in Rome. When he returned to England, however, he immediately presented himself at the Court of George II.[28] The 1720s also witnessed the inception or consolidation of the Welsh socio-Jacobite clubs: the Society of Sea Sergeants in Carmarthenshire, the Cycle of the White Rose in North-East Wales, and the club of '27' in Montgomeryshire. There can be no doubt that the *Leitmotif* of these foundations was sentimental legitimism but also little doubt that they served to transmute potential treason into clubbery and respectable, if partisan, political activity. The Sea Sergeants concentrated their energies on mobilising the tory vote in Carmarthenshire county and borough elections, and served as Councilmen in the safe tory seat of Haverfordwest. In England, too, the discovery of the Atterbury plot in 1722 may have prompted men whose Jacobitism took primarily a liquid form to look for safer ways to express their bonhomie. Philip Jenkins has remarked how 1723 and 1724 saw the foundation of twenty-eight masonic lodges throughout Britain; only seven had been instituted during the previous two years.[29]

The Atterbury débâcle and morality irremediably diminished English Jacobitism. The failure of his plot led not only to Atterbury's exile but also to the emigration and undignified conversion to Catholicism of the whig–Jacobite Lord Wharton and his tory associate, Lord North. More important, it convinced Wyndham, together with Lords Bathurst and

Gower, of the need for tory recognition of the permanence of the Hanoverian regime. Some of the less flexible tory–Jacobite M.P.s withdrew
from politics; others merely died. The very optimistic list of tory
sympathisers compiled by the Atterbury conspirators in 1721 included
eighty-three tory M.P.s who had at some time sat in the 1715–22
Parliament (less than a third of the total number of tories returned to
Parliament during this period). Fifty-two of those listed were dead or
had retired by 1727.[30] Jacobitism attracted no new high-level tory
adherents until the early 1740s, and what is noticeable about the six
tory politicians who reputedly conspired to bring about a Stuart restoration in 1743 is how senior four of them were by the standards of their
age. Wynn was fifty; Sir John Hynde Cotton and Sir Robert Abdy were
fifty-five; the most energetic proponent of an invasion, Lord Barrymore,
was seventy-six; Charles Noel Somerset and Lord Orrery were younger
men but only the latter was still alive by 1757. In other words, most of
these belated conspirators were of a different generation from the bulk
of their party colleagues and five of them had no time to lose if they
wished to achieve a modicum of political power.

It is this diminuendo version of post-Atterburian Jacobitism which
Eveline Cruickshanks has been most concerned to refute.[31] She has argued
that, despite the parliamentary strategy advocated by Wyndham and
Bolingbroke after 1725, the bulk of the tory party remained alienated
from the Hanoverian dynasty and leading tories maintained contact with
the Stuart Court with a view to staging a restoration whenever the
state of European diplomacy permitted. Such an eventuality occurred
with the death of the anti-Jacobite Cardinal Fleury in January 1743:
hence the Franco-tory plot of that year to place Charles Edward Stuart,
the Young Pretender, on the British throne.

In support of this thesis Cruickshanks has printed two lists given to
James Butler, Louis XV's Master of the Horse, when he visited England
in 1743 to assess the extent of domestic support for a Stuart invasion.
One of these documents named 176 of London's Common Councilmen
as favouring a change of dynasty: sixty-nine of these were to subscribe
or join the City Association in support of George II in 1745. The other
list was still more ambitious. It cited almost 270 English and Welsh
peers, M.P.s, and sundry Catholic gentlemen as likely supporters of a
Stuart restoration. Neither the Young Pretender's secretary, John
Murray, nor the French commander, Marshal de Saxe, thought very
highly of these catalogues of potential disaffection and their scepticism
was well founded.[32]

Whoever formulated the second document had a bizarre perception of
English county hierarchies. What would the duke of Devonshire have

said, one wonders, had he been told that Derbyshire – the seat of his great Chatsworth estate – was dominated by the duke of Rutland, Lord Chesterfield, and Sir Nathaniel Curzon? How would Kent's prime electoral magnate, the duke of Dorset, have reacted, had he been informed that his county was '*entirement sous la conduite*' of Lords Westmorland, Thanet, Aylesford, and a host of other lords of more limited Kentish acreage? Was it really to be expected that the whig duke of Rutland, Lord Derby, and Lord Rockingham, Lord Lieutenants of Leicestershire, Lancashire, and Kent respectively, would support a disruptive Jacobite coup? When one turns to the M.P.s listed, it is difficult enough to reconcile the crypto-Jacobitism attributed to 112 tories with the known conduct of many of them in 1744 and 1745; to account for the inclusion of five government supporters, and thirty-seven opposition whigs (including William Pitt, George Grenville, and the Hon. Thomas Watson, a future Lord Lieutenant of Kent), one has to have recourse to the compiler's ignorance, and to the familiar Stuart assumption that parliamentary dissidence was tantamount to incipient disaffection.[33]

Butler's lists illustrate again the deficiencies of French and Stuart archives: they may show that after 1714 some leading tories corresponded and occasionally plotted with Jacobite agents; they do not prove that the bulk of the tory parliamentary party knew of these contacts or endorsed them. So what evidence are we to use? Cruickshanks' assertion that tory family papers are 'non-existent' for the reigns of George I and George II is certainly incorrect, and her argument that the sparsity of tory papers proves that a majority of tories had something to hide is certainly tendentious, but Jacobite tories were unlikely to preserve written evidence of their treason. Are we then to concentrate on the more informal manifestations of tory legitimism, and take seriously the umpteen contemporary references to tory toasts to the King over the water? According to Cruickshanks, yes:

English tories were Jacobites in the sense that their leaders, answering for the party, wanted a restoration of the Stuarts...but they had said again and again that only regular troops could bring it about. With scant regard for logistics, Whig historians have ridiculed them for showing their zeal to the Pretender only by drinking his health in secret. This was so, but after all. *in vino veritas*![34]

The persistence of Stuart invocations and iconography in the eighteenth century and after is certainly a subject which needs attention, but one cannot assume the veracity either of men in their cups or of whig and Jacobite reports of illicit tory toasts. In 1738 Thomas Carte informed the Pretender's secretary that the first after-dinner toast at Sir Roger Mostyn's Flintshire seat was 'constantly The Chevalier'. Since Mostyn's

Hanoverianism was so blatant that he became the only tory between 1716 and 1760 to be appointed a Lord Lieutenant, and since his eldest son, who was tory M.P. for Flintshire in 1738, had forced his county's Jacobite sheriff to proclaim George II in 1727, Carte's report is surely suspect.[35]

Nor is the logistical argument at all clear-cut. The Atterbury fiasco did convince English Jacobites that foreign troops were indispensable to their success. In 1727 Lord Orrery stipulated that 'the number could not be much less than 20 000'. But, as in 1688, no European power would undertake an invasion 'without particular assurances from men of quality, consequence and figure', and such a direct assurance of collaboration was precisely what the tories refused to give. In August 1738 Henry Perrot, Jacobite M.P. for Oxfordshire, addressed a group of tories at Oxford:

He proposed to the gentlemen to give a power to the Duke of Ormonde to represent their sense to any foreign court, in order to procure the assistance they thought necessary to effect a restoration, engaging themselves to make good whatever he should represent or undertake for in their names.

His audience's response was qualified:

They indeed expressed themselves ready to give such a power... [but] they did not care to enter into the consideration of the particular measures proper to make the enterprise and landing of foreign troops successful.

When the tory parliamentary party 'met in greater numbers at London' in February 1739 it withdrew from even this tentative engagement.[36]

Still more suggestive is the behaviour of the conspirators in 1743 when the longstanding demand for foreign support – the lack of which had legitimised tory–Jacobite inactivity – was at last satisfied and the English Jacobites' bluff was effectively called. By late December of that year a French expeditionary force of over 10 000 men had been mobilised, the Brest squadron was ready, and transport-ships for the troops had been assembled at Dunkirk; at which point, Sir John Hynde Cotton, on behalf of his five colleagues, asked for the invasion to be postponed until February 1744. He incurred thereby the possible risk of the British government's discovering the plot (which was what happened) and the certain loss of favourable weather and sailing conditions. His avowed reason was that it would invite government suspicion if leading tories absented themselves from the forthcoming debate on the Hanoverian troops in order to finalise local preparations for the invasion. Since the French were supplying the necessary military equipment, it is not clear what local preparations could have required the personal attention of all the conspirators at this late stage. Nor is it clear why some of them –

especially the aged Lord Barrymore and the peripheral Sir Robert Abdy –
could not have returned to their counties after the vote on the Hanoverians
on 18 January 1744: the practice of most tory M.P.s was, after all, to turn
up in force for set-piece debates and then to trickle homewards in the
wake of parliamentary defeat.[37]

How the tories would have reacted had the French expedition landed
in 1744 or had Charles Edward Stuart launched a French-supported
invasion in England in 1745 rather than landing in Scotland can only
be conjectured. What is certain is that in both these years many tory
politicians demonstrated their loyalty to Hanover in an unequivocal
fashion and that these manifestations of tory probity met with whig
obstruction at the centre and in the localities.

In April 1744 an opposition whig, the Hon. Alexander Hume
Campbell, moved that corresponding with the Pretender's sons should be
made a treasonable offence. His motion was seconded by Nicholas
Fazakerley, tory M.P. for Preston, and according to Bolingbroke 'the
body of the Torys' expressed themselves 'perfectly pleased' with the
proposal.[38] Campbell's bill passed the Commons but it returned from the
Lords with a ministerial amendment that anyone convicted of such
treason should have his lands confiscated in perpetuity – an unprecedented
penalty which was bound to incite tory and libertarian whig opposition.
Fazakerley's speech as he rounded on the government for the blatancy
of its tactic is worth quoting at length.

Ministers never fail to misrepresent those who oppose the measures they
advise, and to persuade his majesty, that they are friends to the Pretender...
This, I suspected, might be the case, with regard to myself, and many other
gentlemen in this House; and...I thought we could not have a better opportunity for endeavouring to remove this mistake, than that of introducing and
promoting this Bill; but, I am afraid, that by what the ministers have taken
care to add to it, in the other House, our endeavours will be rendered unsuccessful; for from the opposition that will probably be made to these
additions, they will take a new occasion to represent us as Jacobites, which is,
in truth, the same with saying, that all those who are not ready to give up
the liberties of their country, are friends to the Pretender...It is easy to see
through their design: they make these misrepresentations with a view to
engross to themselves alone all the honours, offices, and preferments in the
disposal of the crown; but by this means, they make their sovereign the head
of a faction only.[39]

Fazakerley's exposition of the Old Corps' concentration on Jacobitism
has been adopted by many historians of the eighteenth century. It would
seem to need repeating in the face of Cruickshanks' assertion that the
whigs genuinely believed that toryism and Jacobitism were synonymous,
and Clark's argument that the whig–tory antithesis was rooted in the

two parties' inevitably disparate attitudes to the House of Hanover. If they genuinely feared that tory crypto-Jacobitism endangered Hanoverian security, if they perceived Jacobitism as the reason for rather than as a rationalisation of tory proscription, why did the whigs disrupt expressions of tory loyalty? The answer is obvious enough and was intimated in Lecky's silken prose more than a century ago: 'Much as they desired the maintenance of the dynasty, they had little desire to see the Tory Party reconciled to it.'[40]

Whig sabotage of tory rectitude was just as marked in the localities' response to the 1745 invasion. William Grove, tory M.P. for Coventry, was listed as a potential Jacobite in 1743 and presented the city's Loyal Address to the King in March 1744. Eighteen months later he demonstrated that he was indeed on the side of the Georges by urging a Coventry Association against the rebel invasion. A whig report to the duke of Grafton, Warwickshire's Lord Lieutenant, indicates how polarised the counties were by party, and how this antagonism could prejudice effective tory-Hanoverianism.

When the consideration of making this Association useful came to be enter'd upon, the Tories propos'd an application for calling out the Militia which being disapproved by the Corporation & the other Whiggs & a subscription propos'd the Tories have since deserted us... We hear that the Tories met last night, when it was resolved by them that Mr. Grove, who sets out to London tomorrow, should promote some scheme which may anticipate us & in case that did not succeed, then they would joyn the whiggs.

Having been informed of these developments, Thomas Archer, a whig M.P. with extensive electoral interest in Coventry, wrote reassuring the city's whig corporation that both Grove's alternative scheme and a proposal from some Warwickshire tories, that the county militia should be raised, would be safely quashed by the ministry; any provincial anti-Jacobite activity was to be seen to emanate from the centre or from local whigs.[41]

Such whig and ministerial sponsorship tended (and was sometimes intended) to deter tory co-operation. In two of the three counties – Middlesex, Shropshire, and Oxfordshire – where a sizeable number of tories refused to subscribe to associations against the Young Pretender, party scruples and animosity, not disaffection, seem to have been the real obstacles to a gentry consensus.[42] For Sir Roger Newdigate, whig proposals to hand over money to a whig magnate, so that he could raise his own regiment to defend the county, contravened the principle of parliamentary supply and constituted an invitation to aristocratic graft. At the Middlesex county meeting in November 1745 he refused to join in a private subscription against the rebels, 'But was ready to enter into any subscription as soon as it was put in a proper method, so as to be useful for keeping the peace of ye County since I found there was no thought of calling out the Militia which I prefer'd.' George Cooke, another Middlesex landowner and tory M.P. for Tregony, agreed: 'if he subscrib'd he desir'd it might be into the Exchequer'. To argue that all tory malingering was the product of constitutional scruple would be naive, but it should be remembered that some independent whigs of undoubted loyalty – the M.P. for Lancashire, Lord Strange, and George Savile of Yorkshire, for example – showed the same concern and similarly refused to participate.[43]

In Shropshire the tories made no objection in principle to a county association but they did object to the Lord Lieutenant Lord Herbert's 'Want of regard to the Party in that none of them were appointed Deputy Lieutenants'. They also complained of the paucity of tory J.P.s 'in relation to the late Commission of the Peace'. Lord Herbert's insensitivity to the tories' demands for parity of treatment with neighbouring whigs may be contrasted with Archbishop Herring's insistence in Yorkshire that all but avowed Jacobites should be consulted on local defence measures. His political discernment resulted in marked county unanimity, and the tory Members for York, Godfrey Wentworth and George Fox, were amongst the gentry and merchants of both parties who subsequently agreed on a Loyal Address 'in which each pledged himself to the other to defend the established order' and to raise £20 000.[44]

Perhaps the most interesting examples of tory rectitude occurred in Essex. In 1743 it had been this county, so conveniently near to London, which the six tory conspirators had proposed for a French landing. According to French and Stuart sources the plot had won support from several Essex tories, including the two Colchester M.P.s, Charles Gray and Samuel Savill, and one of the county Members, Thomas Bramston. Bramston's co-Member, Sir Robert Abdy, was of course one of the conspirators. In March 1744 Savill and Gray presented Colchester's Loyal Address. On 8 October 1745 Savill, Gray, Bramston, and Abdy attended their county Quarter Sessions meeting and agreed to an Essex Association in response to the Young Pretender's invasion. Gray and Savill went on to subscribe £50 apiece for their county's defence – sums which compare favourably with those donated by whigs of analogous socio-economic status.[45]

None of these actions necessarily disproves the reported Jacobite intrigue of these M.P.s, but they all complicate any assessment of its practical significance. This tory–Jacobite conspiracy resembles the shadowy, hybrid activities of Bolingbroke and Oxford at the end of Anne's reign and, as in this earlier instance, one is compelled to pose two basic questions: what did these ostensible conspirators do on the day and where did they put their money? Charles Gray not only subscribed to the defeat of the Young Pretender, but between 1744 and 1746 he also had over £1000 invested in Bank of England stock – an investment guaranteed by and dependent upon the continuance of the Hanoverian dynasty. Six other tories whom Butler had counted in 1743 as potential rebels – John Affleck of Suffolk, Sir Edmund Isham of Northamptonshire, Sir Henry Marshall of Amersham, George Newland of Gatton, William Strode of Reading, and Randle Wilbraham of Newcastle under Lyme – were together contributing £16 000 in Bank stock to the security of the established order in 1745–6: the same period as Charles Edward Stuart was languishing for want of funds.[46]

III

The majority of tory peers, M.P.s, and their county supporters were innocent of Jacobitism in 1744 and 1745; some of their leaders were not. Sir John Hynde Cotton was a prime tory spokesman in the House of Commons and in 1743 he risked his neck by joining in the invitation to the French to invade on behalf of the Stuarts. When the Young Pretender did invade, Cotton was drawing a court salary as Treasurer of the Chamber – a place he was to retain until his dismissal in July 1746. On 11 March 1747 John Murray, Charles Edward's former secretary turned king's evidence, delighted ministerial whigs by denouncing Cotton as well as Sir Watkin Williams Wynn and Lord Barrymore as Jacobite conspirators. The day after this exposure Sir John paid an ostentatious visit to Leicester House for a discussion with his party's current ally, Frederick, Prince of Wales.[47]

This degree of opportunism is perhaps atypical – the quasi-Catholic Charles Noel Somerset was a more authentic and Sir Watkin a more ingenuous conspirator – but Cotton's audacity is nonetheless a useful indicator. Since they were almost invariably proscribed by the first two Hanoverian monarchs, some leading tories certainly judged it essential to maintain contact with the Stuart Court. At the same time, and very wisely, the party's leadership explored the possibilities at home; responding to the overtures of whig Ministers such as the earl of Sunderland, Lord Carteret, and Henry Pelham, co-operating with dissident whigs like William Pulteney and William Pitt, and aligning with two successive Princes of Wales. It is noticeable that the tory–Jacobite liaison acquired prominence only when the tories were temporarily deprived of whig allies: in the maelstrom of 1715, after the whig reunion of 1720, and after the Patriot whig defection in 1742. Jacobitism, in short, was not the tory *raison d'être* but one political option amongst many, to be considered if and when it became viable. And even those tories who had been prominent exponents of Jacobite intrigue allowed themselves to fall before the final, crucial fence. In 1743–4 they delayed a French expeditionary force which had every chance of success. In 1745, with Charles Edward Stuart forging his way into England and – as Cruickshanks has shown – with substantial French aid assembled and ready to depart, they never even established contact with the Jacobite army; no tory gentleman joined Charles Edward's standard, and by withholding arms, money, and encouragement the party shaped his decision to retreat.[48]

To account for the final tory failure to deliver one has to have recourse to the ideological scruples, not merely of the mass of tory M.P.s, but also of their gentry, clerical, and plebeian supporters. Some months before the Hanoverian Succession the earl of Oxford had jotted down the fundamental objections to a Stuart restoration:

1. Security of our religion which cannot be under a Papist.
2. Securing our ancient rights which cannot be under one bred up in French maxims who comes over here with the [intention] to revive his father's quarrels.[49]

Post-1715 Stuart proclamations always included undertakings to respect the Anglican Church, but historically minded tories may well have remembered that James II had been full of such promises back in 1685. The Pretender's unrelenting Catholicism, his marriage to a Catholic and intolerant Princess (an alliance which Bishop Atterbury had urged him to avoid), the Catholic upbringing of their sons – Charles Edward did not conform to the Anglican Church until 1750 – and the conversion to Catholicism of James' secretary, Lord Hay, in 1725 and of Lords North and Wharton two years later all reinforced the lesson of James II's reign: that a Catholic Stuart would invariably choose to be served by his co-religionists.[50]

The tories were not unsympathetic towards British Catholics. They tended to oppose, as did libertarian whigs, any new proposal for punitive taxation and repressive legislation against recusants. To what extent they reaped their reward in Catholic electoral aid and illicit votes has not been established. In 1722 the tory candidate for Lancashire claimed he had received Catholic support, and in 1734 the whiggish Reverend William Stukeley was to chide a fellow clergyman for rebelling against his whig patron in favour of his county's two (successful) tory candidates: 'I only desire to know on what side the Roman Catholics push their interest in Norfolk? Answer, on the High Church side.' Before accepting Stukeley's testimony one should remember that the duke of Newcastle was bidding for the duke of Norfolk's Catholic influence in the same county contest.[51] And one must distinguish between an understandable tory consideration for the declining Catholic gentry at home and the tory fear that a French- or Italian-bred Catholic monarch would repeal the Test Act, erode what was left of the Church of England's status, and replace the proscription of the tory party with wholesale Anglican exclusion. This fear of expansive Catholicism primed the tory panic in 1736 when dissenting attempts to get the Test Act repealed (shades of 1687!) coincided with Irish agitation in London and rumours of mass conversions to Rome in the capital and outside. The tory Lord Mayor of London, Sir John Williams, wrote to warn Sir Robert Walpole and George II of the urgency of the problem, while Sir John Bland, the supposedly crypto-Jacobite M.P. for Yorkshire, financed an Anglican clergyman to offset the growth of papist sympathies in his own county and urged the Lord Chancellor to take action against missionary activity throughout England.[52]

Since James and his sons — at least after the death of Sweden's Charles XII in 1718 — were primarily dependent for their maintenance and invasion prospects on the Catholic Kings of France and Spain, their popular appeal in England was bound to be vulnerable to the traditional association of Catholicism with anti-libertarian government. The first two Hanoverian Kings were, it is true, scarcely engaging sovereigns. They were foreign, they were initially Lutheran, and they were physically un-attractive. A great deal of romantic Jacobitism as well as some astute Jacobite propaganda hung on the dark and melancholy charms of James Edward and the blonde hair and blue eyes of his son. But if xenophobia and Church of England sentiment prompted popular anti-Hanoverianism they were also likely to redound against low-level Jacobitism.[53] Stuart agents were well aware of this. In 1715 it was reported that the intended slogans for James' invasion of England were 'For the Church against the Whigs and a standing army without making mention of the Pretender or any King'. When the Jacobite army marched through Manchester in 1745 journalists noted that to 'amuse the Ignorant, [they] had on their Standards or Colours, Mottos that they imagined would be grateful, viz, Liberty and Property, Church and Country' — again avoiding any proprietorial legitimist appeal.[54]

The tories too must have been aware that popular alienation from the Hanoverian regime was unlikely to be translated into popular Jacobite activity. In the open constituencies, where the franchise penetrated fairly low down the social scale, the tory share of the vote fell in 1708, 1715, and to a lesser degree 1747: that is, on those occasions when the whigs were able to make their invariable identification of toryism with Jacobitism seem more plausible than they normally could.[55]

In York in 1747 the tories had not only to counter recent memories and, in the case of some of the citizens, direct experience of the invasion, but also to compensate for the Irish (*ergo* papist) descent of one of their candidates, George Fox. A whig broadside informed the city's electorate 'That...the short and long of the Dispute [is], are you for KING GEORGE, or the Pretender? For Popery or the CHURCH of ENGLAND...Gentlemen, I don't love to reflect on my Neighbours, but...it has certainly an odd Appearance, that these same Tories of ours are always on the Same Side with the French and the Papists.' Given Fox's record in 1745 this insinuation was demonstrably false, but it still undermined the York tories' standard and electorally resonant appeal as the party of patriotism and the Church. Fox's supporters were consequently grateful to be able to compromise the election with the whig candidate William Thornton – an arrangement which infuriated those low-level York voters who had responded to the whigs' nationalist propaganda. At the chairing Thornton was carried 'on the right hand of Fox as being first chosen which was a point the Mob insisted on'.[56]

IV

Pragmatism, ideology, and electoral self-interest militated against effectual tory crypto-Jacobitism after 1722. Was Whig belief in tory disaffection still crucial for the maintenance of the two-party system? For some whig M.P.s perhaps it was. William Hay, the sensible and cultivated ministerial Member for Seaford, was happy enough to work with tory M.P.s in the 1730s for a reform of the Poor Law, yet in 1742, when the party seemed on the verge of state employment, his diary is full of stark and panic-stricken references to its antipathy to the House of Hanover. Lord Chancellor Hardwicke had a similarly split if less ingenuous perception of contemporary toryism. In the autumn of 1741 he could consider the accession to office of 'some of the better tories' with equanimity; by February 1742, when such an accession seemed likely, Hardwicke, like Hay, had had second thoughts. He utterly confused Archbishop Secker by first telling him he was 'strong against taking in any Tories: owning no more than that some of them perhaps were not for the pretender' and then, later in the same conversation, remarking that 'the main body of them [the tories] were of the same principles with the Whigs'.[57] Whatever Hardwicke's real opinion, between May and September 1745 he and Henry Pelham abided by an earlier agreement with the tory leadership and issued new Commissions of the Peace, greatly increasing the number of tory J.P.s in seven English counties. As scores of tory gentlemen were being advanced to positions of local influence during a period which overlapped Charles Edward's successful march through Scotland, the ministry was either ludicrously casual in its attitude to domestic security, or had made a more accurate assessment of tory loyalty than some of its propaganda statements would seem to imply.

Sir Robert Walpole was the arch-exponent of tory–Jacobite synonymity, which makes it all the more significant that, on 13 February 1741 and *in extremis*, he abandoned his usual polemic and employed a far more subtle and tripartite analysis of his parliamentary critics: 'Tories, Jacobites, and Patriots...However different their views and principles, they all agree in opposition. The Jacobites distress the government they would subvert; the Tories contend for party prevalence and power.' One of Walpole's closest allies, the Attorney-General, Sir Dudley Ryder, was also prone to using tory and Jacobite as interchangeable political descriptions. Yet in a private minute on the state of opposition in 1748, Ryder drew a distinction very similar to that of his former mentor: 'The end proposed by the Tories is to get into the Ministry. The end by the Jacobites is to promote the Pretender's interest.'[58] Again, it is not merely the binary emphasis which is notable, but the attribution to the tory sector of a central and legitimate political strategy. It was the possibility that this central tory strategy might be successful which really worried the bulk of Walpolian and Pelhamite whigs, and they legitimised this partisan apprehension, particularly to the monarch, by reference to the Jacobite threat. It was the sporadic prospect of a tory incursion into central and local office, and not the unremitting fear of a tory-sponsored Stuart restoration, which was able to hold the whigs together even when their numbers had grown too swollen and their party platform too debased for anything else to do so.

Such a contention will scarcely seem valid given the frequent presentation of mid-century tory M.P.s as independents who were allergic to co-ordinated parliamentary activity and indifferent to state employment. John Owen has quoted with approval Bolingbroke's contemptuous descriptions of his former party: ' "Hewers of wood, and drawers of water"... they seem to proscribe every administration alike, which is to proscribe government itself', and on another occasion, 'strange creatures – I can hardly call them men'. The context of this latter remark was the refusal by many tories to join in Bolingbroke's strategy and support the opposition whig Samuel Sandys' February 1741 motion for Walpole's removal – an abstention which is usually seen as typical of the tory unconcern for parliamentary manoeuvre. Yet if this episode really does demonstrate the tories' innate disinterestedness, how does one explain the party's relentless pursuit of Walpole's destruction less than one year later? How indeed if, as Owen contends, the tories were only concerned to secure constitutional reforms and concessions in local government, does one account for their extreme anger when they were excluded from the high-level ministerial reconstruction of 1742?[59]

Post-1714 tory political ambition has been understated partly because the full implications of the party's political exclusion have not been understood, partly because the extent of tory defection to the whigs has been assumed rather than examined. The lure of place eroded the tory position in the House of Lords, but in the Lower House only thirty-four M.P.s who entered Parliament as tories between 1715 and 1760 are known to have deserted. The tory contingent in the Commons was of course subject to a less visible process of defection in that as the party continued to be proscribed, bright young men – if their constituency allowed them a choice – must inevitably have thought twice before entering Parliament under that party label. Still, as late as 1727, Henry Fox thought it worth his while to contest Hindon as a tory.[60]

Naturally the mid-century tory party included indolent M.P.s as well as men who entered Parliament only out of obedience to a family electoral interest or because of their landed status in a county. It also contained, just as it had done in the reign of Anne, individuals who valued their parliamentary independence too much to accept the constraints attendant on employment. In 1742 Sir John St Aubyn rejected a place on the Admiralty Board: he 'would take no place unless upon the express condition that his freedom and independency in Parliament should remain unquestion'd and uncontroll'd'. St Aubyn's principled immunity to employment was reinforced by his prominence in the tory party, by his landed wealth, and by the consideration that his county seat was likely to complicate accession to office. By an Act of 1706, M.P.s appointed to state office had to offer themselves for re-election in their constituency. By definition government placemen who sat for rotten boroughs ran little risk in seeking election again. But in the large borough and county constituencies contested by-elections were more common, and even an uncontested by-election was likely to prove expensive. Hence in part the diffidence with which some tories greeted the prospect of office: in 1741 ninety-eight of the 135 tory M.P.s were either county representatives or Members of boroughs with over five hundred voters.[61]

So in April 1742, when William Pulteney suggested to the tory M.P. for Herefordshire, Velters Cornewall, that he should apply for a government place, Cornewall's response was both partisan and pragmatic. As he wrote to a friend and constituent, his party's most prominent peers, Lords Bathurst and Gower, had already accepted a share of office:

& ye more of us are taken in ye Broader ye Bottom; consequently ye more agreeable to ye Tories...so that when this popular Ministry is establisht, you perhaps would kindly say that A man must be Felo de se to refuse a very profitable & honourable Employment.

As Cornewall's rationalisation of employment suggests, what really worried him was not the loss of his independence, but whether

Ye generality of my Chief Constituents in Herefordshire will permit me to accept of it; I will write soon to Mr. Hopton...& perhaps 1 or 2 more... that I may feel their pulses as to my takeing A place, and as to my re election.[62]

This eminently sensible attitude to place also governed the tory response to Pelham's offer of a modicum of employment in November 1744. Sir John Hynde Cotton, secure in Lord Ailesbury's pocket borough of Marlborough, cheerfully accepted a place at Court. Sir Edward Dering, who had been returned for Kent in 1733 immediately after the Excise Crisis, was too sensitive to the possibility of a constituency backlash to be able to respond to Pelham's overtures with such unalloyed enthusiasm: 'Dering', noted Lord Fitzwilliam in December 1744, 'is talk'd of...as Commissary General, if he can be rechosen for the county...which is very much doubted.'[63]

The tory leaders appreciated their Members' difficulties and, on those occasions when they were negotiating some access to office, always took care to link demands for employment with an insistence on measures of constitutional reform. Between 1721 and 1723, when members of the party were consulting first with the earl of Sunderland and then with Lord Carteret, they asked for access to place *and* for the restoration of the Triennial Act, a reduction in the size of the Army, and the repeal of the Riot Act.[64] These desiderata were selected to render the negotiations more acceptable to tory backbenchers and legitimise, in the eyes of their constituents, a potential tory incursion into government.

If the party's conscience and its electoral base could be appeased in this fashion, the bulk of tory M.P.s and peers were only too willing to acquiesce in the prospect of employment. In 1742 Legh Master, tory M.P. for Newton, described his reaction to the possibility of his being appointed a Commissioner of the Excise: 'As I would neither act counter to the opinion of my Friends, or the Principles I have always profess'd... neither would I out of any caprice wantonly trifle away & lose the opportunity of serving my family & friends as in such an office I might have an opportunity of doing.' Now Master was the very reverse of a political high-flier. He owed his seat to his uncle (who was Newton's proprietor), his parliamentary attendance was sporadic, and if he made any contribution to debate at Westminster it has gone unrecorded. His comment illustrates the multi-faceted importance of access to patronage — an importance to which Namier failed to do justice when he dismissed the grievances of the tories in 'their exile-from-office period' as 'imaginary in men who did not desire office'. Legh Master may never have dreamed and would certainly not have been capable of becoming a Minister of State; he could and did savour in anticipation the considerable advantages attendant on minor office.[65]

Nor is it enough, indeed it is inconsistent, to argue as Owen has done that the tories nurtured a 'simple desire for local eminence rather than a share in the beneficence of the central administration'. Of course the tories wanted parity with the whigs in the Commissions of the Peace, in the Deputy Lieutenantships, and in the Land Tax Commission; they also (like Master) wanted to be able to advance their relations, their friends, and their constituents in the Church, the Army and Navy, the Law, and the revenue departments. But until the tory leadership gained some access to the political centre, the majority of these local offices and the bulk of this subsidiary patronage would be at the disposal of a uniformly whig administration and would consequently tend to be distributed very much in favour of whig applicants. Sir Nicholas Morice understood this perfectly well when throughout 1721 he busied himself trying to get a minor Excise post for one of his supporters in Newport: 'As to Pethick, ye Commissioner promised me to advance him long since, but, not to dispute ye point, it is not done yet.' Pethick's eventual appointment in January 1722 was a singular concession, as Morice well realised: 'Ye Commissioner is a civil obligeing man & I believe would do more to oblige me if he was left to himselfe, but he must submit to higher powers.'[66]

It was because the parliamentary party and its supporters recognised this connection between the bias of higher powers and the allocation of local patronage that there had been such a tory clamour for place in 1710. Not only had the obvious careerists expected to benefit from their party's electoral coup that year, but so also had tory squires like Richard Beaumont of Yorkshire, a man who was desperate to supplement his landed income with a salaried position. In 1727, when the accession of George II offered the prospect of a mixed administration, the same appreciation of the machinery of patronage led to tory demands that 'the principal persons of the party are employed, & have such a proportion of power as will enable 'em to do. . .Service to their Friends'.[67]

If the importance of direct or indirect access to state patronage was widely felt, and as many tories were clearly amenable to office *on terms*, how did the party expect to penetrate the charmed circle of employment without recourse to a Stuart restoration? The whig supremacy, it is usually supposed, was rooted in Hanoverian dynastic acquiescence; yet how invariable and absolute that acquiescence was, is more difficult to establish than is sometimes allowed. The extant political correspondence of George I is uneven and dispersed; that of George II fragmentary.[68] For both Kings' attitude to the tories we rely heavily on whig and German reportage, and, as B. W. Hill has remarked, Lord Hervey's very biased court diaries hardly suggest that the monarchical stance in the 1730s was so stable as to permit whig complacency. Hervey knew well enough that George II and Caroline periodically dangled the prospect of a tory administration before the eyes of their Ministers to keep Walpole and his friends on their toes. So the various Walpolian panics he recorded between 1733 and 1737, when it seemed that George might adulterate the whig bases of his government, suggest that something more serious was happening than the King's normal petulance or the Queen's malice.[69]

There can of course be no doubt that the rumoured extent and the limited actuality of tory crypto-Jacobitism inspired Hanoverian distrust of that party, and that George I's desire for complete religious toleration and his own and his son's Euro-centric foreign policies were at odds with tory Anglicanism and insularity. But George I hardly found Robert Walpole a proponent of complete religious toleration either, and few of George II's Ministers, with the exception of that erstwhile tory, Lord Carteret, were markedly sympathetic to his Hanoverian commitments. And what of the whig Jacobites? The duke of Marlborough, earl Cowper, the earl of Sunderland, possibly Lords Orford and Chesterfield, were all implicated in Stuart intrigue; the Pretender's most flamboyant converts were the young Lord Wharton and Lord Rialton, grandson of the earl of Godolphin. If these deviants did not detract from whig acceptability why should not the Hanoverian Kings have drawn a distinction between known crypto-Jacobite tories and their more innocuous colleagues?[70]

To an extent they did. Less than three years after the Hanoverian Succession the Prince of Wales assured the loyal Suffolk tory, Sir Thomas Hanmer, 'qu'il avoit un vif repentir d'avoir, sur des perfides conseils, regardé les tories comme ses ennemis'. George's more subtle perception of English party politics was derived, like his father's concurrent disillusionment, from experience of the political presumption attendant on undiluted whiggery. Both King and heir had become sensitive to the logic behind Bernard Mandeville's inquiry of the victorious whigs in 1714: 'What will you say, when the King turns out the Whigs, and takes these Tories in again that you have so much rail'd against, as he'll be forced to do at last? He was an absolute Prince before, Do you think he'll ever stand under the impertinent Tutorship of Whig Parliaments?'[71] Some tories were too suspect and some whigs too able for a pure tory administration to have been viable after 1714, but the prospect of a

mixed administration – a ministerial format which had been the norm
in post-revolutionary Britain and the invariable preference of William III
and Queen Anne – was persistent and attractive. George I in 1717, 1721,
and 1725, and his son in 1727, 1744, and 1746 (and these are only the
instances for which we possess definite evidence) not only considered
such a political solution but also went some way towards exploring its
practicality.

That these royal initiatives did not result in a partial tory return to
power may be primarily ascribed to contingency and Sir Robert Walpole
– in that order. But even though they failed, as soon as we recognise that
the first two Hanoverian monarchs were prepared to entertain some
flexibility in party choice, the mid-century tory party appears less impoverished and the periodic nervousness of its whig opponents more
explicable. In October 1742 when Walpole, now Lord Orford, warned
his successor that the whigs had been 'brought. . .into such danger, that
the tories think they have now an opportunity of making a push for the
whole', he was not writing as an old man fixated on the party battles
of the past, but rather reminding Pelham of a political fact of life which
he himself had always borne in mind: that the whigs' monopoly of the
centre was not guaranteed either by monarchical bias or by tory impotence.
The decision of William Pulteney and his Patriot allies, in the same year,
to realign with Orford's Old Corps successors rather than form a mixed
administration with their *quondam* allies, bears witness to the whigs'
fundamental cohesion and to their fear of the partisan repercussions of
tory access to state patronage and royal favour.[72]

Considering that the tories after 1714 always had the prospect of
limited royal recognition, and remembering that as the eighteenth century
progressed the whig group became so swollen as to be almost inevitably
friable, the tories' room for manoeuvre at Westminster was such that
they did not usually need to commit themselves to Jacobite skullduggery,
or to sink into the dour and indiscriminate opposition of a squirearchical
rump. Horace Walpole's threefold identification of tory options was a
concession to his century's taste for epigram; it was not composed in
accordance with historical fact.

PART II

The Ingredients of Tory Survival

3

The Tory Party in Parliament

Since the tories after 1714 have so frequently been described as Jacobite fifth-columnists or as political independents, it is scarcely surprising that their leadership and parliamentary organisation should have been ignored or more commonly denied. Neglect has also been encouraged by the lack of easily available evidence. Only two tory Commoners in this period, Thomas Carew and Sir Roger Newdigate, and only one of the party's noble families, the earls of Oxford and Mortimer, are represented by a substantial cache of political papers.[1] Reliance instead on the ill-informed and often contemptuous assessments of the tory performance supplied by some whig observers, or an assumption that the apparent paucity of tory papers presupposes a concomitant lack of tory parliamentary endeavour, have been both convenient and consonant with preconceptions about the party's role in the mid eighteenth century.

The disorganised quality of Augustan toryism as compared with the efficiency of the Junto Lords and their whig adherents is of course part and parcel of the political instability so often and, as I have already suggested, too immoderately ascribed to the period. Geoffrey Holmes' excellent account of the frequently partisan but invariably independent tory country gentlemen and of 'the seemingly limitless tory capacity for fragmentation' has tended to obscure the same author's salutary reminder that the Oxford administration of 1710–14 suffered only one major defeat in four parliamentary sessions. Tory M.P.s were often difficult to manage; they were not unmanageable. And in the latter part of Anne's reign, some of the longstanding obstacles to tory unison had fallen away. Sir Edward Seymour and Lord Rochester, who had each tended to distract some tory peers and M.P.s from the Harleian centre, were both dead by 1711. The earl of Nottingham's defection to the whigs over the Treaty of Utrecht was not emulated by any of his tory friends or relations, and only liberated Oxford from one of his sharpest party critics.[2]

Nor was the fusion between the Harley and Foley imports of the 1690s and mainstream tory M.P.s as unfinished by 1714 as Keith Feiling once suggested. Their capacity for ideological and practical *rapprochement* was advertised in the friendship and working alliance between the High-Church William Bromley, M.P. for his party's most quintessential seat, the University of Oxford, and that product of a whig, quasi-Puritan family, Robert Harley, earl of Oxford. The Harleyites retained and were to retain after 1714 a distinct identity within the tory party, but it was not so much tory backbench incompatibility with Country ideology which underlay such tensions as remained between the two groups, as Oxford's own tactical disinclination to break off all ties with the whigs. His preference for a mixed administration and his belief that concurrence in a tory policy of 'Thorough' would result in the party supremacy of his rival, Henry St John, Viscount Bolingbroke, led him to intrigue after 1712 with whig Lords such as Cowper and Halifax and to resist a tory monopoly on place at the centre and in local government. It was no accident that the only Welsh county not to have been given a new and predominantly tory Commission of the Peace by Lord Chancellor Harcourt in 1713 was Oxford's own stamping-ground of Radnorshire, or that, of the many English whig J.P.s purged in the same year, those in the Lord Treasurer's home county of Herefordshire were treated with comparative moderation.[3]

Even if state patronage had been deployed as unilaterally as Harcourt and Bolingbroke desired, it would still have been impossible to appease every proclaimed tory politician. In 1710 the English and Welsh constituencies returned 332 tory M.P.s; in 1713 the corresponding total was 363, inflating the tory party in the Commons beyond the possibility of ideological uniformity or its leaders' close surveillance. Accentuating this logistical difficulty was the strain on the party's nerves and morale imposed by the potential crisis in the Succession. Since their contention was about personal primacy rather than alternative dynasties and since both men wanted to keep their options open, neither Oxford nor Bolingbroke would clarify their respective positions on the Succession. This apparent ambiguity at the centre permitted the emergence in 1713 of a Hanoverian or whimsical tory pressure-group in the House of Commons of between fifty and sixty M.P.s and of a Jacobite cadre of about the same number.[4]

Proscription solved some of these tory problems very quickly. By the time all the 1715 election petitions had been processed the number of tory M.P.s had fallen to just over 190. The Hanoverian Succession (which had been the sole basis of their voting agreement with the whigs), and the near-absolute tory proscription implemented in the wake of the 1715 rebellion, served to reintegrate the whimsical tories with their colleagues. In 1714 the group's two leading Commoners, Sir Thomas Hanmer and Ralph Freman, refused George I's offer of employment, and the following year saw the reversion to opposition of their counterparts in the Lords,

Abingdon, Anglesey, Aylesford, and Archbishop Dawes. The earl of Nottingham stayed with the ministry until 1716 and his parliamentary attendance was to slump with age and the passing of the Septennial Act; nonetheless by 1717 his proxy vote at least was restored to tory orthodoxy, being entrusted to Lord Guilford.[5] Exclusion from state office also permitted and was to ensure until the 1750s a degree of policy cohesion. Since all tories were compelled into an opposition stance, the dichotomy between the party's court and Country wings was normally obscured, just as it had been in the lean years between 1705 and 1710.

Proscription preserved the tory party's identity; it did not encourage its parliamentary efficiency. Bolingbroke's flight to France and Oxford's imprisonment in 1715 deprived the tories of their most substantial and experienced politicians. Initially it was not clear who was to replace them, and the process by which a tory leader would emerge was bound to be more arbitrary now that his party status and authority would not be reinforced by possession of a principal office of state. It is well known that tory M.P.s were peculiarly lax in their attendance at Westminster: it is not however true. Backbenchers of both parties tended to be recalcitrant, but on the evidence of their performance in 1715 the tories were marginally better. If one examines the eighty divisions in the House of Commons that year in which M.P.s voted on strict party lines, the average tory division rate was 98 M.Ps, 50 per cent of their Commons contingent; the whig average was 150 M.P.s or 45 per cent.[6]

A 50 per cent attendance rate was of course no way to run a successful opposition. The tories were quite capable of producing an excellent turn-out for a specific parliamentary crisis. Just under four-fifths of the party was present for the Commons divisions on the Septennial Bill in April 1716 and the repeal of the Occasional Conformity and Schism Acts in January 1719. In the House of Lords divisions on the latter piece of legislation fifty-five tory peers out of a possible sixty-two were present to vote against it; less than half of these made a practice of attending the House for more prosaic business.[7]

Selective tory attendance continued to be the norm even after the whig schism of 1717 provided the party with the prospect of voting in the majority. When the High-Church Dr Snape was chosen to preach the House of Commons Restoration Day sermon on 13 May 1717, eighty-four tories were present for the occasion. Snape was elected only because fifty-six dissident whigs, wanting to embarrass Stanhope's administration, also lent him their support. Before the winter session of that year a large number of tory M.P.s made a concerted decision not to attend, so that when the House was called over on 23 December, sixty-seven of them were absent. Another call of the House was ordered for

23 January 1718, whereupon some tory M.P.s responded like Sir John
Stonhouse, the Member for Berkshire, who turned up on the appointed
day and went home the day after, 'notwithstanding the earnest persuasions of his best friends'. George Clarke, tory M.P. for Oxford, sought
to account for his colleagues' irresponsible behaviour to a disgruntled
constituent: 'There is no persuading Gentlemen to come & stay in
towne, or attend when they are here...For my owne part, I am afraid
that a majority is not to be depended upon, for people act with different
views, & there is no common principle in which they agree.'[8]

Clarke's emphasis on policy variance as the root cause of tory disarray
was prompted by his party's incompatibility with Walpole's clique of
opposition whigs, but his analysis was also applicable to tensions within
the tory group itself. Such dissonance derived in part from a major
and persistent organisational defect. When one reads how in April 1714
Oxford and Bolingbroke summoned a meeting of thirty prominent tories
and proposed that they 'should meet twice a week for mutual confidence',
one is struck not so much by the wisdom of this initiative (which seems
never in fact to have been implemented) but by amazement that a
similar expedient had not been adopted much earlier. In George I's reign
as in that of Queen Anne, leading tories lacked both a regularised system
of intra-party consultation and means to transmit their policy decisions
to their more influential supporters. To this internal obstacle to efficient
and coherent tory parliamentary opposition was added the distraction
which was Jacobitism. To an inadequately organised and provincially
orientated group of men, the Stuart solution to proscription could seem
more attractive and more plausible than a prolonged parliamentary
campaign. A violent restoration had dramatic appeal for the talented and
embittered young men of the party – most notably the clique attached
to Sir William Wyndham – and intriguing in a country house or (as
was Wyndham's habit) on a hunting party was consonant with secrecy
and social ease.[9]

The tories' fluctuating parliamentary experience between 1715 and
1760 divides into three periods of development. In the first ten years of
proscription these problems were simply not resolved: hence in large
part the tory failure to stage a partial political recovery in the crucial
interval before Walpolian predominance. Wyndham's accession to the
tory leadership and to pro-Hanoverian respectability after 1724 inaugurated a period of qualified recovery, which also saw the emergence
of durable and less personalised forms of party control: London-based
clubs, which helped the tories to retain a coherent parliamentary presence
in the third and final phase after Wyndham's death in 1740.

I

The political demolition of Bolingbroke and Oxford in 1715 did more than deprive the party of their guidance *pro tempore*, it compromised their authority in the long term. Since many tories had regarded the projected parliamentary inquiry into Utrecht as a partisan device intended to take the lives of the tory Ministers (a diagnosis in which some whigs enthusiastically concurred), Bolingbroke's retreat in March 1715 did not immediately estrange party opinion. It was his recruitment by James III and his subsequent desertion of the Stuart cause which antagonised both Hanoverian and Jacobite tories. After 1715 Stuart agents in England worked to corrode his party reputation, so that by September 1716 Thomas Hearne had been informed of the new St Germains orthodoxy – entirely the reverse of its propaganda line one year earlier: 'My Ld Bullingbroke hath been a great villain...My Ld Oxford is very honest &...had managed things for the King's restoration but that Bullingbroke hindered every thing.' More acute Jacobite-tories like Wyndham and Lord Bathurst were also initially contemptuous of Bolingbroke's letters of advice and of his secretary, John Brinsden, when he visited England in 1717: alienated, one suspects, less because their mentor had abandoned James, than because he was currently purveying tory information to the whig ministry.[10]

Oxford's fall from party grace had preceded and was partly redeemed by his imprisonment. His shadowy, daedal intrigues during the latter years of Anne's reign and his scurrying attempts to conciliate George I after his accession disgusted straightforward tory M.P.s like Sir Thomas Cave, who responded Mercutio-like to the impeachment proceedings against both Oxford and the exiled Bolingbroke: 'if they meddle with none but these two in this manner, I'm not of opinion to stay to defend 'em'. In the House of Lords, in part because of his creations in 1711, Oxford's position was stronger. Over fifty tory peers attended the debate on his impeachment on 9 July 1715, forty-seven of them signing the subsequent Protest. The Protest on Bolingbroke's impeachment attracted only fifteen signatures.[11]

Oxford's two-year confinement in the Tower damaged his health and confirmed his tendency to neurosis and mistrust. He developed a self-righteous perception of himself as prime political martyr of the whigs as well as the victim of tory ingratitude after 1710. Lord Harley's comment of 1721 suggests both his father's recognition of the tories' need for direction and the rationalisation of his failure to provide it: 'they [the tories] have been long at sea, and stand in great need of a good pilot, and when they are safe on shore hang the pilot'. This bitterness was expressed in political inertia, a disinclination to engage in partisan activity which extended to all the Harley clan in the first decade of proscription. They allowed their electoral interests in Cambridgeshire and Herefordshire to slide; Oxford's son and heir, Edward Harley, refused to come into Parliament until 1722 and did nothing when he got there; Auditor Harley was equally aloof, and this supineness in adversity was legitimised by an almost Miltonic sense of political predestination. (*Samson Agonistes*, with its hero's passive fortitude rewarded by an ultimate God-given victory, had accompanied Oxford to the Tower.) So in 1720, at the height of the South Sea crisis and when all political permutations seemed possible, Auditor Harley was still assuring his brother, 'That Providence who so wonderfully conducted & preserved you, does not at present seem to afford any opportunity for you to Act.'[12]

Oxford's political distinction could still make itself felt. His speech against the repeal of the Occasional Conformity Act was considered impressive, and he instigated the Scottish peers' resistance to the Peerage Bill in 1719. During Atterbury's trial in 1723 he triumphed over his personal dislike of the bishop and his own encroaching disabilities, and led the House of Lords' campaign in his defence: 'Always at the House', recorded the breathlessly admiring Mrs Charles Caesar, and never dining till late in the evening.[13] But Oxford refused to take responsibility for a continuous policy line, and his visits to London were too sporadic for him to supervise (even had he wished to do so) the minutiae of tory parliamentary attendance and voting behaviour. In the House of Lords his concern, like his presence, was uneven: 'I have not heard of any thing which requires immediate attendance', he informed a fellow tory peer in November 1719, just one month before the Peerage Bill crisis, 'perhaps when the scene opens something worth going up may appear, but I desire your Lordship will let me know your opinion for I shall regulate myself by that.'[14]

With Oxford and Bolingbroke disqualified by choice and contingency, and since the earl of Anglesey, a tory peer of considerable ability, was also politically unstable and holding office in Ireland throughout 1715, the leadership was bound to devolve on a Commoner. There was the former Speaker, Sir Thomas Hanmer, who had frequently demonstrated his personal disdain for state employment and who was unlikely therefore to be greatly perturbed or prompted into defection by the tories' novel exclusion. Hanmer's own independence did not imply unconcern for his party's claims to government, but his cultivated and aloof demeanour, so aptly conveyed by his mannered oratory (he 'tickled the ears', thought one whig critic, rather than 'convincing the understanding'), equipped him more for high-level consultation than for parliamentary management. This personal limitation was partly offset by a working alliance with the able Hertfordshire tory Ralph Freman.[15] When Hanmer – 'ye greatest man in England with ye Prince' – promised the Hanoverian heir in 1719 that the tories would oppose the Peerage Bill, it was Freman who went about lobbying individual tories and who moved for a Call of the House on 14 April, ensuring good tory attendance on that day and the bill's deferral. The intelligence and the evident loyalty of both these men made them ideally suited to lead tory negotiations with the whig elite. This same pro-Hanoverian rectitude meant however that neither Hanmer nor Freman was able to work wholeheartedly for tory reconstruction since each always felt obliged to dissociate himself from the tory right wing. In October 1722, when the suspension of Habeas Corpus was under discussion, Hanmer was prepared to argue that it should be suspended for six months only; he was not prepared to join William Shippen and the more partisan tories in denying the very existence of the Atterbury plot: he 'told some of his party . . . that if they were at that Sport he must vote with the Court or leave the House, & accordingly left it'.[16]

Shippen's antics should not give the impression that after 1714 he led a distinct Jacobite contingent in the Commons or that he translated his genuine legitimist sympathies into active plotting. His role was more subtle and essentially individualistic. In 1715 his passivity led to suspicions that he had betrayed another Jacobite tory, John Anstis, to the government. In 1717 Bishop Atterbury planned to use him to collect money for a Swedish–Jacobite invasion; instead, a purely verbal assault on the House of Hanover ensured that the tory M.P. was safely incarcerated in the Tower. In 1722 his house was searched but no firm evidence of his complicity in the Atterbury plot was ever found.[17]

What Shippen did endeavour to do, with considerable success, was to hinder any tory conjunction with either ministerial or dissident whigs and to ensure thereby that the Jacobite solution to tory proscription was kept to the fore. In June 1717, when Robert Walpole was working to ingratiate himself with the tories by getting Oxford's impeachment quashed, Shippen reminded the House that it was Walpole who had initially engineered the impeachments. He went on to speculate aloud as to whether Walpole's novel humanity had anything to do with his now being out of office: 'That he did not mention this as a reflection on that gentleman, for whom he ever had a great respect; but that he was afraid this would lessen him in the esteem of others.'[18] Shippen's sly and generally virulent parliamentary style was often effective, and on the frequent occasions when he had his speeches printed they were immensely popular. Apart from this wayward talent and the occasional effort to secure good tory attendance for any debate which impinged upon the Church of England, his contribution to tory parliamentary' activity was almost entirely negative. In the first decade of proscription, his unapologetic anti-Hanoverianism compromised any tory bid for political respectability. In the 1730s he acted as the party's tame eccentric, ostentatiously refusing to subscribe to the *Craftsman* and allowing himself to be condescended to by Sir Robert Walpole, who savoured the propaganda value of his overt but sterile Jacobitism. Shippen tended nonetheless to be included in any high-level tory consultation – partly because he could contribute his experience and an undeniably shrewd mind, partly because Wyndham preferred to keep him under surveillance lest he succeed in distracting tory M.P.s from the party's coalition agreement with the Patriot whigs.[19]

With Freman, Hanmer, and Shippen disqualified by their respective polarisation within the party, it was the former Secretary of State, William Bromley, who emerged as the most plausible candidate for the tory leadership in George I's early reign. His range of friendships within the party was extensive and he commanded respect even from those politicians who acknowledged that his intellect was second-rate. More important, Bromley was prepared and qualified to straddle the differences within his party. He was a close friend of Hanmer, whom he had persuaded to accept the Speakership in 1713, but he also accepted the need to keep himself informed of tory–Jacobite activity if only so as to keep it under control.[20] His attempts to reconcile the Hanoverian and pro-Stuart lobbies were not always successful. In the Habeas Corpus debate of 1722, which had so offended Hanmer, Bromley sought to placate both groups and attract independent whig support. He proposed 'A Committee of ye Whole House upon it, & to proceed upon ye Amendment; this the Old Whigs, 'twas thought, would generally come into, & we should make a better figure on ye first Division.' In fact Bromley's suggestion satisfied nobody. One of his friends, the Warwickshire tory Robert Digby, was left lamenting: 'I am sorry Mr. Bromley's judgement does not fall in with, or rather so cement others as to produce an Unanimity & intelligence of what is to be done.'[21]

The ill-health which dogged him after 1718 and the attitude of the earl of Oxford were more insuperable limitations on the scope and success of Bromley's party activity. Though he was sometimes critical of the Lord Treasurer's conduct in 1713 and 1714, loyalty to him had become the mainspring of Bromley's political involvement: 'My dependence is entirely on your great abilities', he wrote to Oxford in August 1721, 'Your perfect knowledge of men and of our constitution, your sagacity and dexterity to extricate us out of our difficulties.' He sought the older man's advice on whether and when he should attend Parliament and on how he should respond to the political advances of Walpole, Sunderland, and the Prince of Wales: all too often Oxford's apparent political indifference perplexed and immobilised his friend in the Commons.[22]

In November 1721 he did instruct Bromley to open negotiations with Sir William Wyndham and Lords Gower and Bathurst. It would be difficult to exaggerate the potential importance of this initiative. Before 1714 Wyndham and Bathurst had been among Bolingbroke's closest party allies; since the Hanoverian Succession they and Gower had dabbled in Jacobite intrigue and had encouraged in that direction their many friends and relations in the party. By approaching Bromley they were demonstrating an advance in political maturity, and a willingness to renounce the Stuart cause and the prolonged and destructive feud between the Oxford and Bolingbroke camps. In December Bromley and Wyndham made some progress on an agreement for future parliamentary collaboration, but their discussions were compromised by Oxford's persistent and inexplicable refusal to journey to London and lend his authority and approval to the scheme. As Dr Stratford reported to Lord Harley:

Sir William Wyndham and those who were supposed to have headed a party in opposition to your father, now make their court entirely to Mr. Bromley, and as he has declared he will act with no man but your father, had your father been on the spot, I believe all old breaches had been made up by this time, and Mr. Bromley had brought the whole Tory party once again under your father. But your father having failed Mr. Bromley, he is going into the country again next week, and I cannot say whether there will ever be so fair a juncture again.[23]

Allowing for Stratford's partisan hyperbole, it does seem that an opportunity to gain a measure of tory unity which would have contained the demoralising effects of the Atterbury plot, even had it not been able to forestall it, had been sacrificed to Oxford's political paralysis.

The potential for a limited tory recovery at Oxford's death in 1724 — and there was such a potential — was bound to be confined to the House of Commons. As the creation of four pro-tory peers in 1703 and 'Harley's dozen' evinced, the party's majority in the Upper House had always been fragile and was dependent on its possession of the Court. At George I's accession only eleven of the twenty-six bishops were tory and of these Crewe of Durham, Manningham of Chichester, Ottley of St David's, Blackall of Exeter, and Hooper of Bath and Wells were too old, too apolitical or too distant to attend Parliament with any regularity.

This episcopal rump was not of course liable to eviction, though at an early stage of the Hanoverian regime some victorious whig politicians urged the abrogation of the bishops' parliamentary rights – a proposal vetoed by the more prescient Walpole. The same permanence did not apply to the Scottish representative peers. In 1715 tory Lords from North of the border were either excluded in the rigged electoral process or were returned to Westminster transmuted into whigs; Lords Montrose, Loudoun, and Orkney, all tory office-holders under Anne, opted for the latter course.[24]

The erosion of the English tory peers was less rapid than has sometimes been supposed. Only thirteen committed themselves to defection during the first Hanoverian Parliament. Lords Byron, Delawarr, and Pembroke had ever been flexible in their party allegiance and were predictable casualties of tory proscription. Less predictable but enforced by poverty was the apostasy of Lord Clarendon who, by 1719, was accepting the ministerial whip as well as ministerial hand-outs, and who voted for the repeal of the Occasional Conformity and Schism Acts. He was joined in this aberration from High-Church rectitude by the former tory Lords Hatton, Jersey, Yarmouth, Saye and Sele, and Maynard.[25] Some tory peers demonstrated an unexpected fidelity. George I rewarded the mild Lord Paget for his steady Hanoverianism by making him earl of Uxbridge, an act which served only to stimulate him into greater tory activism in the Lords. Lord Masham was made Remembrancer of the Exchequer in 1716 yet continued to entrust his proxy to fellow tories and join in some of their Protests. It was in fact much more common for an aristocratic shift in party allegiance to take place only when a title changed hands. The earl of Anglesey was resolute in his toryism until his death in 1737; his son discreetly took his seat as a ministerial supporter. The earl of Dartmouth inverted this process by waiting until his son, Henry Legge, had been appointed Secretary to the Lord Lieutenant of Ireland in 1739 with a guarantee of a Secretaryship to the Treasury before agreeing to transfer his proxy vote from one of his tory friends to the duke of Grafton.[26]

While the decline of the English tory peers was gradual, their minority status in the House of Lords was an immediate result of the events of 1714 and 1715. At Queen Anne's death the tories had only six more English temporal peers than had the whigs, and this margin was swiftly reversed by the creation of new government peers and bishops and by the death and attainder of tory stalwarts. Many of the tory peers who remained could see little point in attending only to be out-voted. 'I am very confident that whatever is proposed will be carried', wrote Lord Mansel in 1723 when Oxford asked him to be present at the Atterbury debates, 'therefore my being there will be of no further use than having one protester more upon the books.' The event proved him correct. In May 1723 more than forty tory peers assembled in London for the division on Atterbury's Bill of Pains and Penalties; they did so knowing that on 26 April the ministry had aired its strength by rounding up 120 compliant peers.[27]

It was this invariably justified pessimism which the errant whig Lord Cowper sought to dissipate: 'when one could not capture an enemy fort', he is supposed to have remarked, 'one had to bombard it at least'. For over two years his opposition cabal of about twenty tory peers and a few whig oddities like the duke of Wharton and Lord Coningsby forced an unprecedented number of House of Lords divisions – thirty-six in the 1721–2 session and thirty-seven between October 1722 and May 1723 – more than double the average annual division rate achieved between 1714 and 1721. Their inevitable parliamentary defeats were converted into propaganda triumphs by way of carefully written Protests which were communicated to the London press and published in pamphlet form.[28]

Such activism was a clear advance on negative absenteeism but its limitations were twofold. Cowper was felt to be essential to the cabal's efficacy, and when he fell ill in June 1721 he received regular tributes to his indispensability from his second-in-command, Lord Bathurst: 'the truth of it is my Lord we have had no Spirit left since your Lordship has been absent'. More seriously Cowper's methods were only likely to attract support and be productive if the administration was insecure. So long as Walpole was contending with Sunderland or Lord Carteret for prime royal favour such a condition could apply, but to lay siege or advertise nuisance value to an entrenched and unified ministry from such a minority position was futile. The waning in vitality of the Upper House in the mid eighteenth century reflects in large part tory recognition of this fact. After 1723 the sessional division rate fell sharply until 1730, when the tory conjunction with the Patriot whigs permitted some revival. Between 1743 and 1760, when the tory peers were almost isolated in opposition and their effective membership had fallen to below twenty (and after 1756 even this tory residuum was neutralised by its adhesion to Pitt), recorded divisions in the Lords fell to an average of three a year.[29]

The organisation of Cowper's cabal had been precise. Every week various members had assembled at Lord Orrery's London house to discuss strategy and an intricate system of whipping had been devised. Cowper and eleven tory peers including Bathurst, Archbishop Dawes, and Lord Foley had each assumed responsibility for two or more other cabal members, informing them of prospective debates and making the necessary proxy arrangements.[30]

Subsequent tory organisation in the Lords was less regularised. The limited numbers involved encouraged a reliance on social intercourse for communication and would certainly have made any formal device like the whig peers' pre-sessional assemblies at the Secretary of State's residence seem quite inappropriate. Special meetings tended to be held only if a contentious debate demanding a written Protest was imminent. 'I saw Lord Anglesey in the House yesterday', wrote Lord Aylesford to Dartmouth early in 1729, 'but no conferences yet.' Aylesford's enthusiasm was only answered in March when Bathurst summoned a meeting of his fellow peers 'to concert what was proper to be done in this session of Parliament – it was agreed that the state of the Kingdom should be brought into [the] house of Lords, then to manage the debates so that a protest advantageous to the cause might be made'. The Protest duly appeared on 18 March with the safety of Gibraltar as its ostensible concern and with the signatures of seventeen tory Lords appended.[31]

As the proxy books reveal, the tories made extensive use of this limited solution to absenteeism. Lord Abingdon found the device so convenient, and the number of absent tory Lords so great, that in May 1742 he moved that peers should be allowed to hold three proxy votes instead of the customary two. In times of parliamentary crisis tory peers were expected to make the necessary proxy arrangements; if they did not, one of the party's noble activists – Gower, Bathurst, or the Wiltshire magnate, Lord Bruce – took care to remind them of their duty. In readiness for the Lords debate on the South Sea inquiry in May 1733, Bruce surveyed the proxy lists as a matter of course, commandeered Anglesey's proxy, and sent a blank proxy form off to the invariably domesticated Lord Dartmouth.[32] A similar initiative secured proxies from Lords Aylesford, Craven, Boyle, Gainsborough, Thanet, Leigh, Stafford, and St John well in advance of the motion for Walpole's removal in February 1741. It was consequently a measure of the party's poverty in the Upper House, and not (in some contrast with the Commons) of its organisational or policy dissonance, that only twenty-seven tory votes were available on the day of the Lords division.[33]

Until 1730 it was taken for granted that tory peers would confine their proxies to each other. When Lord Bingley was forced to leave London during the debates on Bolingbroke's reinstatement in May 1725, he left his own proxy with Gower and instructed a friend to find a home for Dartmouth's vote, which he had been supervising: 'but pray remember to... [find] some tory Lord as Lord Strafford or Gower'.

Dartmouth's proxy was ultimately entrusted to the suitably partisan Lord Masham.[34] Even after 1730 only the more moderate tory peers, or those more responsive to Bolingbroke's tactical polemics – men such as Gower and the earl of Thanet – were prepared occasionally to exchange proxies with opposition whigs. Right-wing tory peers like Beaufort, Scarsdale, and Lichfield never made any such concession, while successive Lords Foley and Oxford tended to express their cousinage and their distinctive brand of toryism by assigning their proxies to each other.

Though the tory presence in the Upper House became progressively more residual, individual peers remained prominent in the general running of the party. The conjunction between Gower, Bathurst, and Wyndham, with the restored Bolingbroke acting as political consultant to this triad, was crucial to the tory recovery in the 1720s. Gower's defection in 1745 and Bathurst's slightly earlier apostasy – his name disappears from tory Protests after 1743 – shattered tory morale and effectively emasculated what was left of concerted tory activity in the House of Lords.

II

It is difficult, probably impossible, to form a satisfactory estimate of Wyndham's political ability. We have the tributes of two not unbiased historians of the time, Tindal and Smollett, to his 'wonderful powers of eloquence', and Speaker Onslow's panegyric, 'the most made for a great man of any one that I have known in this age'; but these and many other contemporary eulogies lack the substantiation which a cache of Wyndham papers and a return to high office after his dismissal from the Chancellorship of the Exchequer in 1714 might have provided. The occasional anecdote – the House sitting in respectful silence while he waited to recover from a fainting bout and resume his speech – gives some indication of his prestige and personal force, while a reading of his recorded speeches confirms Onslow's judgement of his intelligence and clarity of mind. What is certain is that by 1725 Wyndham was generally regarded as the tory spokesman in the Commons and bore the peculiar constraints of that role. In February 1726 when he commended the Treaty of Hanover and 'all the address except the last clause', he found himself under attack from some tory M.P.s for his excessive compliancy: 'he had no authority from them to say this, for they approved neither'.[35]

There was in fact always a danger, as Wyndham himself was aware, that his rather individualistic politics would alienate mainstream tory opinion. He abandoned Jacobitism in the early 1720s and, influenced by Bolingbroke's polemics and his own second marriage to a Dutch woman, evolved a more liberal position on Dissent. By 1738 the former proponent of the Schism Act was being lobbied (albeit unsuccessfully) by the Dissenting Deputies in their campaign to repeal the Test Act. Less controversial, so far as his own party was concerned, was Wyndham's developing interest in the press and in the more open politics which the press permitted. When the Commons discussed the newspaper reportage of parliamentary debates in April 1738, the tory leader was the only M.P. recorded as having spoken in support of full and accurate press coverage; the Patriot spokesman, William Pulteney, declared himself absolutely opposed to the practice.[36]

What saved Wyndham from party isolation was his suitably bucolic veneer (his hunting prowess is well attested) and, more important, his own skill and the support he received from his cousin Lord Gower. 'There is no body living', wrote Wyndham to that peer in 1724, 'whose Commands carry with them such Weight to me as your's do...my intimacies have never been extensive.' Wyndham's appraisal of his own social selectivity was apt and it was therefore of considerable importance that Gower brought with him a formidable array of tory connections. Not only did he have two brothers in the House of Commons in the 1730s, but a sister and one of his brothers had also married into the Grosvenor family of Cheshire, which produced three tory M.P.s in the same decade. Another sister married the fourth earl of Clarendon and in 1732 her son, Viscount Cornbury, became the prestigious if wayward tory M.P. for Oxford University. John Proby, elected for Stamford in 1734, was yet another brother-in-law of Gower and one of Wyndham's most efficient party whips.[37] Gower enjoyed a reputation for absolute party integrity – understandably so, since it was known that the ministry had been trying and failing to win him over since the late 1720s – and among more traditionalist tory M.P.s his sponsorship of Wyndham served as a guarantee of the tory leader's own orthodoxy. 'No man within my memory', wrote Dr William King, seeking to convey the magnitude of Gower's defection, 'was more esteemed and reverenced ...the Tories...placed the greatest confidence in him and did nothing without his advice and approbation.'[38]

Wyndham's connection with Lord Bathurst was scarcely less productive. The tory peer had two brothers and two sons in the Commons and his family was related by marriage to Lord Bruce, an active tory whip in the Lords and the electoral patron of Marlborough (one of the few tory pocket boroughs). Bruce's sister had married the tory earl of Cardigan and that Lord's proxy was usually at the disposal of Bathurst or Gower. Together, these two peers not only provided Wyndham with an impressive base in the Commons, but were also able and content to second his policy direction in party counsels and in the House of Lords. Neither man was a first-rate parliamentary performer, but they both spoke and attended regularly. Gower acted as teller for the tories and their Patriot allies in forty divisions between 1715 and 1743 and Bathurst served this function on sixty-five occasions in the same period.[39]

Such influence as Bolingbroke exerted over tory parliamentary activity after 1725 (as distinct from his contribution to the formation and tactics of the anti-Walpolian confederation) was largely mediated through these three men. And even with them his non-party stance was sometimes an embarrassment. In 1734 he infuriated Bathurst by urging him to compromise Gloucestershire's representation with a whig. The younger man, whose politics were more conventional, successfully ran two tories ('We are very proud of our victory, it being to be observ'd that there have not been two Tories sent up out of this county not ever since the Revolution'). Wyndham regarded Bolingbroke with a deference which was not unmixed with pity and took care to cater to the old man's continuing desire for political involvement. He sought his advice on strategy and occasionally had resort to him for the odd classical reference for his set speeches. He was never Bolingbroke's colourless parliamentary succedaneum and ignored or modified his mentor's advice if it conflicted with his own more informed perception of tory backbench sentiment.[40] In February 1737, when Pulteney moved for an increase in Prince Frederick's allowance, Wyndham by-passed the author of *The Patriot King* and allowed tory M.P.s free rein on the division: forty-five of them subsequently absented themselves. As the tory leader recognised, some of his M.P.s disliked the Hanoverian heir and many more were unwilling to coerce George II into increasing his allowance. Wyndham also knew that Walpole was waiting to capitalise on any schism within the tory ranks. That Minister had earlier approached Shippen and told him that if he would oppose the motion and bring 'over some of the Torys to do the same', £20 000 would be given to the widow of an executed Jacobite, Lady Derwentwater. To his honour Shippen refused, but Wyndham was not prepared to strain his own credit with the tory backbenchers and risk driving them into Shippen's arms for the sake of Bolingbroke's grand design.[41]

As undisputed leader of the tory contingent in the Commons Wyndham had no successor. Almost two years after his death in 1740, the Warwickshire M.P. Edward Digby was still lamenting, 'We want Sir William Wyndham very much as head of the party for I think we know not well how to conduct ourselves.' The men whom George Bubb Dodington identified in 1741 as collectively representing the tory party were less than impressive: Lords Bathurst, Gower, Thanet, and Oxford, and in the House of Commons, Sir John Hynde Cotton, Sir Watkin Williams Wynn, Lord Charles Noel Somerset, and Nicholas Fazakerley. Thanet was a nonentity; Bathurst and Gower were to defect and, as we shall see, Edward Harley, who became earl of Oxford in 1741, was hard-working and able, but unqualified for partisan activity on behalf of the tory parliamentary party as a whole. Of the four designated Commoners (and Dodington could legitimately have included the Cornish tory, Sir John St Aubyn, and Wyndham's replacement at Somerset, Thomas Prowse, in this oligarchy), Wynn, Somerset, and the far more cynical and talented Cotton were crypto-Jacobite.[42]

As a politician Cotton stood high in the second division. He was a frequent and mordant speaker in the Commons, and according to Archdeacon Coxe his organisational zeal led him to visit every influential tory Commoner and peer during the summer so as to maintain intra-party communication outside the parliamentary session. His political contacts were not confined to his own party. In the early 1740s he worked closely with Dodington and William Pitt and like both men he was inclined to subordinate scruple to ambition. Sarah Marlborough, characteristically perhaps, believed that even Cotton's steady refusal to defect was rooted in self-interest: 'As he happened to be allways of the Tory side...he thought he should make a better figure in being the head of a party than in leaving it.'[43] After the tory coalition with Pelham in November 1744 Cotton accepted the office of Treasurer of the Chamber, a lucrative place which was usually seen and had often served – most notably in Pelham's own case – as a springboard for further advancement. Yet unlike the Leveson-Gowers, the Bathursts, and the Gores, who all received office between 1742 and 1744, Cotton chose to revert to opposition with the bulk of his party in 1745. It was typical of the man that he nonetheless refused voluntarily to give up his office, arguing that 'he kept so much from the enemy'. Such adhesion to employment, however partisan in rationalisation, temporarily damaged Cotton's intra-party reputation and his name was conspicuously absent from the tory whip sent out in December 1745.[44]

Despite the party prominence in the 1740s of Cotton and, to a lesser extent, of Beaufort and Wynn, it would be wrong to characterise the tory 'front bench' in this period as uniformly Jacobite. Not only were these men ambiguous conspirators, but this facet of their party activity was also challenged by Fazakerley and Thomas Prowse. In March 1747, after Murray had denounced Cotton and Wynn as Jacobite conspirators, Prowse called an emergency meeting of about forty tory M.P.s and subsequently asked the Speaker for parliamentary clarification of the imputation so as to prevent its redounding against the party as a whole: 'Mr Onslow intimated that he believed the parties concerned would not choose it. Prowse replied: "That I cannot help, others know themselves best."'[45]

After Wyndham, Prowse was by far the shrewdest parliamentarian proscribed toryism produced. Both the duke of Newcastle and Horace Walpole listed him and his fellow West Country M.P., William Northey, as being among the most regular and efficient speakers in the Commons. Prowse was to reject whig offers of employment in 1741, 1742, and 1744; in 1760 he refused the Speakership; in 1765 he declined the duke of Cumberland's invitation to join the ministry; and only two months before his death in 1767 he turned down a similar offer from Chatham. Yet despite this record of personal abnegation, Prowse was determined that the tories as a group should have access to and accept the responsibilities of state employment under the Hanoverians. He was on friendly terms with Henry Pelham, and after that Minister's death in 1754 attempted to reach an understanding on behalf of his party with the duke of Newcastle. When this initiative failed he and Northey turned to Pitt.[46] This brand of unemotional, conciliatory toryism was occasionally challenged by two very individualistic tory M.P.s: the plutocratic Member for London, William Beckford, and the one-time crypto-Jacobite Sir John Philipps. In the mid 1750s both men favoured a tory alliance with Henry Fox, and it was this policy discrepancy among its leaders which underlay the unprecedented tory cross-voting on the Mitchell election petition in March 1755. Both Philipps and Beckford were subsequently reconciled to Pitt, but their rather incongruous backgrounds – Philipps was the son of a whig M.P. and a distant cousin of Sir Robert Walpole, while Beckford's landed status was recent and founded on the profits of West Indian sugar – tended to limit their influence within the party. This remained the case even after 1760 when Northey accepted a place at Court and ill-health and disillusionment with post-proscription politics led Prowse to withdraw from Parliament. In October 1761 George Grenville notified Hardwicke that 'Sir Charles Mordaunt & the soberer part' together with Lords Lichfield, Bruce, and Oxford were the only tories worth consulting: 'Ald. Beckford and Sir John Philipps pretended to answer for them but could not.'[47]

III

I have described the premier exponents of parliamentary toryism in some detail because their names and their variegated talents are usually forgotten. There can be no doubt that able men who aspired to direct the tory contingent were available throughout the mid eighteenth century; it should also be apparent that with the exception of Wyndham none was of first-class calibre. Even Wyndham had to cater to the distinct if normally co-operating interest-groups within his party. The Harleyite and crypto-Jacobite sectors were both small but both had attracted men too prestigious or with too much nuisance value to be ignored. The solid bloc of county tories – men for whom someone like Beckford would always remain parvenu – expected to have their parliamentary collaboration negotiated and not assumed. With a joint or at the very least a consultative leadership as the tory norm and with none of the machinery of the Cabinet or the Cockpit available, the need for regular meetings of the tory elite became even more apparent than it had been before 1715.

Occasional congeries of a few selected M.P.s and the odd mass-meeting demanded no long-term organisational investment, and until the late 1720s these remained the only arrangements for party communication. In April 1725 Lord Bathurst held a 'public meeting of some chosen tories' at his London house in order to obtain a consensus for the impending parliamentary debate on Bolingbroke's reinstatement. He deliberately invited some Jacobite–tory M.P.s such as Sir Thomas Sebright so as to anticipate their hostility to the motion and, in the event, only five tory Commoners voted against it.[48]

This kind of *ad hoc* meeting remained the accepted format for the drafting of bills or parliamentary petitions sponsored by the party – occasions when one or more of the tory lawyers would normally be present. In March 1736, when the University of Oxford's endowments were threatened by the Mortmain Bill, Wyndham, Wynn, Shippen, and Baptist Leveson-Gower assembled at the London lodgings of Dr Clarke, one of the University's tory M.P.s, and Nicholas Fazakerley – perhaps the party's most prominent lawyer and yet another M.P. who was to be related by marriage to the Gowers – was appointed to draft the University's petition against the legislation. When the failure of the tory Oxfordshire petition in 1755 threatened to adulterate the freeholder franchise and hence the party's county base, the petition's managers, Sir Roger Newdigate and Sir Charles Mordaunt, organised a series of meetings with William Northey. They commissioned William Blackstone to write a pamphlet in support of their case and also took advice from two tory lawyer M.P.s, Randle Wilbraham and Richard Crowle. On 29 February 1756 they 'din'd at Sir James Dashwood's' – one of the unsuccessful Oxfordshire candidates – and agreed to 'consider of motion about copy-holders'. Their discussions were to culminate in Sir John Philipps' introducing and passing a bill to clarify the voting rights of copyholders in county constituencies.[49]

Tory politicians also had at their disposal more informal but established means for their occasional rendezvous. The honorary degree ceremony at Oxford and the annual alcoholic romps of that institution's High Borlase Society always attracted a sizeable number of tory M.P.s and peers and were sometimes used for party discussions. Welsh, Cheshire, and Lancashire tories could meet at the Wigan races; those from the Midlands at the Burford races. Neither of these events could rival the popularity or morale-boosting capacity of the annual race-meeting at Lichfield. It was there in 1748 that the prosperous Sir Watkin Williams Wynn ran a horse called 'Old England' and, to the delight of many country gentlemen, that entity for once emerged victorious.[50]

To make party business more palatable by including it in a format which also provided for liquid refreshments, gossip, and the occasional wager would seem to have been an obvious solution to the traditional tory allergy to conventional party discipline. Yet with the exception of the October Club, which was the creation of a group of dissident backbenchers and not a supervised instrument for party control, Augustan toryism had lacked an effective socio-political club. There had been no tory counterpart to the whig Kit-Cat Club, 'a social assembly of the leaders and many members of the Whig party... [which] was a sort of permanent joint committee of the party in the two Houses, meeting regularly to concert political measures in an informal manner'. Ever since the 1670s whig inventiveness in the sphere of organisation had been derived from that party's more extensive experience of an opposition function. The rigours of proscription may similarly have prompted the development in the 1720s of two tory societies to which W. F. Lord's description of the Kit-Cat's composition and attributes can be partially applied: the Honourable Board of Loyal Brotherhood which met every Tuesday during the parliamentary session, and Edward Harley's Board, initiated in 1727 and assembling every Thursday at the Cocoa Tree coffee-house, Pall Mall.[51]

The Loyal Brotherhood had been founded in 1709 by the second duke of Beaufort. Its transformation from a rowdy if staunchly high-tory drinking-club was effected by a qualitative change in its membership. Having previously been the resort of suitably principled clergymen and gentry and of solid but limited Commoners such as Alexander Pendarves and George Dashwood, the Board confined itself to about twenty-five members of the tory parliamentary party. By 1730 it had attracted to its ranks Lord Gower, Lord Charles Noel Somerset, Sir John Hynde Cotton, Sir Watkin Williams Wynn, and Sir William Wyndham.[52]

It has been suggested that the Board's function was purely convivial, and it is true that the extant minute books are too skeletal to indicate the content of its weekly meetings. As with the Kit-Cat Club however, too rigid a distinction between social congeries and meetings for political discussion would almost certainly be inappropriate. Party clubs fulfilled both functions, and that tories of this central importance could meet at a fixed time and place every week during the parliamentary session was bound to facilitate party communication and the decision-making process. There seems good reason to believe that in 1733 Wyndham and his fellow Brother, Humphry Parsons, then M.P. for London, used these weekly meetings to help concert the City's campaign against the Excise Bill; nine members of the Board were subsequently invited to the mayoral banquet held to celebrate the bill's defeat. On 1 May 1749 thirteen peers and 103 M.P.s, drawn in the main from the tory party but with the addition of some Leicester House whigs, met at the Board's current headquarters, the St Albans Tavern, and were there addressed by the club's president, the duke of Beaufort. The tory leadership was seeking to advertise its coalition with the Prince of Wales and more specifically to deflect a proposed ministerial visitation of the University of Oxford. Since Sir James Dashwood, M.P. for Oxfordshire, and the two Members for Oxford, Thomas Rowney and Philip Herbert, were also attached to the Brotherhood, the Board's responsibility for this successful coup seems undeniable.[53]

The Loyal Brotherhood's origins, as the name suggests, were legitimist. By 1730 this Jacobite commitment was residual but many of the club's members still came from what can be fairly described as the tory right wing. This indeed was one of the Board's attractions for Wyndham in that it gave him access to high tories such as Lords Lichfield and Scarsdale and to complacent county M.P.s like Sir Walter Bagot, who might otherwise have remained aloof from him and his strategy of coalition with the Patriots. (Instead they all subscribed to the *Craftsman*!) Yet when Edward Harley entered Parliament as M.P. for Herefordshire in 1727, it was probably the Board's ostensibly high-tory bias, together with his family's proprietorial if distant attitude towards tory activity, which encouraged him to establish an alternative tory society.[54]

Harley's Board took its tone from its membership – fourteen of the twenty tory M.P.s it admitted before 1742 sat for county constituencies – and from its founder. Unquestionably loyal to the Hanoverian dynasty and a close friend of the Attorney-General, Philip Yorke, Harley was a man distinguished by 'cool good sense' as well as over-burdened by his own moral rectitude. 'One cannot', he wrote to his wife in 1731, in his sententious but indubitably sincere fashion, 'bear too publick a testimony against pensions & corruption.'[55] His Board was intended to bear such a testimony: to carry out solid reforming activity in the Commons and to press for legislation which would buttress the necessarily beneficial and purifying influence of the independent landed gentry. In March 1730 Harley carried a bill to prevent the packing of juries and enforce their property qualifications. In 1732 Thomas Bramston, M.P. for Maldon, secured an act to regulate the landed qualifications of J.P.s, and in 1733 Bramston combined with another Board member, the very able and tragically short-lived William Bromley the younger (drawn predictably into the Harleian orbit), to introduce a bill which would have shifted responsibility for road maintenance from the poorer to the more affluent inhabitants of each parish. Most notably perhaps, it was two members of the Harley Board, Bromley and Sir John St Aubyn, who moved on 13 March 1734 the repeal of the Septennial Act, arguing that shorter Parliaments would not only cut electoral bribery, but prevent the socio-political displacement of those lesser country gentlemen who could not afford the increased costs of septennial elections.[56]

Apart from acting as a pressure-group for Country toryism, the Board contributed to its members' parliamentary efficiency in more mundane ways. In February 1734, after the death of his steward had forced the Northamptonshire M.P., Sir Justinian Isham, to leave London and attend to his estate, the club took care to keep him informed of the course of parliamentary business. Consequently on 10 March Isham hastened back to Westminster 'Upon account of a Motion I heard was to be made on Tuesday for repealing ye Septennial Bill'. When Sir Roger Newdigate was canvassing Middlesex in 1747, he was furnished with an obvious and potent source of electoral aid: 'Board at ye Cocoa Tree', he noted on Thursday 30 April, 'Lord Oxford promis'd me his assistance. Mr. [Robert] Harley his vote & interest, Mr. Bramston his vote and interest.'[57]

Both these tory societies demonstrated their recognition of what has often eluded subsequent historians: that the independent attitudes characteristic of many tory M.P.s did not preclude party control but rather placed a premium on sensitive and consultative leadership. Given that prominent tories were unable to use 'the attractive power' of royal bounty to beguile their supporters into good attendance and bloc voting, the result was not parliamentary atomisation but rather greater concessions to intra-party democracy. The facilities provided by the two Boards served not only to bring together various tory activists, but also to transmit policy decisions to and obtain a consensus from the parliamentary party as a whole.[58]

In 1738 the Brotherhood decided to hold its weekly meetings at the

Fountain Tavern in the Strand, a locale with a long and emotive high-tory history. In 1685 it had been the venue of 250 tory–royalist M.P.s meeting before the first session of James II's first and only Parliament. In the autumn of 1704 William Bromley had held a series of tory meetings there whereby it was agreed to 'tack' an Occasional Conformity Bill on to the Land Tax grant. The Board's patronage revived the tavern's political role and encouraged the tory parliamentary party and its whig allies to resort there for policy discussions. The most celebrated of these debates occurred on 12 February 1742, when 235 peers and M.P.s met to determine opposition strategy after the resignation of Sir Robert Walpole. On 15 March 1743 over sixty tories, including eleven members of the Loyal Brotherhood, assembled at the Fountain and 'solemnly engaged themselves and likewise promised to use their utmost interest with their absent Friends to meet at the House on the first Day of the next session of Parliament and to give a constant & due Attendance there'.[59]

In December 1743 the Brotherhood's three most active Commoners, Cotton, Wynn, and Sir John Philipps, sought to formalise the opposition's rather haphazard and variegated organisation. Together with three Patriot whigs, William Pitt, Edmund Waller, and George Bubb Dodington, they formed a central committee 'to prepare & draw up all ye Questions' and, as Lord Hartington reported, 'they have now got into a method of not telling their People what they intend to propose but only summons [sic] them upon business'. Such peremptory methods and the abrupt cessation of mass party meetings at the Fountain Tavern were highly unpopular, particularly with the tory M.P.s – hence their complaints when the tory leadership negotiated a coalition with Pelham in November 1744 without making any real attempt to consult backbench opinion. 'How happened it that there was not one Meeting at your beloved Fountain-Tavern?' jibed a whig pamphleteer, as he surveyed the subsequent tory bickering. 'Were not your Leaders frequently called upon to summon one, in order to submit their Actions to the Publick Censure? Did they not as constantly decline it?'[60]

Whether the Harley Board's decision to establish itself at the Cocoa Tree was conscious policy is not clear, but by opting for this locale the club ensured that its members were brought into regular contact with mainstream tory M.P.s and peers for whom the coffee-house had traditionally served as a social centre and as a venue for discussion with parliamentary colleagues and visiting constituents. Under the stimulus of the Harley Board this tory connection became more formalised. By the 1740s the coffee-house had become a private party club; by the 1750s and 1760s its name was employed by whig politicians and pamphleteers as a synonym for the tory parliamentary group, and with good reason. One visitor to the Cocoa Tree in the autumn of 1754 found that according to its post-electoral calculations its members made up 81 per cent of the tory contingent in the Commons: 'At the Cocoa Tree Numbers are counted, strength is computed, & it is agreed that they consist of Numbers not to be despised and that 90 may carry some weight.'[61]

Those of its members who were London-based or simply more politically attuned were accustomed to assemble at the club before each parliamentary session in order to send out whips to any absent tory M.P.: 'Our Gentlemen at ye Cocoa Tree have been Writing to their Friends to be up by monday ye 27th Instant', noted a London lawyer in November 1749.[62] Once Members had arrived in London the club sought to keep them informed of parliamentary business and to ensure their attendance for crucial divisions. It is unfortunate that the one detailed description of this procedure which has survived was written by a man disillusioned with the club's efficacy. Henry Shiffner, who contested Minehead in the Luttrell–tory interest in 1754, had hoped to employ the Cocoa Tree's organisational machinery in support of his subsequent electoral petition:

A Motion is made, & Attendance, close Attendance is promised; Notice is given of the Day, & all goes swimmingly till the Critical Minute; then one is out of Town, another at Home, a Great many at the Bottle, & hardly any at the place of Action...This was the very Fact on the Night that my Petition was committed.

Shiffner was a new tory candidate and Prowse had already warned him that the club was husbanding its limited resources for the much more significant Oxfordshire dispute. Newdigate and Mordaunt were both members of the Harley Board and, as managers of the latter petition, naturally had recourse to the Cocoa Tree: in the first division on the Oxfordshire election on 18 November 1754, they secured the attendance of eighty-eight tory M.P.s.[63]

The Cocoa Tree, like the Fountain Tavern, was also used for mass party meetings at which leading tories could advance a policy line and endeavour to secure their supporters' agreement. In April 1758 Sir John Philipps threatened to lead a tory revolt against Pitt's scheme to give monetary aid to Prussia and thereby to compromise the tories' current association with the ministry. Thomas Prowse, who was a member of the Harley Board, immediately summoned a meeting of tory Lords and Commoners at the Cocoa Tree. Twelve reputable tory M.P.s were selected to address the gathering on behalf of the Prussian grant, and pressure was exerted on Philipps 'to declare in the Cocoa Tree on Sunday when the great Assembly is held, that he thinks the measure right'. The meeting took place on 18 April, and on the following day Pitt's proposal for

£670 000 in Prussian aid was allowed to pass the Commons without a division.[64]

Partly because the tories gradually evolved these more sophisticated and centralised forms of organisation, they tended to be less dependent on that system of local whips which had been such a material component of party control during Anne's reign. Certainly during the early stages of its proscription the party was indebted to the West Country activism of Wyndham, Bathurst, and Gower, whose landed and electoral influence in Somerset, Gloucestershire, Staffordshire, and North Shropshire enabled them to mobilise tory M.P.s in all these counties in addition to those attached to them by kinship and amity. So in October 1718 Bishop Atterbury wrote to Lord Gower to ask that he be present at the opening of the parliamentary session '& would persuade your friends to be there also', in readiness for the expected assault on the Occasional Conformity Act. Three years later, after Bathurst, Wyndham, and Shippen had met to discuss party strategy in the wake of the Atterbury crisis, they instructed Gower to mobilise their friends in the West: 'We desire... that you will give Notice to all Members within ye Week to be there at ye opening of ye Session.'[65]

In Wales local whips remained important throughout – partly because of the distance from London, partly because Welsh toryism was peculiarly focused and dependent upon the exertions of local magnates. Lord Charles Noel Somerset, who became duke of Beaufort in 1745, was accustomed to dispatch pre-sessional whips to the Glamorgan and Monmouth tory M.P.s. When the onset of gout increasingly enforced his residence at Bath, he also chivvied into parliamentary attendance any valetudinarian tory he found lingering there.[66] Sir Watkin Williams Wynn was tory overlord of Denbighshire and of a great deal more. His very name and even the manner of his death – he was unhorsed while out hunting rabbits – seem to embody the bucolic tradition to an almost ludicrous degree. Yet this aura of rural integrity, underpinned by a ruthless exploitation of his local power-base, gave him a unique status within the tory party which had nothing to do with his very mediocre parliamentary talents.

It was not only tory M.P.s from North Wales whom Wynn harried into attendance and supervised when they got to London but also the Cheshire M.P.s (Sir Robert Grosvenor was a member of Wynn's Cycle of the White Rose) and the Lancashire tories, whom he directed through his friend Lord Barrymore, M.P. for Wigan, and by way of his own involvement in Liverpool's local government. In return for their compliance Wynn was sometimes willing to place his electoral machine, which came complete with the coercive power of his armed Welsh tenantry and his own hard cash, at the disposal of his tory clients. Sir Richard Grosvenor benefited greatly from such assistance at the Chester mayoral election of 1732, and its recognised efficacy was such that in 1744 Thomas Prowse, writing from the Cocoa Tree, had to remind the tory candidate for Glamorgan, Sir Charles Kemys Tynte, that 'The Election was out of his [Wynn's] province (North Wales) and therefore I believe an Application to Him to attend you will be to no purpose.'[67]

It was perhaps fortunate not only for the forces of law and order but also for the continuity of tory organisation that the party's dependence on dynasts such as Wynn was limited and diminishing. Regional organisation relied for its efficacy on the authority, the volume of activity, and, most crucially, the longevity of the responsible local whip. Wynn's death in 1749 left his estate in debt, his family with no adult heir, and his suzerainty over three counties in shreds. Nor was the social and landed structure of some counties at all consonant with the emergence of one generally acknowledged party custodian. Velters Cornewall, who represented Herefordshire from 1722 to 1768, also sought to influence tory M.P.s in Worcestershire and Shropshire. In 1747 he was able to implement the tory electoral alliance with Leicester House in all three counties; but having to deal with a dispersed and independent squirearchy, unable to draw on that sense of regional identity and tory kinship which another party whip, Sir John St Aubyn, could exploit in Cornwall, and with nothing like the wealth of Gower and Wynn, Cornewall had only the most tenuous influence over the parliamentary performance of these counties' M.P.s. When the House of Commons was called over on 4 December 1740, he duly acted as tory spokesman for his region, but as he complained, 'I excus'd my defaulting compatriots as well as I coud, one on his ladys ye 2d on his own & ye 3d on his Mother's Account, so that neither of 'em was taken into Custody, tho' I hadn't ye honour of A Line from either of 'em.'[68]

IV

We have seen how, after an initial period of disarray, the tories responded to proscription by evolving London-based societies which could synchronise the party's parliamentary performance, and that in some counties metropolitan party direction was supplemented by local initiative. How receptive and how politicised were the men at whom these organisational expedients were aimed?

It is a pleasant and noteworthy irony that Sir Roger Newdigate, the tory M.P. cited by both Sir Lewis Namier and John Brooke as the acme of the independent country gentleman, achieved an average sessional attendance rate of 65 per cent between 1754 and 1759 – a period of comparative parliamentary quiescence. As his diary entries prove, Newdigate was in fact one of the most active tories of his day, but many of the more authentically apolitical tories were accustomed to attend Westminster regularly, if with limited enthusiasm, out of a sense of duty to their constituency and their county status. Sir Justinian Isham devoted just two sentences of his diary to the parliamentary session of 1731: 'May 7: The Parliament was prorogued. I attended the whole session except two journeys I made about business into ye country.' The fact that so many tory M.P.s represented county constituencies meant that the demands of local legislation guaranteed a certain level of their attendance. Sir Justinian's father, a man of identical name, constituency, and temperament, was appointed between January and March 1725 to eighteen parliamentary committees – most of them to do with private bills on roads, internal navigation, and enclosure rulings.[69]

The attendance rate of county tories who were also prominent in the party's hierarchy could be quite outstanding. Until he was appointed an officer in the Somerset militia in 1759, Prowse was reputed never to have missed a day's parliamentary business. When some Somerset whigs circulated a rumour that he had been absent from an important division in December 1741, he got the Bristol M.P., Edward Southwell, to reassure local tory agents that this was 'false and injurious tho' he [Prowse] had a fever, he came Cloak'd up and Voted...and during a favourite daughter's long illness and the very morning she died he never was absent from the House one hour'. As Prowse's speedy reaction to this grass-roots slander demonstrates, a tory M.P.'s sense of duty could be reinforced by insecurity. A county member's position was such that his parliamentary assiduity or otherwise might figure in the London and provincial press, and in an open constituency lax behaviour could compromise electoral prospects. On 16 March 1722 the *Freeholder's Journal* printed a list of absentees from the division on the Septennial Bill and suggested that their conduct should be taken into account at the imminent general election. William Peyto, tory M.P. for Warwickshire and one of the guilty, responded in dramatic fashion. On 22 March he inserted a notice in the *Whitehall Evening Post* advertising a meeting at Warwick at which he promised to vindicate his behaviour: 'The Freeholders, as well as the Gentlemen and clergy are desired to be there.'[70]

Of course many tory M.P.s did not represent vulnerable constituencies and of course the vast majority were much less motivated than the redoubtable Prowse. Some indeed went through Parliament leaving barely a trace of their passage in its journals. Of the 227 M.P.s who were returned as tories and who took their seats during the 1715–22 Parliament, more than half are not recorded as having spoken, acted as teller in a Commons division, or been appointed to a committee. About forty tory M.P.s in this early period, one quarter of them lawyers, bore the brunt of speaking for their party and counting its votes.[71] The comment which best sums up the parliamentary responses of the paradigmatic tory M.P. – the man who was neither one of these hard-core activists nor incorrigibly absentee – was supplied by George Bubb Dodington after the death of the Prince of Wales in March 1751. Seeking to avert the fragmentation of the tory association with Leicester House, Sir John Hynde Cotton had decided to whip up every tory M.P., 'acquainting them at the same time that nothing was to be propos'd to them, but to sit still and wait Court' – a strategy which Dodington rightly derided 'From experience of the disposition of those gentlemen, who I thought would neither come, if nothing was propos'd, nor stay, if there was nothing to do: but yet would implicitly follow a few of their Lordships in one or the other.'[72] Tory M.P.s and peers tended to be highly responsive to direction when it was offered and especially when it was offered with a specific and generally accepted end in view; the party was rarely able to maintain a respectable level of attendance at Westminster if there was no party point at stake or if there was no prospect of a party initiative's achieving success.

The most pithy rejoinder on the inutility of attending Parliament merely to be reminded of one's minority position came from the late-seventeenth-century tory, Sir Charles Sedley, who when rebuked for strolling in the Mall during a debate of some importance replied 'What should I do therein I know how the matter will go, and an honest man signifys no more in that house to rectifye it, than a Drop of Essence to perfume a pail full of stale piss.' In 1719 the tory M.P. for Newport, Sir Nicholas Morice, was more genteel but the logic was identical: 'It is extremely hard...to ride four hundred miles to be baffled & laughed att for no wise man can think there is ye least prospect of succeeding when it has been evident that this Parliament never denied ye Court, one individual thing they have asked.' Such a negative response to an unpromising parliamentary situation was often anchored in the country gentleman's traditional aversion to London's crowds, squalor, and expense. One can sense the apprehension compressed into Morice's plea to his City-based brother, when steeling himself for attendance in September 1722: 'Please don't take ye lodgings I had when last in town, they being pestered with buggs.'[73]

This sort of reluctance and facile defeatism also characterised many whig backbenchers, as did the tendency of some tory M.P.s to leave London early for Christmas and then to linger at home well into the

New Year. In 1732 Parliament reassembled on 13 January and Sir Justinian Isham set out for London nine days later; in 1736 Parliament met on 15 January and Isham did not turn up until the end of the month. The superb tory attendance achieved in the final assault on Walpole was in part a tribute to the tory leaders' anticipation of both these party failings. On 5 and 9 January 1742 they got the tory Common Council-man Richard Nutt to insert a printed whip in his flagrantly partisan journal, the *London Evening Post*, demanding attendance:

Not on the 20th, or 19th or on the 18th, in the Evening, but on the 18th, at the Meeting of the House...The old Excuse...for remaining idle in the Country cannot now be pleaded, that all Attendance is Fruitless, because there are no hopes of Success: There are hopes; nor can it be said that the attendance of a single Person is of no consequence.[74]

Such special if usually less blatant appeals were standard tory practice in periods of parliamentary crisis. Early in 1717 Sir Thomas Hanmer and William Bromley sent out requests for attendance so that the party might benefit from the impending whig schism. Central whipping however was rare in the first decade of proscription, many tories responding to the atomised state of their leadership by taking individual responsibility for alerting their friends. It was Lord Barrymore who urged the Cheshire tory, Sir Richard Grosvenor, to attend the debates on the Septennial Bill, and Sir Thomas Cave dispatched similar instructions to the Amersham M.P., Viscount Fermanagh. Both initiatives were successful.[75] No tory whips to M.P.s outside London appear to have survived for the 1730s, but one might hazard a guess that methods to secure attendance became more centralised under Wyndham; they certainly became more effective. 'All that can be said', wrote the Patriot Lord Cobham in December 1734, in an otherwise pessimistic survey of the opposition, 'is that Sir Wyndham has promised the Tories shall be in Town.' Ministerial commentators duly noted the high level of tory attendance when Parliament met again in January 1735.[76]

In the four years after Wyndham's death it became the regular practice for a fluctuating group of tory and Patriot politicians to dispatch whips to their respective supporters before each session of Parliament. In December 1743 tory and whig members of the opposition received a printed whip authorised by thirteen M.P.s, including Cotton and Wynn. With a certain deliberation the signatories extended their appeal to those tories who were contemplating an extended Christmas break: 'The great Question of the HANOVER TROOPS will undoubtedly be forc'd on immediately after the Holydays.' When the Hanoverians were voted on 18 January 1744, the tory party achieved a House of Commons attendance rate of 94 per cent. This was exceptional, but in the seventeen Commons divisions held between 1716 and 1755 for which a voting list of some kind has survived the party appears to have secured a respectable average attendance rate of 76 per cent. Between 1730 and 1744, when the coalition with the Patriots lent some validity to the business of opposition, this rose to 81 per cent – a figure which compares favourably with that achieved by either ministerial or opposition whigs. In the fourteen divisions between 1716 and 1754 where we know the voting behaviour of every tory M.P. present, there are only twenty-two instances of individuals voting against the party line, thirteen of these defections occurring over the Septennial and Peerage Bills when the party was in partial disarray and lacking its subsequent organisational expedients.[77]

The high tory attendance achieved at these key divisions derived in part from special efforts on the part of the leadership and the emotive nature of the issues involved: septennial Parliaments, Place Bills and Hanoverians. Was the impressive cohesion of the tory vote demonstrated on these occasions also exceptional? Such evidence as we possess suggests that it was not. Horace Walpole had no love for the tories, but his letters to Horace Mann are littered with references to the solidarity of the tory vote in the Commons.[78] As their party never numbered more than 150 M.P.s after 1727 and as they always sat together on the left-hand side of the House of Commons, the tories were highly self-conscious as a group and renegade voters were correspondingly visible. When William Vaughan, tory M.P. for Merioneth, allowed a whig relation to persuade him into voting with the Court in the Army debate of February 1738, he was promptly tackled by Watkin Williams Wynn; four days later another tory M.P. was noting Vaughan's reversion to party docility.[79]

There were only three situations which could seriously fragment the tory vote. The party could waver when it lacked unified direction or when its leadership was believed to be acting in an arbitrary or factious manner. Hence in part the tory débâcle over the 1741 motion to remove Walpole. Cotton and Wynn had themselves been ill-informed of this opposition whig measure and had assumed rather than negotiated party concurrence. The result is illustrated in the behaviour of Sir Herbert Pakington, tory M.P. for Worcestershire, who was 'sent for out of the country in violent haste', and complied in so far as he hastened to London, but then 'voted directly against them'. Secondly, tory M.P.s, like their whig counterparts, usually voted in accordance with the economic interests of their constituents on bills relating to trade, roads, and internal navigation. So in the broad wheels debate of February 1755, Nicholas Fazakerley wanted punitive duties imposed on narrow-wheeled vehicles and found himself at odds with his party colleagues, Thomas Prowse and William

Northey, who had the rather different roads and transport facilities of Somerset and Wiltshire to consider.[80]

Tory unity could also suffer during times of Jacobite crisis, the more conscientious or less secure tories tending to vote with the Court at such times in order to affirm their loyalty. On 15 February 1744, after George II had informed Parliament of the prospective French invasion, an opposition whig M.P. moved for a constitutional amendment to the Commons' Loyal Address – an amendment which most tories, many of them for constitutional reasons, supported. Velters Cornewall however joined the ministry in defeating it. He was immediately taken to task by Sir John Hynde Cotton, who disingenuously twitted him for succumbing to the usual calculated alarmism on matters Jacobite: 'I told him', wrote Cornewall, 'That I made a great difference between ye King's talking of ye Pretender & a Court member's lugging him in head & shoulders on failure of argument to ye Question, which often happen'd.'[81]

In the mid eighteenth century politicians of the first rank did not employ the adjective 'tory' or the noun 'tory party' merely as shibboleths (had they been nothing more, their usage would still have shaped contemporary behaviour and assumptions), but because at the political centre these terms could be fastened to a recognisable and coherent group in Parliament. Organisational expedients were, it is true, a less material component of the tory party's durability than the persistence of its traditional and distinctive policy attitudes. In 1778 it could still be said of Sir William Bagot, M.P. for Staffordshire, that he 'continued to take a lead in the Cocoa Tree club', but since tory ideology had by then splintered in the face of changing political, parliamentary, and extra-parliamentary conditions, agencies like the Cocoa Tree could no longer hold together all their original sponsors. But even though it did not guarantee the tories' discrete identity after 1760, organisation was indispensable for the peculiar tactical imperatives posed by proscription.[82]

After 1715 it was only by demonstrating parliamentary efficiency and cohesion that the tories could tempt or harass a Hanoverian monarch, or a whig administration in need of support, into negotiations. Only by showing a capacity for bloc voting and good attendance could the tories attract dissident whig allies in possession of those spectacular parliamentary talents which they themselves usually lacked. William Pulteney after 1725, that almost brilliant failure, the earl of Egmont, after 1747, and William Pitt in 1755 were all compelled into association with the tories and their mundane parliamentary virtues. Indeed it was partly because the tory party could still be so effective in the Commons that its opposition whig allies often regarded it with some ambivalence. 'It is generally agreed', wrote a government supporter Sir Robert Wilmot in January 1742, '...That the Tories would come into any Terms, & that the Patriots being sensible of that are so afraid of being left in the Lurch that they only wait for the first good offer.'[83] A group of disorganised and absentee country gentlemen would scarcely have engendered such trepidation in the minds of its auxiliaries.

The tories' capacity for party organisation was no less crucial for the party's morale. Before 1760 it was extremely rare for tory politicians to be invited to assemblies and levees at St James'; at Westminster they could usually rely on the hostility of the administration and at best a relationship of convenience and/or mutual mistrust with opposition and independent whigs. The Cocoa Tree Club emerges from Sir Roger Newdigate's closely written diaries as a life-line: a guaranteed refuge which was also a centre for consultation and decision. And the tories' sporadic ability to summon up very nearly their full parliamentary strength, like their common tactic of walking out of the Commons en bloc to demonstrate their concerted if impotent disapproval, catered to a sense of professionalism and gave an impression of political grit. There is partisan confidence as well as partisan mischief in Heneage Finch's compliment to the Patriot whig Lord Malton: 'The Whigs for once in their lives', wrote the Maidstone M.P. in 1742, 'have whipped in better than the Tories.'[84]

Tory parliamentary assiduity also had a more public dimension, though not as much publicity as some tories desired. In 1722 the M.P. for Hastings, Archibald Hutcheson, wanted lists of every Commons division published; in 1738 Wyndham argued that the substance and exponents of parliamentary debates should appear in newsprint. Tory constituencies were increasingly encouraged to dispatch Instructions to their M.P.s — documents which were designed for partisan advantage, but which demanded that their recipients be seen to be present and occasionally active at St Stephen's. When the tory M.P. for Merioneth, William Vaughan, stayed away from the division on the Hanoverian troops in December 1742, his 'constituents' instructed him in his duty: 'We had no representative present to declare our sense of so extraordinary a measure ...exert an English spirit.' Sir Lewis Namier once suggested (using an anachronistic criterion of party to prove party's non-operation in the eighteenth century) that party discipline could be achieved only if M.P.s were dependent on their party for their seats. But constituency pressure could sometimes supplement more formal tory organisation. Vaughan was dependent for his seat largely on his family's estate, but it was still a county seat, and it was still advisable that he be seen to act in conformity with xenophobic and anti-Army sentiment. When the Hanoverians were voted again in 1744 and 1746, Vaughan was present and in the opposition lobby.[85]

A few especially vulnerable tories were pressurised to a much greater degree. When Edward Southwell, *de facto* tory M.P. for Bristol, voted for the ministerial candidates at the Chippenham election petition in January 1742, his local sponsors assailed him with irate letters and electoral blackmail and demanded detailed accounts of his subsequent parliamentary conduct. As Southwell complained to one of Bristol's tory activists, 'If I am to suffer or be run down for every single private vote in an affair where none but those who hear the Arguments & pleadings, can be judges, It is certain that no man can be more a Slave, than the Representative of so populous a City.'[86] Southwell's relationship with his constituency was unique, but his connection between a constituency's size and the degree of its M.P.'s responsibility was more widely relevant. The tory party's minority position enforced and permitted an unusual degree of internal organisation. Given the party's mid-century electoral base, some tory M.P.s must also have been confirmed in their duty and orthodoxy within Westminster by the consideration of their large and potentially volatile electorates without.

4

The Content of Toryism

In 1740 a whig lawyer, Henry Berkeley, jotted down some advice to an aspiring M.P. He could, thought Berkeley, 'In conscience take up with any party at present, at least as I conceive, who imagine them not divided by the plain & easy understood principles of Whig & Tory, but by favour & dislike of Sir Robert's Ministry.' He went on to add a qualification: 'I say *in Conscience*, because there are several other things that may draw you or me or any Man with the most upright heart into Party, as Education; Prejudice; the Persuasions of, or the desire of serving one's friends; I may add ambition.' Many historians would agree with Berkeley in emptying Hanoverian toryism as well as Hanoverian whiggism of distinctive principle; those few who have acknowledged a continuing tory identity in this period have also tended to attribute it solely to culture and environment, though not of course to ambition. 'Tories', it is claimed, 'were born, not made'; 'post-1715 Toryism' was 'a tradition rather than a policy'; or again, 'The Tory party. . .held no principles of government which conflicted with those of the victorious Whigs, its coherence was traditional.'[1]

There is no doubt at all that heredity, friendship, and marriage patterns, as well as youthful indoctrination, did contribute to the party's survival. Of the 617 tory M.P.s who entered Parliament between 1715 and 1760 217 were the sons of tory M.P.s; 269 had gone to Oxford University as against only 76 to Cambridge; 120 were linked to other tory families by their own marriages.[2] But the environmental explanation of party choice is as inadequate as invocations of an undefined tory tradition. One still needs to ask why it was that the family background of so many M.P.s was a tory one, why they chose to consort with other tory families, and why so many were sent to one English University in preference to the other.

I

For many tories, selecting Oxford – Charles I's headquarters in the Civil War and the defender of Anglican supremacy in the face of James II's suspension of the Test Act – was as much an ideological statement as a family custom. The University consolidated high-tory attitudes and was also able to instil them: hence the whig campaigns to bring the institution under ministerial control in 1717 and 1749. In 1720 it had admitted John and Erasmus Philipps, sons of a whig and Puritan M.P. and cousins of Robert Walpole. Erasmus described in his diary how he spent his student days: 'Went a Foxhunting with Geo. Henry Lee, Earl of Litchfield, John Leveson Gower, Lord Gower, Marqs. of Carnarvon, Sr Wm Wyndham, Bart., Mr Villiers (Brother to Villiers, Earl of Jersey).' Given these confrères and their membership of the equally partisan Pembroke College – extreme even by Oxford standards – the Philipps brothers' eventual entry into Parliament as tory M.P.s may have shocked their father but should have come as no surprise.[3]

The influence of Oxford and specially chosen private tutors, as well as the existing bias of tory country house libraries, must have helped forge distinctive tory reading habits. Recent quantitative research on eighteenth-century subscription lists and on the book purchases of ninety-one M.P.s between 1670 and 1760 suggests that, despite the flux of parliamentary alignments after 1715, whigs as varied as Robert Walpole, George Bubb Dodington, Henry Pelham, and William Pulteney tended to favour roughly the same authors. Their book selections were in marked contrast with those of tory M.P.s like Sir Richard Grosvenor, Sir Justinian Isham and his son, and Abel Ketelby, whose common bias was reflected in a different subscription pattern.[4]

One reason for this literary disparity was the two parties' continuing debate over seventeenth-century English history. Royalist piety ensured that before his death in 1744 the tory Lord Mansel had acquired four different lives of Charles I, an account of his sufferings, and his complete writings. In 1716 Henry Cantrell (who had been appointed to the vicarage of St Alkmunds by the tory mayor of Derby), in 1731 Bishop Atterbury, in 1732 William Shippen, and in 1739 John Davys, incumbent of the tory earl of Northampton's living of Castle Ashby, all published defences of the Martyr King and vindicated Lord Clarendon's *History of the Rebellion* from its many whig detractors.[5] The moderate tory earl of Dartmouth sought consolation for his political exclusion in refuting, section by section, the whig Bishop Gilbert Burnet's *History of My Own Times* (or, as William Bromley styled it in 1723, 'this libel, this collection of vile low scandal'). 1740 saw the posthumous publication of Roger North's *Examen*. Its editor hoped that it would correct the whiggish accounts of Charles II and James II supplied by White Kennett's *Complete History of England* of 1706, as well as challenging John Oldmixon's *Critical History* of 1724, another whig production which had attracted nonconformist subscribers like Edmund Calamy and Thomas Bradbury.[6]

In February 1744 several tory peers and M.P.s, four Oxford colleges, and representatives of the three great tory London guilds – the Vintners, the Goldsmiths, and the Grocers – agreed to subscribe to the Nonjuror Thomas Carte's projected history of England. It was predictable that contributions for this four-volume partisan extravaganza should have been entrusted to the tory banking house of Childs; predictable too that the enterprise attracted few whig sponsors and that some of those who did participate, the earl of Egmont and Viscount Perceval amongst them, soon fell into arrears. As late as 1758 a reviewer of *The Case of the Royal Martyr Considered*, written by an Oxford graduate influenced by Carte, feared that its tory extremism 'instead of healing divisions, will, by irritating both parties mutually, rather help to widen the unhappy breaches which faction has made among the natives of these Kingdoms'. In the same year David Hume's essay 'Of the Coalition of Parties' identified 'greater moderation...in representing past events' as the crucial factor in a whig–tory fusion: this atypical neutrality was to be Hume's declared objective in his own historical work.[7]

Some tories inherited their adulation of Charles I: the bulk of the right-wing tory M.P.s who had attached themselves to the October Club in 1710 had been of royalist ancestry. But even tories who lacked this hereditary commitment – families like the Lisles, Cartwrights, Blagraves, St Johns, and Whitlocks, who had been Parliamentarian, even regicide, in the Civil War – found retrospective royalism valuable. It stabilised traditional party attitudes to the Crown and Dissent and provided a major tory argument against standing armies. J. G. A. Pocock has remarked on, but does not account for, the fact that after 1714 parliamentary debates on the renewal of the Mutiny Bill contained many more references to the excesses of the New Model Army than had previously been the case. This polemical shift was due quite simply to tory prominence in the opposition after that date. In 1717 Shippen linked the Army and the Septennial Act in a common Civil War obloquy: 'A Parliament Army (consisting of about the number now demanded) once committed greater Outrages...than all the Armies of the Crown have ever done; and THAT ARMY was the creature of A PARLIAMENT, which had established itself.' During the Army debate in the connotative year of 1749 Lord Oxford employed an argument which would have been familiar to the whig earl of Shaftesbury in the 1670s: that military power and the influence of the House of Lords were inversely proportionate. As used by a tory, this debating ploy acquired a royalist tinge: 'It is but an hundred years and a few months since an English army...

raised and maintained by the House of Commons...imbrued their hands in the blood of their Sovereign, and abolished the House of Lords.'[8]

In the mid eighteenth century as in the 1690s, the cult of Charles the Martyr helped to sustain a fundamentally monarchical party deprived of contact with and the confidence of the current dynasty. And though tributes to Charles I could serve as a disguise for Jacobitism, tory politicians most often used them to remind the Hanoverian Kings which party had the sanctity of the Crown closest to its heart. On 30 January 1735 eight young whigs, including two Walpolian M.P.s and a Patriot Member, were discovered celebrating Charles I's execution and had to be rescued from an irate London mob. A sombre earl of Oxford noted how the participants had lit 'a bonfire and drank some outrageous healths in relation to the murther of King Charles the First...it is a great pitty but that they had been made examples of'. The tory press agreed, and the *Grub Street Journal* was one of the partisan newspapers which drew the moral:

> At last, 'tis plain, some Whigs are as of yore;
> The same in forty-eight and thirty-four;
> Kings and all Kingly government they hate;
> And Whig and Roundhead differ but in date.
> Take care, great GEORGE, who's next: for those who dine
> On sacred CHARLES'S head, would sup on thine.[9]

More sedately, tory politicians could advertise their principles by defending Parliament's commemoration of 30 January. In 1755 Henry Fox urged the Commons to abandon this ceremony, and it is indicative that he won support from two outstandingly independent whigs: Sir Francis Dashwood, M.P. for New Romney, and the Lancashire Member, Lord Strange, who was to renew the motion in 1763. Authentic Country whiggism had always led both men to vote with the tories in support of Place Bills and against standing armies; this same brand of whiggism necessitated their rejection of tory monarchical piety. When Fox's proposal was debated on 28 January it was noted that Strange and Dashwood, 'a hater of all Kings', spoke in its favour, but Thomas Prowse, the tory leader in the Commons, was adamantly against it and 'was religious on the occasion'.[10]

Partisan interpretation of the events of 1649 and 1688 also legitimised tory antipathy to Dissent. The Jacobite tory Lord Lansdowne put the case in simple fashion on 19 December 1718 when he claimed that non-conformists should for ever be deprived of civil rights for their murder of 'the best of men and of Kings. He who renounced the purple to preserve the lawn.' Not content with regicide the Presbyterians and fanatics of the Civil War had gone on to destroy the Stuart dynasty. As one tory pamphleteer argued (fallaciously), James II's conversion to Catholicism was the product of his exile in France 'by the factious Rebellion originally caus'd'. After his succession, it had been unscrupulous Protestant dissenters and Quakers like William Penn and Robert Barclay who had seduced James into destruction by encouraging him to repeal the Test Act and to abandon his most steadfast allies – the Church of England and the tories.[11]

The same virulence could also inform tory parliamentary argument and it provoked, as it was often intended to do, a corresponding whig extremism which could then be labelled as quasi-republican and sectarian. The 1753 debates on the Jew Bill developed in both Houses into a discussion of 1649, the Popish Plot, 1688, and the comparatively recent Sacheverell affair. Lord Temple (who was to regret his words when William Pitt was in need of tory allies) told his fellow peers that tory opposition to the Naturalisation Bill was typical of 'High Church Principles, calling them without any Ceremony *detestable*...He drew a Comparison between ye present Days and those of Charles ye 2d when the furious High Church Zealots declar'd that Presbyterianism was more dangerous to ye Protestant Religion than Popery itself.' Temple's selective history was matched in the Commons by William Northey, tory M.P. for Calne. Replying to whig denunciations of Queen Anne's last ministry he offered the House his interpretation of the Sacheverell crisis and the Treaty of Utrecht, events which had occurred some ten years before his birth.

In his [Sacheverell's] person our established Church itself was attacked; for by his prosecution and Sentence, one of its most essential doctrines was condemned, and the rebellious doctrines of 1649 revived...The treaty of Utrecht ...[was] absolutely necessary; and if there was any thing amiss in that treaty, it was occasioned by the obstinacy of our allies abroad, and the perverseness of a party at home.

A similar identification of the tory party with non-resistance informed the former Secretary of State Sir Thomas Robinson's parliamentary attack on the Cocoa Tree (used indicatively as a synonym for the tory contingent) in 1757. He 'said the creed of those gentlemen was in the preface to Clarendon's *History*': that is, the archetypally high-tory, High-Church preface composed in 1701 by Lord Rochester, a champion of Convocation and cousin to Queen Anne.[12]

Partisan tradition and partisan history permeated mid-eighteenth-century parliamentary debate to a much greater degree than is usually recognised. Did the content as distinct from the catch-phrases of politics provide for a distinctive and enduring tory ideology? At first glance conditions after 1714 scarcely seem congenial to such a survival. The whig appropriation of the Hanoverian dynasty and Walpole's careful alliance with the Anglican hierarchy are supposed to have compromised the tory party's monarchism and its vaunted and symbiotic association with the Church of England. The tories' minority status enforced successive alliances with dissident whigs and a concentration in Parliament on issues which could attract their support; consequently it has also been assumed that the need for opposition unity blended whig and tory critics of the Walpolian and Pelhamite state into a neutral and ideologically homogeneous Country party.

Some historians would indeed argue that the materials providing for a Court–Country rather than a whig–tory split in British politics anticipated the peculiar tactical imperatives posed by the Hanoverian Succession. J. G. A. Pocock, his friends, and his imitators have described how English theorists in the seventeenth century appropriated Machiavelli's critique of the corrupt state and his insistence on civic *virtù* as its only salvation. James Harrington's *Oceana*, the pamphlets and speeches of the first earl of Shaftesbury and his whig colleagues, the productions of the so-called neo-Harringtonians – radical whigs such as Walter Moyle, John Toland, Robert Molesworth, and John Trenchard – and the writings and political thought of Robert Harley and, after 1714, of Lord Bolingbroke have all been scanned for this ideological plagiarism and none of them has been found wanting. In so far as it affected parliamentary argument the neo-Harringtonian or Country tradition involved opposition to standing armies, placemen, electoral bribery, and long Parliaments, and an insistence that since land was indispensable to political independence, landed men should monopolise central and local office. With these ideas Shaftesbury and the early whigs had attacked Charles II and the duke of York in the 1670s and early 1680s. As a result of James II's assault on the Church of England and William III's alien origin and political disregard they became tory property as well, and this partial transference of anti-executive arguments from whigs to tories was facilitated by the latter party's junction with the neo-Harringtonian Robert Harley in the 1690s. After 1715 proscription cemented the tories to an opposition stance, yet many whigs retained residual Country sentiments despite their party's productive relationship with the Hanoverian dynasty. This, it has been argued, made for a fundamental consensus between whig and tory, and was the context for Bolingbroke's political analysis. He and his literary aides claimed that as both parties had participated in the Revolution Settlement and partook of the same Country tradition, the conflict of whig versus tory was obsolete. *Soi-disant* whigs and *soi-disant* tories should unite in a Country opposition to Walpole's corrupt Court party:

'In these two are confusedly blended together all other former distinctions.'[13]

Such a bald summary does not do justice to the complexity and detail of Pocock's analysis and it is not my intention to challenge the importance of the tradition in political argument which he has described. What I would dispute is the Country programme's capacity to absorb the more proprietorial party attitudes of its exponents. Because they were not excluded from the executive to the same extent, because there was a difference in their constituency bases, and because their attitudes to the central government were shaped by historical and partisan tradition and not merely by their current experience, whig and tory dissidents employed Country arguments in rather different ways. The tories criticised standing armies in neo-Harringtonian but also in royalist terms. When the party pressed for higher landed qualifications for J.P.s in 1719, 1722, 1745, and 1747, its spokesmen echoed Trenchard and Molesworth; its immediate and peculiar concern was to hit out at those whig J.P.s of small acreage who had supplanted tories on the Commissions of the Peace. And Georgian toryism was far more than a variant of the Country programme. Having examined Bolingbroke's tactical expedient – for that in effect is what the *Craftsman*'s party analysis was – in the light of tory and dissident whig practice, one has to turn to the two institutions which continued to lend distinction to tory parliamentary and extra-parliamentary attitudes: the Crown and the Church of England.

II

Bolingbroke's political emphases have been expounded with much subtlety by Quentin Skinner. Concentrating on the parliamentary campaign against Walpole in the 1730s, Skinner argues that Bolingbroke – who is assumed to have supervised strategy – instigated the opposition's near-annual attack on standing armies and placemen. These institutions were selected because the premier whig theorists of the seventeenth century had condemned them as tending inevitably towards the destruction of public and individual liberty. By reminding Walpole and his followers 'of the views held by the accredited theorists of their own party' and by showing that Walpole disregarded these tenets, the opposition discredited the ministry's pretensions to authentic whiggery. By citing 'the whig canon' in support of its criticism of the executive, the anti-Walpolian confederation could also evade the contemporary identification of formed opposition with treason.[14]

It is of course possible to account for the opposition's platform in less sophisticated fashion. Ever since the late seventeenth century their common aversion to standing armies and placemen had provided for parliamentary co-operation between dissident whigs and tories. In the 1730s these institutions were obvious targets for a mixed opposition: not only did they theoretically endanger individual liberty, but the patronage they afforded also stabilised Walpole's administration. Their cost was borne by indirect as well as by direct taxation, so their criticism was in part dictated by the opposition's need for extra-parliamentary popularity. There is however no doubt that many tory M.P.s in the 1730s – particularly the more Jacobite ones – savoured the ideological camouflage and potential for embarrassment which appropriating primitive whig arguments gave. In the Army debates of 1738 William Shippen and Lord Noel Somerset vied with each other in jogging the somnolent party conscience of the ministry by quoting the best whig authors against the military. Lest the administration miss the point, Sir John Hynde Cotton remarked, 'These, Sir, are the principles, if I am rightly informed, that once characterised the true Whigs. Let gentlemen apply these characters to their present conduct, and then, laying their hands on their hearts, let them ask of themselves, if they are Whigs?'[15]

Such a tactic would of course have been futile had M.P.s not retained a sense of partisan distinctions. And the tactic was not of Bolingbroke's devising. Since the late 1690s pamphleteers acting in the tory interest, like Charles D'Avenant, and Robert Harley in 'Plain English to All Who Are Honest', had taunted court whigs with their dereliction of original whig principles. In the early years of the Hanoverian regime when Lord Molesworth and Moyle subordinated radicalism to party sentiment and aligned with the ministry tory M.P.s had had a field-day. How, they inquired, could these worthy theorists reconcile their libertarian writings with support for the Septennial Act? Chandler's account of the debate on the Mutiny Bill in February 1718 shows the same ideological sabotage at work. Auditor Harley, 'To shew the Danger of a Standing Army govern'd by Martial Law, quoted a Book written by a noble Member of the House, intitled an Account of Denmark . . . Lord Molesworth (Author of that Book) endeavour'd to shew, "That this was not a parallel Case".' Whereupon John Hungerford, tory M.P. for Scarborough, pounced on the reeling Molesworth with yet more apposite quotations from the moderate tory Bishop Robinson's *Account of Sweden* – a book, as Molesworth well knew, often bound and sold together with his own.[16]

Exchanges like this demonstrate tory familiarity with whig authors as well as the longevity of the parliamentary tactic of unmanning one's ministerial opponent by references to his party's manifesto; whether they demonstrate tory concurrence in an ideological amalgam with Country whiggism is more questionable. The tories may have appropriated the language of radical whig theorists; they were not indebted solely to the neo-Harringtonian tradition or to their coalition with Harley's New Country Party for an anti-executive stance.

As Mark Goldie has emphasised, tory resistance to the encroachments of the Court had been aroused by James II's interference in the rights of the Church of England and indeed in the rights of tory landowners. In 1685 Sir Edward Seymour, a prominent Devon tory and former ally of Danby, accused the Crown of manipulating borough charters so as to fill Westminster with its creatures – unwonted dissidence which owed a great deal to the new charters' erosion of Seymour's electoral influence. In the post-revolutionary Convocation controversy the tory spokesman Francis Atterbury countered William Wake's insistence on the Church's subordination to the State by claiming that the ecclesiastical parliament should meet by right and not be dependent upon royal *dictat*, legitimising tory oppositionism by anchoring it yet again to the cause of Church autonomy. Certainly Atterbury used whig history and ideas to buttress his argument, but he was exploiting them for traditionally tory and clericalist ends.[17]

Throughout the mid eighteenth century tory resistance to the executive was lent a special quality by the party's proscription. As one whig pamphleteer reminded Sir Watkin Williams Wynn in 1745, when the party was in coalition with Henry Pelham, once the tories relinquished their 'Old Sentiments you cannot pretend to hold People by the band of PRINCIPLE but must rely on that of preferments'.[18] Such preferments were rarely available. And even when leading tories were within reach of state promotion, because they were negotiating on behalf of a party, they could not afford the cynicism of Patriot whigs like Samuel Sandys, who led the Place Bill campaign in the 1730s, accepted office without conditions in 1742, and opposed the tory Place Bill of the same year. In the winter of 1744 tory spokesmen asked Pelham for a restricted Place Bill and the disfranchisement of Customs and Excise officers. By the Carlton House declaration of 1747 they obtained Frederick's promise that his accession would be accompanied by 'Inquiries into the great number of abuses in Offices' and the exclusion of army officers from the Commons. That the Army be reduced was a condition of the tory negotiations with Prince George in 1718, with Frederick in 1737, and with Pelham in 1744: in each case a lack of royal or ministerial compliance disrupted tory collaboration. The stress which resulted if the party did renege on its traditional principles was demonstrated in its association with William Pitt.

In 1756 Samuel Johnson was employed as editor of the Pittite journal, the *Literary Magazine*. The articles in which the tory writer attacked the duke of Newcastle for involving Britain in a dishonest war with France indicated some of the tensions which were built into the tories' parliamentary agreement with Pitt. The latter politician had criticised the ministry not so much for its large-scale and costly European involvement as for its military ineptitude and delay. His tory allies were to succumb for a time to his patriotic triumphs (just as tory M.P.s had initially succumbed to the achievements of the duke of Marlborough), but as the Seven Years War progressed and became increasingly expensive many of them reverted to their habitual insularity.[19]

Once Pitt had taken charge of the war Johnson was dismissed from his editorship, but the tories still had their constituents and their political opponents to remind them of the falsity of their position. In 1758 William Blackstone challenged his University's M.P., Sir Roger Newdigate, to justify tory complacency: Pitt had 'declaimed it is true against the Army, but saddled us with a larger than was ever granted before'. In 1759 George Bubb Dodington, who was attached to the earl of Bute and therefore eager to corrode the tory conjunction with Pitt, produced a viciously effective pamphlet, *The Honest Grief of a Tory*. He reminded the party that by allying with the duke of Newcastle Pitt had founded his ostensibly patriot regime on Old Corps corruption and was now up to his neck in a continental war; 'I have always understood the Maxim of employing the Force of France upon the Continent, to be a Whig, a Court Maxim...I have lived to see this Party [the tories] give their Aid and Influence to support the Mischiefs it must necessarily produce.'[20] The tories had become the victims of their own long-term tactic. Instead of upbraiding state whiggism by references to 'the whig canon', newly establishment toryism was being taunted with the arguments of its recent and dissident past. Robert Walpole after 1717, William Pulteney after 1742, and William Pitt when he joined the ministry in 1746 had all shown themselves singularly immune to accusations of political inconstancy; the tories could not be so impervious. In the last two years of George II's reign tory support for Pitt dwindled visibly. By 1759 Sir Roger Newdigate, like his party's leaders, Thomas Prowse and William Northey, had taken refuge in rural integrity and accepted a commission in the recently established county militia – institutions which the tories had frequently advocated as the proper alternative to standing armies.

For one part of the Country programme – shorter Parliaments – the tories did not relax their efforts during the Newcastle–Pitt administration. In the light of Skinner's analysis of opposition tactics in the 1730s it might seem strange that the anti-Walpolian confederation did not make regular attempts to repeal the Septennial Act. Successive whig theorists had championed short Parliaments, and what could have been better calculated to disarm Walpolian objections than the reminder that the great Junto whig, Lord Somers, had taken a leading part in securing the Triennial Act of 1694? Bolingbroke was unable to incorporate short Parliaments into the opposition programme because, despite its neo-Harringtonian pedigree, the issue split the coalition on party lines. There were sound electoral reasons for this. Of the eighty-two opposition whig M.P.s who have been identified in the 1734 Parliament, only nine represented English counties. Five of these – George Bowes of Durham, Robert Vyner of Lincolnshire, Sir Edward Stanley of Lancashire, Thomas Scawen of Surrey, and John Hanbury of Monmouthshire – can be more properly described as independent whigs, whose opposition stance had preceded Pulteney's less disinterested initiative. Ten more Patriot M.P.s sat for malleable Scottish constituencies, while no less than forty-four represented those small and susceptible English boroughs which the tories were so prone to condemn.[21] For men with this consti-tuency base frequent elections were likely to be far more expensive and uncertain than for the tories who were entrenched in the English counties and accustomed to the larger and less bribable boroughs.

It was only with great difficulty that Bolingbroke obtained Patriot co-operation for the tory motion to repeal the Septennial Act in March 1734: 'it seemed', the whigs protested, 'to imply a dereliction of their principles'. In 1739 and 1740 tory proposals to revive the motion en-countered a Patriot veto. In March 1742, when two tory M.P.s did move to repeal the Septennial Act, Pulteney, Sandys, Sir John Rushout, Phillips Gybbon, and Edmund Waller – all leading opposition whig politicians who had made their terms with the ministry – joined 'several other Patriots' in voting against the motion.[22] On 20 February 1758 Sir John Glynne, tory M.P. for Flint boroughs, seconded by Sir John Philipps, proposed that the duration of Parliament be shortened, making clear 'they meant to have them chose annually'. The motion was de-feated by 190 votes to 87, every tory M.P. present supporting it, and almost every whig, including Pitt's closest allies, voting against it.[23] Whig intransigence reflected historical as well as current partisanship. The Septennial Act was rightly regarded as the crucial inauguration of the party's supremacy. A return to triennial Parliaments would have endangered whig electoral investments and diminished whig ministerial control of the House of Commons.

There were some whig peers and M.P.s who put the Country plat-form, including its insistence on short Parliaments, before partisan advantage. Lord Shaftesbury, Lord Strange, Sir Francis Dashwood, Sir

Robert Vyner, and the former tory turned City independent, Sir John Barnard, were as averse to improper ministerial influence, to the stock market, and to the displacement of landed men as any tory politician. It is these sterling independents, as distinct from the Patriot opportunists, whom John Owen has cited as demonstrating the Country platform's capacity to attract both whig and tory.[24] Owen is right to dispel any assumption that the tories had a monopoly on disinterested criticism of the Old Corps regime (there was of course nothing disinterested about the tory criticism of long Parliaments and non-landed placemen), but his authentic whigs were very thin on the ground. He estimates that out of 73 English county M.P.s not holding office in the 1715–22 Parliament only 2 were independent whigs. In the 1727–34 Parliament the proportion was 6 out of 71, and in the next three Parliaments 9 out of 77, 10 out of 68, and 2 out of 66. In other words the only time when whigs came near to forming a sixth of these so-called independent county M.P.s was the period of opposition to Walpole; which perhaps suggests that it was the excesses and personality of that Minister rather than the machinery of mid-eighteenth-century government which was the primary irritant to Hanoverian Country whiggism.

And precisely because of their ideological purity, these independent whigs were always eager to stress their distinction from the tories. Dashwood and Strange dissociated themselves from tory adulation of Charles I. John Sambrooke, whig M.P. for Wenlock from 1727 to 1734, admitted to voting with the tories against Walpole and his ministers when he thought the latter 'in the wrong & acting contrary to the Interest of their Country & Whig principles', but was anxious to refer anyone who thought he had abandoned his party 'to ask, what are my Politicall Principalls of the Master of the Rolls...whom I mention as a known avowed whig, though attached singly to Principles & not men'. The Master of the Rolls was Sir Joseph Jekyll. As one of the managers of Sacheverell's impeachment, a renowned anti-clerical, and 'a great patron of the freethinkers', as well as an opponent of standing armies and corruption, he was a fitting referee for an independent whig but scarcely to be confused with a tory dissident. Nor was Jekyll, any more than another independent whig, Robert Vyner, at all enthusiastic about Lord Bolingbroke's notion of a bland Country opposition. To Vyner the *Craftsman*'s rhetoric was 'cant'. To Jekyll any organised opposition was incompatible with the individualism essential to political independence: 'A Country Party will not do...every member...independent of any Party should speak out according to the Dictates of his Conscience. That a sort of man so acting may be called Patriot and no other.'[25]

Hence the dilemma after 1725 of Bolingbroke and, to a lesser degree, of Pulteney and Wyndham: Patriot whigs were anti-Walpolian but still partisan, independent whigs were unmanageable, and the tories felt their distinction from both groups. All three men recognised that Walpole's defeat predicated a parliamentary confederation of these diverse oppositionists. All three tacitly recognised party differences by adopting a parliamentary platform which could appeal to the parties' common Country inheritance and so, it was hoped, conceal their divergencies. Only Bolingbroke affected to believe that this jerry-built opposition was a coherent and durable political alignment. According to his biographer of 1752 even Bolingbroke was aware 'That though this was the best Expedient, yet is was no more than an Expedient; and that how well soever the Threads of Party might be twisted, they would infallibly separate, and show themselves when the line of Opposition was cut.'[26]

Suspicion of the man as well as partisan bias prevented many tories from concurring with Bolingbroke's analysis of contemporary politics (for one must distinguish between tory acquiescence in the validity of a Country party and tory recognition that a temporary coalition with the Patriot whigs was the only feasible parliamentary strategy). Tory M.P.s remembered Bolingbroke's rumoured deism, his association with and subsequent desertion of the Pretender, and his intrigues with Stanhope and Sunderland in which he bartered tory and Jacobite information for re-entry into political life; in April 1725 only fifty-two of them – less than a third of the party in the Commons – attended and voted to remove his Act of Attainder. In 1741 an influential pamphlet, *The Sentiments of a Tory*, dismissed the *Dissertation upon Parties* as 'Methodism in politics', compared Bolingbroke's shifting politics to the career of the first earl of Shaftesbury (it is indicative that by tory standards this was a derogatory, not a favourable, parallel), and with considerable prescience argued that tory compliance in a Country amalgam would only facilitate the party's continued proscription:

The Reason why he [Bolingbroke] proposed this extraordinary Scheme and took so much Pain to reduce his Notion in Politicks into a System grounded thereon, was plainly this, that the Bulk of those who were to form the Party he was to use might not perceive how small the Number of those Men were, who, in case of Success, were to reap the Benefit of their Labours...But if he, or any of his Disciples, are so sanguine as to imagine, that a certain Body of Men, who have always distinguished themselves by a steady Adherence to Church and Crown, were the Dupes of this Chimerical Notion, and resolved to maintain it at the Expense of their old established Principles, they are mistaken.

Samuel Johnson for one was delighted with this polemic. He referred to the pamphlet in the *Gentleman's Magazine* as the creed of the 'High-heel'd

Party' and gloried in its conclusiveness: 'To this Apology no Reply was attempted.'[27]

The same year witnessed the Worcestershire county contest in which two tories, Edmund Lechmere and Edmund Pytts, defeated two Patriot whigs – one of them being an intimate of Bolingbroke's, George Lyttelton. Sir Charles Hanbury Williams, ministerial M.P. for Monmouthshire, seized upon the incident to versify the disparity between Bolingbroke's fluent and cerebral political style and the ingrained responses of tory country gentlemen. Lyttelton was allotted a suitably precious lament: 'Oh my poor Country, I thy fate deplore, / Still rent by faction and by party tore. / Has all-accomplish'd St John, first of men, / That demi-god, then, vainly drawn his pen?' Lechmere (no less suitably intent upon his cow-herding) is not impressed: 'My principles to you I'll freely state / I love the Church and Whiggism I hate.'[28]

Not all tories were so strident; they had after all been exposed to anti-party arguments before. Robert Harley had always emphasised whig and tory ideological similarities so as to further his desired end of a mixed administration. In the early 1720s independent whig and tory journalists had also argued that the corruption of the whig establishment required a binary party opposition – a format which had been temporarily implemented when whig and tory purists had collaborated in the parliamentary Committee of Inquiry into the South Sea scandal. One of the committee members had been the tory M.P. Archibald Hutcheson. Of Hutcheson's attachment to neo-Harringtonian doctrines there can be no doubt. His classic speech against the Septennial Bill contained images culled directly from various Shaftesburian pamphlets of the 1670s, and he interpreted the new legislation as an affront to the Ancient Constitution, characterised, he maintained, by 'at least annual new Parliaments'. These polemics and his South Sea inquiries drew Hutcheson into the company of radical whig theorists. In 1722 he planned to contest Westminster in partnership with Lord Molesworth, and he joined the influential tory M.P., Sir Thomas Hanmer, in urging John Trenchard to stand at the same general election: 'I would to God there were a few such Whigs as you are in the house & such Tories as my honoured friend [Hanmer] for I am sure such would unite in the preservation of the Liberties of Brittain against all those who would infamously Endeavour to sell & betray them.'[29]

Hutcheson's political analysis reached an audience outside Parliament. He contributed to the radical *Freeholder's Journal* which reputedly sold a regular eight thousand copies until its demise in 1723. In various leading articles and in his own pamphlets Hutcheson argued that party distinctions had been annulled by the Revolution and that good men, whatever their nominal alignment, should close ranks in opposition to an avaricious State. As he told Lord Cowper in April 1722 when sending him his most recent essay, 'My Chief View therein is to persuade honest Whigs and Tories to unite against the Common Enemys of the liberties of the Kingdom; and I hope the Writers of the different parties will employ their Pens for that purpose, instead of irritating one another.'[30]

Hutcheson rehearsed the rationale of the *Craftsman*, but like Bolingbroke and like the neo-Harringtonian Harley, he was to a considerable extent outside the tory mainstream. Hutcheson had been a whimsical tory before 1714 and the Worsley list compiled for George I in 1715 classified him as a whig. From the parliamentary diary of the Kent tory Sir Edward Knatchbull he emerges as a well-meaning oddity, while Mrs Caesar, an ingenuous lady who knew both Jacobite and Harleyite tory politicians, considered him 'some times a little Wild'. Hutcheson himself admitted that he thought 'differently in some things, from other Gentlemen with whom I generally agree'. Most especially he thought differently on matters concerning the monarchy and the Church. He voted against the 1714 Schism Act and he later claimed that, had he not been abroad in 1718, he would have supported its repeal as well as the abrogation of the Occasional Conformity Act. The *Freeholder's Journal* was more orthodox in its Anglicanism, but it advanced contract theory and stigmatised non-resistance.[31]

Church and Crown similarly obstructed tory liaison with Hutcheson's radical whig allies. John Trenchard and Thomas Gordon might use their journalistic essays, 'Cato's Letters', to comment on the obsolescence of 'old names of distinction and faction', but neither whig was able to resist sniping at the tory cult of Charles the Martyr or indulging in facile anti-clericalism. In January 1722 the high-tory *Applebee's Original Weekly Journal* labelled both men as republican: 'I suppose I need not give you the Anatomy of a Commonwealth...the wounds which it formerly made in the Royal Family of the Stuarts are felt to this day.' In 1723 in the wake of the Atterbury crisis 'Cato' launched an attack on the tory-dominated London Charity Schools, claiming that they had been penetrated by Jacobite teachers.[32] This may have been true of a minority of schools but the whig objection went much deeper. Like Bernard Mandeville in his recently published *Essay on Charity and Charity Schools*, Trenchard and Gordon criticised the schools for extending Anglican influence and diverting the poor from their proper station in life. Suspicion of education and sometimes of organised charity as tending only to plebeian indolence had often characterised whiggism. John Locke had queried the suitability of a classical education for tradesmen. In 1698 the radical theorist Andrew Fletcher attacked charity schools as well as almshouses and hospitals for the poor. In 1741 William Pulteney warned the Commons that charity schools were agencies of social insubordination. Ignorance, wrote the whig M.P. Soame Jenyns in 1757, was the 'opiate' of the poor.[33]

The avowed tory position was rather different though fundamentally no less hierarchical. The tory complexion of the majority of urban mobs and the party's greater exposure to large electorates may have been conducive to a more relaxed attitude towards the aspiring canaille. Certainly tory squirearchical propaganda stressed the identity of interest and even of culture which should ideally exist between landlord, tenant, and labourer. The *London Evening Post* reported the socially inclusive Christmas celebrations of a Hertfordshire tory:

His House was open to entertain the Neighbourhood all the Holidays; and particularly on Tuesday was provided a Dinner for the poor Farmers and Labourers in that Parish, where the Season was celebrated with a decent Joyfulness, and long life to their liberal Benefactor, as well as Prosperity to Old England, was drunk with the greatest Cheerfulness. – A true English Hospitality, observed by all Gentlemen of Fortune in this Kingdom, till foreign Fashions and foreign Attachments so vitiated the Palate, as to reject the Appearance of Freeborn Britons.

In such a milieu, it was implied, the squire's authority was guaranteed by consent and indeed by political consensus; individual improvement within such harmony could only benefit the community. In March 1723, at the same time as the debate on charity schools was raging in London, Baron Price, former tory M.P. for Weobley, delivered an assize sermon in Wales and 'said a great deal in favour of Charity Schools, particularly what an advantage it was to Farmers and Husbandmen who cannot read or write to have servants who could do both'.[34]

But is was the charity schools' religious rather than their social utility which attracted most tory advocates. For Anglican philanthropists like Lord Thanet and Auditor Harley (who was to be elected Chairman of the Trustees of the Charity Schools of London in 1725) and for the many English and Welsh tory peers and M.P.s who subscribed to the S.P.C.K., the Church of England charity schools were 'a most useful and pious design'. They enabled wealthy individuals to fulfil their station's charitable obligations, they indoctrinated children in partisan religious principles, and they exemplified the tory belief that the Anglican Church had a formative role to play in the organisation of secular society. In 1723 Gordon and Trenchard were not only charged with irreligion by the predominantly tory Grand Jury of Middlesex (Robert Vyner, one of the few Country whigs on the jury, dissociated himself

from the condemnation) but were also castigated by the tory press –
even by the *Freeholder's Journal*. With metropolitan tory opinion so
critical, it was scarcely surprising that a conventional tory squire, Thomas
Smith of Shaw House, Wiltshire, should have denounced Thomas
Gordon in his diary at this time as 'the writer as 'tis said, of the Independent Whig and London Journal, both bad papers'.[35]

III

The survival of distinctly tory attitudes prevented the party's amalga-
mation with dissident whiggery; how far did their Hanoverian context
deprive these attitudes of positive expression? Both the French historian
Rapin-Thoyras in 1717, and the duke of Newcastle's chaplain, Samuel
Squire, in his survey of English parties in 1748, argued that since tory
royalism had been strained by the Glorious Revolution and nullified by
the change of dynasty in 1714, any residual adherence to the Crown
could be focused only on the Stuarts.[36]

Some tory M.P.s did find George I and his son intrinsically as well as
politically unsympathetic. They were, thought Sir John Hynde Cotton,
of 'a race of foreigners whose title we do not dispute, but whose want
of paternal affection to us we cannot avoid suspecting'. This alienation
drove some crypto-Jacobite tories into an incongruous acceptance of
the citizens' right to resist their monarch. In the Army debate of 1738
the suspect Lord Noel Somerset deviated from his party's usual distinction between the inviolability of the King and the responsibility of his
Ministers: 'His present Majesty...will consider, that, although by our
Constitution the King can be guilty of no crime, yet by endeavouring
to overturn the Constitution in order to skreen a favourite criminal, he
may bring the resentment of the people upon himself and that the
people's resentment may, upon such occasions, exceed the bounds of our
constitution.' As had been the case since the 1690s, this Jacobite propensity to resistance made for collaboration between some pro-Stuart and
republican activists. The Independent Electors of Westminster, initiated
in 1741, was a constituency society which went on to attract predominantly tory, but also dissident whig, republican, and Jacobite sympathisers. It was possibly this mongrel body that Henry Fielding had in
mind when he described, in a pamphlet of 1747, a London Alderman
who was at one and the same time voting tory, hankering for a Stuart
restoration, and gloating over the achievements of 1649 and Oliver
Cromwell.

Since then we must have a King, I am pretty indifferent as to the Person,
and would in my choice consult the Good of Old England only. Whenever

therefore we want a Redress of Grievances under any King, what can be so desirable as an Exchange? For by such Exchange we shall more probably be Gainers than Losers...I am a Jacobite upon republican Principles.[37]

But for the majority of tories concern 'for the Prerogative abstractedly considered' survived the change of dynasty and checked the temptation to disaffection. The party could usually reconcile this concern with parliamentary opposition by distinguishing between the King and his Ministers, and by concentrating on those discretionary powers of the Crown which would not augment whig ministerial control. Initiatives like the 1726 tory bill to limit the sale of crown lands catered to the party's royalist image and, like the tory championship of more crucial monarchical privileges, were designed to attract Hanoverian attention. When Lord Oxford spoke against the Peerage Bill in 1719, asserting that 'he would never give his vote for lopping off so valuable a branch of the prerogative', his argument was shaped by a tory and typically Harleyite concern to preserve the royal capacity for political intervention; it was also astute. As Oxford realised, neither the Prince of Wales nor George I was enamoured of this piece of legislation. It was only unfortunate that Robert Walpole had reached the same conclusion and, by attacking the bill, prevented the tories from posing as the sole guardians of legitimate royal influence.[38]

Tory concern to advertise superior consideration for the Crown was a complicating factor in the party's coalition with the Patriot whigs. The burden of an interesting pamphlet, *The Loyal or Revolutional Tory* (1733), was that the party's history uniquely qualified it to act as a royal auxiliary, and that it would be foolish to compromise this traditional posture by too close a collusion with republican and anti-clerical whigs. This argument had some substance. Samuel Sandys and Daniel Pulteney were both rumoured to harbour republican sympathies and William Pulteney periodically dismayed many of his tory allies by urging the duty of resistance to unworthy monarchs.[39] In the debate on the repeal of the Septennial Act Pulteney relieved his irritation at having to support short Parliaments by linking them with the predominance of the popular will: 'This government is founded upon resistance; it was the principle of resistance that brought about the revolution, which cannot be justified upon any other principle.' As he wrote to another opposition whig, 'The Torys did not much approve of it, being so contrary to their notions of passive obedience and seeming to justifye the Revolution.' It was not in fact Pulteney's vindication of 1688 which had been the problem, but rather his insistence that it was incompatible with the doctrine of non-resistance – something which tory historiography had always denied.[40]

Earlier in 1734 the Patriot Lord Morpeth had moved that no military officer should be removed without a court martial or an Address of Parliament – a piece of retaliation for the royal dismissal of Lords Cobham and Bolton from their regiments for their opposition to the Excise Bill. Wyndham supported the motion in his usual co-operative manner; his backbenchers were more receptive to the taunts of the administration. Had not Queen Anne's tory administration urged the royal removal of the duke of Marlborough, inquired Walpole; had not Wyndham rewarded the actor Booth for his performance in 1713 in Addison's *Cato*, which showed the dangers of politically presumptuous military men? Sir William Yonge, a future Secretary of War, joined in the fun. He wondered how men who cherished the prerogative could support a motion whereby the King 'would not have so much Power left him as the Stadtholder of the Republick of Holland' – an invidious parallel selected for a tory audience. Real and assisted tory disapproval was so patent that the Patriot leaders abandoned the motion before it came to a vote.[41] Seven years later Samuel Sandys' motion that George II be asked to dismiss Walpole foundered on the same tory scruples. Admittedly the fifty-odd tory M.P.s who opposed or abstained from the motion were swayed by the partisan consideration that the Minister's fall was unlikely to result in their own employment, and by partisan disgust at Sandys' speech which had likened Walpole's offences to Lord Oxford's treason at the Treaty of Utrecht, but their pamphlet apologia, *The Sentiments of a Tory*, also dwelt on the sanctity of royal privilege: 'Since the Executive power is in the King by law, he is at liberty to act as he thinks proper as to the choice of ministers and use of their councils.'[42]

Old Corps recognition and occasional exploitation of tory monarchical bias was bound up with the fear that it might attract Hanoverian attention – especially if a whig administration clashed with royal ambition. In 1744 Pelham had lured the tories into coalition by representing to them 'that it was now their time to wipe off the slur that had so long laid on them – and that by rescueing the King from the Bondage which was intended for him, they would act upon their avowd Principles, which were a peculiar Tenderness for the Crown'. He had reason to recall this argument after the contretemps of February 1746 when he, together with Newcastle, Hardwicke, and forty Old Corps politicians, resigned to enforce their rival Lord Granville's dismissal. Not only did George II respond by an unsuccessful appeal to the tories (unsuccessful because they hated Granville and his continental policies), but Horace Walpole also pointed the moral of the incident in a series of pamphlets: 'Have the Tories shewed a want of reverence for the King? Have *they* obtruded themselves upon him into his very closet?'[43]

The lesson was not lost on the Hanoverian heir. In July 1747 Frederick issued the Carlton House declaration pledging himself to end proscription and intimating a particular tenderness for tory policies and politicians. In December his newspaper the *Remembrancer* commenced publication, condemning the Pelhamite coup of the previous year as a 'Bold Encroachment on the Prerogative', a final illustration of how 'modern or corrupt whigs' had invaded the freedom of prince and people alike. The next reign would be characterised 'By shewing equal countenance to Men of equal Rank and Merit, distributing impartially the favours of the Crown'. Frederick's hack journalist, James Ralph, was eventually bought off by the ministry, and the duke of Newcastle also took care to prosecute John Shebbeare, a radical–tory pamphleteer who produced in 1755 one of the most lucid expositions of the divergence between whig and tory attitudes to the Crown. A monopoly on royal favour, he argued, had no more converted the whigs into an authentic court party than proscription had alienated the tories from the Crown.

The Tories have no inclination to oppose the King, they bend their force against the Minister alone, whose power they see every year so enormously increasing; and the Minister has no inclination to augment the royal prerogative, and only advances his own power: thus it appears that the Whigs are still Whigs, tho' in power; and the Tories still the same, tho' out of it.[44]

In the following decade embattled Old Corps and Rockinghamite polemicists were to accuse George III and Bute of founding their government 'upon tories and tory maxims'. Their assertion was demonstrably bogus in terms of ministerial policy and personnel; its propaganda resonance was enormous because it harped on the whigs' longstanding fear that a Hanoverian king might one day exploit the tory monarchism of which they themselves had always been aware.[45]

IV

In 1731 Edmund Gibson, bishop of London, cautioned the inhabitants of his diocese against all political dissension and condemned the current parliamentary opposition in particular: 'All Slanders cast upon the Ministry, do really end in the Dishonour of the Prince...A practice, which the Church of England can never approve, if for no other reason, for the sake of that pious Prince, King Charles the First.' This assertion of Anglican support for Walpole's administration and the calculated association of political dissent with resistance to the Lord's Anointed would seem to exemplify the impossibility of the tories' maintaining their proprietorial attitude to the Church of England after 1714. If the Anglican establishment was cosseted rather than imperilled by a whig regime, why should it look to the tory party for its defence? How could the 'Church in Danger' argument retain its efficacy when Old Dissent was on the decline and popular Anglicanism supposedly waning? Keith Feiling at least was convinced that the tory–Anglican connection dwindled in the mid eighteenth century and that it was this which predicated the party's ideological bankruptcy: the bond 'from which they derived their first creed thus became limp and flaccid'.[46]

Had the tory–Anglican entente been based upon a sympathetic episcopacy its prospects would indeed have been bleak. At Atterbury's trial in 1723 the only tory prelate available to speak in his defence was Francis Gastrell, bishop of Chester. With Gastrell's death in 1725 and that of the moderate George Hooper, bishop of Bath and Wells, two years later, the Bench became entirely whig. Much has been made of Queen Caroline's advancement of tory clerics after 1727. All that this boiled down to in practice was the promotion of Thomas Sherlock to the see of Bangor in 1728 and some of his high-tory friends, such as Henry Stebbing, who became a King's Chaplain in 1732. What distinguished these appointments was first the whig opposition to their implementation – as late as 1748 Pelham and Newcastle were nervous lest Sherlock's translation to London give 'too much encouragement to the tory clergy' – and second the fact that they were exceptional and rendered nugatory by Sherlock's and Stebbing's habitual compliance in whig administrative and electoral demands.[47]

More committed tory churchmen had little chance of reaching the higher ecclesiastical ranks. George Horne, who was to be made a dean and then a bishop by George III, noted in his commonplace book how as President of Magdalen College, Oxford, and as a follower of the High-Church philosopher and scientist John Hutchinson he (and his peers) had stood no chance of preferment before 1760 – not surprisingly, as Hutchinsonianism was an uncompromisingly tory movement. It denounced the Arian and Socinian heresies in which some whig latitudinarian churchmen had dabbled, and its central text, *Moses's Principia* of 1724, condemned the whigs' pet scientist, Isaac Newton, as atheistical in tendency.[48] Geology and the elements, argued Hutchinson, confirmed the veracity of the Scriptures and the Bible was a guide to the ordering of the State; kings were analogous to Christ and the Fall of Man was a dreadful warning of the result of citizens lapsing from passive obedience. It was to be expected that Hutchinsonianism would sweep the University of Oxford in the late 1740s and 1750s, and its major clerical exponents were no less predictable. Horne led the University's campaign against dissenting relief in 1779; the equally tory Dr Nathan Wetherall, Master of University College, delivered a sermon at Oxford on 30 January 1755 which was a plea for absolute passive obedience; and Williams Stevens, 'a Tory of the old Filmer stamp', was appointed Secretary to the Governors of Queen Anne's Bounty.[49]

Hanoverian bishops were men of a different type and their tory press was astringent. When Lord Oxford noted that the outrageously Low-Church bishop of Bangor, Benjamin Hoadly, had been promoted in 1722 as payment for his South Sea complicity – that it was Hoadly who had persuaded the company's cashier, Robert Knight, to abscond and so prevented his revealing the full extent of ministerial graft – he may have been misinformed; what is significant is Oxford's assumption that this was how whig prelates won their sees. 'Bangor's merit was his. . . keeping the Directors to hold their tongues, & was the go between the Ministry and the Directors by which he got the see of Hereford.' In 1735 when Oxford's uncle Auditor Harley, 'whose whole life had been one preparation for Futurity', lay dying it was the saintly bishop of Sodor and Man, a veteran opponent of heresy and worldliness, whom the family called in to administer the sacrament.[50]

This distrust of the episcopate was not so much a departure from as a development of pre-1714 tory attitudes. Ever since the 1690s the struggles between the Upper and Lower Houses of Convocation had testified to the whig liaison with the bishops and tory association with the lesser clergy. It was at the tory-dominated Lower House, up in arms against an erastian sermon by Bishop Hoadly, that the whig closure of Convocation in 1717 was aimed. Tory politicians were to urge Convocation's recall in 1722 and 1742. In 1717 their campaign against the closure was hampered partly by self-interest – some tory admissions to government seemed inevitable after the whig schism and the closure had been instigated by George I – and partly by their disjunction from the bishops. Unwilling at this stage to break with the Court, the whig Archbishop Wake rejected Lord Strafford's proposal that the bishops and the tory peers should combine in a parliamentary condemnation of Convocation's suspension and Hoadly's theology.[51]

Since the bishops were rarely sympathetic, the tories often had to resort to unorthodox allies in ecclesiastical affairs. In 1701 Sir John Pakington, tory M.P. for Worcestershire, had introduced a bill to curb the translation of bishops and so prevent prelates from succumbing to the Court in return for lucrative advancement. In 1731 this motion was renewed, only this time the tories looked to the anti-clerical whigs, who disliked bishops of whatever bias, to assist them. The bill was introduced by the opposition whig M.P. for Hindon, George Heathcote, and seconded by the tory M.P. for Devon, William Courtenay. Two years later the tory M.P. for Derbyshire, Sir Nathaniel Curzon, chaired a parliamentary committee to regulate the ecclesiastical courts. Curzon and the twenty-six other tory M.P.s attached to the committee wanted the courts' powers (and particularly the capacity for patronage they gave to the bishops) to be defined in order that ecclesiastical jurisdiction be properly respected. Many of the whig members of the committee hoped that definition of the courts' powers would be a prelude to their reduction. This disparity was made clear in the parties' reactions to the Quaker Tithe Bill of 1736. As Edward Harley noted, the bill would in fact have exempted the Quakers 'from the payment by putting the recovery of Tythes under the jurisdiction of the Justice of the Peace & taking them out of the Power of the Ecclesiastical Courts'. The bill accordingly met with government and opposition whig support in the Commons and was adamantly opposed by tories in both Houses.[52]

As Pakington's 1701 bill indicates, the tory–Anglican nexus had never been dependent on the higher, more careerist clergymen. Tory bishops had been in the minority throughout the reigns of William III and Queen Anne, and it was the parsons, before the Hanoverian Succession as after, who formed the backbone of clerical toryism. Though Convocation deprived them of organisational expression, their attachment to the tory party and tory concern for their welfare could still be implemented at parish level, and this more humble but persistent tory-Anglicanism deserves attention. Too many historians have concentrated on the parliamentary *coups de théâtre* – the Quaker Tithe and Mortmain controversies of 1736 and the Jew Bill debates of 1753 – and have argued from the rarity of such crises that tory commitment to the Church of England was deprived of all point. This is not true. Clerical poverty, the lack of church accommodation, and the competing attractions of Dissent affected almost every English and Welsh county and, whatever the content of parliamentary debate, tory M.P.s and peers had to react to these problems and so came up to Westminster with their Anglican loyalties and intolerance already forged.[53]

We do not know how many of the 5700 or so English benefices belonging to private landowners had tory patrons. In 1745 *The Clergyman's Intelligencer* listed 210 benefices as being in the gift of tory M.P.s alone, and the party's peerage also had its share of livings: the duke of Beaufort and his wife appointed to thirty-one. In 1736 Wyndham told the Commons that the predominantly tory Oxford colleges had 290 livings at their disposal, and tory investment in metropolitan politics meant that many of the London and Westminster vestry lectureships as well as aldermanic and mayoral chaplaincies were available for sympathetic clergymen.[54] For whether the patron was head of an Oxford house or a tory layman, his largesse tended to go to men suitably disposed in their politics. Archbishop Sharp's eldest son was accommodated in the tory

Blackett family's curacy of Hexham. Jonathan Swift got a tory friend appointed chaplain to the crypto-Jacobite Alderman Barber when he was made Lord Mayor of London. Benjamin Robertshaw, who was appointed vicar of the tory pocket borough and parish of Amersham in 1728, had earlier secured testimonials from Wyndham, Lord Gower, and Sir John Hynde Cotton. His verdict on the anti-clerical Mortmain Act of 1736 was as indicative of his loyalties as were his referees: 'such are ye blessings entail'd upon us by Republicans & Whigs'.[55]

Tory politicians' interest in the orthodoxy of their own parsons was combined with a more general insistence that Anglican clergymen receive an adequate though not excessive income, and a desire to fill those vacant livings – estimated at over four thousand in 1737 – which could afford no parson at all. In 1714 Queen Anne's tory Commons had ordered that no curate should earn less than £20 or more than £50 *per annum*. In 1717 Sir William Pole, M.P. for Honiton, chaired a predominantly tory committee to devise more effectual ways of collecting clerical revenue.[56] Tory wills showed the same concern. When the great Bristol philanthropist Edward Colston died in 1721 he left £6000 to augment the salaries of poor clergymen. He also demonstrated one of his party's meeting-points with the new evangelism – the belief that affluence was as corrosive of clerical integrity as extreme poverty – by stipulating that no more than £100 should be allocated to each living. This insistence on clerical asceticism (coupled with the consideration that the dignatories of the Church were by this stage invariably whig) prompted William Beckford's proposal in 1748 that clerics earning more than £200 *per annum* should be subject to income tax.[57]

The clerical charity of Queen Anne's Bounty, set up in 1704, gave the tories organisational machinery with which to aid impoverished clergy and supply vicars for parishes which would otherwise have been left untended. Between 1714 and 1736 fifty-five tory peers and M.P.s, as well as tory gentlemen like Sir Richard Newdigate and Oxford Fellows like Dr William Stratford, subscribed at least once, and the Governors were able to purchase and fund 516 livings in England and Wales. Tory contributions represented more than altruism. By an Act of 1715, drawn up under tory auspices and allowed through because George I wanted to conciliate the Hanoverian tory Archbishop Dawes, donors who gave more than £200 in lands, money, or tithes to a poor living acquired the right to nominate its incumbent. So when Frederick Tylney, former tory M.P. for Whitchurch, enriched East Tuddenham parish by £200 in 1723, when Charles Cholmondeley, M.P. for Cheshire, gave £200 to the parish of Ince in 1724, and when Sir John Kaye, M.P. for Yorkshire, Watkin Williams Wynn, M.P. for Denbighshire, and Thomas Strangways, M.P.

for Dorset, made similarly munificent donations, they were benefiting the Anglican Church, countering the influence of dissenting preachers, and extending tory ecclesiastical patronage.[58]

Its checks to Dissent, its increase of tory clerical patronage, and indeed its provision of Anglican parsons made Queen Anne's Bounty anathema to many whigs. As Walpole's hack writer William Arnall made clear when he defended a Patriot motion of 1730 to curtail tithes, few whigs of any persuasion were as committed to the maintenance of a clerical presence as were the tories: 'Supposing that there would be in consequence of such a Law, a gradual diminution of the maintenance of the clergy...How would this affect Society, but by lessening the Numbers and reducing the Power of the Clergy?...It would ease the Landed-Interest of a grievous and oppressive Burden.'[59] The whig-sponsored anti-clericalism of the 1730s, which found expression in the Tithe Bill, in Arnall's and numerous other pamphlet presentations of the clergy as a drain on the State, and in Butler's lament in his *Analogy* that Christianity had come to be regarded 'not so much as a subject of enquiry ...as a principal subject of mirth and ridicule', was to contribute to the restriction of Queen Anne's Bounty by way of the Mortmain Act of 1736.[60]

The Mortmain Act was also a symptom of Walpole's break with his ecclesiastical adviser Bishop Gibson. In 1725 Arthur Onslow, the future Speaker, and Walter Plumer, a potential Patriot whig, had brought in a similar bill to regulate landed endowments to the Church. Walpole had abided by his entente with the bishops and joined in defeating the proposal. In 1736 he had no such scruples. The Mortmain Bill was introduced into the Commons by Sir Joseph Jekyll and met with ministerial as well as Patriot support. The tories were bitterly opposed, not only because the bill would cripple bequests to Queen Anne's Bounty, but also because it would redound against landed endowments to other charitable institutions – the whigs, in other words, were betraying their habitual suspicion of corporate Anglican philanthropy. 'The true design of many of the House was against all publick Charity', noted Edward Harley, 'Which appeared by the Warmth & Bitterness of their Speeches against the two Universities, the Charity Schools, Queen Anne's Bounty to the poor Clergy, & to the Clergy in General. None more forward in these Invectives than Mr. Sandys & the Patriots (as they are termed).'[61] Harley did not confine his protests to his diary. He presented a petition against the bill from the Trustees of the Charity Schools; the Governors of Queen Anne's Bounty and the two Universities also petitioned. In the House of Lords, Gower, Strafford, Bathurst, and Abingdon – 'leaders in the high-church or tory party' as one contemporary styled them –

managed to get the bill modified as far as the Universities were concerned. The other two petitions failed, and as a parliamentary report of 1828 on English charities established, the Mortmain Act restricted the benevolence of the aristocracy and gentry for the rest of the century.[62]

The events of 1736 demonstrated that once the artificial brake supplied by Walpole's ecclesiastical policy was removed, whig anti-clericalism would revive and seek public expression. Clerical reaction to the Mortmain Act and to the concurrent Quaker Tithe Bill was also a tribute to the tories' continuing identification with Anglican welfare. Under Gibson's management clergymen all over England signed petitions against the Quaker Tithe bill. It was probably no accident that twenty-eight of the thirty-eight petitions came from dioceses or parishes in constituencies represented by tory M.P.s. When the earl of Egmont visited his former tutor Bishop Smalbroke of Lichfield in May 1736, he found him fulminating against the ministry's betrayal.

He talk'd in a Strain as if the Bishop of London & the other Bishops was resolved to break with Sir Robert...I ask'd him where they would go, for if they break with Sir Robert they break with all the Government Whigs: and as to the discontented Whigs, they were the Clergys greatest Enemies...He reply'd this was all true, but somewhere they must go, the Torys were still friends to the Church upon principle.[63]

Walpole was much too shrewd to let this episcopal alienation get out of hand, but even when the whig-ecclesiastical entente was operative, there was, as Smalbroke recognised, a difference between this politic arrangement and the more positive tory concern for Anglican influence, material welfare, and doctrinal orthodoxy. Anyone who reads the letter books of Archbishop King of Dublin or considers the Hanoverian experience of Archbishop Wake of Canterbury and Bishop Gibson – all staunch whig churchmen who ended their careers as disillusioned and neglected men – will be wary of the familiar assertion that Walpole anaesthetised ecclesiastical suspicions of whig intentions.[64] The notion that Walpole's Church policy endeared him to the tory gentlemen on the back benches also needs to be modified.

On 19 January 1719 Lords Harley and Guernsey had moved for a bill to restrain the growth of Socinianism. Robert and Horatio Walpole and sixteen other dissident whig M.P.s who had just voted with the tories against the repeal of the Occasional Conformity and Schism Acts promptly rejoined the ministerial whigs to defeat this more constructive gesture towards Anglican orthodoxy. In 1721 Lord Willoughby de Broke, tory dean of Windsor, introduced a bill into the Upper House ostensibly designed to suppress blasphemy; it was in fact intended to buttress the

Thirty-Nine Articles against contemporary Arian and Socinian contro-
versialists and to increase magistrates' control over dissenting preachers.
This bill received tory and limited episcopal support. All the whig peers
present opposed it, including Walpole's brother-in-law, Lord Townshend,
and Lord Cowper, a devout churchman who was a friend of Archbishop
Wake and a political ally of the tories.[65]

Walpole's whiggish tolerance of avant-garde theologians did not of
course extend to a radical commitment to Dissent. The *regium donum* –
a subsidy to dissenting ministers' widows which was reintroduced in
1723 – and the various Acts indemnifying dissenters who had failed to
take the sacrament as laid down by the Test and Corporation Acts were
his administration's sole legislative concessions to Dissent. But just as the
tories recognised that Walpole's concern for the Church was passive and
pragmatic, so they interpreted his resistance to nonconformist demands
as one of the more cynical components of his statesmanship. In March
1736, when Watkin Williams Wynn described for his father how tory
M.P.s had obtained ministerial support in their opposition to the
projected repeal of the Test Act, his tone was ironic and his discrimination
explicit.

You are rightly inform'd as to my being in ye Front of the Battle...Sir
Robert Walpole brought up ye Rear...whether they [the ministry] deal in
sincerity or not, I will not pretend to say; in this instance their sentiments
& ours tally'd though upon different Principles. Theirs were founded in
policy ours upon ye basis of our Constitution in Church & State.[66]

Logically the animosity between tories and dissenters should have
waned. As one pamphleteer who styled himself a 'Modern Tory' reasoned
in 1736, both groups were relegated to second-class citizenship and their
continued estrangement only served ministerial interests. Bolingbroke
used the same argument throughout the 1730s, particularly during the
Excise Crisis when the *Craftsman* made some feeble attempts to moderate
tory prejudice and entice dissenting votes into the opposition fold: 'Can
the dissenters hesitate about the option they are to make?'[67] They could;
on the whole they did; and with the exception of Bolingbroke's immediate
allies, Sir William Wyndham and Lord Bathurst, tory M.P.s and peers
remained equally intractable. In 1734 and 1735 Quaker and dissenting
agents lobbied government and opposition M.P.s on a possible repeal of
the Test Act. Their reports show that the only county where the tories
were at all responsive was Gloucestershire, where Bathurst had been able
to moderate party hostility. Otherwise the nonconformists tacitly acknowledged tory bias by confining their inquiries to the various whig M.P.s
available. In Worcestershire they ignored the two county tories, Sir
Herbert Pakington and Edmund Lechmere, and solicited instead the

Patriots, Samuel Sandys and Sir John Rushout, and a government M.P., Colonel Bowles of Bewdley. When the delegates reached Oxfordshire they simply gave up: 'No acquaintance with nor interest in any of the Members of Parliament for the County.'[68]

Most mid-century tory M.P.s did accept the muted religious liberalism of the 1689 Toleration Act. Criticising the Quaker Tithe Bill Sir John St Aubyn took care to stress that 'In points of religious worship, compulsion ought never to be tried but Truth is to have the fair Opportunity of Working by its own force upon the natural ingenuity of the Mind.' Where most tories deviated from most whigs was in their insistence that while religious persecution was wrong, giving legislative encouragement to sects outside or alien to the Anglican Church was worse. This was the declared rationale of the tory opposition to both the Quakers Affirmation Act of 1722 and the Quaker Tithe Bill of 1736. In an all-tory Lords' Protest against the former concession, the signatories condemned the ministry's erastian rationalisation of extended toleration:

The inducement mentioned in the Bill towards granting the Quakers those favours, that they are well affected to the Government...might, we apprehend, be improved into a reason for granting the like favours to Deists, Arians, Jews, and even to Heathens...as no man should be persecuted for his opinions, so neither should any man, who is known to avow principles destructive of Christianity, however useful he may otherwise be to the State, be encouraged by a law, made purposely in his favour, to continue in those principles.[69]

It was this insistence – as well as more straightforward electoral considerations – which prompted tory opposition to the whig-sponsored bills of 1746–7 and 1751 to naturalise foreign Protestants, and of course to the Jew Bill of 1753. In advancing these bills as in their championship of the Naturalisation Act of 1709, the whigs had linked appeals to toleration with references to the economic benefits of easier immigration. Economic *laissez-faire* was normally consonant with tory principles, but not when it facilitated the import and acceptance of religious dissidents. The Anglican Church was also the national Church, and government policy must not outrage her peculiar status. There was a great difference, Thomas Prowse told the Commons in 1753, 'between that of giving the Jews the protection of the Laws whilst they live honestly and peaceably amongst us, and that of naturalising or associating them into our society'.[70]

The tory response to the new Dissent was necessarily more complex. The Glorious Revolution damaged the Church of England and the tory party in several ways but the subsequent Anglican schism, whereby six tory bishops and over four hundred clergymen opted for eviction rather than moral and theological equivocation, was not entirely disadvantageous.

Together with the party's concern for ecclesiastical and social reform and its advocacy of a vigorous and ascetic pastoral presence, the stark integrity of the Nonjurors may have been one of the tories' attractions for those pious, formerly Puritan families like the Harleys, the Mackworths, and the Philippses, who joined the party in such numbers in the late seventeenth and eighteenth centuries. This ideological congruence between Anglican and dissenting purists could operate in reverse. The tory Nonjuror William Law was employed as tutor to Edward Gibbon, father of the historian and a future tory M.P. for Petersfield. By the 1730s Law's religious intensity had found expression in Quaker mysticism. In the same way High-Church asceticism and fear of the pastoral consequences of the whig captivity of the Church could mutate into Methodism.[71]

One of the most evocative paeans to the tory notion of clerical probity appeared in 1731. It described an Anglican parson whose Christian charity ('There were no Beggars in his Town') was matched only by the success of his Anglican intolerance ('There was not a Dissenter or Papist in his Parish'):

> No Wild Disputes found him off his guard,
> Nor those who followed late Socinus' Plan
> Degraded God incarnate to a Man;
> Nor those who wresting Texts with greater slight.
> With Heav'n, as taught by elder Arius, fight.
> Reas'ners! who no Absurdity can see
> In a new-made dependent Deity.
> Amongst his Corn no Tares neglected sprung:
> That free-born Subjects ought to rule their King.

The allusion to passive obedience and the parson's aversion to the Arian and Socinian heresies were alike indicative of the political bias of the author, Samuel Wesley, brother to John and Charles, and a protégé of Bishop Atterbury and Auditor Harley.[72]

John Wesley was less orthodox than his elder brother but of identical partisan bias. As he admitted when defending Samuel from posthumous accusations of Jacobitism, 'Many of those who gave him this title did not distinguish between a Jacobite and a Tory, whereby I mean, "one who believes God, not the People, to be the Origin of all Civil Power". In this sense he was a Tory; so was my father; so am I.' Like the tory parliamentary party he saw the defects of the Hanoverian Church as an invitation to reform, not as a cause for defection or contempt: 'We no more look upon these filthy abuses which adhere to our Church as part of the building than we look upon any filth which may adhere to the walls of Westminster Abbey as a part of that structure.'[73]

Given these attitudes, Wesley's Oxford background, and his insistence that his followers should not secede from the Anglican Church, it was not surprising that the tory response to Methodism was a mixed one. Some Jacobite tories were hostile. The pro-Stuart *Fog's Weekly Journal* made the first known attack on the embryonic Oxford sect, the Holy Club, in December 1732, and in 1740 the duke of Beaufort supervised a riot against the Welsh Methodist, Howell Harris, at Monmouth races. Other Welsh tories, especially those of Puritan ancestry, were markedly sympathetic. John and Erasmus Philipps corresponded with Wesley and introduced George Whitefield to the tory-dominated S.P.C.K.[74]

Tory receptivity was not confined to Wales. In Bristol it was the tory printing house of S. and F. Farley which undertook the first edition of Charles Wesley's hymns in 1741. In Cheshire one of John Wesley's allies was the solid tory squire, Richard Davenport of Calverley Hall, who had introduced himself to Wesley after hearing him preach at Bath. Richard and Rowland Hill, sons of the tory M.P. for Lichfield, became ardent Methodist ministers. In Lincolnshire Sir Neville Hickman, who had contested the county in the tory interest in 1724, scandalised his county neighbours by allowing Wesley to preach at Hickman Hall in Gainsborough and by thanking him after the sermon. The Methodists encountered ferocious persecution from some Cornish tory gentry, but one of the county's leading evangelicals, George Thomson, was presented to his benefice by John Molesworth and became the son-in-law of Sir Nicholas Trevanion, than whom it would have been difficult to find two men more tory.[75] Only in the later 1740s, when Methodism was attracting large numbers of old-style nonconformists, when its itinerant preachers were making inroads into tory parishes, and especially when John Wesley responded to the anti-Jacobite hysteria of 1744–5 by urging his followers to vote for ministerial candidates, did the tory response to the movement become more uniformly hostile.

The tories also showed some sympathy for an evangelical sect closely related to the Methodists, the Moravian Brethren – logically so, as in England it accepted the Thirty-Nine Articles and attracted a fair number of nonjuring and tory disciples, including Charles Kincham, the High-Church rector of Durmer in Hampshire, and James Hutton, the son of a nonjuring parson and next-door neighbour to Samuel Wesley. On 6 April 1747 that ambiguous tory, General Oglethorpe, moved that the Moravian settlers in America should be exempted from the Oath of Allegiance for conscientious reasons. He was promptly supported by Humphrey Sydenham, tory M.P. for Exeter. Two years later the Brethren sought further concessions from Parliament and, as their leader Count Zinzendorff noted, they met with opposition not only from the bishops but also from ministerial whigs. Partly, one suspects, because of whig

and episcopal hostility, the Moravian Bill received tory support, Oglethorpe being seconded on this occasion by Velters Cornewall.[76]

I would not wish to place undue emphasis on tory acquiescence in the
new Dissent. The party's reaction was mixed, its relationship with the
Methodists deteriorated, and in numerical terms both the Methodists and
the Moravians were of limited importance in this period. What is significant is the consistency of the tory–Anglican position. Dissident groups
within the Church of England or doctrinally close to it were to be
distinguished from those sects which had rejected Anglican tutelage and
were associated in the tory mind with Civil War guilt. Critical themselves
of some aspects of the eighteenth-century Church, the tories could sym-
pathise with positive attempts at its reform though not with those who
responded to Anglican deficiencies by secession, hostility, or indifference.

One reason why David Hume's essay 'Of the Parties in Great Britain'
is so unsatisfactory is that it combines accurate political observation with
fallacious analysis. Hume recognised that despite propaganda denials
conventional party divisions continued to matter: why else should dissenters with a grievance against the State still support a whig administration, and the lesser Anglican clergy persist in their tory adherence? But
the apparent illogicality of this survival exasperated him. The tory party
had participated in the Glorious Revolution and had invariably criticised
the executive: how could it plausibly distinguish itself as the party of
non-resistance and the prerogative? Hume extricated himself from his
own erroneous assumptions by arguing that the tories owed their
distinct quality to their attachment to the House of Stuart. Hume was
wrong.[77]

What is striking about tory political argument in the late seventeenth
and eighteenth centuries is its capacity to adapt to dynastic and parliamentary flux while still retaining traditional emphases. Successive tory
bishops, politicians, and pamphleteers demonstrated, to their own satisfaction at least, that non-resistance correctly understood was compatible
with tory participation in the Glorious Revolution. And even if tory
polemicists had failed so to accommodate the Revolution, the party's
Civil War memories would have dictated both a reverence for kingship
and a belief that the interests of the monarch and the integrity of the
Church of England were inseparable: the tories consistently placed the
preservation of this latter connection before attachment to a specific
dynasty. Between 1714 and 1760 tory monarchical piety drew its
emotional sustenance more from Charles the Martyr than from the substantial persons of George I and his successor. But since both of these
monarchs were nominally Anglican they were preferable to their dynastic

competitor, and in 1715 when George Berkeley wrote to dissuade his fellow tories from Jacobite rebellion it was to the Church and to the obligation of non-resistance that he confidently appealed.[78]

After 1714 the tory parliamentary party criticised, as its more errant M.P.s had done since 1685, any undue aggrandisement of the executive, especially if it contravened peculiarly tory interests, as long Parliaments and, to a lesser degree, landless bureaucrats undoubtedly did. The party usually took care to distinguish between this criticism and its concern for the discretionary powers of the Crown – the prerogative, that is, as the earl of Dartmouth defined it: 'a power lodged in the Crown for which there is no Law, but not repugnant to any Law'. When in 1738 Boling-broke tacitly acknowledged the impracticality of the Country amalgam he had advocated in the *Dissertation upon Parties* (1733–4), and opted for a Patriot King to serve as a fulcrum for the variegated opposition, his new theory may have been prompted by these persistent tory monarchical scruples as well as by the fortuitous availability of Frederick, Prince of Wales. Certainly Bolingbroke revealed his own party origins and catered to his tory readers' acquaintance with Filmer. The ideal polity as des-cribed in *The Idea of a Patriot King* 'is that of a patriarchical family'.[79]

The Church of England was in danger throughout the mid eighteenth century. It was imperilled by the supremacy of the whigs, who had always insisted on its subordination to secular authority. It was weakened by the poverty of many of its clergy and by the government's refusal after 1725 to bring the number of churches into line with the size and concentration of the population. It was vulnerable to the Enlightenment and made even more so by the closure of Convocation – its agency of internal reform and theological debate – and by its chief officers' real or reported concentration on temporal affairs. Old Dissent had, it is true, lost some of its missionary zeal and was contained by the administration. England remained in many ways an obsessively religious nation. (A comparison of the number of theological tracts and sermons listed each month in the *Gentleman's Magazine* with the number of scientific, political, and historical works also listed provides an illuminating gloss on the Age of Reason.) But many tories believed or claimed to believe that, becalmed as it was under whig administration, the Church was facilitating spiritual apathy, a decline in public and private morality, and perhaps a weakening in social control.[80]

Whoever wrote the lines for some anti-ministerial street theatre organised by tory and opposition whig politicians in London in 1733 was a worried man and possibly more radical than his sponsors intended. 'Religion's a politick Law', declared 'the Citizens' in *The Honest Electors*,

Devised by the Prigs of the School.
To keep the Rabble in awe,
And amuse the poor ignorant Fool.
Oh why should not B[ishop]s do good.
According to Conscience give vote.
The Reason is soon understood
That they have their lessons by rote.[81]

The remedies which the 'Citizens' went on to propose were hardly adequate for this breakdown in popular religious acquiescence: a new Convocation, a remodelled episcopate, and an assault on deviant theologians. Under whig auspices even these palliatives were unavailable. Tory politicians and gentry had to make do with the indoctrination supplied by Anglican charity schools, with disseminating simple religious and moral literature through the S.P.C.K., with funding new churches, and with keeping watch over the number and integrity of Anglican parsons who might arrest religious enervation in the rural parishes at least. The same enforced reliance on indirect expedients prompted initial and limited tory concurrence in Methodism. Wesley and his followers could penetrate the urban areas and, like its tory matrix, the movement sought to correct the spiritual flaccidity and popular alienation afflicting the Hanoverian Church.

It would obviously be wrong to claim that the content of toryism remained stable from James II to George II; the tories – like most political groupings – modified their attitudes to meet changing circumstances. But it would also be wrong to ignore the fundamental continuity in the tory stance on kingship, the Church, nonconformity and the organisation of the State. Even the mutations of toryism affirm this continuity. Hutchinsonianism went on to influence Newman and Pusey, thus forming a link between the Nonjurors and High Churchmen of the early eighteenth century and the Oxford Movement of the nineteenth. In the period of proscription this persistence in party emphases coupled with party organisation preserved the tory identity throughout and despite the necessary alliances with dissident whigs. In 1762 the earl of Lichfield, President of the Board of Brothers, made a list of the toasts currently in use by this elite tory society: 'Church and King, prosperity & Old England', 'City of Oxford', 'Elections free & Members Incorrupt', 'Fewer Jews & more Christians', 'That we may keep our Money at Home & Credit abroad', and 'Fewer Soldiers & less Taxes'.[82] The October Club would have cheered.

The Tory Party in the Constituencies

In Anne's reign the tories lost only one general election and that by a narrow margin; in 1715 220 tory M.P.s were returned to Parliament and in the 1761 election barely half that number. Accounting for this declension and for the party's limited survival is complicated by the dichotomous intent and chronology of most historians of the eighteenth-century electoral system. Sir Lewis Namier concentrated his own and his research students' attention on the post-1754 period and on the pliant, colourless, and lucre-drenched electoral mores of the lesser boroughs. His famous survey in *The Structure of Politics at the Accession of George III* devotes ten pages to the counties, twenty to the great borough constituencies, and 102 to Harwich, Orford, and the Cornish boroughs — an allocation which reflects the unreformed system's allocation of seats, but not the electoral conditions experienced by the mass of English voters and the bulk of tory parliamentary candidates. More recent work on the Augustan electorate has been both lively and tendentious. Geoffrey Holmes, J. H. Plumb, and W. A. Speck have dwelt on examples of non-deferential voting, on the multiplicity of contested elections under the 1694 Triennial Act, and on the antics of a growing and politicised electorate.[1] Such evidence can obscure the fact that electoral sclerosis was already advancing. By 1690 about 38 per cent of borough seats were under private or government patronage. More than one quarter of England's 203 boroughs were not contested or were contested only once at general elections between 1700 and 1713.[2]

Yet it is tempting to assume that both pre-1715 and post-1754 schools have supplied a comprehensive electoral survey, that it was the intervening period which was crucial to the growth of electoral oligarchy, and that the tory quietus was a function of this process. In the mid eighteenth century, Speck writes, 'political issues were no longer so fundamental...since the vote no longer mattered it was worth selling to the highest bidder'. It is usually supposed that in this game of electoral seduction the tory country gentleman was bound to lose out to his more lavish whig competitor, especially after the 1716 Septennial Act had strengthened patron control, eroded voter initiative, and *arguably* inflated electoral costs.[3] Since tory M.P.s were committed to repealing the Septennial Act, presumably they believed that it was indeed detrimental to their interests; still, it needs to be stressed that in so far as early Hanoverian Britain experienced an increase in, as distinct from a continuity of, electoral oligarchy, this process did not always favour the whigs.

In 1741 only four English counties were contested; the same general election saw thirty-one of England's forty county constituencies returning at least one tory M.P. Having won both seats in Somerset in 1715, in Berkshire, Shropshire, and Suffolk in 1727, in Gloucestershire in 1734, and in Leicestershire in 1741, the tories basked in the representative system's tendency to *rigor mortis*, and held these acquisitions unchallenged until George III's reign.

In the boroughs the electoral stasis which Namier described for the 1750s and 1760s was a gradual and piecemeal creation. The fact that England experienced more borough contests in the first six general elections of the Hanoverian era than in the six general elections of Anne's reign – 494 as against 487 – is in part an indication of how fiercely tory candidates and their supporters resisted electoral oblivion. And, as the regional variations in tory constituency decline demonstrate, borough stultification was not a constant. In the North-East of England, an area spanning Yorkshire (which had supplied the whig party with almost one sixth of its safe seats even in Anne's reign), the Lowther empire of Cumberland and Westmorland, the duke of Newcastle's county of Nottinghamshire, and the old puritan heartland of East Anglia, only nine tory M.P.s were elected in 1761, a 70 per cent decline from the 1715 figure. Yet the eleven Midland counties – Bedfordshire, Buckinghamshire, Cheshire, Derbyshire, Lancashire, Leicestershire, Northamptonshire, Oxfordshire, Shropshire, Staffordshire, and Warwickshire – returned forty-one tory M.P.s in 1761, only seven less than in the 1715 election.[4]

The party's tenacity in the Midlands was due partly to the region's royalist tradition, but primarily to its electoral structure. Its twenty-two county seats were always dominated by tories and it contained only seventeen borough constituencies – less than 17 per cent of England's borough seats. Whereas nine of these Midland boroughs had more than 1000 voters and therefore at least an occasional prospect of open and politicised voting, only four were of the burgage franchise type, which was most conducive to patron control. These conditions made for tory success and made the Midlands anomalous. Elsewhere burgage voters were common. They made up almost 28 per cent of the North-Eastern electorate and were crucial to the Lowthers' success and to tory decline

in that region. England's 203 burgage, freeman, inhabitant, and corporation boroughs together returned 73 per cent of all M.P.s, and over 70
per cent of these borough Members represented electorates of under 500.
The South-West – Berkshire, Cornwall, Devon, Dorset, Gloucestershire,
Hampshire, Herefordshire, Monmouthshire, Somerset, and Wiltshire –
contained ninety-two borough constituencies: over 45 per cent of
England's boroughs, but only 25 per cent of its borough electorate. It
was in this region, in these predominantly petty boroughs, that the tories
suffered their biggest numerical decline, with ninety-one M.P.s returned
in 1715 and only forty in 1761.

As Romney Sedgwick's analysis of the 1713 and 1715 election results
in England (see below) makes clear, this pattern of tory decline was not
the result of a gradual narrowing of the electoral system, but followed
immediately on the accession of George I.[5] My own estimate of each

	No. of voters (to nearest 100)	No. of Members	1713		1715		Whig gain
			Tories	Whigs	Tories	Whigs	
Counties (40)	159000	80	65	15	49	31	16
Boroughs under 100 (74)	3500	146	100	46	47	99	53

party's performance in these two categories of seats would be slightly
different, but the burden of the table is indisputable. The extant poll
figures reveal that in 1715 each party won roughly the same number of
votes – about 46 000. For many seats poll figures do not survive and
many seats were not contested; since however the tories retained a
majority of the county constituencies in 1715, they must have retained a
majority of the electorate. But the active or passive choice of England's
160 000-odd freeholders could be and was reversed by seventy-four
petty boroughs whose voters formed less than 1.5 per cent of the
country's total electorate. The fact that the whig performance in these
boroughs was almost a mirror-image of the 1713 result shows that even
at this stage their voters were ductile, and that the unreformed system
tended to bestow a majority of seats on that group of men to which the
Crown had already given political predominance.

I

To present tory electoral decline in this way, as a foregone conclusion
of tory political dispossession, is open to at least two objections. Some
contemporaries judged that the 1722 election could have witnessed a

tory recovery. Only 'too much bribery on one side and indolence on the other', thought one journalist, had given Walpole his victory.[6] It might also be argued that this interpretation over-estimates the electoral influence of ministerial patronage.

Certainly the Atterbury plot distracted some tory funds and attention from the 1722 campaign, and so did a facile defeatism born of proscription. Only 221 tory candidates are known to have stood in English constituencies in 1722 as against at least 294 in 1715. Sir John Barlow withdrew from canvassing Worcestershire on the grounds that as 'an honest man & a Tory' (and, he might have added, as a man in debt) a parliamentary seat was simply not worth his time and effort. Worcestershire's representation was accordingly divided between the parties without a contest. In Surrey and Buckinghamshire single tories were obliged to canvass in partnership with dissident whigs. Such unnatural conjunctions provoked disagreement between *enragé* and moderate tory activists – the Gloucester tories are a case in point – and infuriated those voters who had grown used to the partisan excitement and monetary benefits attendant on contested elections.[7] 'Is [it] not absurd', argued a 'Bucks. Freeholder' – who had had seven opportunities to vote between January 1701 and September 1713 and had been fobbed off by a compromise between his county's whig and tory elites in 1715 and 1722 – 'to send up two representatives of different principles to Parliament for the same place...if they should vote differently, which of them shall be said to speak the sense of the county?' In Leicestershire the tories made a belated decision to share the county between their own nominee, Edmund Morris, and the whig/Rutland-interest candidate, Lord William Manners. Some Leicester artisans promptly set up another tory candidate, Thomas Wrigley. The High Sheriff refused to allow these plebeian ultras to poll, but their subsequent parliamentary petition was probably correct in claiming that Wrigley could have beaten Manners with ease.[8]

In some of the large boroughs, too, the tories failed in 1722 to exploit voter alienation from an administration linked by pamphleteers and the press with Riot and Septennial Acts and high-level corruption. In Reading the citizens themselves had to call in two tory candidates who were reportedly 'chosen gratis'. In Nottingham only one tory candidate came forward. He lost to the second whig by just fifty-two votes, and almost all of his own votes were plumpers. In Bristol William Hart canvassed as a single tory, came third by just over 100 votes, and secured almost 1400 plumpers from the 1743 votes cast in his favour.[9] No tory stood for Colchester, Derby, or Worcester; only one canvassed at Leicester, Preston, and York. All these constituencies were characterised by substantial grass-roots toryism and, as later elections were to demon-strate, all were amenable to tory success.

Yet it would be wrong to place too much emphasis on missed tory opportunities. In terms of votes cast, the tories won the 1722 election, just as they won the 1734 and 1741 elections. To take the crude guide of those seventy-seven English county and borough contests where tories opposed whigs and poll figures have survived, the 114 tory candidates known to have been involved polled 14 000 votes more than the 153 whig participants. But neither votes cast in their favour, nor all the large constituencies the tories won or might have won, could offset what William Bromley called 'the great dead weight' of the petty boroughs. The seventeen English county contests of 1722 produced twenty-four victorious tories and only eight government whig M.P.s. Only thirty-eight English boroughs with under a hundred voters were contested in 1722 and this category of seat returned 138 whig M.P.s as against only 27 tories.[10] Had the election been held one year earlier, as the whig premier, Lord Sunderland, promised some tory politicians, post-South Sea popular alienation might have been more electorally productive, but in the majority of English boroughs, in Scotland, and in the cinque ports such animus would not have counted for much. Postponement of the election was unfortunate for the tories rather because it gave whig morale more time to recover from the party's 1717–20 schism and the South Sea scandal, and the administration time to organise an election campaign which was widely regarded – with how much justice is not known – as unprecedentedly corrupt.

Not that corruption in the sense of monetary bribes to voters formed a very important part of any eighteenth-century government's electoral armoury. Detailed evidence of how little secret service money was ex-pended on elections, and historians' remarks on how limited was the administration's capacity for direct electoral control (in 1761 only thirty-one English borough seats were under government patronage), are useful only for showing what government electoral influence was *not*. Its real significance lay in the patronage made available by crown favour. Tory politicians were fully cognisant of this advantage because it had been theirs during Anne's reign. Between 1701 and 1706 Westmorland's leading tory peer, Lord Thanet, together with the tory Members for the county and Appleby, had obtained offices worth over £3190 *per annum* for their influential local supporters.[11] And whether it was a case of legal promotion for an attorney gifted in electoral craft, or advancement for the returning officer (in 1727 the tory position in the borough of Christchurch was undermined when the returning officer's son was presented to 'a good benefice...by a great man'), or a place on the Land Tax Commission for an impoverished squire with electoral weight, such baits to key constituents had often more electoral effect than indiscriminate and pecuniary bribes, and were always more accessible to government candidates than to their opponents. This, thought his biographer, was the reason for the whig Robert Nugent's electoral victory at Bristol in 1754, a city previously represented by two tories:

It was a general complaint among the citizens, that they had not a friend to whom they could apply for obtaining any favour from the great officers of State...that in the disposal of Government-places, belonging to their port and city, it was hard and grating to them to see such numbers of strangers preferred, whilst several of their own tradesmen, reduced by misfortunes, wanted bread.[12]

With a third of England's boroughs situated on the coast, there were ready-made opportunities for government influence via Customs and Excise men, shipbuilding contracts, and naval employment. Seaboard counties were also vulnerable. In the Kent election of 1715, 148 freeholders who had voted tory in 1713 and switched their allegiance two years later came from just six parishes, Chatham, Deptford, Gillingham, Gravesend, Greenwich, and Woolwich – areas seething with employment prospects in the naval dockyards, hospital, and ordnance and victualling office, provided that employees acknowledged the fluctuating bias of the Admiralty. Even the decayed port of Chester had its cache of Excise appointments which the government whig Sir Robert Salusbury Cotton could use in 1734 to buy off Cheshire freeholders of influence or extended family. 'It is a matter of great comfort to me, that Sir Robert Walpole has promised you this place for honest Parson Worthington's nephew', wrote one of Cotton's aides in the county election; 'as to Mr. Pierpoint', an Excise appointment was 'absolutely necessary...there is his Grand-father, Brother-in-Law, and at least two or three very near relations gained absolutely'.[13]

Since no 1734 Cheshire poll book has survived, it is not known whether Cotton's antics did any more than confirm the county's rejection of him as a proponent of the Excise Bill. The efficacy of the system whereby more elegant employments were used after 1714 to beguile tory electoral patrons is however beyond doubt. When Walpole gave Thomas Holmes increased administrative leeway in the Isle of Wight in the 1730s, and when Pelham made Henry Bankes a K.C. in 1747 and Henry Rolle a peer in 1748, they may not have increased their administrations' direct electoral influence, but they were converting former tory M.P.s into ministerial supporters, and ensuring that their respective family boroughs – Newton, Corfe Castle, and Barnstaple –

would return only sympathetic M.P.s in the future. The tories had
fortunately never been as dependent on aristocratic electoral patrons as
had their competitors, but the Crown's seduction of its peerage still cost
the party some safe borough seats. In 1734 the new Lord Brooke followed his father's example and nominated two tory candidates for the
pliant borough of Warwick. To the horror of the family's steward,
their return was reversed by a whig House of Commons. 'The calamitys
that have happened', he wrote, '. . . will not alter our principles, break
our unanimity, or render us less zealous', but of course they did. Brooke
learnt his lesson, joined his family's Warwick interest to that of a local
whig, acquired an earldom in 1746, and was Lord Lieutenant of Warwickshire three years later.[14]

As the 1734 Warwick petition demonstrates, one way in which an
administration could increase its parliamentary majority was to use its
existing one. Particularly after the 1715, 1722, and 1747 general elections, tory electoral petitions tended to be consigned to parliamentary
oblivion, while whig petitions, in the phrase of Henry Pelham's secretary,
were determined 'as Justice requires and Whiggs desire'. Hence Archibald Hutcheson's unsuccessful motion in 1722 that election petitions be
heard by a select committee of thirty-six M.P.s – an embryonic version
of Grenville's Election Act of 1770.[15] Control of the House also enabled
the administration to determine a disputed borough charter or franchise
to whig advantage. In 1718 Banbury's new charter gave the borough to
the whigs. Two years later parliamentary restrictions on Boston corporation's right to appoint freemen prevented the tories from gaining control
of both its seats. Some tory electoral patrons were consequently nervous
about pushing their interest to the full lest they invite parliamentary
retaliation. In 1722 Mrs Luttrell, acting lord of the manor of Minehead,
agreed that Sir William Wyndham should represent the borough with
another tory, Robert Mansel. After a not disinterested warning from
Lord Chandos that such a partnership would provoke a whig parliamentary assault on Minehead's charter, she dropped Wyndham and ran
Mansel in conjunction with a government candidate.[16]

If one considers these post-1714 whig advantages, and if one also
remembers that the Crown was usually able to ensure that sheriffs in
election years would be whig, just as partisan Lord Chancellors made
certain that the majority of J.P.s (who could exert enormous influence
over voters) were whig, then the problem to be investigated is not why
the tory position in the constituencies deteriorated in this period, but
rather how the party was able to survive at all.

By 1761 only twenty of the 255 borough seats under private patron
control were firmly under tory control. Cardiff, Beaumaris, and Haver-

fordwest were obedient to the Windsor, Bulkeley, and Philipps families. Lord Bruce, the Grosvenors, the Foleys, the Drakes, and the Leghs usually nominated both M.P.s for Marlborough, Chester, Droitwich, Amersham, and Newton respectively. The Listers and Curzons joined to nominate the Members for Clitheroe. The earl of Abingdon had regained control of one seat at Westbury, and his new Wiltshire neighbour, William Beckford, had beguiled the corporation of Salisbury. Jonathan Rashleigh controlled one seat at Fowey, and after 1722 Monmouth's deceptively large electorate of two thousand invariably acquiesced in the election of the current duke of Beaufort's tory nominee.[17] The bulk of tories had been forced to seek refuge in those large constituencies where government pressures were less potent and patron control more uncertain. Constituencies with over five hundred voters had accounted for less than 29 per cent of tory English borough M.P.s in 1715; by 1761 they accounted for over 57 per cent. In 1761 tory M.P.s made up less than one fifth of the House of Commons but the party still held 50 per cent of the English and Welsh county seats.[18] In a period of tentacular electoral oligarchy, the tories were often compelled to extend their acquaintance with demotic constituencies. This compulsion modified tory electoral techniques; it did not prompt the parliamentary party to modify the representative system.

II

The persistence of tory attitudes amongst large sections of the English and Welsh landed elite was a guarantee of both the party's electoral survival and its electoral conservatism. Not that the socio-political arrangements of many counties entirely corroborate Speck's claim that in the mid eighteenth century 'the political nation was largely united into one governing class'. In Shropshire whig and tory landowners co-operated to obtain legislation but they patronised different social events. The Shropshire whigs had their St Uvedale's Club which assembled four times a year at the Red Lion Tavern in Shrewsbury, while at the Raven in the same city, the local tory gentry met as the 'Fraternity of the True Blue'.[19] Even when Shropshire tories visited London they could refresh their own allegiance and consult their county's invariably tory M.P.s at the capital's Shropshire Club. Such careful socialising made possible a neighbourly vigilance which stabilised partisan alignments. When Thomas Palmer, tory M.P. for Bridgwater, betrayed some sympathy for the whig nominee at the 1734 Somerset county meeting, he was ostracised by his tory friends and 'found it necessary to send to those manors where he had an interest to secure them' for the tory candidate Sir William

Wyndham.[20] Only occasionally would whig and tory landowners compromise county seats out of a sense of common social interest rather than out of necessity, and even then such an atypical consensus might be resisted from below.

From 1701 to 1734 the bulk of Hertfordshire's county M.P.s were tory and kept so by the Royston Club, a society of staunchly tory East Anglian and Hertfordshire landowners. In 1734 one of the sitting tory Members, Charles Caesar, was suspected of ministerial proclivities and dropped in favour of an independent whig, William Plumer, who was also admitted to the Royston Club. By 1754 the club and the county's representation demonstrated an unusual degree of cross-party collaboration and socialising. The candidates that year were Paggen Hale, a ministerialist who was rendered acceptable by his marital connections with a tory family, and Charles Gore, a one-time tory who had defected in 1744. Agreeable as this duo was to the bulk of the Royston Club, it exasperated some of Hertfordshire's lesser and more purist tory gentry; it also angered the county's freeholders, who had been able to vote seven times between 1705 and 1736 but, because of their superiors' complacency, not since. Activists from both interest-groups set up a rival tory candidate and rebel Royston Club member, Edward Gardiner. He came third in the 1754 contest but gained over a thousand plumpers, and as the Royston Club's historian recorded, 'the divisions in the county on the general election...occasioned an almost total desertion of this club'. Indeed, the election put paid to Hertfordshire's polite consensus. The county was contested at six general elections between 1761 and 1802 – three more times than any other English county.[21]

In county terms the 'political nation' was united and impregnable only when one party predominated. As described by Sir Roger Newdigate, the 1753 Warwickshire meeting was both exclusive and complacent. A select assembly of the county's landowners smirked at the late arrival of the disgruntled sheriff (the only whig who bothered to attend) and casually nominated two of their number who were returned, as was usual, without a contest. This was a comparatively open meeting. In 1731 and 1734 Berkshire's representation was settled by a paper agreement between sixteen tory gentlemen.[22] In Wiltshire the choice of a county M.P. was confined to and decided by six tory families; in Cornwall, five tory families; in Northamptonshire, three. Even in counties like Leicestershire where landed society was more variegated, tory candidates were usually pre-selected at *sub rosa* meetings of the sort held on 28 June 1747. 'We shall meet as if it were by accident', wrote one of the five participants, 'for an affair of this kind must be secret lest others take offence.' The following day their decision was ratified and lent a semblance of gentry, clerical, and limited freeholder agreement by a 'general' meeting at the Craven Inn, Leicester.[23]

The great cathedral cities were often represented and managed by the same clique of tory landowners as regulated their county M.P.s. In December 1740 Richard Hopton, formerly tory M.P. for Herefordshire, met the county's current Members, Edward Harley and Velters Cornewall, and Sir John Morgan, who was resigning the task of representing Hereford's 1400 freemen. Their purpose, wrote Hopton, was 'to think of a Gentleman to join my Cousin Winford in offering their services to the City', and their choice fell on Hopton's son, who fortunately came equipped with his wife's fortune of £30 000. Canvassing was to begin a fortnight after the selection process: 'It is not designed to give any money, but only to try how far ye honest interest at first blow will go.' An analysis of the 1741 Hereford result (968 freemen polled, only 69 split their votes between the whig and tory candidates, and the tory majority was less than 30) suggests that whatever the attractive power of the 'honest interest' (the Junto Lord Wharton's synonym for the early, anti-executive whigs, which mid-century tories frequently and indicatively appropriated), it had been supplemented by rigorous campaigning and considerable expense. One tory source implies that each of the party's candidates had been expected to spend £400–£500, in addition to the contributions of their gentry sympathisers.[24]

We need to remember arrangements such as these when assessing the popularist and anti-corruption rhetoric so often employed by tory candidates. When a whig contested Northamptonshire in 1730, he could legitimately describe himself as an opponent of local tory oligarchy. And tory county oligarchies were often rendered more insidious by the fact that their members were mainly substantial landowners and not prominent absentee landlords. From 1708 to 1734 Gilfrid Lawson was able to maintain a tory presence in Cumberland despite the encroaching empire of the Lowthers, because, as Lord Lonsdale diagnosed, he 'made it his business for a long time to know every part of the county thoroughly', as well as all 'the yeomen who are men of business', and this understanding of how each locality functioned lent precision to his canvass.[25] Greater familiarity could also extract a greater degree of deference – using that term in its classical sense of a political acquiescence which was often voluntary and habitual. In the Herefordshire contest of 1754 the single whig candidate, Robert Price, received far less efficient support from his party's great landlords than did the tory duo from the substantial gentry. The parish of Ross in Greytree Hundred was in the sphere of influence of both the whig dean of Hereford and the similarly partisan Herbert Westfaling, yet a third of its seventy-five freeholders gave at least one of their votes to the tories. In Shobdon, the home parish of the county's whig Lord Lieutenant, Lord Bateman, who had instigated Price's candidature, only nine of the twenty-one freeholders plumped for whiggism. The contrast between this piecemeal whig response and the solidarity of the tory parishes is stark. Thirteen of the fourteen freeholders in Sir John Morgan's parish of Kinnersley voted tory; the freeholders resident in the Cope Hopton's village of Stretton were tory to a man.[26]

By combining their influence and experience a clique of tory families could often keep at bay a country's more showy whig aristocrats. And as E. G. Forrester pointed out long ago, the titles which were increasingly concentrated on the whig side in elections did not necessarily imply a commensurate superiority of acreage. Even the great duke of Bedford owned only a tenth of Bedfordshire, which was one reason why the tories were able to maintain a presence in the county and the county town. A peer who could supplement his territorial interest with as much political status, industry, and cash as the duke of Newcastle was, it is true, unbeatable. But such lavish activists were rare, and the tories could usually underwrite the most expensive county contests by collaboration and ingenuity.[27] In the 1734 Yorkshire contest the whig Lord Malton alone was reported to have spent £15 000. The tory landowners coordinating Sir Miles Stapylton's canvass resorted to their monopoly of York's local press to publicise a more democratic tory subscription. In 1747 Sir Walter Wagstaffe Bagot, whose uncouth name was a byword for electoral stinginess, was able to withstand the electoral weight of the Leveson-Gowers and a parliamentary petition against his return for Staffordshire by drawing on a special fund raised by his county's irate tory gentry.[28]

If tory county M.P.s were eighteenth-century England's class representatives *par excellence*, their relationship with their constituency was often more concessionary and diffident than Namier's description might suggest. Tory like whig county M.P.s were expected to instigate and supervise local legislation. This meant intensive participation in parliamentary committees, and such activity should be regarded as an indispensable and continuous form of constituency organisation. Nor could tory county M.P.s feel as secure as a retrospective examination of electoral statistics might suggest. The tory monopoly on Cornwall's county seats went uncontested between 1710 and 1774, but there was a prospect of a whig incursion in 1744, 1748, and 1753, and a near-successful whig assault in 1760. The ever-present prospect of a challenge and the knowledge, confirmed by the Grand Guignol which was the Oxfordshire election of 1754, that no county was invulnerable, meant that some basic organisational machinery had always to be maintained. At each of these emergencies Cornwall's tory elite was willing and able to circularise the freeholders as well as the county's out-voters.[29]

In other words, beneath the complacent veneer and considerable substance of tory county oligarchy, there was always the knowledge that large electorates were *potentially* volatile, and the fear that in the event of a whig-sponsored local rebellion, national whig predominance might ensure its success. In 1727 the tory candidates for Shropshire did not take their uncontested election for granted; instead they spent six weeks making 'personal application' to every accessible freeholder. In 1741 a Leicestershire contest was inevitable and this enforced even greater deviations from the nuances of normal class relations. 'Every Freeholder is also a freespeaker', wrote the tory Wrightson Mundy after several weeks' hard canvassing; '. . .I have frequently met with rebukes from sagacious voters for not pays [sic] my obeisance to 'em earlier, but when I have entreated their vote, they have sagely reply'd. . .that it was long till the Elections; & that time must be taken to consider of it.'[30] In fact the Leicestershire tories had an easy win, but their pre-election nervousness is a warning against any monolithic interpretation of eighteenth-century voter mentality.

Certainly self-interest was a major determinant in eighteenth- as in twentieth-century English voting behaviour. Instead of opting for a national party traditionally associated with the advancement of their class or interest-group, eighteenth-century voters pursued their advantage in a more direct and individualistic fashion and in a much more localist context. Freeholders considered their adjacent landlords; urban voters could be influenced by their employers; tradesmen could be swayed by corporation contracts or by the bias of their wealthier customers. If none of these links of clientage applied, votes could be magnetised by monetary bribes, free food, or free ale, 'ye *primum mobile* of ye vulgar' as one Cheshire whig remarked in 1734. But since the representative system usually allowed them two votes apiece, eighteenth-century voters often combined self-interest with principle, necessary deference with what one contemporary electioneer called 'a natural kicking against power'.[31]

It was largely because he catered to both of these voter tendencies that Sir Walter Blackett remained tory M.P. for Newcastle upon Tyne from 1734 to 1777. He practised lavish, pro-Anglican paternalism: each New Year's day 'some hundreds of poor persons', selected by the churchwardens, were given bread, meat, and sixpence; he showed an efficient concern for the city's mercantile elite; and he exploited commercial clientage to the full. At every election Blackett 'was usually attended by about five hundred gentlemen, tradesmen and others, some of whom had weight with almost every freeman'. Yet Blackett also took care to advertise his toryism and contempt for the government. As Namier observed, in a phrase which reveals his own prejudices, Blackett appealed by way of 'private benefactions and Opposition cant'.[32]

A similar dualism could obtain in contested county elections. In the 1741 general election Worcestershire's freeholders were confronted with an unusually subtle choice. They could opt for two opposition whig candidates, Viscount Deerhurst and George Lyttelton, or for two tories, Edmund Lechmere and Edmund Pytts. Of the 3827 freeholders recorded in the poll book, fewer than a sixth split their votes between the two sets of candidates. This result could indicate sophisticated party identification, or the efficiency of the rival electoral coercion exercised by two local magnates, the tory Lord Foley and the opposition whig Lord Coventry. The experience of the Irish-born Worcestershire landlord, Lord Bellamont, suggests that the answer lies somewhere between these two poles.[33]

Bellamont was a rather ineffectual and often absentee whig. In 1741 sixteen of his twenty-five freehold tenants defied his instructions and voted for both Lechmere and Pytts; six more gave one of their votes to the tory duo. The vicar of one of the family's livings sought to account for this defection:

By letting your Lordship know what upon observation I have always found to be true, that the inclinations of the people in this part of the County with regard to Elections have generally been with the Tory interest, & that when any of your Lordship's Ancestors have made any figures at an Election, it has been when they have gone that way. When the Freeholders are to vote that way, they go in to an Election cheerfully & willingly: But if they are to vote the other way, they are drag'd as it were by compulsion. And tho' Lord Deerhurst be unexceptionable as to his character...yet 'tis apprehended he is set up on the other interest. And that is the reason why the Freeholders are less inclined to vote for him than otherwise.

Doing justice to a real complexity, he added: 'Not but that if your Lordship had thought fit to have declared your mind in time, & to have invited the Freeholders to a small treat, very few of the three parishes would have refused to have given Lord Deerhurst a vote.'[34]

III

Particularly where Dissent was electorally entrenched – in Cheshire, Essex, Hertfordshire, Gloucestershire, and Lancashire nonconformists made up a fifth of each county's electorate – innate freeholder toryism was often rooted in Anglican prejudice.[35] Religious intolerance was compounded when activists from one or other of the camps were engaged in a struggle for temporal influence over their fellow citizens. Resistance to Coventry's dissenting corporation was bound to assume a tory guise, just as those freemen who criticised Maidstone's High-Anglican corporation and its presiding magnate, the tory Lord Aylesford, were largely nonconformist and stridently whig. Although mid-century Old Dissent was rarely an expansive force, tory electoral propaganda during the 1753–4 Jew Bill crisis shows how instinctively the party resorted to religious xenophobia. The tory nominees for Newton in Lancashire indulged in an electorally gratuitous parade through their pocket borough so as to corroborate their partisan identity: 'The Ribbands worn on the Occasion were blue, with these words, No Jews; Christianity and the Constitution.' 'The principles of whiggism, at the best', *Jackson's Oxford Journal* told its county's voters in 1754, 'are lax and latitudinarian… they are for introducing a wild medley of all sorts of impieties from Judaism down to Quakerism.'[36] At the Bristol election of that year only eight out of the thirty-four Anglican clergymen who voted polled for the whig candidate, who received instead the votes of four Presbyterian teachers, three Anabaptists, and three Quaker preachers. In his copy of the 1754 Abingdon poll book one tory noted with pride the bias of his candidate John Morton's allies and that of his enemies: 'there was not one Dissenter poll'd John Morton', but 'the number of Churchmen' who favoured the whig candidate, Henry Thrale, 'were not half the number that poll'd John Morton'.[37]

Echoes of the 'Church in Danger' theme can be found in every contested election in 1754 in which tories participated. And while this was in part a peculiar excrescence of the Jewish Naturalisation Bill, its more normal and electorally productive background was the rapport which so often obtained between tory M.P.s and gentry and the lesser Anglican clergy. John Ivory Talbot, tory M.P. for Ludgershall and later for Wiltshire, made it his business to dine with the 'Clergy of the Neighbourhood' once every month. Sir William Massingberd of Bratoft Hall was no less assiduous between elections, and this groundwork ensured that a fortnight before the 1721 Lincolnshire contest he had ready-made electoral agents at his service: 'I have writ to all the clergymen between this place and Boston to acquaint them when the election begins and to desire them to be active in the getting their parishioners together and mounting such as are unprovided of horses.'[38]

Incumbents of tory livings were automatically engaged in their patron's partisan activities. During the invasion scare of 1744 Thomas Carte risked government postal espionage to advise William Drake, then in Italy, of the need for a good resident clergyman in his family borough of

Amersham: 'I hope he will not think of putting in any body who will not reside with & converse with the townsmen with that ease & friendliness which is necessary to keep them in good humour.' Carte's indiscreet communication was as usual superfluous. The former rector of Amersham, Benjamin Robertshaw, had already persuaded the Drakes to purchase numerous scot and lot tenements in the town. 'Though ye purchase of old houses is no very gainfull bargain', he had written, 'Yet it may prevent a monstrous expense in case of an opposition; & may also be means of keeping peace and good neighbourhood in ye Borough.' He was quite right. Amersham had been contested three times between 1728 and 1735. After the Drakes' property consolidation the borough was inviolate and left undisturbed until its disqualification in 1832.[39]

Because of the discretionary implementation of the tithe system the parson could exert economic as well as ideological pressure. In 1740 the Devon tories had to run their own candidate in partnership with an opposition whig, Theophilus Fortescue. As a whig, Fortescue wanted to approach the county's dissenters, who formed at least a sixth of its electorate. He was promptly brought to heel by the tory Chancellor of Exeter diocese, Theophilus Blackall: 'I should think a publick Declaration of your sincere Attachment to ye Constitution of the Church of England...would on the contrary gain you five Votes for ye Loss of one.' Further recalcitrance on Fortescue's part only brought more elaboration on the Church's capacity to sway votes:

The Clergy...are a body of men by no means to be despised by any one who offers himself as a Candidate for ye County. Had they an Influence over ye People in no other Respect, yet the Composition for Tithes in these parts is everywhere so very low, that there are not perhaps many parishes wherein the Minister cannot command more votes than the Squire.[40]

The parson's electoral bias was bound to be modified by the whig administration's appropriation of the higher Church appointments. Hanoverian bishops were not as uniformly partisan as Walpole and Gibson would have liked to believe. Robert Clavering, appointed bishop of Peterborough in 1729, reportedly favoured the tory candidate in the Northamptonshire by-election of the following year, and he certainly gave Sir Justinian Isham an assurance of his benevolence in 1734.[41] But the bulk of post-1714 bishoprics, prebends, and deanships were more carefully allocated, and at election-time ardent whig dignatories were in a position to appeal to the ambitions of their clerical subordinates, as well as to the deference and insecurity of the devout. In 1741 some of Hereford's normally tory clergymen were enticed into the whig fold by Samuel Croxall, archdeacon of Salop and a former royal chaplain. The city tories promptly made their conventional Anglican propaganda more discriminatory: 'Be not deluded by *false Preachers*.' Thirteen years later the sermons and coercion of Samuel Creswick, dean of Wells, were instrumental in finally eroding the tory position in that borough.[42]

More generally, the electoral inclination of the clergy reflected each county's pattern of ecclesiastical patronage. In Sussex the Crown owned twenty-three livings, the bishop of Chichester twenty-nine, and the dukes of Dorset and Newcastle appointed to another fourteen. With such generous leeway for ministerial influence, it was scarcely surprising that whig propaganda in the county always took care to cater to the clergy. Conversely, one source of tory electoral strength in Cheshire was that the county contained no royal livings at all and several active tory patrons. Between 1713 and 1747, 159 out of 177 Cheshire clergymen identified firmly with one or other party: 115 voted tory, and 61, including 10 dissenting ministers, voted whig in one or more of the elections held in this period. Only when Bishop Peploe succeeded to the bishopric of Chester in 1725 did the whigs begin to dent the tories' Anglican monopoly. The prebends selected by Peploe, as well as the parsons he appointed to his thirteen episcopal livings in Cheshire, were expected to and usually did vote whig. And the corrosive nature of patronage was shown when some of the parsons appointed to episcopal livings by Peploe's tory predecessor were bullied after 1725 into subduing their original party bias. The poor and therefore vulnerable rector of Tatteshall (worth £13 *per annum*) and the vicar of Over (£18 *per annum*) had both voted tory in the 1715 election. They retained their penurious livings until the mid century, but neither dared practise tory partisanship at the polls again.[43]

The conflict between Church and Chapel, between bishop and parson, was only one aspect of a wider tendency for locally determined alignments to ensure recourse to binary party terminology. Parliament's bias may have been fixed between 1714 and 1760; not so the bias of mayors, coroners, churchwardens, verderers, and workhouse guardians, all of whom could exercise coercive and monetary powers over their local neighbours and their votes. Henry Fielding's caveat in 1749 is more than a satire on the pretensions of parish-pump politicians: 'The great are deceived if they imagine they have appropriated ambition and vanity to themselves... Schemes have indeed been laid in the vestry which would hardly disgrace the conclave. Here is a ministry, and here is an opposition...parties and factions, equal to those which are to be found in courts.' Historians are certainly deceived if they ignore these local conflicts, or if they cite the interest they aroused as proof that the eighteenth-century populace was apolitical. Given poor communications, extensive illiteracy, and limited centralisation, it was to be expected that most men would regard agencies of local government with more concern than they did a distant and still introspective Westminster. This was to remain the case until the Victorian era, and in the eighteenth century the fact that local alignments so often employed whig and tory nomenclature and slogans helped to preserve their emotive quality in the constituencies, despite the comparative stasis at the centre.[44]

Although there were no parliamentary contests in Norwich between 1715 and 1727 and no tory M.P. represented the city during the period of proscription, its inhabitants still saw their politics in party terms. A local weaver's diary records twenty-one elections for councillors and sheriffs between 1721 and 1729, all of them contested on party lines. A piece of reportage by the *Norwich Mercury* in 1742 renders the clarity as well as the closeness of the local contest: 'The state of the Common Council stands thus – Whigs 32, Tories 28.' Exeter underwent only two parliamentary contests between 1715 and 1761, but in 1735, 1736, 1738, and 1740 the city's mayoral elections were so contentious that they gave rise to their own poll books. In the 1738 contest 1424 Exeter freemen voted for the whig or tory candidates, about two hundred more than had turned out for the 1734 city parliamentary contest.[45] These hectic and often disruptive local elections were not confined to major cities. In 1722 twenty voters were arrested at Greenwich after the election of a churchwarden had been disputed 'On account of a party cause...ye majority of ye poll... was on ye side of ye Tory party.' Nor was gentry and aristocratic dominance in the counties immune to these substratal convulsions. Shropshire politics in the mid eighteenth century has sometimes been described as a polite landed consensus whereby the county representation went to the tories and the borough seats to the whigs. At grass-roots level it was not always so tidy. In 1748 and 1749 the fear that a tory candidate would be successful in contested elections for the Mastership of the county's House of Correction led to emergency meetings of the local whig magistrates and to the intervention of the Lord Lieutenant, the earl of Powis.[46]

Though eighteenth-century local elections were humbler and less politicised ventures than their nineteenth-century counterparts, contemporaries could still view them as skirmishes in a wider political battle. The whigs' bill of 1716 to 'reform' close vestries in London, Westminster, and Southwark was as much a piece of high-political calculation as were the Sturges Bourne Vestry Acts in the nineteenth century. Its immediate targets were the clerics and churchwardens active in these vestries, and its long-term aim was the bridling of metropolitan toryism.[47]

One can see the same recognition at Westminster that units of local government could serve as party auxiliaries in the whig response to Richard Beckford's Bristol Night Watch Bill of 1755. Beckford wanted night watchmen to be chosen by a wide franchise to prevent Bristol's whig corporation from using these positions as electoral bribes. He was assisted in his campaign by the city's High-Anglican Corporation of the Poor. Since carefully allocated charity was an important ingredient of eighteenth-century electioneering – the Bristol Corporation of the Poor cemented poor voters to the tory cause by gifts of coal at Christmas and free coffins for their children – this organisation was itself a prime example of how local agencies could fuel political conflict: 'It has power', wrote the tory parliamentary reformer, Thomas Carew, in 1765, '. . . else the contests or Elections for a Guardian of the Poor would never have been so high or so strongly solicited for.' In 1755 whig M.P.s of all varieties showed their joint recognition that Beckford's bill would redound to the tories' electoral advantage by voting against it. And because Bristol's Corporation of the Poor has shown itself to be an effective pressure-group, it was increasingly besieged in the second half of the eighteenth century by the city's whig dissenters.[48]

IV

Extensive gentry allegiance, Anglican prejudice, and the exigencies of local government were inbuilt pre-conditions of tory electoral survival; constituency organisation required both creativity and initiative. Secure in his advantage of William Adam's unparalleled cache of papers on whig organisation in the 1790 election, Donald Ginter has dismissed the less documented constituency tactics of earlier opposition alignments as sporadic and 'not outwardly oriented'. Recalcitrant M.P.s, he argues, saw to their own and their immediate friends' elections, but rarely regarded a general election 'as an opportunity to expand the bases of their political power beyond the bounds of their connection'. Yet tory magnates and M.P.s in the mid eighteenth century do seem to have viewed individual electioneering within a wider partisan context. In 1727 the change of monarch misled Lord Strafford into nation-wide optimism: 'the torys are resolved all over England to make their strongest efforts to get the majority in this next Parliament'. Seven years later, William Noel described his successful corruption of Stamford as his personal contribution to a post-Excise Bill tory comeback: 'The new Parliament would be a Tory Parliament as he expressed it.'[49]

Some tory borough patrons did place considerations of family and friendship before the demands of party. Thomas Winnington deserted to the whigs in 1729 but he was accommodated at his tory uncle Lord Foley's borough of Droitwich until 1741. These politics of kinship tended however to be confined to constituencies where no independent voters or staunch gentry were in a position to object (thus Robert Walpole had been able to support his tory uncle Horatio at the family's burgage borough of Castle Rising), and even in pocket boroughs such concessions were not invariable. In 1722 Sir Nicholas Morice threw his brother out of the family's borough of Newport in retaliation for his support of the Septennial Act.[50] And it was far more common for tory politicians to regard their diminishing hoard of patronage boroughs as sanctuaries for talented party colleagues. In 1722 the tory lawyer Thomas Lutwyche had to resign from Appleby because its proprietor, Lord Thanet, wanted the seat for his eldest son. He applied to Lord Gower, who promptly consulted with Sir William Wyndham. Wyndham talked to his co-Member for Somerset, the tory William Helyar, and Lutwyche was shunted into Callington, where Helyar's son-in-law, Sir John Coryton, controlled a seat. Twenty years later these rescue operations were still sufficiently common for a Welsh whig to find no consolation in Sir John Philipps' contested election: 'I am apt enough to believe the tories will bring him in for some borough if he loses Carmarthen.'[51]

With the exception of the 1715 and 1722 elections, in which some Jacobite or very high tories canvassed in opposition to their pro-Hanoverian colleagues (this happened in Cambridgeshire and London and in each case permanently damaged local tory interests), it was rare for tories so to oppose each other. As late as 1761 and in a contest which has been cited as exemplifying the emptiness of party loyalties, the tory brewer Thomas Best refused to stand for Canterbury in partnership with a whig. To do so would have given Best ministerial support, but it would also have entailed his opposing another tory candidate, Richard Milles. Best and Milles went on to canvass and win Canterbury, acting in conjunction.[52]

Not only did tories within a constituency normally assist each other, but if they had influence elsewhere they were also expected to exercise it on behalf of their compeers. In 1722 Lord Cardigan notified Sir Justinian Isham that his servant's freehold vote would be required by Lords Exeter and Gainsborough at the imminent Rutland contest: 'I dare say you will not refuse those Lords this favour, since you are sure that their interest will be always ready to serve you...I hope your interest in Leicestershire will be for Sir Geoffrey Palmer & Mr. Morris [i.e. the tory candidates for that county].' Northamptonshire's tories duly received recompense for their electoral extroversion. When George Compton was returned for the county town in 1734, his voters included the tory M.P.s for Warwickshire, Leicestershire, Tavistock, and Bedford, as well as Richard Lowndes, who was to be returned for Buckinghamshire in 1741.[53]

Tory M.P.s and gentry also made themselves available to any partisan corporation which wanted to cement its control by the creation of honorary freemen. When the historian Edward Gibbon's father contested Southampton as a tory in 1741, its sympathetic corporation appointed 117 new freemen to assist his election: 'a supply was readily obtained of respectable volunteers who flocked from all parts of England to support the cause of their political friends'. The most dramatic instance of these tory freemen creations – indicative both of the party's acquiescence in electoral corruption and of its sense of collective identity – was Worcester corporation's protracted inflation of the city's tory vote. Between 1731 and 1747 sixty-three tory M.P.s, including stalwarts like Sir John Hynde Cotton, Sir James Dashwood, Sir John Philipps, Lord Harley, and Thomas Carew, were made honorary Worcester freemen. In all, 431 freemen were appointed in this period and the predictability of their party bias is a tribute to the corporation's resolution. In 1735 it selected eight Bristol merchants who were to be the founding fathers of the city's tory caucus, the Steadfast Society. In 1736 it appointed a batch of Oxford heads of houses, a flurry of Anglican clergymen (including the vicar of Lacock, appointee of the tory M.P. for Wiltshire) and, to round off the year, Captain Webb, the duke of Beaufort's Gentleman of the Horse. In this way, in a borough where Dissent and the influence of adjacent whig landowners were both strong, the corporation managed to return single tory M.P.s in 1734, 1744, and 1747. Appalled at such efficient tory exploitation of a standard electoral device, an equally corrupt and partisan House of Commons disallowed the latter election, and on 11 February 1748 disfranchised all of Worcester's honorary and tory freemen by a single resolution.[54]

The tories were less gregarious with their money than with their votes. Although there were rumours of a nation-wide tory subscription in 1750, and in 1754 the Cocoa Tree supervised a press campaign to finance the Oxfordshire contest and petition, there is no evidence that the party evolved a central election fund.[55] Regional tory subscriptions were fairly common, however. After Sir John Glynne contested Flint borough in 1734 and lost the election, a subsequent parliamentary petition, and £4000 in the process, he refused to risk his solvency again in 1741. Richard Williams, brother of Watkin Williams Wynn, was chosen to canvass the borough on a tory subscription which raised almost £1600. Sir Robert Grosvenor donated £200 and lesser subscripions came from other Cheshire tories as well as from Lancashire and North Wales. In 1715 and 1741 various Midland tories contributed to their party's campaigns in Leicestershire. Regional munificence had not abated in 1762 when yet another county contest seemed probable. 'I am vastly pleas'd at it, as a thing highly necessary to support the old interest', wrote the Northamptonshire M.P., Sir Edmund Isham, of the new

Leicestershire subscription; 'I have thrown something into the common stock.'[56]

Mid-century toryism could rely on inter-constituency co-operation and a rather amateurish electoral solidarity; some tory sympathisers wanted more. In the early 1740s Thomas Carte compiled his 'Scheme for the Counties', which began by contrasting the tories' enormous reserves of gentry and popular support with their current electoral attenuation. Carte's solution was a binary one. He wanted a London-based committee of about a dozen tory M.P.s under the direction of the duke of Beaufort, to supervise electoral strategy and inter-regional collaboration; he also advocated the 'setting up in all Market towns or larger Parishes Clubs of Independent Electors'. As long as tory candidates concentrated on the conventional monetary and coercive appeals, they were playing a game in which their ministerial opponents were likely to be better equipped. A nation-wide system of constituency societies would regularise the tory canvass and reduce its cost by augmenting the voters' sense of their political responsibility.[57]

Much of Carte's scheme is eccentric, but, as he acknowledged, it was tory practice systematised and writ large. In 1745 the duke of Beaufort founded the Bull Club at Cirencester. Its format was modest enough: a group of local gentry and responsible citizens which Beaufort intended should monitor tory electoral interests at Cirencester in the wake of Lord Bathurst's defection to the Court. Far more democratic was the Charter Club at Colchester. In 1742 the borough's charter had been withdrawn for corruption. The 'chief townsmen' did little to recover it, and Colchester's two tory M.P.s, Charles Gray and Samuel Savill, encouraged a group of 'humbler freemen' to campaign for a new charter. Their regular meetings at the King's Head Tavern facilitated the M.P.s' rapport with their huge electorate, provided for contact between rural and urban tory sympathisers, and, in the end, secured a renovated charter.[58]

One finds further examples of tory acquiescence in grass-roots organisation in the Half Moon Club of Cheapside, London, the Bean Club of Birmingham, and the Independent Electors Society of Coventry. But the avowed inspiration of the 'Scheme for the Counties' was twofold. I describe the activities of the Independent Electors of Westminster in Chapter 6; it is worth mentioning here that in 1747 they arrogated to themselves the functions of Carte's London oligarchy and advertised in the London press their right to select suitable candidates 'for each of the other Counties of Great Britain'.[59] More significant as a constituency experiment, and much more realistic in its ambitions, was the Steadfast Society of Bristol.

In Bristol in December 1737 some tory Merchant Venturers inaugurated

A large club of the principal person of the city...and set up at the same time a great many lesser ones; these last taking their rules and directions from the former, which gives them instructions from time to time, and countenanced them at all times; so that their harmony in about a year's time made them absolute masters of the city.[60]

This was an exaggeration, but the society's impact can be gauged from its electoral record and the speed with which Bristol's whigs, despite their possession of the corporation, set up a Union Society in order to compete. Between 1715 and 1737 only one tory had been returned for Bristol. In 1739 the Steadfast Society secured the return of a *de facto* tory; it scored another success in the 1742 by-election; and in 1747 the tories captured both seats. This achievement was based on the popular toryism latent in Bristol's huge electorate, mobilised, as Carte described, by way of a chain of parish societies. So, after the 1756 by-election, the society voted its thanks to the 'Independent Society of the Parish of St Michael for their Subscription of Thirty Pounds'. And St Michael's voting record reflects the partisan clarity and gain to be derived from durable, low-level organisation. In the 1722 Bristol contest 127 of its parishoners had voted: 64 for the whigs, 42 for the tory candidate, and 21 splitting their votes. In 1754 152 St Michael's freemen polled: 76 for the tory candidates, 76 for the whig, and none splitting his vote. The parish societies also ratified constituency Instructions and the selection of candidates. In 1768 the Steadfast elite chose the one-time woollen draper Matthew Brickdale to share the city's representation with a whig nominee, but this was less the act of a mercantile oligarchy than John Brooke has supposed: 'They sent a copy of their resolution to every parish of the principal people to give their consent of which about 600 signed it & then & not before they applied to the Union.'[61]

The societies' co-ordinated funding protected tory candidates from the dilemma faced by William Hart in 1727 when, for the second time, he contested Bristol as a single tory and had to withdraw from the poll in the face of horrendous election bills. And like the Birmingham Bean Club in its relation to Warwickshire, the Steadfast Society provided a point of contact between the commercial toryism of the city and the landed, high-political toryism of the adjacent counties.[62] In 1748 Norborne Berkeley, tory M.P. for Gloucestershire and a colliery owner, was made President of the society; two years later, the position was filled by Thomas Prowse, M.P. for Somerset; and in 1752, by the duke of Beaufort himself. These partisan contacts were not confined to electoral and civic hand-outs on the part of the tory elite and grateful deference on the part of Bristol's tory merchants. How an organised constituency society might impinge on a party at Westminster was shown in the Steadfast Society's indirect election of Sir John Philipps in 1754. Defeated at Bristol that year, Philipps was returned for Petersfield – according to Josiah Tucker, with the aid of £1700 from the society. One of Newcastle's spies notified his master that 'great matters are to be brought on the tapis this Parliament in regard to commerce so as to make Sir John's having a seat in it, necessary in several capacitys'. In February 1755 Philipps moved, unsuccessfully, to abolish the press-gang system. He and his party had strong libertarian motives for so doing, but of course naval press-gangs preyed on the crews of mercantile vessels. It was no accident that the Merchant Venturers who composed the Steadfast Society should have organised a concurrent subscription 'for the better support & Defence of several Prosecutions of Persons injured & oppressed by Press-Gangs'.[63]

If Carte's independent elector societies had some basis in constituency fact, the same is not true of his tory London oligarchy. By the 1740s both the Cocoa Tree and the St Albans Tavern were contributing to their habitués' national party perspective by serving as clearing-houses for informed electoral gossip, but neither club seems to have attempted a directive role. Yet the Glamorgan by-election of 1745 suggests that, had the various components of tory parliamentary and constituency organisation been regulated and combined, their electoral achievement might have been considerable.[64]

On 26 November 1744 Bussy Mansel, tory M.P. for Glamorgan, succeeded to his family's peerage. The news reached Thomas Prowse three days later in London. 'I instantly went to the House of Commons', he wrote to Sir Charles Kemys Tynte, a Somerset and Glamorgan landowner, 'and talked the Matter over with several of our Friends, who were clearly of Opinion that you ought to be the Man.' On 30 November Beaufort arrived in London and, as Prowse informed his friend, 'Was told by Sir Watkin Williams that Admiral Mathews had declared himself a candidate for Glamorganshire...upon which the Duke sent me to meet Him at the Cocoa Tree about an hour ago, and...his grace desires you will immediately offer yourself a Candidate.' The same day Beaufort dispatched letters to Lords Windsor and Mansel (the three peers between them were to provide £2000 as an election fund) and 'Directions' to his own Glamorgan tenants. Sir Watkin Williams Wynn secured a promise from the Westminster M.P., Charles Edwin, not to push his rival tory interest at Glamorgan. When he proved recalcitrant, Wynn resorted to the Independent Electors of Westminster, who successfully pressurised their M.P. into withdrawing from the contest. Meanwhile, Lord Gower tried to persuade the whig Mathews to accept a vacant seat at Portsmouth. The tory leadership was currently negotiating a coalition with Pelham, and Cotton, Wynn, and Gower tried to make the Glamorgan election part of the deal. As Prowse explained, 'Great professions are now made with regard to Tories, and as this is required as a pledge of their security, you will readily agree with me that such a bequest is likely to be granted.'

All these manoeuvres were compromised when Mathews chose to persist in his candidature. With a contest now unavoidable, Prowse undertook 'to canvass the voters that are in London', and Beaufort sent Tynte his electoral instructions, presciently advising him to watch out for the sheriff: 'If you find they are likely to begin their old Tricks I will do what I can to get Sir Watkin Williams Wynn to come among you. I don't think it would be amiss for you to get it hinted... that you expect him.' It was in fact the whig sheriff's duplicity which cost Tynte the election: he polled 641 votes to Mathews' 688. The tories' response to this failure was as concerted as their preparations for the contest had been. On 14 March 1745 Beaufort returned Tynte for his pocket borough of Monmouth. On 11 April the Commons concluded its inquiry into the indecisive sea battle of Toulon in which Mathews had fought. According to Horace Walpole, 'The Tories, all but one single man, voted against Mathews, whom they have not forgiven for lately opposing one of their friends in Monmouthshire [*recte* Glamorgan] and for carrying his election.'[65] Mathews was court-martialled and in 1747 took himself off to the whig borough of Carmarthen, Glamorgan being restored to tory auspices by its election of Charles Edwin.

It is possible that tory conduct of the 1745 Glamorgan contest was as exceptional as the survival of its documentation: that the concerted metropolitan endeavours to forestall a duplication of tory candidates, to supply the chosen candidate with monetary and coercive aid, and to mobilise the out-voters derived only from Beaufort's personal interest in the constituency. But even if this were the case, it remains true that here, as in the Bristol caucus system, tory sympathisers showed themselves capable of a more positive response to electoral pressures than mere muddling through. The Foxite whigs' organisation in the 1780s and 1790s marked an increase in scale but only rarely in content on the constituency expedients of their dissident tory predecessors. When William Windham set up the Independent Club and its parish offshoots in Norwich in 1783, when Charles James Fox triumphed by way of a similar system in Westminster, and when the erstwhile tory turned

Foxite, Edward Bouverie, inaugurated the Independent Electors Club at Northampton, the format and even the names of these societies – all in constituencies where low-level toryism had been evident in the mid century – were second-hand.[66]

Where, is might be argued, the tories were deficient in comparison with some late-eighteenth-century whigs was in their failure to recognise that sophisticated electoral techniques were not enough; that only a reform of the electoral system could salvage a party bereft of royal favour. Such an argument would be not only anachronistic but also wrong. As we shall see, some tory writers and politicians did advocate limited parliamentary reform from the 1730s onwards. The parliamentary party never espoused the issue *en bloc* and it had good reasons for not doing so.

Tory spokesmen often criticised the Septennial Act for increasing electoral bribery and what Sir William Wyndham called the 'unnatural' influence of government placemen. Such affluent strangers, declared Watkin Williams Wynn in 1734, subverted the 'natural' electoral influence of 'Gentlemen who live in the neighbourhood; gentlemen who give them [the voters] daily employment, by buying in their shops and markets...gentlemen whose ancestors have, perhaps, often represented that very place in parliament.' These invocations of a dispossessed gentry class can obscure the fact that many tory candidates were neither impoverished squires nor handicapped by the need to bribe. For if, as one Gloucester whig calculated in 1751, contested elections always cost tory participants one third more than they did government candidates, who had official pressures and perks at their disposal, then what is remarkable in this period is not the number of tory squireens squeezed out of the electoral circus by escalating costs, but rather the party's survival rate. Even in the 1761 general election, the least volatile of the eighteenth century, half the boroughs with over five hundred voters were contested. Concentrated in these large boroughs as they increasingly were, the tories had no alternative but to spend.[67]

In the other tory bastion, the counties, contests were sparse in this period but exorbitant when they did occur. J. A. Phillips has cited the Oxfordshire contest of 1754 as a cliché for the century's reputed electoral corruption, and it was certainly the model for Hogarth's prints on the venality and burlesque of contemporary electioneering. It was also a contest which cost the two tory candidates, Lord Wenman and Sir James Dashwood, at least £20 000 of their own and their supporters' money.[68] Inevitably, the more that tory candidates invested in current electoral mores, the less likely they were to change them.

And it is by no means clear what changes in the franchise or distribution of seats would have redounded to the tories' unmitigated advantage. A glance at the party's hierarchy indicates some of the problems. Lord Noel Somerset, Lord Gower, Sir Watkin Williams Wynn, Sir John Philipps, Sir John Hynde Cotton, and William Northey were all borough magnates or incumbents of rotten boroughs. True, all these men, with the possible exception of Northey, would have had the entrenched landed status and wealth to penetrate Parliament had the minor boroughs been abolished, but what of the tory *arrivistes*? William Beckford could advance from canvassing Penryn as a recently arrived West Indian in 1747, via a seat in the corrupt borough of Shaftesbury, to metropolitan glory and reformist attitudes; but not every tory capitalist had his style. The banker Henry Hoare had to make do with a seat at the corporation borough of Salisbury and the vicarious satisfaction of lending his tory son-in-law, Lord Bruce, £13 000 to purchase the rotten borough of Great Bedwyn.[69]

Even if the rotten boroughs had been not disfranchised but purified, as some tory reformers urged, by admitting neighbouring freeholders to their electorates, the logic of such a reform would have been invidious. It would have raised the question of whether obsolete and variegated borough franchises should be replaced by a standard qualification. As Fox, Lord Grey, and some proscribed tories foresaw, a respectable and standardised borough franchise would increase voters' immunity to bribery and illicit coercion; in the mid eighteenth century it would also have disfranchised many indigent tory voters in the great towns. In the 1727 Bedford contest 95 per cent of the voters who had their right to poll queried had voted tory. In 1734 more than one tenth of the votes secured by the tory candidate at Bristol came from men reportedly in receipt of charity. The tory candidate for Westminster in 1741, Charles Edwin, drew much of his support from the poorer city districts and the lesser tradesmen.[70]

Would the tories have benefited had the number of county seats been increased? Perhaps, but the size of the party's actual county investment was both an incentive to them to advocate this reform and a crippling hostage to fortune. If county seats were inflated the social and organisational mechanisms, whereby select groups of tory landowning families were able to monopolise shire representation, might be rendered ineffective and outflanked by other interest-groups. In 1761 some of Hertfordshire's freeholders staged a repeat of their 1754 rebellion. They set up another outsider, an independent whig this time, who won his seat with the aid of both dissenting and menial tory voters. The moral must have been clear enough to Hertfordshire's tory gentry. Any modification in the personnel and practice of county elections might inaugurate a new kind of politics in which poor Anglican voters would feel more rapport with their poor dissenting neighbours than with their tory landlord.[71]

Mid-century tories must have known that their party's main electoral weakness was a decline in candidates. After 1734 the number of tory candidates at general elections who took their canvass through to the poll never rose above 200; by 1754 it had fallen below 130.[72] This decline was a symptom not of tory gentry penury but rather of tory proscription. The party kept many of its county families; it would attract the rich, the dissident, and the eccentric; but until it regained state employment, it could not attract the middle-of-the-road individual who was in search of a profitable parliamentary career. And to mid-eighteenth-century tories, as to most late-eighteenth and early-nineteenth-century whigs, regaining access to power seemed a more plausible and attractive way of reversing their electoral minority than launching an assault on the representative system. Only in 1830, when extensive agitation outside Parliament coincided with the prospect of their return to power, did the whigs pledge themselves to undertake parliamentary reform. In the mid eighteenth century there were no such public pressures.

The same localist concentration which gave durability to whig and tory nomenclature was also some guarantee of continued acquiescence in the unreformed system, provided that it retained flexibility. In 1757, when tory landowners co-operated with the Birmingham Bean Club's entrepreneurs to petition Parliament for the duty-free import of American bar-iron into all English ports, they were keeping the town's Warwickshire freeholders content and postponing its agitation for independent representation. In 1766 the Birmingham industrialist Samuel Garbett wrote that he had 'An old acquaintance with Sir Charles Mordaunt and Mr. Bromley, the [tory] Member for this county Warwickshire and must apply thro' them and some of their friends...who would be offended if in my own name I should petition Parliament thro' any other hands.' As Garbett implied, the unreformed system's capacity to cater to new economic and social pressures could stifle autonomous middle-class endeavour (which of course was part of the intention), but this inconvenience was usually tolerated. Even Garbett's subsequent complaint, 'We sorely want somebody who is not only intelligent but with enlarged views to take the lead in considering our commerce as a subject of politicks', was not a *cri de coeur* for a Birmingham M.P., but rather an appeal for more informed landed sponsorship.[73] Contemporary artisans and labourers may have been less complacent, but it is at least arguable that criticising the tory party for omitting to advance parliamentary reform is inappropriate on two counts. It is not clear that moderate parliamentary reform would have automatically provided for a tory parliamentary majority, though manhood suffrage might have done. It is also possible that in its limited enthusiasm for parliamentary reform as in so much else, the proscribed tory party was in tune with the opinion of the majority of Englishmen outside Parliament.

The Fabric of the Tory Appeal

The extent of extra-parliamentary toryism was an eighteenth-century commonplace. 'Two thirds of the nation were Tories', William Pulteney told the King in 1742; two-thirds of the gentry and nine-tenths of the clergy, argued George Lyttelton in 1747. The pamphleteers located tory support lower down the social scale. Those tempted to vote tory, warned a ministerialist in 1734, should ponder on the likely beneficiaries of a tory administration: 'I think I need not say, how agreeable it will be to Judgements and Inclinations of...the Mob of England.' 'Tradesmen, Shopkeepers, Tories and Jacobites' were the party's proclaimed allies in the 1749 Westminster by-election: 'True, they have got the Mob on their side', the government candidate was made to admit, 'but have not we the Army?'[1] The historians – then as subsequently – tended to remark on the tory party's popularity while failing to explain it. 'Their leaders were men of property and extraordinary abilities', ventured John Almon in 1762; 'Possessed of these advantages, it was impossible their speeches and remonstrances should fail of making a sensible impression on the minds of the people; and by taking the popular side of every question, though hardly ever successfully, they initiated themselves intirely into their favour.' This is as unsatisfactory as basing estimates of popular toryism on the opposition bias of the provincial press and the open constituencies. It seems likely that the majority of people in early Hanoverian Britain were 'agin the government': the majority of people often are. How can one distinguish the tory party's rapport with the excluded from the appeal of other contemporary dissidents?[2]

I

One answer presupposes that the tories were the economic as well as the political losers of the eighteenth century. Christopher Hill, Isaac Kramnick, Robert Malcolmson, and E. P. Thompson superimpose tory attitudes on the lesser landed gentry, a class supposedly threatened and demoralised by wartime taxation, the machinations of whig financiers, increasing centralisation, and the real estate operations of the great whig

landlords. Popular toryism sprang from and depended on an alliance –
based according to Kramnick on paternalism and according to Thompson
on the anger and frustration generated by a common socio-economic dispossession – between these rural unfortunates and the labouring poor.
For the squirearchy, whig supremacy meant diminishing local and
political influence and a possible reduction in acreage; for the farmer,
labourer, or villager, an assault on customary rights and a governmental
clamp-down on popular protest.[3] A hierarchical but benevolent society,
wrote Oliver Goldsmith in 1764, had given way to a new hierarchy with
different and illegitimate values:

> Fictitious bonds, the bonds of wealth and law,
> Still gather strength, and force unwilling awe.[4]

The fact that the analyses of eighteenth-century society supplied by
modern historians are so similar to the denunciations of *parti pris* writers
and poets such as Goldsmith, Bolingbroke, John Gay, and Jonathan Swift
should perhaps make one pause. Tory apologists and politicians were
bound to dissociate themselves from the less attractive aspects of eighteenth-century society and link them with whig predominance. In 1743
Lord Oxford suggested that the tories' exclusion from office and court
society enabled them to traverse the rift between sheltered privilege and
the suffering multitudes:

There are many in this House who see no other scenes than the magnificence
of feasts, the gaieties of balls, and the splendour of a court; and it is not
much to be wondered at, if they do not easily believe, what it is often their
interest to doubt, that this luxury is supported by the distress of millions...
It is my custom, when the business of the parliament is over, to retire to
my estate in the country, where I...take a calm and deliberate survey of the
condition of those that inhabit the towns and villages about me; I mingle in
their conversation, and hear their complaints; I enter their houses, and find
by their condition, that their complaints are just.

This reads rather like the propaganda of the Young England movement,
and there is indeed some continuity in the tory social critique. One has
only to turn to some of Oxford's party allies for proof that no more in
the eighteenth than in the nineteenth century, was there consistency in
tory social practice. The tory earl of Uxbridge was an absentee Staffordshire landlord who prosecuted local men for game offences on no fewer
than eighty occasions between 1750 and 1765. He also fought a long and
successful battle to erode common rights on Cannock Chase, assisted by
neighbouring tory J.P.s. In the 1730s and 1740s the Beaufort family's
copper-mining made inroads on common land in Glamorgan – a process
which was challenged for partisan and economic reasons by lesser landowners, who were predominantly whig.[5]

Tory paternalism did of course exist. Georgian fiction delineated its acceptable and unacceptable faces in Squire Allworthy and Lady Catherine de Bourgh. The first practised charity and hospitality out of a sense of his station's responsibilities to neighbours and inferiors; the second perverted these virtues into the ingredients of an intrusive local tyranny. Both strategies had their real-life tory exponents and increased the party's support. Even before the Drakes converted Amersham into a pocket borough, its inhabitants had been welded into social harmony and political compliance by the family's benevolence and by the attentions of successive, carefully chosen tory parsons. When a whig candidate equipped with 'very large sums of money' contested Amersham in 1727, he was confronted by a powerful tory electoral interest rooted in plebeian solidarity. The Drake tenants told him 'they could not think of selling their landlord'.[6] A similarly scrupulous supervision of his employees and dependents enabled Watkin Williams Wynn to identify and deal ruthlessly with any Denbighshire recalcitrants. A crippled woman in receipt of a small pension from the family was turned off Wynnstay estate immediately she was seen giving verbal support to Wynn's opponent in the 1722 county election.[7]

Paternalism's inbuilt ambiguity was no less apparent in industry. In 1713 the iron magnate Ambrose Crowley III, the founder, according to one historian, of 'probably the greatest industrial organisation of his age', compiled a Law Book for the regulation of his workers. 'The familiar landscape of disciplined industrial capitalism', remarks Thompson of this document, 'with the time-sheet, the time-keeper, the informers and the fines.' All true. But what is also true is that in this same year Crowley, a former Quaker converted to tory-Jacobitism, stood for the rotten borough of Andover on the interest of the duke of Beaufort. His son and successor in the business, John Crowley, was a Jacobite suspect in 1715 and returned as tory M.P. for Okehampton in 1722. The Crowley Law Book is a monument to tory paternalism. It provided for factory chaplains 'to read prayers as is directed by the Church of England established by Law every Sunday' and for factory schoolmasters. In 1724 John Crowley appointed a full-time factory doctor ('all workmen's and officers' children are to be relieved gratis') and like his father administered an insurance scheme for impoverished or injured workers. Those attitudes usually bracketed together as paternalism were economically janus-faced: they had often humanised and legitimised rural hierarchies; they also helped erode those hierarchies and their values by facilitating early industrial organisation.[8]

Crowley's enterprise serves as a reminder that the tory parliamentary party was not the squirearchy writ large. Some of its M.P.s came from unorthodox social backgrounds, many of them benefited from contemporary economic diversification, and most of its members in both Houses were affluent men. All things being equal (and tory radicalism occurred when all things were not equal) it was to be expected that tory politicians would demonstrate a legislative concern for property similar to that of their whig counterparts and a similar legislative animus against those who threatened it.

Not that either party was as calculated in its assault on the socially dispossessed as some historians have suggested. If one looks at the Lords debate on the 1724 Physicians' Bill 'for securing executed bodies' for dissection, what is striking is not the peers' desire that unruly plebs be consigned to the anatomists as well as to the hangman, as 'part of the policy of class discipline', but their repugnance towards the whole practice: 'the Physicians (they imagin'd) had some sinister end in it'. Walpole's brother-in-law, Lord Townshend, remarked on the Tyburn crowd's attempts to rescue bodies from the surgeons and praised its initiative: 'the mobb show'd a merciful disposition in hindering dissections, & it ought to be encourag'd'. The tory Lord Trevor made a different objection to the bill. If dissection were the rule, 'a person of consideration ...convicted of capital crimes' might be exposed to this humiliation. His intervention was prescient. Lord Ferrers, who was hanged and dissected for the murder of his steward in 1760, was also a tory.[9]

In the House of Commons tory M.P.s were predictably concerned to buttress the Game Laws. They were responsible for a tougher Act in 1718, and in 1719 John Hungerford, one of the party's leading lawyers, presented a bill for the 'further punishment of such persons as shall unlawfully kill or destroy Deer in parks, paddocks or enclosed ground'. In 1724 Hungerford was to be one of nine tory M.P.s appointed to a parliamentary committee on farm labourers, a committee recently cited as exemplifying the Walpolian concern for 'a more authoritarian resolution to the problems of power and order'.[10] The Black Act is no less problematical as a model for divergent whig and tory social attitudes. The parliamentary committee which sought to amend the Act in 1731 was chaired by a tory; a similar initiative in 1732, whereby the Act's applicability was restricted and some of its penalties reduced, was stagemanaged by a government whig apparently acting with Walpole's approval.[11]

Whether the tories' minority status on the Commissions of the Peace after 1714 was accompanied by a qualitative change in county justice is a subject which awaits the local historians. There is evidence that the purging of some tory J.P.s met with grass-roots opposition. By Sir George Beaumont's removal from the Leicestershire Bench, wrote Nichols, 'The poor were the only sufferers, who in him found an impartial magistrate and a steady friend; but, so great and general was the discontent upon that account, that it was afterwards thought proper to restore him.' Beaumont came from a gentry family which had been associated with Leicester's civic organisation since the sixteenth century. Between 1714 and 1718 tories of this moderate if entrenched landed status formed the bulk of Lord Chancellor Cowper's victims, not only in Leicestershire, but also in Cheshire, Cornwall, Hampshire, Northamptonshire, and most of Wales. It is possible that J.P.s from this landed category had most contact and cultural affinity with their poorer neighbours and were most inclined to be regular in their assize attendance: hence perhaps the popular sense of bereavement at their removal. Certainly the slogan 'No King George's Justices' became part of the armoury of the early Hanoverian crowd.[12]

The politicians capitalised on this sentiment and tended to connect any harsh or insensitive legislation in the counties with their party's lack of magistrates. On 16 July 1715 a tory moved that a clause be added to the Riot Act 'that an Account may be laid before this House of what persons are at present in the Commissions of the Peace; and also what Persons were in the Commissions at the demise of her Majesty'. In 1741 Benjamin Bathurst argued that pressed seamen often appealed in vain to their J.P., 'some abandoned prostitute dignified with a commission only to influence elections, and awe those whom excises and riot acts cannot subdue'. As a component of the tories' radical persona this argument was important, but, in view of the common identification of toryism and social concern with the declining gentry, it is interesting that the party's solution to the purported deterioration in local justice was higher landed qualifications for J.P.s. By 1747 the tory leadership wanted Justices to be worth at least £300 *per annum* as assessed by the Land Tax Commission – a provision which in some counties at least would have redounded against the minor gentry.[13]

One comes back therefore to the validity or otherwise of assuming that the squirearchy was predominantly tory. The success and occasional radicalism of the alliance between the marquess of Rockingham, Sir George Savile, and the Yorkshire gentry in the Wilkite and Wyvillite eras is a reminder that in the Northern counties especially, the whigs had their own independent and squirearchical tradition. A survey of 1755 listed thirteen English counties with fewer than twenty great estates apiece: presumably these were also the most propitious counties for lesser landowners. Five of them (Herefordshire, Lancashire, Leicestershire, Warwickshire, and Worcestershire) were duly tory in their county politics; four more (Cumberland, Huntingdonshire, Monmouthshire, and Northumberland) were among the few English counties in the eighteenth century that showed a consistent preference for whig knights of the shire and had done so even in Queen Anne's reign.[14] If sympathetic justice was a concomitant of limited acreage, whig squireens must have been available in some post-1714 Commissions of the Peace to intercede for the rural poor, and it has yet to be proved that even affluent whig J.P.s were less attached to the moral economy than were the substantial tory J.P.s who survived Cowper's purges.

On 18 April 1732 at the Easter Quarter Sessions at Boothall, Gloucester, the magistrates fixed wage levels for all labourers and servants in the county. They had their orders printed in the *Gloucester Journal* and displayed on the doors of every parish church in the county. Several tory J.P.s were present on this occasion but so were Sir John Guise, a former whig Member for the county, and its current whig M.P., Sir John Dutton. In 1738 weavers at Melksham in Wiltshire rioted in protest at their employers' use of truck in lieu of money wages. The government sent in troops and three weavers were hanged. The episode gave rise to a pamphlet by the whig J.P. William Temple – a clothier, a friend of the political economist Josiah Tucker, and a posthumous hero of J. R. McCulloch. Like most economic commentators in the first half of the eighteenth century, Temple argued that low wages were the indispensable spur to industry; more unusually he asserted that magisterial intervention on behalf of the labouring poor was always ill-advised: 'If the Poor had no Laws to rely on for support in their Extremities, they would behave in a more decent and becoming manner to their Masters and Superiors.' Temple seems an ideal whig social villain. It is complicating but true that in the 1760s he went on to subsidise John Wilkes' popularist endeavours and that one of the few J.P.s complimented in his pamphlet for their 'utmost Efforts, Care, and Diligence, to suppress the Riot, and detect the Offenders, even to the hazard of their Lives' was John Ivory-Talbot, tory M.P. for Wiltshire.[15]

I have concentrated on the case against superior tory social concern and have done so in deliberately cavalier fashion because it seems to me unsatisfactory and misleading to single out either paternalism (however one construes that term) or the tories' empathy with the dispossessed as the mainspring of the party's eighteenth-century popularity. Linking the tories with a social attitude which has connotations of archaism, or stressing, as Thompson does, their inadaptability to the new economic order, tends to make tory popularism of antiquarian interest only. By the 1760s John Wilkes and his allies can be allowed (by some) to have inaugurated the alternative politics of the traditionally excluded, but the tory oppositionists of the Walpolian and Pelhamite era must be consigned to the historical attic as nostalgic revanchists. More important, because

Thompson describes the tories as bucolic traditionalists, he can see no reason why they should or could have forged an association with those urban, commercial, and professional classes which were also excluded from the full benefits of Hanoverian society. Hence in part his need to condemn the mid-century middle classes to impotent acquiescence in the whig regime, if not to clientage: they were, he asserts, 'consenting adults in their own corruption'. Yet in some of his essays, at least, Hume identified 'the middling rank' of the people as being the most responsive to the tory platform, and if popular toryism existed anywhere, it was in the great commercial cities of London, Norwich, Coventry, Newcastle, and Bristol and in the expanding though unrepresented industrial towns, Birmingham, Manchester, and Leeds.[16]

Instead of assuming what cannot be proved – that the tories were more socially sympathetic than their opponents – it is worth approaching their popularity by way of Josiah Tucker's singular analysis. The 'Independence of the lower and middling People in regard to the Great, but a Dependence of the Great upon them', was, he wrote in 1757, the key to understanding some of the antics of England's elite:

The People are independent, because they have nothing to fear, and very little to hope from the Power of the Great; but the Great are rendered dependent upon them; because, without the Assistance or Approbation of the People, they cannot be considerable either in the Senate, or out of it; they cannot either be Ministers themselves, or raise an effectual Opposition to the Ministry of others...Hence that diffusive Charity...so conspicuous in Persons of Fortune in this Country; hence those noble Instances of public Beneficence for the Relief of the Poor, in Times of Scarcity and general Distress; hence also that Rivalship and Emulation in some of the Members of the Legislature, to patronise a public-spirited Scheme.

Much of this is conscious hyperbole. Few plebs or tradesmen in eighteenth-century England were required invariably to cringe before the great; hardly any were economically independent of their superiors.[17] Tucker was right however – though his observation does not accord with the subsequent presentation of early Georgian politics as insulated and contracting – in noting that dissident politicians needed, or believed they needed, reinforcement from outside Parliament. The gradual reification of a miscellany of public aspirations and complaints into articulate and co-ordinated popular protest owed much to a succession of high-level opportunists: John Wilkes and the Rockinghamite whigs in George III's reign and, in the two preceding reigns, the tories. Wilkes was but one man and was soon silenced by parliamentary acceptance. The Rockinghams' exclusion from administration was rarely total and often self-inflicted. The tories were a substantial and affluent section of Britain's landed elite and they were exposed to extensive political discrimination for forty-five years. It is scarcely surprising that they explored the advantages to be gained from extra-parliamentary contacts and did so in a much more impulsive fashion than did the majority of whig politicians before 1790.

Even before its proscription the party had acquired distinctive qualifications for an extra-parliamentary strategy. After 1688 it was able to strengthen its position in the populous constituencies; indeed, so confident were some tory M.P.s, that in 1701 they urged the abolition of all parliamentary boroughs with under fifty voters. During the Exclusion Crisis London's street politics had been vociferously whig. By 1692 the City's Common Council had a tory majority (drawn particularly from the larger and poorer wards) and Thomas Langham, tory deputy alderman for Bishopsgate, was leading an abortive campaign to extend the City franchise. Just as the Junto whigs reneged on their party's anti-executive tradition only to see it increasingly appropriated by tory parliamentarians, so the post-revolutionary flux in party attitudes was also illustrated by the fact that the prime opponent of Langham's civic democracy was none other than the former whig-republican, John Wildman.[18]

The roots of tory popularity pre-date even the Glorious Revolution. Tory royalists had always tended to criticise excises as well as governmental expense and interference in trade and the localities. After 1714 these emphases could be developed into a more radical assault on the supposed parasitism of the Walpolian–Pelhamite State. In the seventeenth and eighteenth centuries the power of tory-Anglicanism was socially far more widespread than is sometimes assumed, not least because Church of England loyalties were interwoven with popular patriotism. The operation of this latter sentiment in the eighteenth century has been much less explored than that of the more fashionable notion of class, and yet Chatham, Lord George Gordon, and, in a different sense, John Wilkes all emulated the tories in exploiting English nationalism's potential as a bridge between the gentleman politician and the mobility.

II

Asserting the popularity of tory-Anglicanism may seem perverse, given the reputed condition of the Hanoverian Church: its chief officers creatures of the whig State, its parsons the flunkeys and parochial spies of the local squire, and its hold on popular culture, like its congregations, diminishing with every decade. Such a view of the Church is however very largely a view from above.[19] Few men and women had anything to do with whig bishops. For most of them the predominantly tory parsons were the most visible and accessible representatives of the Church, and in the first half of the eighteenth century these men evoked more respect than hostility. Clerical diffidence and low food prices made the tithe system more acceptable than it became after the 1740s, when rural clergymen began to agitate for the full economic value of their tithes. Until 1760 clergymen seldom in fact 'officered the same law as the gentry': how could they, when the toryism of the bulk of the clergy tended to exclude them from Commissions of the Peace? At the accession of George III only 11 per cent of magistrates were clergymen. The poverty and dissident politics of many parsons facilitated popular discrimination between them and a self-indulgent ecclesiastical hierarchy and its secular counterpart. How else would a Reading tory vicar have had the credibility to precipitate a freeman rebellion against the borough's whig candidates, when he preached in 1722 against the evils of bribery and corruption?[20]

Moreover the Anglican parson was always more than a religious or political idealogue, just as his church was more than a large, half-empty building. The spire and the church clock were material ingredients of the rural landscape; cathedrals were objects of civic pride. The demolition of Lincoln Cathedral spire in 1726 provoked High-Church rioting in the city. The diary of Benjamin Rogers, rector of Carlton, Bedfordshire, from 1720 to 1771, reveals social snobbery, mediocre piety, and minimal charisma, but also its author's indispensability to his parishoners, church-going or no. He wrote out and witnessed their wills; he supplied them with dubious medical prescriptions; he attended their harvest celebrations; and he voted tory at every local election. By such multifarious petty services a parson could gain considerable sway over his village. How else would so many rural clergymen have been able to incite mob violence against itinerant Methodist preachers?[21]

True, church attendance was declining, as it had been since the late seventeenth century. A survey of several parishes in the tory stronghold of Oxfordshire indicates that only 911 of their inhabitants took Anglican communion in 1738 – less than 5 per cent of their total population.[22] But Anglican sentiment was not co-extensive with formal worship. In the industrial towns, where church accommodation was woefully inadequate for the population, High-Church catch-phrases remained the most common expressions of tory loyalty. A Leeds vicar recorded that at the Yorkshire contest of 1734 the tory candidate, Sir Miles Stapylton, 'had more votes of both clergy and laity in this parish than out of any one parish in the county'. Leeds only had two Anglican churches, yet Stapylton's appeal had been entirely orthodox. When the whig petition against his return was abandoned in May 1736, one of the town's dis-

senters noted the local Anglican rejoicing 'and the ridiculing of such as
were quiet by many of the High Party'. In Birmingham there was a
continuity in Anglican-inspired mobbing from the Sacheverell outbreak
of 1710, through the anti-Methodist and anti-Quaker riots of 1751 and
1759, to the Church and King demonstrations of the 1790s: it was a
town, wrote one nonconformist commentator in the latter decade, 'distinguished for the narrow spirit of its priests'.[23]

Mid-eighteenth-century Manchester had a population of 18 000, two
churches, and a vigorous local press preoccupied with the duality of
Church and Dissent. Here is a whig caricature of a Mancunian tory in
1748:

I learned to cry Down with the Rump manfully; to drink Church and King
as oft as I dined; to hate all Whigs and Presbyterians cordially; & to believe
all Clergy, but Whig Parsons, God's Vicars upon Earth.

But it was more than a caricature. Here is a Mancunian tory's rebuttal
of whig charges of Jacobitism just one year later:

The World will be very apt to dispute the Sincerity of a Charge of Rebellion
against us by Men; who are at the same Time defending the very worst
Instance of it, that Grand Presbyterian one of 1641.[24]

As this stylised exchange suggests, in counties like Lancashire where
Civil War memories were strong, assertive Anglican prejudice and tory
voting could both be ramifications of a romantic monarchism which had
more to do with nationalism than with either the Stuart or the Hanoverian dynasties. In 1733 and despite the rival attractions of the Excise
Crisis, Cheshire's tory voters linked their party's proprietorial slogans
with a catalogue of national emergencies overcome.

> Then down with the Pope
> Let him swing on a Rope,
> Since the fifth day of November;
> Down with that curs'd String,
> That murder'd Charles our King,
> These things we well remember:
> And down boys with all those
> That are the Church's Foes,
> May the Church and the King bear the sway boys.

To the Bristol tory mob the Church of England was 'Mother Church'
or 'Great Harry's noble Labour'. The slogans of the city's election crowd
in 1754 conflated Anglican prejudice, xenophobia, and class interest:
'No General Naturalization! No Jews! No French Bottle-Makers! No
Lowering Wages of Labouring Men to 4d a Day and Garlick!'[25] This

suggests some popular acquaintance with whig arguments for the Naturalisation Act of 1709 (repealed by the tories in 1712) and in support of the Naturalisation Bills of 1746–7, 1748, and 1751 (all successfully opposed by the tories): that easier immigration for Protestant artisans would swell the labour market and depress wages. 'Our labourers and mechanics, 'tis said...live too high and extravagantly', wrote one tory pamphleteer in 1748, mimicking the whig case so as to prey on workers' insecurity, whereas foreign labourers lived 'upon herbs and roots and drink water' and could be expected to import their lower living standards and expectations with them.[26]

Tory propagandists were equally adept at linking a genuine social or economic grievance with the machinations of religious dissidents. As early as 1748 the *Worcester Journal* was informing Wolverhampton's inhabitants that their problems could be attributed to the town's alien population. The paper fixed upon local objections to newly installed turnpikes and reported that Wolverhampton's turnpike commission was dominated by whigs and dissenters. 'As a specimen of the Administration of the said prevailing Party, they appointed a Quaker to be Treasurer, a Presbyterian to be Surveyor of the roads and Dissenters of different Denominations to be the Gate-Keepers.' When men in authority really were nonconformist, High-Church, high-tory slogans could become the most appropriate media for protest from below. In Gloucestershire and Wiltshire in the 1720s some of the rioting weavers deviated from their occupation's traditional whiggism and used tory slogans to affront the largely Quaker clothiers.[27] In constituencies where dissent was entrenched in local government – Nottingham, Bristol, Coventry, and Norwich – Anglican catch-phrases were likewise used to taunt superiors. The Norwich anti-Methodist riots of 1751 snowballed into a protest at the corporation, its rule, and its considerable corruption. The tory rioters' shouts of 'Down with the Meeting House' were scarcely suitable for an itinerant preacher; they were designed to provoke the Norwich city militia, the Honourable Artillery Company, which had a high nonconformist membership and a polarising role as local whig mafia.[28]

Tory–Anglicanism was a protean and versatile emotion; it was also socially diverse. High-Church mobs could riot; tory gentlemen could sponsor church-building; and urban *arrivistes* could mimic their betters and be seen attending services at a prestigious church or cathedral. So in Norwich the richer tory tradesmen strove to live in Mancroft ward – a royalist bastion in the Civil War – and patronised St Peter Mancroft's, the city's most splendid church, partly because it also attracted the neighbouring tory landowners. Still more comprehensive was the tories' anti-executive stance. What most provoked criticism of the Hanoverian

state was not the inegality of its electoral system nor even the imbalance
of wealth and power (which was too much the norm to kindle collective
protest) but rather its comparatively novel and increasingly efficient
interference in men's lives and pockets. The notion of the State as expensive predator informed Sir Coventry Carew's address to the Cornish freeholders in 1744: 'Lords, Placemen, Expectants of Places & Smugglers,
are to a Man join'd against the natural Interest of your County.' Ten
years later Orator Henley arranged one of his most popular orations
around a gloss on the biblical prophecy 'The Locusts, that is Placemen
(from Locus, a Place) shall consume thy field.'[29]

What placemen in fact consume is public money, and anti-executive
polemics had some foundation in the trend of contemporary taxation.
Between 1715 and 1760 British governments derived an estimated 72
per cent of tax revenue from indirect taxes.[30] Excises were levied on soap,
candles, leather, malt, salt, and tea (by the 1740s an article of popular
consumption), and by 1754 the tory pamphleteer John Shebbeare claimed
that 'out of every Twenty Shillings. . .laid out to purchase the Necessaries of Life, Fourteen was doomed to the paying Taxes'. Two years
later the Pittite economist Joseph Massie argued that the Salt Tax alone
might cost an artisan earning 7s 6d a week a third of that sum every
year; a gentleman worth £1000 would pay only 14s 2d towards the
duty. These are both partisan estimates, but it was generally accepted
that indirect taxes were socially regressive: indeed, administrations
may have intended them to be so. 'The lighter the taxes, the greater
the danger. Easy, imperceptible taxes the most dangerous', argued
Walpole's memorandum on the 1733 Excise Bill. It would be difficult to find a cruder exposition of indirect taxation as a form of social
control.[31]

Given this fiscal background, popular apprehension that Walpole's
proposal might lead to a general excise was intelligible, and should not
be dismissed as the synthetic product of incitement from above. 'We pay
for our Light / Both by Day and by Night', declaimed the best-selling
anti-Excise ballad, 'Malt, Salt, Shoes, Newes and our Soap / Oh! Spare
us, good Bob / And drop this new Job, / Or at last we cant pay for a
Rope.' Nor was the tory party's exploitation of this fear and its opposition
to a bill which would have cut the Land Tax as opportunistic or as
incongruous as some historians have maintained. Like so many components of the tory platform, aversion to excises was rooted in seventeenth-century history. Tory commentators like Swift and Blackstone
chose to forget that Charles I had sought to levy excises, and remarked
instead on the Parliamentarians' successful implementation of this form
of tax to pay the New Model Army. After 1649 hatred of excises was a

component of royalism at all levels of society and some of the Common-weath tracts it inspired were reprinted in 1733.[32] In a debate on excises in March 1694 the West Country tory Sir Edward Seymour referred to their Civil War pedigree and attacked indirect taxation on socially com-passionate grounds. His party colleagues warned that an excise on specific commodities would lead to a general excise, than which, argued Paul Foley, some tories 'had rather give 6s per £ on land'. In 1711 some tory backbenchers rebelled against Oxford's projected leather excise; in 1723 the party divided against Walpole's introduction of duties on tea and coffee; and in 1756 George Cooke, tory M.P. for Middlesex, success-fully challenged ministerial proposals to levy taxes on bricks and tiles.[33]

The tories had sound partisan reasons for their fiscal criticism. Excise collection meant further penetration of the counties by government officials, whereas the Land Tax, as Colin Brooks had noted, 'was operated locally, and not centrally or bureaucratically'. This objection sharpened after the Treasury tightened its grip on Excise departmental patronage in the 1730s. The more minor Excise posts tended to be at the disposal of local whig magnates and were some of the most sought-after electoral bribes. Tory peers and M.P.s retaliated by parliamentary proposals that Excise and other revenue officials be disfranchised, reduced in number, or subjected to income tax, as well as by heart- (and purse-) rending diatribes like William Dowdeswell's of 1764 on 'the grievances of the excise laws' – in this case the Cider Tax – 'upon ignorant countrymen'. It all struck a sympathetic chord amongst taxpayers. Excise officers were disliked (and, as their occasional murder demonstrated, often hated) for their right of search in shops and private houses, for their interference in small-scale smuggling, for the heavy fines which non-payment of duties involved, and for the long stays in debtors' prisons to which the inability to pay such fines could reduce the poorer tradesman or bankrupt merchant.[34]

In as much as tory spokesmen linked the Land Tax with the political predominance of the landowning classes, the party's advocacy of direct taxation was based on social conservatism as well as social compassion. Sir William Wyndham used both popular and class-bound arguments to stigmatise the Salt Tax in 1732: 'A poor man, who has no property, ought not certainly to be charged for the defence of property; he has nothing but his liberty to contend for...Liberty may be equally dear to every man, but surely he that has the largest property, ought to contribute most to the public expence.' Isaac Kramnick reads this as a paternalist's rejection of the whig ministry's Lockian defence of indirect taxation: that all men are indebted to and should contribute towards the running of the policeman state. He goes on to cite Lord Bathurst's speech against the same duty as a nostalgic evocation of a world with 'no bourgeois values, and no Locke':

In all cases it is hard, it is cruel to tax the poor journey men and day labourer, because it is not to be presumed that they can get anything more than their bare subsistence by their daily labour. The profits that may be made go all to the benefit of the master who employs them. He it is that has the whole benefit of their labour and therefore ought to pay the taxes.[35]

But in this same speech Bathurst went on to assert that indirect taxation would in the long term injure the bourgeois employer rather than the labourer himself:

By such taxes we enhance the price of the very necessaries of life, [the poor] cannot possibly subsist upon the same wages they subsisted on formerly; they must starve or otherwise their wages must be raised, and thus at last the master that employs them must pay the taxes that are laid upon the poor he employs.

William Kennedy argued that these two conflicting identifications of the social victims of the Salt Tax showed that tory opposition lacked doctrinal coherence. Might it not also be the case that Bathurst was casting his net as widely as possible? The anti-taxation argument was profitable for the tories precisely because it not only had an immediate popular appeal, but was also attractive to those trading and mercantile classes which were likely to be more prominent in mid-eighteenth-century electorates than the labouring poor.[36]

Sir John Barnard's motion (March 1737) to reduce the interest on the National Debt to 3 per cent attracted tory parliamentary support partly because it attacked the City financiers, partly, as Edward Harley noted, because it would 'take off some of the Heavy Taxes which oppress the Poor *and* the Manufacturers'. When the tory clergyman Thomas Andrews published his *Essay on Riots* (1739) vindicating Wiltshire's rioting weavers, he focused on socially regressive taxation as a prime cause of popular discontent and made the same dual identification of its victims: 'By these Taxes Trade is oppressed, by them the Necessaries of Life are raised to the Poor; consequently the taking them off would relieve them and give life to trade.' The need to cut taxation looms large in tory electoral propaganda, and retail and domestic traders' receptivity to this emphasis contributed to the party's strength in England's commercial cities. Of the thirty-odd retail traders who are known to have been active in London local politics during William III's reign, nineteen were tories. Of all the tory councillors elected in Norwich between 1720 and 1739, 57 per cent came from this same occupational group.[37]

The obverse but equally attractive side of this condemnation of place-men and their cost to the public was that the tories themselves, as pros-cribed men with independent landed incomes, were neither leeches on the public nor creatures of the State. A squib from the 1747 Coventry by-election has its tory hero 'John, who though a poor Man, is his own Master' contrasting the city's tory M.P., William Grove, with the current whig candidate: 'I voted for Mr. Grove last time, I love him, and will always poll for him while I live; he is to be depended upon; but if we chuse Mr. Bird he will directly go off to the Court.'[38] Such propaganda made a virtue out of ineluctable tory exclusion but, as the tories' experience after 1760 was to demonstrate, it was likely to rebound on them when-ever they re-entered employment.

The contemporary historian Tindal described how Lord Gower's individual *volte-face* in 1745 was received in his native Staffordshire: 'the Common people were heated, even to madness, against those who, as they said, had betrayed them by coming into the service of his Majesty'. The mainspring of the Lichfield riots of 1747 was not, as Eveline Cruickshanks has supposed, Gower's defection from Jacobitism, but his defection from toryism to the executive. The local tory gentry set out to exploit the indignation this aroused and they did so in socially provocative terms. In 1748 they initiated a race-meeting at Lichfield to rival that held annually by Gower in the same borough. The *Worcester Journal* was sent a notice to indicate how interested patrons might distinguish between the two events:

To all *Placemen, Pensioners, Officers of the Excise, Post-Masters, Window Peepers etc. etc. etc.* There are two races advertised for Lichfield the one in August, the other in September: To prevent mistakes, 'tis proper to address you with the following Caution. The former [the tory races] will probably be crowded with Country Squires, Freeholders, Yeomen, Mechanicks, and such like...by the sweat of their Brows ye are enabled to live like Gentlemen.

In contrast to this carefully selected and clearly virtuous social amalgam, the actual and aspirant drones of society should take themselves off to the September races where 'Your new Patron [Gower] exhibits himself ...if any officer, Military or Ecclesiastical, wants an Advance let him attend and his Fortune is made.'[39]

As well as stressing their own independence of ministerial emolu-ments, the tories tended to urge their supporters to assert themselves autonomously against corruption. During the 1722 election campaign Archibald Hutcheson asked readers of the *Freeholder's Journal* to send him information of any instance of electoral coercion 'assuring them of a faithful publication which is the only means of making the whole

Nation truly sensible of the Corruption used in every Part of it'. Subsequent issues described the civic vigilance of the Harwich, Exeter, and Reading voters. At the Hereford election of 1741 fifteen voters initially accepted a bribe from the ministerial candidates and then 'produc'd it publickly at the time of polling & voted against the Corrupters'. Since fewer than thirty votes separated the two successful tory candidates from the whig runner-up, this piece of supposedly spontaneous voter resistance was duly lauded by the tory printer of the consequent poll book. A more concerted demonstration took place in the small borough of Abingdon in 1754, when the whig candidate, Henry Thrale, who had lavished over £1500 on the contest, was defeated by the tory John Morton. A group of Abingdon voters had accepted Thrale's bounty only to reject it before voting: 'They had received twenty, thirty and fifty pounds not by them taken as the Price of their Votes, but that they might become Instruments of exemplary Punishment to those who dared to seduce them...This conduct it seems was the effect of an uniform Resolution taken among them.'[40]

It is irrelevant whether or not these episodes were accurately reported, nor does it matter that tory candidates in other constituencies resorted to bribery and clientage as a matter of course: as with the party's patronage of the Independent Elector societies in Westminster, Grantham, and Coventry, the tories were publicly identifying themselves with voter resistance to electoral emasculation. The same process was at work when tory M.P.s occasionally rehearsed Wilkes' device of championing borough revolts against magnate control.

By the mid eighteenth century Derby had succumbed to the domination of the whig Stanhope and Cavendish families but the borough retained a large number of tory sympathisers. In the 1742 by-election the tory candidate received extensive support from frame-work knitters, tailors, brickmakers, wool-combers, and tanners – minor artisans of a sort poorly represented on the whig poll list. Six years later Derby's burgesses rejected the Stanhope nominee and invited the family's agent, Thomas Rivett, to stand as an independent candidate. As one journalist reported, they also begged support from 'the Neighbouring Gentlemen of Fortune' and the paper proceeded to identify these sponsors: Sir Nathaniel Curzon, tory M.P. for Derbyshire, who voted immediately after Derby's mayor; Curzon's son, the tory Member for Clitheroe; and Sir Robert Burdett, Wrightson Mundy, Sir Charles Sedley, and James Shuttleworth – tory M.P.s for Tamworth, Leicestershire, Nottingham, and Preston respectively.[41]

III

It would be quite wrong to suppose that the tory constituency experience was invariably different from that pecuniary and issue-free norm so cunningly set forth in Namier's analyses: it was not. It is however difficult to see why the tories should so often have employed an anti-bribery platform if it was always incompatible with contemporary voter mentality. It is also difficult to accept Namier's contention that voter attitudes in the larger constituencies were essentially the same as those in the rotten boroughs. Certainly many tory M.P.s, dependent on the more open constituencies and with limited patronage resources, believed themselves to be compelled into a more subtly accommodating relationship with their electors than was customary in the eighteenth century.[42]

In keeping with their dislike of socially regressive taxation, many tories – such as John Wesley – urged that road maintenance should be the responsibility of a county's affluent inhabitants, rather than 'saddling the poor people with the vile impositions of turnpikes for ever'. In 1731 and 1733 Thomas Bramston and William Bromley introduced a bill to 'render more equal...the methods by which persons are charged towards the repairing of Highways'. Later in the same decade tory gentry in both Gloucestershire and Herefordshire demonstrated a reluctance to prosecute turnpike rioters. After the Ledbury riots of 1735 some of the culprits had to be transferred to whig-dominated Worcester to ensure their rigorous trial.[43] To a considerable extent this tory attitude was dictated from below. As soon as the M.P. for Hereford, Thomas Geers Winford, deviated from his party's line and joined a local turnpike trust, the county's leader, Lord Oxford, was warned of the electoral consequences. Winford, wrote a tory agent from Hereford in October 1733, 'has not the hearts of the Citizens...the Turnpike (of which they take him for a Patron) is much disrelished, & set there against him'. There were about 1400 voters in Hereford. In 1727 that munificent whig, Lord Chandos, had calculated that to bribe even a third of them would have been 'extravagantly expensive'. In 1734 Oxford was near to bankruptcy. Herefordshire's tory gentry were not as poor as Lord Egmont's subsequent electoral survey was to maintain, but neither were they fond of exorbitant electoral expenditure: a genuflection to grass-roots opinion was cheaper and just as effective. Winford was made to withdraw before the general election and the 1734 Hereford contest returned two tories.[44]

The need to cater to voters' social and economic grievances obtained in the first half of the eighteenth century even in large boroughs susceptible to a family interest. After the contest at Newcastle under Lyme in 1734 Lord Gower evicted any tenant-cottager who failed to vote for his candidates; before the election, however, the family had felt obliged to issue broadsheets to the borough's five hundred voters, assuring them 'that we never did, nor ever will consent to the inclosing of any part of the ...Town Fields or Common Grounds'. In April 1732 Sir Richard Grosvenor's opposition to a whig parliamentary proposal to revive Chester's declining trade by widening the River Dee alienated the city's 1500 voters and almost cost him the seat. The Cheshire whigs published division lists to show how the county's tory M.P.s had voted on the issue, and by July local anti-Grosvenor and pro-navigation rioting threatened to disrupt the mayoral elections on which tory control of the city depended. The situation was saved only by Sir Richard Grosvenor's death, the electoral techniques of Watkin Williams Wynn, and the Grosvenors' public promise that the new tory M.P. for Chester, Sir Charles Bunbury, would introduce his own Dee Navigation Bill.[45]

Large constituencies also demanded more attentive nursing between elections. In 1730 the Manchester whigs proposed to establish a workhouse governed by a self-selecting Board of Guardians. Since Manchester contained a large number of Lancashire freeholders and a charitable institution of this kind was bound to influence votes, one of the town's tory activists, John Byrom, started a campaign to have the Guardians popularly elected and so dilute their whig complexion. On 26 January 1731 he met the county's two tory M.P.s, Randle Wilbraham and Nicholas Fazakerly, at the Cocoa Tree and agreed to organise a petition to Parliament 'to be signed by as many as possible' of the town's residents. Byrom's subsequent propaganda against a workhouse oligarchy ran counter to any association of the franchise with a certain level of property; government, even the government of a workhouse, could be legitimised only by popular consent: 'We look upon ourselves [as] embarked in THE GOOD SHIP MANCHESTER, and whenever we apprehend her in the least danger, are ready to work as hard as if we were never so considerable sharers in her cargo.' The Manchester petition, carefully monitored by tories in both Houses, was successful. At a celebratory dinner the Lancashire tory M.P.s were perhaps made aware of the possible repercussions of advancing urban democracy: 'the conversation turned at last upon the subordination that was necessary to be amongst people', recorded Byrom; 'I contended for an equality, and for the poor people.'[46]

The tory association with the Independent Electors of Westminster provides much more extensive illustration of how electoral self-interest could marry the party to low-level, radical politics. The Independents were not a tory creation. A group of middling tradesmen, lawyers, and Common Councilmen had assembled in 1741 to support the Westminster candidature of the opposition whigs Viscount Perceval and Admiral Vernon. When Perceval went over to the ministry in 1742 many of the Independents disowned him, and as he later noted, a sub-group of about sixty, 'mostly of ye lowest rank', persisted in meeting on a monthly basis at the Crown and Anchor Tavern. It was the vociferous extremism of this plebeian rump which helped forge the anti-democratic emphasis of Perceval's brilliant pamphlet *Faction detected by the Evidence of Facts*, and it was this same group which the tories sought to annex.[47]

It can indeed be argued that the high-political crisis of 1742 by which Pulteney and his friends joined the Old Corps in government and left their tory allies in the lurch was a crucial stage in tory radicalisation. Deserted by many of its Westminster allies, the party looked without, and predictably became much more aware of the need for fundamental reform. 'We must so act', a tory spokesman is supposed to have told a Fountain Tavern meeting, 'as every Individual, if possible, may feel himself interested in our Endeavours, and actually become a Gainer by the Event.' So it is that tory pamphlets in 1742 and 1743 bristle with demands for the repeal of the Black Act and Riot Act, for reform of the representative system, and for a broader base in local government. To force themselves into administration, Perceval warned, the tories would 'bait the People by the Project of an Encrease of Popular Power, by proposing Alterations in the Constitution, the Effects of which, and consequently the necessary Measure of which, the common sort are by no means able to understand'.[48]

The Independent Electors were part of this more assertive and, in practical terms, largely sterile tory radicalism; they also had a more routine constituency function. That many of Westminster's poorer voters could be responsive to the tory appeal had been demonstrated when the party won both seats by a margin of over 1600 votes in March 1722. Tory patronage of the Independents was an attempt to make contact with this tory/opposition stratum, swamped as it was by court and whig aristocratic influence, and coax it into electoral efficacy by other means than hard cash. The Independents canvassed potential tory voters, issued propaganda, and seem to have raised electoral subscriptions; in return they demanded a say in the selection of opposition candidates for Westminster and were also consulted on the Middlesex tory candidature in 1747. How far the society's members collaborated with the tory parliamentary party is not clear. In 1749 the tory leadership was sufficiently influential to dissuade the Independents from selecting the quasi-Jacobite Sir Thomas Dyke as their candidate for the City by-election and 'to render them unanimous' for the moderate tory, George Cooke, who was more acceptable to the party's current ally, the Prince of Wales. Thomas

Carew, tory M.P. for Minehead, acted as link-man between the Independents and the Cocoa Tree, endeavouring to discipline the former and communicating the society's legislative and local needs to his colleagues.[49]

In April 1746 Viscount Perceval introduced a bill to increase duties on coal imported into Westminster and to appoint new officials to supervise them. The avowed aim was to curb illicit sales of coal but the new bill was bound to raise prices, and the Independents, who seem to have had smuggling contacts, reacted strongly. Samuel Johns, a solicitor in the Court of Chancery and the Independents' 'Field Marshal General & Commander in Chief', wrote and distributed a broadsheet inquiring of the citizens 'Whether it is not an insolent Presumption to apply to the Parliament to obtain New Taxes and New Place-men?...the same Reason will hold in all Trades, that wherever there is a Fraud there must be a kind of Excisemen or Surveyor, will not this be introducing a general Excise?' Johns' initiative was supported in the Commons by Carew and other tory M.P.s. They managed to delay the Coal Bill until June and then tried to get it deferred until August. They failed, just as the Independents failed as a constituency society. By the 1750s hostile politicians claimed, probably with some justice, that the society used its organisation and popular contacts only to extract more extensive electoral bribes.[50]

But even if the Independents dwindled into greed, they deserve attention as one of the many complex and sometimes semi-criminal strands which contributed to the more familiar City dissidence of the 1760s. Their association with the tories was also significant. Working in the shadow of the Court and unable to compete with the duke of Bedford's bruisers and extensive commercial patronage, the tories experimented with a broader constituency strategy and a civic rather than an individual appeal. Tory peers and M.P.s made a show of seeking the Independents' consent at election meetings and acted as stewards at their annual dinners. Tory M.P.s inside Westminster made some attempts to co-ordinate their activities with a radical lobby outside and, as Carew's papers show, schemes were devised at the Cocoa Tree for a reform in the City's ward government and for improvements in its street lighting.[51]

Tory M.P.s and candidates tended to stress their receptivity to their electors' political opinions as well as their attention to local needs. It is not known when constituency pledges were first attempted in England; they certainly antedated the Wilkite era. In 1722 several constituencies demanded undertakings from their candidates that they would work to restore triennial Parliaments. Not all tories were sympathetic. Sir John Barlow, canvassing Worcestershire, refused to have his parliamentary conduct so regulated: 'If I am to be treated not as a free agent [but] as a tool to be told unless I do so & so that they & theirs will never give their votes for me & mine...it is a little too hard.'[52] Nonetheless, attempts to secure pledges appear to have continued in some of the larger boroughs, and Edward Southwell's association with Bristol's Steadfast Society shows just how extensive their influence could be.

In 1739 the Steadfast Society found itself without a suitable tory candidate for the city by-election and approached Southwell, an independent whig, offering him its backing if he would pledge himself to act in Parliament as a *de facto* tory. Southwell recorded the conditions and his acquiescence therein in his journal:

1st.   If I should be for a bill for Triennial Parliaments...

2d.   If I should be ever against the repeal of the Test Act...

3dly.   If I should be against a Standing Army in Time of Peace, I answered most Certainly.

4.   If I should be for a bill to restrain Placemen from being Members of Parliament...I answered, that I thought such a Bill most essential to the Constitution.

A cross-section of the Steadfast Society's leadership at this time shows again that urban toryism could co-exist fruitfully with middling class occupational groups of the sort so attracted to the Wilkite Associations. The men who received Southwell's pledges in October 1739 included two lawyers, two drapers, a distiller, two tobacconists, and various petty merchants.[53]

For Southwell, Steadfast Society support meant funding and the automatic electoral aid of the Gloucestershire and Somerset tory gentry. It also meant that once he was elected these counties' tory M.P.s supervised his conduct in Parliament, and the society expected him to provide regular information on his voting habits as well as accounts of debates and relevant division lists. So his vote against Sandys' motion that Walpole be removed in February 1741 was pardoned only when he explained that the tory party as a whole had split over the issue. 'I enclose you a copy of my Speech', he wrote to one of the Steadfast agents three days after this division, 'That you may see the Arguments which weighed with me which I must submit to yours and my friends candour to whom I will never conceal the least part of my Conduct nor claim your Approbation or Interest longer than you shall freely think I deserve it.' To compare the meekness of this language with Edmund Burke's rebuke to his Bristol constituents in November 1774 after they had attempted to instruct him is to be made aware of just how limited was the Rockingham whig's perception of the extra-parliamentary nation. The development of provincial political activism and the politicians' response to it were more uneven than the crescendo version of eighteenth-century English radicalism would suggest.[54]

Constituency Instructions also stressed the M.P.'s accountability to the represented and were far more widely used than pledges. After 1739, when William Pulteney dissociated himself and his opposition whigs from the constituency campaign against the Convention of Pardo, Instructions became increasingly identified with the tory party. It is in fact an indication of the political exclusiveness latent even in the heroic brand of whiggism that Algernon Sidney condemned the constitutional implications of this device, employing the same slightly condescending attitude towards the represented as Viscount Perceval: 'When I differ from your Sentiments', Perceval told the Westminster Independents after rejecting their Instructions in 1742, 'I shall do it with the greatest Reluctance, and then only when I am convinced that your true Interests must extort it from me.'[55] The extra-parliamentary classes could not know their own interests best. The proclaimed tory attitude was quite different. For Thomas Carew, speaking in 1745, M.P.s were the people's attorneys; for Velters Cornewall in 1756, 'No more than their trustees *pro tempore* . . . if they should, *ex mero motu*, instruct us, and we grow restive, and scorn their advice, we shall be then no longer good and faithful stewards, but be turned adrift, and richly deserve it, at the next general election.' This was potent (and popular) stuff; it should not obscure the fact that most Instructions were synthetic, formulated by the M.P.s themselves or at an assize meeting of a county's tory gentry. Only in the larger and better organised constituencies was there an element of popular participation. In 1739 the Steadfast Society, on orders from London, composed Instructions to its tory M.P. to promote a Place Bill. The finished document was partly authentic, however, in that it was circulated among 'the Electors in the severall Parishes for their Concurrence'.[56]

Whatever their origin, Instructions tended to refer to the sovereignty of the popular will and treat M.P.s' compliance as automatic. In 1753 Cirencester was one of fifteen tory constituencies to instruct against the Jew Bill: 'The voice of the People has fully declared itself; that voice, which is in some sense the voice of God. . .It is with the greatest pleasure and zeal that we have joined it. Your regard, gentlemen, to it or to us, we cannot doubt of.'[57] Most Instructions – especially the more dogmatic ones – were reprinted in the London and provincial press. If they were the product of a particular crisis and would sell, they were collected together and published in pamphlet form. The anti-Walpolian Instructions of 1740–2 appeared as *Great Britain's Memorial*. The 1756 Instructions for an inquiry into Britain's loss of Minorca were printed with the title *The Voice of the People* and could be purchased for 12d.

A tory M.P. would usually take care to thank his constituents for letting him know their ostensible opinions, and these carefully worded replies also found their way into print. In April 1742 Thomas Carew wrote to his Minehead constituents assuring them that their recent Instructions would be attended to and informing them of his parliamentary progress:

Great part of my time has been taken up on that most important part of my duty, the Regard of the woollen manufacture...The publick papers have of late given so full an account of most of those Transactions & the great fatigue I have gone through ever since the Parliament sat has obliged me to depend upon your acceptance of those papers but in case any thing were omitted by them, I should keep up a literary Correspondence with my Friends.[58]

As in Southwell's communications with the Steadfast Society, the M.P. is here presented as the attentive guardian of the welfare of his constituents, who are not mere passive beneficiaries, but men who have a right to be informed of their representative's political activity. Whatever these proclaimed tory attitudes owed to considerations of etiquette or propaganda, they could impose considerable constraints on the conduct of tory M.P.s.

In November 1742 the high-tory Chamber of Exeter, dominated by the city's merchants and wealthier tradesmen, dispatched Instructions to Humphrey Sydenham and Sir Henry Northcote demanding constitutional reform and urging the two tory M.P.s not to grant supplies until concessions were forthcoming. Northcote wrote apologetically to Exeter's town clerk that Sydenham had been 'extremely nettled' at the tone of the Instructions and refused to have them printed in the London press. Northcote was concerned lest this recalcitrance reflect upon him: 'I must desire you to Communicate the Contents of this Letter to the Mayor and Chamber, that they may not think me guilty of any neglect in this affair.' Since five years were to elapse before the next general election Sydenham's offence on this occasion escaped penalty. In 1753 he ignored Exeter's Instructions again and voted for the Jewish Naturalisation Bill. The Chamber promptly publicised this defection and nominated another candidate for the forthcoming election. In 1754 Sydenham was defeated in an all-tory contest.[59]

Many contemporaries recognised the wider implications of Instructions. The protests over the Jew Bill and the predominantly tory Addresses at the loss of Minorca were, thought one pamphleteer, 'a Proof that the Sense of the Nation may differ from the Sense of Parliament; and that therefore the Voice of Parliament is not the only Evidence of the Sense of the Nation'. From this it was but a short step to suggesting that the representative system be adjusted so that Parliament did reflect the national will. Even earlier in 1740 a tory pamphleteer had vindicated his party's recent campaign of Instructions and shown that its attacks on indirect taxation might evolve into something more dangerous. Those who condemned the participation of 'the meaner sort' in Instructions, he argued, should ask themselves

Where are these mean People? Is there a Man in England who does not either drink Beer, wear Shoes, or now and then smoak a Pipe of Tobacco? Can he do any of these without contributing to the Support of the Government?... all who support a Thing, have a natural Interest in the Thing they support... it follows that every [sic] the meanest Man in the Kingdom has an interest in the Publick...amongst a free People, who has a Right to control the Majority?[60]

Since large and open constituencies were conducive to tory electoral success, since the party had made productive contact with many of the new industrial towns, and since tory M.P.s had shown themselves capable of superior receptivity to extra-parliamentary opinion, parliamentary reform might seem to be an obvious solution to tory proscription. As early as 1722 Archibald Hutcheson, returned for Hastings by thirty-three of its seventy-odd voters, was told that in this cinque port there were 'about 1000 men, besides the electors; and he is informed that he would have had the Voice of about four of five of them, had they been entitled to vote'. Yet Hutcheson acted no further on this information than proposing that Parliament compile a list of rotten boroughs and examine the potential for influence therein.[61] No tory M.P. in this period seems to have made the transition from advocating the abolition of petty boroughs to advocating their effective eradication by a wider suffrage. The redistribution of seats was a pill more easily swallowed.

Predictably, it was the post-Excise election of 1734 which first elicited serious reform proposals – the administration's victory, albeit with a reduced majority, finally demonstrating that a nation-wide agitation could be neutralised by the imbalance of the representative system. In July 1734 Bolingbroke submitted an essay to the *Craftsman* lauding the superior rationality of the Instrument of Government's redistribution of seats in 1653. He correlated each county's representation with its current contribution to the Land Tax, noting that by this criterion Cornwall, with its forty-two M.P.s, merited only eight seats: 'Wealth is the rule, by which Equality ought to be regulated...From this Computation it appears how unequally the Election of Members is at present.' At every successive general election the tory and dissident whig press returned to the attack, so when John Almon's reform manifesto appeared in the *Political Register* in March 1768 it marked not the inception of the reform campaign but rather a continuation of an opposition tradition. Similarly the connection between representation and the payment of taxes had become a commonplace long before the Stamp Act crisis: tory polemicists had earlier cited payments to the Land Tax and Window Tax and, occasionally, moveable property as suitable qualifications for enfranchisement.[62]

What tended to distinguish the pre-1760 tory contribution to the parliamentary reform debate was an insistence on the need for public agitation. Parliament could not be expected voluntarily to reform itself. In 1747 the tory *Westminster Journal* printed a series of articles demanding the disfranchisement of rotten boroughs and the reallocation of the seats to unrepresented towns which were 'populous, and greatly concerned in manufactures': 'Tho' that remedy cannot be instant, it may be soon, if properly sought for. The large towns who have no choice, tho' great weight in the community, may petition the whole representative body in their own behalf.' By the 1750s William Beckford's *Monitor* was advocating parliamentary reform even in non-election years, and so was the tory provincial press. In 1759 'Britannicus' in *Jopson's Coventry Mercury* demanded redistribution of seats as well as payment of M.P.s – an indication that the tory incitement of reform could have uncongenial consequences for a party attached to land as the indispensable qualification for office.[63]

Like John Wilkes, tory M.P.s and pamphleteers argued that the principle of popular election should be extended to local administration. In April 1755 Peniston Powney, M.P. for Berkshire, informed the House that

The freeholders (who are often called the people, and are the true proprietors of the nation and the land) had originally...the election not only of all sheriffs, but of all other magistrates, civil or military...The freeholders had originally the election of the conservators of the peace, who are out of date by introducing justices, who have their power not by election of the freeholders as formerly, but are named by the King.

This insistence on the primacy of the English freeholder, though an ingredient of radical attitudes right through to Thomas Paine and beyond, points to one of the discordances necessarily present in the tory argument for parliamentary reform. It has sometimes been claimed that the tories hesitated to advance reform lest it strengthen the manufacturing and commercial classes, but this is to postulate an antagonism which the tories' urban experience in the mid eighteenth century hardly corroborates.[64] The party had reason to be confident of its electoral prospects in the event of the unrepresented towns' enfranchisement; it had no way of knowing how its electoral base in the counties, supported as it was by traditional tory landlord influence, would be affected by a dilution in the freeholder franchise. The invariable tory commendation of the Instrument of Government reinforces the point: that scheme was attractive both because it did give representation to manufacturing towns and because it gave the majority of seats to the counties on a very restricted franchise.

A pamphlet exchange between the whig dean of Gloucester, Josiah Tucker, and Charles Gray, tory M.P. for Colchester, epitomises the comparative radicalism of the tory position as well as its confinement. Both men supported Poor Law reform, but in his *Essay on Trade* (1749) Tucker argued that the indigent should be disfranchised for their own moral and economic good. As he later wrote to Lord Townshend, 'No effectual Cure can be had for ye Evil, till ye Common People are excluded from their present Influence in the Business of Elections.'[65] In his reply to the *Essay*, Gray, who was accustomed to an electorate of over two thousand and to regular contact with Colchester's labouring freemen through the city's Charter Club, denied that the franchise was socially detrimental. If petty boroughs had succumbed to bribery, they could be purified by allowing freeholders from the adjacent county worth over £30 *per annum* to vote in their elections: 'this it is imagined would throw the right of Election into the proper hands, without disfranchising any borough'. Gray submitted this socially conservative proposal to the 1751 parliamentary committee on the Poor Law; it was never heard of again.[66]

Tory acquiescence in franchise reform was bound to be complicated by the party's aversion to Dissent. The affluence and social respectability of Old Dissent in the eighteenth century should not be overstated. In the election for forty Hospital Guardians at Exeter in 1700, when every man paying 2d a week to the poor rate was allowed to vote, the whig/ dissenting interest 'carried every Member'. The likely partisan repercussions of anything approaching manhood suffrage must have been clear enough to Exeter's tory M.P.s.[67]

New Dissent was even more plebeian and it is just possible that Methodism in particular acted as a kind of ideological Trojan horse amongst poorer tory voters in some of the populous constituencies. The Wesleyan religious and social critique had much in common with the tory appeal. Tory M.P.s attacked placemen and rotten boroughs; so did Wesley. Tories condemned press-gangs, turnpikes and the wastefulness of whig aristocrats; so did Wesley. Given Wesley's own origins and politics it was to be expected that the whig authorities would make their usual ideological conflation and that in 1744–5 these quasi-tory evangelicals should have been accused of Jacobitism. Wesley over-reacted. In his *Word to a Freeholder* (1747) he urged his followers to evince their loyalty by voting for government candidates, and a movement which had emerged within the tory tradition was turned against its sponsors.⁶⁸ In 1714 a whig pamphleteer had noted how Bristol's Loyal Society (an early attempt at tory constituency organisation) had 'engag'd the Colliers of Kingswood in their Interest, & whenever they want them, those filthy ruffians are ready to enter the City to their assistance...The High Church colliers hardly ever heard of religion, till Sacheverell was the Word, given them by the Faction.' These same High-Church colliers were to be the most picaresque converts of Whitefield and Wesley. By the mid 1750s commentators were noting a slight but perceptible shift in the composition of each party's vote in Bristol. 'The mob is all of our side', wrote the whig Josiah Tucker with surprise, 'great numbers of the low and middling tradesmen of theirs.'⁶⁹

Even had it wished to do so, the tory party would have found it difficult to moderate its attitude to Dissent: assertive Anglicanism was too crucial to its ideology and popular support. The party was therefore segregated from a sizeable and potentially dissident group in British society and could in this respect be outflanked after 1760 by John Wilkes. Wilkes was far more conventional in some of his *political* attitudes than were his tory forebears. His response to the tory pamphleteer John Shebbeare, who criticised almost everything about the Hanoverian State, would have satisfied Sir Robert himself: Shebbeare, thought Wilkes, 'traduced the Revolution' of 1688. But while Wilkes was a gentleman and a whig, he was also after 1763 a political outcast; the majority of tories, by that date, were not. The constituency reaction to the party's return to political respectability bears eloquent testimony to the popularity of the tories' former and more disreputable stance. The tory M.P. Thomas Bunbury's appointment as secretary to the British Embassy in France was 'a new phaenomenon in the hemisphere of Suffolk. The freeholders of that county had not been accustomed to see their representatives in place, and they drew a melancholy presage from it of what was soon to follow.' A one-time tory voter in Newcastle noted with some asperity that the city's M.P., Sir Walter Blackett, was no longer 'the opposer, but the favourite of the Court: he attends the Levee, is noticed by the King & bowed to by the Ministers'.⁷⁰

Yet tories who bemoaned the end of their radical phase could still feel proprietorial about their successor. 'What says the Body of *your friends*, the Torys?' Lord Temple inquired of Wilkes in November 1762. He was far from being entirely ironical. Wilkes had contacts at the highest level of the tory party – Lord Lichfield, Norborne Berkeley, and the more significant if less bonhomous William Beckford. His début in extra-parliamentary agitation had occurred in 1756, when he joined some Berkshire and Bedfordshire tories in formulating the latter county's Address on Minorca.[71] In 1768 the *St James's Chronicle* was to remark how the voters in the eastern division of Middlesex, who had given Wilkes his best support, had also rallied to George Cooke, the tory who was returned for that county in 1750 and who 'greatly availed himself of this numerous body of little freeholders'. As an early exercise in psephology this claim was only partially correct; it is nonetheless significant that the comparison between tory and Wilkite electoral support was made. In Bristol, Newcastle, Coventry, Norwich, Colchester, and most of all in the metropolis there was undoubtedly some concordance between former tory and subsequent radical allegiance. In London the tory Half Moon Club and the Independent Electors of Westminster were both associated with the new movement. Since the latter society had already absorbed the number 45 into its internal organisation, and since the Independent Elector Alexander Murray had been paraded through the City to shouts of 'Murray and Liberty' in 1751, this transition must have been a comfortable one, made even more so, perhaps, by the Wilkite employment of blue ribbons and songs of an emotive and indicative ancestry: 'Hearts of Oak' and 'True Blue Will Never Stain'.[72]

Georgian toryism incited extra-parliamentary dissidence without being able fully to accommodate it. The party combined a longstanding and popular suspicion of the executive with a rooted inclination towards a stratified, stable society where land determined political responsibility. The tories, thought Lord Shelburne, as he looked back to the period of their proscription, 'were the landed interest of England who desired to see an honourable, dignified government conducted with order and due economy and due subordination' – a rather hackneyed description which accords well with Henry Fielding's various tory squires, but which must also have been applicable to many of the party's real-life county supporters. The parliamentary tory party was tempted and sometimes compelled into a very different socio-political stance. A common hatred of the whig regime encouraged tory M.P.s to identify themselves at least rhetorically with the socially and politically dispossessed, and the electorate to regard a tory vote (like a liberal vote a century or more after) as a means to vex the mighty.[73] Humphry Parsons' speech against the Excise Bill, which was handed about London in manuscript, is an example of this binary syndrome in operation: its defiance of great men and home-spun language serves to narrow the gap between the tory

M.P. and his constituents, giving the latter a vicarious experience of
protest:

I have no Obligation to the Gentlemen, nor the Ministry – He [Walpole]
Knows it – And they did oppose me, but I don't care for them – I carried it
& shall carry it again in spight of their Teeth – There are a great many
without Doors, that desired me to oppose it, And I am desired by those who
sent me hither, & by those who did not send me – But here I am, & I am
now their Member for all that – And I don't like the Excise – And I think
it an Hard Case upon Folks – And I am heartily against it Sir – That I am.[74]

Tory M.P.s not only served as spokesmen for extra-parliamentary discontent, they also urged the new world of the politically excluded to
exert itself so as to redress the corruption and inadequacies of the old world
of oligarchical politics. Constituencies were invited to instruct their M.P.s
and so render them more fully representative. Towns were encouraged
to petition for their better government and for their ultimate representation. The individual voter was urged to practise *virtù* rather than short-
sighted greed. All these emphases may have been designed primarily for
partisan benefit but they do blur J. G. A. Pocock's distinction in mid-
eighteenth-century Anglophone radicalism between the American insistence on the need for autonomous civic action and the English confinement within a reformist 'Country' tradition.[75]

Ambivalence towards Dissent, their own conservatism, and of course
the social and economic conditions which obtained in the first half of
the eighteenth century prevented the tories from exploiting their radical
daring to the full. So too, perhaps, did the availability of other party
options. Wilkes after 1763, like Milton's fallen angels, had to rebel
against conventional politics if he was not to relapse into oblivion. The
tories after 1714 were proscribed; an extra-parliamentary strategy was
a possible solution and they partially explored it, but their proscription
was not irreversible. Always available, to distract from and enervate tory
popularism, was the prospect of a tory return to power by high-political
or parliamentary manoeuvre, which would preclude a more extensive
and possibly subversive assault on the political and social order.

PART III

Single-Party Government Assailed

A Dark Hole with Blind Guides: 1714–24

The year 1714 witnessed not only the Hanoverian Succession, but also one of the most remarkable *coups d'état* ever staged. When Anne died the tories had a Commons majority of 208. The whigs' concurrent reduction to 171 Members admittedly marked their post-1688 nadir, but their minority status at Westminster and in the constituencies had been the post-revolutionary norm. How was it, then, that Bolingbroke's prediction of March 1714 came to be fulfilled: 'The minority, and that minority unpopular, must get the better of the majority who have the sense of the nation on their side'?[1]

Much was owing to whig ruthlessness – a ruthlessness born of desperation and rendered effective by the superior organisation and cohesion of an embattled minority. Knowing they had rarely achieved power by due constitutional process, the whigs at the end of Anne's reign showed themselves willing to employ violence. After the Pretender's announcement in March 1714 that he would not convert to Anglicanism there is no evidence that any of Anne's tory ministers seriously considered his restoration. Neither after March nor before is there any firm evidence of tory military preparations to forestall the Hanoverian Succession. Some whigs, by contrast, were willing to risk civil war. Since 1712 the duke of Marlborough had been urging the Emperor and the Dutch and Hanoverian governments to invade Britain and overthrow the tory administration. By 1714 George Ludwig, the Elector of Hanover, had agreed that Marlborough would lead an invasion if a Stuart restoration seemed likely at Anne's death.[2] The Scottish whigs had already formulated their own emergency strategy and had stockpiled weapons in Edinburgh. By the calculated hysteria of their propaganda and by their Westminster alarmism, the whigs sought throughout 1714 to panic the Queen either into changing her administration or into her grave. In April the duke of Bolton moved that a reward be placed on the Pretender's head if he entered Britain, implying that such an incursion was the ministerial and royal intention. Later that month, and with whig connivance, the Elector's representative,

George von Schütz, demanded that the electoral prince be allowed to take his seat in the House of Lords as duke of Cambridge.[3] For personal and political reasons the Queen was bound to veto this proposal, and so seem to substantiate whig claims that she and her ministers were crypto-Jacobite. Indeed, whig polemicists insisted that self-preservation allowed the tories no choice but to be Jacobite. The six thousand copies of John Dunton's *Neck or Nothing* dispersed about this time warned that any tory peer or M.P. 'who declared for the Peace [of Utrecht], and yet declares against the Pretender; such must be void of common honesty, or common sense'.[4]

Neither Anne nor the premier tories allowed themselves to be tempted into the violence or political extremism which some whigs desired. In the last month of her life Anne made plans for a new mixed administration, led by Marlborough and Bolingbroke, on which the Elector would be consulted. Both Oxford and Bolingbroke had anticipated such an alteration, and in the spring and summer of 1714 it was concern for their careers in the current reign as well as a desire to insure against the future dynasty which prompted their separate approaches to leading whigs. Even before Oxford resigned on 27 July, Bolingbroke had arranged 'to engage Ld Albemarle to negotiate for em wth ye Court of Hanover'. When Anne was on her death-bed, it was the tory Lord Chancellor Harcourt, not, as has often been supposed, the Hanoverian Kaspar von Bothmer, who ensured that the earl of Shrewsbury, a flexible but pro-Hanoverian whig, would be named as the new Lord Treasurer.[5] Why, then, were tory politicians, after such vaunted moderation, hounded out of power in 1714–15? Why were the whigs able to effect in 1714 what they had been endeavouring to achieve since 1688: the identification of the tory party with Jacobitism and its subsequent proscription by the constitutional monarch?

I

The new King was not thought to be averse to the tory party as a whole. Schütz, Bothmer, and the Hanoverian Resident, Kreienberg, had certainly done their best to shape their master's partisan bias. The information they sent him was derived almost exclusively from whig sources, and, largely because of the tory administration's internal wrangles, there was no influential tory representative at the Hanoverian Court to counter these selective reports. Hanover did manage to establish contact with the leading whimsical M.P., Sir Thomas Hanmer, and through him with the Secretary of State, William Bromley. In May 1714 Hanmer's equivalents in the House of Lords – Nottingham,

Anglesey, Abingdon, and Archbishop Dawes – had been informed that the Elector and his advisers were determined to conciliate the Church tories, 'qui...leur paroissent les veritables interpretes de la plus saine partie de toute la nation, aquoy L'on n'a pas manqué de faire beaucoup d'attention'.[6]

This pledge was partly designed to keep the whimsical tories co-operative in the run-up to the Hanoverian Succession, but even the whig leaders acknowledged the Elector's avowed preference for a mixed administration. They made sure that he stopped in Holland in September, on the way to his new kingdom, so that he could be lectured on tory unsuitability and whig virtues by the Dutch government. James Craggs' letter to George's Secretary of Embassies, Jean de Robethon, just two weeks into the new reign, betrays a similar anxiety:

I shall be the first to rejoice to see that the King may succeed in annihilating parties, and in employing, without distinction, those who are best affected and most capable. But I own I distrust a sudden change, and cannot help remarking to you, that a great change in offices is necessary in order to be able to say, that you are not governed by a party.

Later in the year the new Secretary of State, Lord Townshend, protected the earl of Dartmouth from impeachment and tried to keep Lord Lansdowne's brother-in-law, Sir John Stanley, in place as Commissioner of the Customs. As contemporaries recognised, these acts derived less from his own moderation than from his assumption that 'the King's inclination was to have a mixture of Whigs and Tories'.[7]

His most expert biographer has claimed that what George in fact wanted was a king's party in which his leading German ministers, a majority of whigs, and a subordinate but stable group of loyal tories could be usefully contained. But his prejudices and prime political aides scarcely equipped him to construct such an amalgam. Although normally shrewd and moderate, he could be both obsessive and intransigent about European affairs. His disgust when Harley broke the Grand Alliance and negotiated a separate peace with France had been lasting and un-comprehending. The crudity of his response – the announcement in the whig *Daily Courant* in December 1711 that he would regard such a peace and its makers with absolute hostility – showed an unusual lack of judgement. It provoked English nationalistic resentment, exacerbated tory insecurity and encouraged Jacobite intrigue.[8] George's invariable concentration on war and foreign policy was bound to favour whig rather than the more insular tory politicians. In the crucial early years of his reign his preoccupation with Hanoverian expansion in North Germany was to mean that he was less concerned with preserving that flexibility in domestic politics which only a two or multi-party system could ensure. Having granted the whigs primacy in return for their compliance with his foreign policy, he was to discover that he had shackled himself (and his successor) to men whose political creed allowed coercion of the monarch.[9]

In 1714 some moderate whigs had been available to second tory arguments that it would be unwise to dismiss or punish every tory politician implicated in the Treaty of Utrecht. Bishop Potter of Oxford was to recall that

Lord Halifax, upon the turn of things in the beginning of George the First's reign, was very earnest with the great mass of his friends, to proceed moderately in the disposal of places, and was very desirous that men of ability and character, though Tories and in with the former ministry, might not be turned out, but continued in full favour.[10]

But Halifax died in 1715, and his fellow moderate, Lord Shrewsbury, was, as always, too diffident and indolent to make any impact on the King's ministerial choice. A minority of George's German advisers – von Görtz and the elder von Fabrice for example – was sympathetic to tory promotions, and in the first half of the reign a small group of Hanoverian courtiers was always available to lobby in the same cause. It was incontestable, wrote one of these in 1717, that the maintenance of a two-party system would have been to George's advantage: 'Les suites me confirment dans cette opinion de plus en plus.'[11] But in 1714–15 what counted was the whig bias and the greater ability of von Bothmer and von Bernstorff. Their advice coincided with that offered by self-styled moderates like Lord Cowper, by whigs with a grudge against the Oxford regime like the duke of Marlborough, and by supremely confident and adept Junto men like Robert Walpole. The subsequent unfair or tactless tory dismissals and excessive persecution provoked bitterness and over-reaction – that self-perpetuating, polarising cycle which a Harleyite peer lamented in 1715: 'The Tories complain of oppression & are impatient to provoke it, and the Whigs suspect the Tories & unite them in despair.'[12]

If the new dynasty was to retain the whimsical tories and appeal to the self-interest of their ambitious colleagues, it needed to demonstrate some correlation between loyalty and reward. This was only partially done. The earl of Nottingham, a renegade since 1711, was made Lord President and given places for his immediate relations. He was not allowed to serve as an intermediary through whom more orthodox but aspiring tories could be attached to the administration. Edward Nicholas, the Shaftesbury M.P., who had been an inevitable office-holder for seventeen years, John Bland, Nottingham's nephew-in-law and a future dealer in Jacobitism, and the influential Lancashire tory Richard Shuttleworth all applied to Nottingham's clique for some small access to patronage, and all in vain.[13]

The Finches themselves were remorselessly jostled by those whigs who wanted monopoly status. Lord Aylesford had accepted the Duchy of Lancaster on the agreed condition that it would carry an increased salary of £1500 *per annum*. George ordered his new Paymaster General, Robert Walpole, to formulate the warrant accordingly. Walpole somehow neglected to get the document signed by the King or the salary paid. Given the Nottingham clan's appetite for money, such restraint may have been justified; much less so was Townshend's peremptory demand in August 1715 that Aylesford dispose of certain livings in the duchy in favour of his whig nominees. This kind of whig harassment influenced tory opinion in general. 'Lord Nottingham & his Brother, Anglesey & Abingdon are hard pursued', wrote the Carlisle tory Sir Christopher Musgrave a few months after George's accession, 'so I take [it] those sort of Men called Toryes are bound hand & foot, & if they keep their Lives and Estates, they must owne the Whiggs to be men of moderation.' 'War', announced the impetuous but pro-Hanoverian Lord Anglesey, 'had been declared on the whole tory party.'[14]

Tory alienation and mistrust contributed to Sir Thomas Hanmer's and William Bromley's refusals to take office as Chancellor and Teller of the Exchequer. They feared that if they accepted office the tories would be deprived of leadership in the Commons and that, having achieved this end, the whigs would engineer their dismissal or treat them in the same cavalier manner as they did Nottingham and his friends. Hanmer declared that he would not take office unless Bromley remained Secretary of State or more places were made available for tories. Bromley would come in only if his post carried some guarantee of permanence. These conditions were not met and the incident enabled whig politicians to argue that it was tory intransigence which prevented a mixed administration. 'It was interpreted', wrote the unscrupulous ex-tory James Brydges in December 1714, as 'an unwillingness to come into his Service upon ye foot of acting in conjunction with ye Whigs & gave ...such a turn in ye King's mind, if one may judge by ye effects, as has inclin'd him perfectly to the Interest of ye Whigs.'[15]

At the highest level this was true, though how far the King was informed of and understood what was done in the lower echelons of state office is not always clear. By October twenty-five tory Privy Councillors, including Oxford, Bolingbroke, Lord Chancellor Harcourt, the duke of Ormonde (the former Captain-General), and the Secretary of

State for Scotland, the earl of Mar, had been dismissed. By January 1715 half the Lord Lieutenancies had been shuffled and only four tories retained theirs. Tories were purged from the higher judicial posts: Lord Trevor, to cite one of the major victims, gave way to Sir Peter King as Lord Chief Justice of the Common Pleas. Thirty tories were removed from the more important court positions and twenty colonels were dismissed from, or forced to sell, their regiments for their attachment to the Oxford administration and/or for supposed Jacobite tendencies.[16]

The whigs, like their tory predecessors, tacitly acquiesced in the emergence of a non-party civil service by allowing departmental officials below (and sometimes at) the rank of Chief Clerk to retain their posts. Sixteen of the Treasury officials listed on 1 August 1714 had appeared on the list issued in March 1702; ten of them were still in office in June 1727. Tory proscription filtered down to these lower administrative ranks only with the death or resignation of the Augustan generation, appointment to even minor state employments in the mid eighteenth century usually depending on a man's access to whig patrons. Higher ranking tory officials in the Army and Navy Boards, in the Admiralty, in the Board of Trade, and in the revenue departments went out in 1714 and early 1715.[17]

Tory horror at the scale and rigour of the purges was sharpened by their arbitrary implementation. The consistent Hanoverianism of Sir William Pole, a well-respected tory M.P. and Master of the Household since 1712, did not save him from dismissal. In August 1715 he was still unemployed and his arrears of pay were still owing. A less worthy but more dangerous tory, the earl of Strafford, was rightly removed from his inappropriate post as First Lord of the Admiralty; more unwisely, he was left uncompensated. Even his pension was terminated in February 1715. He would cheerfully have supported any administration which paid him, and he was still begging the Hanoverian ministers for a place in 1717; by 1720 he had lapsed into Jacobitism, as had an erstwhile whimsical tory, the earl of Orrery, who was dismissed from the Lord Lieutenancy of Somerset in the autumn of 1715.[18]

G. M. Trevelyan once suggested that the Hanoverian regime made up for these occasionally capricious removals by allowing local government to go its way undisturbed: 'The Tory squires were left unprovoked.' This would have been politic; however, it was not the case. Between September 1714 and the general election in March 1715 all but two of the English county Commissions were remodelled by Lord Chancellor Cowper. Some counties, like Leicestershire, where eighteen tory J.P.s appointed by Lord Chancellor Harcourt went out in 1715, got a whig-dominated Bench at the first attempt; others – Middlesex, Buckinghamshire, Hertfordshire, Oxfordshire, and Warwickshire – needed to be purged two or three times before the right partisan complexion was achieved. Recalcitrant J.P.s in the tory bastions of Wiltshire, Stafford-shire, and Berkshire were still being weeded out in 1719.[19] According to Cowper's own account to George, his remodelling of the Commissions was moderate enough. Tory J.P.s, he claimed, were not purged 'on bare general suspicion; unless they who solicited their removal, would give in writing some particular instance of objection to their conduct'. This policy-statement tells us what Cowper believed the King wanted to hear; it scarcely squares with some of the new Commissions actually issued. Why should Sir Thomas Hanmer, an affluent landowner and the whimsical tory whom George was most concerned to employ, have been dropped from Suffolk's magistracy when Charles Caesar, a tory M.P. of precarious fortune and crypto-Jacobite tendencies, was allowed to retain his place on the Hertfordshire Commission? Cowper was a Hertfordshire man and certainly aware of Caesar's politics. It is at least possible that he judged a known and peripheral dissident to be less of a threat to the whig position than a prestigious and loyal tory whom the King desired to honour.[20]

It was perhaps the minor incidents which contributed most to the gangland quality of high-political life in the first months of Hanoverian rule. Several tory commentators reported how Charles Aldworth, the tory M.P. for Windsor, was provoked into a duel by a whig army officer's accusations of Jacobitism. The taunts were true enough, but Aldworth was physically handicapped, and his assailant, who killed him, knew it. The new Secretary of State for the South, Lord Stanhope, having bribed one of Bolingbroke's footmen to spy on his master, made sure that Bolingbroke learnt he was under surveillance, but not by whom. In London the duke of Newcastle organised bands of toughs to counter the City's grass-roots toryism and intimidate the tory presses. When Sir Thomas Cave was the victim of a double return for Leicester-shire, in February 1715, he found he could not get his version of the contest reported in the *Evening Post*. 'The Tory writers here dare not insert matters of fact', reported one of his friends from the capital, 'whereas the Whigs put in their papers the greatest falsehoods imagin-able. The publick must needs be imposed on if they can hear only their side.'[21]

I have described the process of tory alienation in some detail, and of course from the tory point of view, because it forms the background to the party's parliamentary defeatism in the 1715 session and to the active involvement of a few M.P.s and peers and the tacit concurrence of others in the Jacobite rebellion of that year. How the tories should have responded to these major and minor grievances was clear to their more astute leaders. A Hanoverian tory pamphlet quoted one of them:

What then Gentlemen? said he, we must take it for a misfortune, and must wait peaceably for a time to open His Majesty's Eyes and if possible, to bring him to believe us, as we believe our selves, to be honester Men and better Friends to his Interest than the Whigs; but as for Resentment! What can you pretend to? or who have you next? You know there's no body next but Popery and the Pretender.

Popery was abhorrent and the Pretender lacked intrinsic appeal ('It is an impracticable man', Sir William Wyndham had told Lord Lansdowne in July 1714, 'and will never be brought in'). What reduced Wyndham to working with Lansdowne in the 1715 conspiracy and what stymied the party as a whole was the failure of Oxford and Bolingbroke to place their joint authority behind a responsible strategy for tory survival.[22]

Oxford had hoped for much from George's preference for a mixed administration. On 18 August 1714 he, Edward and Thomas Harley, and the earl of Dartmouth, dined with Bothmer and Kreienberg to discuss tory prospects in the new reign. Bothmer was non-committal but at the end of the month Oxford was still convinced that 'Neither party of the two denominations (Whig and Tory) separately can form any such [administration] as is practicable.' This confidence was partly designed to keep his supporters in spirits and his enemies at bay, but he does seem to have been beguiled by his own political diagnosis. He behaved as though his credit with the Hanoverian dynasty was sufficiently good to provide not only for his personal safety but also for his future employment. Bolingbroke's suggestion that they should co-operate in the face of an inevitable whig assault was ostentatiously rebuffed. 'Does he think after what has passed, they who are clear themselves will come in to save him', wrote one Harleyite of Bolingbroke's initiative; '...old quarrels must be forgotten, we must unite again, no doubt of it; and it is to be hoped the church party will unite, but exclusively of them.'[23]

Oxford let it be known that he would accede to any impeachment proceedings against his former colleague. He may also have instigated the publication in October of Defoe's pamphlet *The Secret History of the White Staff*, which portrayed him as consistent in his devotion to Hanover despite the wiles of Bolingbroke, Harcourt, and Bishop Atterbury. The widespread belief that he had collaborated in this denial of tory ministerial responsibility alienated party opinion, and his campaign to dissociate himself from Bolingbroke was badly misjudged.[24]

Oxford's behaviour arose from his fundamental acquiescence in the

Hanoverian Succession. His prolonged and tortuous intrigues with the French envoy, Abbé Gaultier, had been intended to protect his position in domestic politics rather than restore the Stuart dynasty. But Hanover, predictably, opted for a less subtle interpretation. 'That Lord Oxford is devoted irrecoverably to the Pretender and to the King of France', Robethon had recorded in February 1713, 'is what we had no doubts of long ago.' But there was more to the new King's hatred of Oxford than this. It is possible that Oxford's anti-executive past was known and distrusted by an ambitious monarch with a conventional view of the prerogative; the Hanoverian Court had welcomed Harley's fall from office in 1708 – long before he was seriously associated with Jacobite intrigue. Certainly George knew that Oxford and not the flamboyant Bolingbroke had been chiefly responsible for the timing and content of the Treaty of Utrecht. Even before the peace Hanoverian diplomats, like their Dutch and Austrian counterparts, had marked down Oxford, with his 'dark, perplexed and unintelligible' political style, as the personification of perfidious Albion. The King, noted Dr John Arbuthnot in October 1714, spoke 'more contemptibly' of Oxford 'than of any body; & in very hard terms, has not he managed finely at last?'[25]

Royal antagonism finally registered with its object and in November Oxford sent Lord Bingley (one of the twelve tory peers he had created in 1711) to sue for Bolingbroke's assistance. Bingley returned with a cool assurance of support in common party ends and a rejection of any future personal collaboration. The whigs naturally took care to widen the division between the two tory leaders. Acting on behalf of Bothmer, James Brydges wrote to Bolingbroke assuring him of the administration's benevolence – on terms:

I dont find but that everybody would be glad to have your Lordship escape ye Storm, which must inevitably break upon some or other...every one wishes my Lord Oxford may be ye man to be made ye Sacrifice...I heartily wish it may stop there, & ye most likely means for your friends to effect it, I think is not to endeavour too much to divert ye present indignation from him.[26]

While the most prominent tories adopted a policy of *sauve qui peut*, the business of guiding the parliamentary party fell to more peripheral and less able men. The earl of Peterborough, Lord Trevor, and the duke of Ormonde held meetings to try to secure agreement on a party counter-offensive. The bishop of Rochester busied himself composing the pamphlet which was to be commonly regarded as the tories' electoral manifesto. *English Advice to the Freeholders of England* predicted that a whig victory would lead to a Riot Act, to the repeal of the Triennial Act, and to a legislative assault on the Church of England. Even more presciently, Atterbury warned the King of the danger of too facile an acquiescence in whig electoral ambitions:

If the King himself can be supposed to have any Inclination to balance or break Parties, 'tis his Interest to have such a House of Commons as may check the House of Lords; by which means he might be at Liberty to act, as he should think fit. If he is now so swayed by a few Whigs, how will he be over-ruled by two Houses of the same Principles?

Atterbury's anticipation of royal ductility, coupled with his criminally stupid comparison of the Hanoverian and Stuart dynastic religions ('Lutheranism and Popery in many Things differ only as that which is absurd differs from that which is more so'), only contributed to George's concurrence in whig partisan endeavour. On 15 January 1715, reputedly at Walpole's suggestion, the King issued a proclamation effectively urging the constituencies to return whig M.P.s.[27]

Royal rhetoric, as distinct from royal influence, had very little impact on the election result. Much has been made of the tories' 'rout' in the English counties and of the 'massive swing to the whigs' in the larger constituencies in 1715.[28] This emphasis is perhaps misleading. What defeated the tories, in this election and in its four successors at least, was the electoral system rather than the electorate.

As always when the party was associated with Jacobite intrigue, there was a limited swing against the tories in some open constituencies. But this factor cost them comparatively few seats. They lost eighteen of the English and Welsh county seats they had gained in the 1713 election and won one other. One seat in Monmouthshire fell to the whigs because the tory Beaufort family had no adult heir. Both county seats in Kent, and one each in Worcestershire, Shropshire, Norfolk, and Bedfordshire, were lost by fewer than two hundred votes; four of the other losses – single seats in Hampshire, Anglesey, Buckinghamshire, and Cheshire – were due not to tory defeats but to tory decisions to compromise these counties with the whigs. In some counties – Kent, for example – the tory gentry demonstrated a similar lack of partisan confidence by absenting themselves from the polls. 'Many of ye tories', wrote one sympathiser, 'sit still & let ye World go as it will...Country Gentlemen being weary of spending Money to no purpose, & only for ye sake of Persons who mind not their Country but their own Interest' – an oblique condemnation of the Oxford administration's internal wrangles and its apparent squandering of two electoral coups.[29] In the largest borough constituencies – those with over a thousand voters – the party won or retained twenty-five seats, and some of its thirteen losses had nothing to do with tory unpopularity. The Beaufort minority cost the party its M.P. at Monmouth. In Bristol the two unsuccessful tory candidates actually polled more votes than their whig opponents; their achievement was cancelled out by the city's whig sheriff and a whig-dominated Committee of Elections.[30]

The bulk of tory losses occurred in quite different constituencies. In 1713 the cinque ports had returned seven tory M.P.s; in 1715 they returned two. In 1713 royal and Treasury influence had helped the tories win a hundred seats in English boroughs with fewer than a hundred voters; over forty of these were lost in 1715. Toryism as distinct from Jacobitism had never had much relevance North of the border and Scottish M.P.s were usually poor, malleable, and the product of tiny electorates. Self-interest, a lack of partisan commitment, and governmental coercion ensured that forty-two of the forty-five Scots returned to the Commons in 1715 were nominally whig. Given the party's disarray, the imbalance of the representative system, and royal and ministerial electoral influence, the fact that the tories emerged with some 220 M.P.s testifies to their enormous and rooted constituency strength.[31]

When Parliament reassembled on 17 March 1715 270 whigs and 150 tories were present. By 6 April tory attendance was down to 129 M.P.s. United and confident of defeat, they walked out 'to a man' when Sir William Wyndham was censured for criticising the bias of the King's pre-election proclamation (the 'Pamphlet Proclamation' as tory balladeers styled it). On the same day Walpole announced that impeachment proceedings would be initiated against the former ministry. By the end of August Oxford had been consigned to the Tower; Bills of Attainder had been passed against Bolingbroke and Ormonde, who had both fled to France and to the service of the Pretender; barely twenty tory M.P.s continued to attend the Commons to vote in their leaders' defence.[32]

The Jacobite invasion of Scotland in the autumn of 1715 and the proven complicity of a few tories in the Lansdowne–Ormonde plot seemed to substantiate what the impeachers had only been able to assert: that before its demise, Oxford's administration had schemed to restore the pretender and that it was this design which had been put into belated execution. Two tory M.P.s, Ralph Freman and Lord Guernsey, were the first to propose a Commons Address of Loyalty in the face of the Pretender's invasion, but this overt rectitude and the paucity of tory treason were alike beside the point.[33] The '15 put a premium on unity at the centre, legitimised garrison politics, and led unerringly to the removal of those few tories who had clung on to state or court employment. In November Lord Uxbridge lost his place as Lord of the Bedchamber. In February 1716 Lords Anglesey and Rochester lost their Irish posts and the earl of Nottingham was dismissed. Nottingham's fall was accompanied by that of his brother Lord Aylesford; Aylesford's son, Lord

Guernsey, resigned from the Jewel Office, and Nottingham's son-in-law, Sir Roger Mostyn, was removed from the Lord Lieutenancy of Flintshire. Sir John Walter, the Oxford M.P., and Archibald Hutcheson were two more casualties of whig consolidation. At high-political level tory proscription was almost complete. It was chance and tory blunders, rather than the prejudice of George I or the acumen of Robert Walpole, which prevented this situation from being reversed during the next seven years.

II

The potential for the tory party's recovery was easily apparent. The great whig party of 1715 had been forged by the impeachment proceedings and the Jacobite threat and was as insecure as the great tory party of 1713. Country whig M.P.s had all along been nervous of the centralist tendencies of some of their leaders. In May 1715 they joined tory M.P.s in an attack upon placemen. In the same month Walter Moyle complained that the ministry's additional allowance for the Prince of Wales only endangered 'ye Constitution by makeing ye Court independent of ye Parliament'. Whig diffidence was again in evidence on 2 February 1716 when a tory motion to adjourn the House during a debate on the rebel captives was defeated by only 162 votes to 155. Thomas Brodrick, at this stage a government whig, noted 'how ill our people attend', whereas 'the toryes (within call) attended to a man, and several of them came to the town the night before from remote parts'. He also commented on the defection at this division of forty whig M.P.s who disapproved of the ministry's rigorous treatment of some of the prisoners. Two months later forty-three whigs joined over 140 tories in opposing the Septennial Bill.[34]

More serious than Country whig qualms was the increasing dissonance within the whig elite. By mid 1716 Horace Walpole's correspondent in London, Anthony Corbière, was noting how rumours of a quarrel between George and his heir and of tensions in the whig administration had lowered the price of government stock. In August he passed on information culled from tory sources 'that Lord Carnarvon [the former James Brydges, suitably rewarded] will be made High Treasurer and Lord Townshend Lieutenant of Ireland'. In the same month another whig observer reported that a mixed administration was being discussed which would take in two very mild tories, Lords Pembroke and Carleton, as well as the earl of Shrewsbury and members of the Nottingham clan.[35]

How near these machinations came to success is unknown and does not much matter. What needs to be stressed is that many contemporaries did not believe that the whig administration had been cemented in power or, conversely, that tory exclusion was irremediable. The belief that the tory party was going through a lean period of strictly limited duration explains why tory defections in this early period were so sparse. Few English peers and only nine tory M.P.s changed sides in the 1715-22 Parliament. The majority of tory politicians – including careerists like Harcourt and Trevor – tended to agree with Lord Strafford, who wrote in November 1719, warning a potentially recalcitrant Aldeburgh voter to think twice before he switched his party allegiance,

Let him consider how often Ministers Change in England, & that it is not probable that the Torys shou'd stay out of imployments much longer; I believe you have heard enough to satisfie him, that they had like to have been brought into imployments, even before the King return'd from Hanover & when they do come in...you know what power I shall then have and how I may serve my friends & be even with my enemys.[36]

Indeed, it seemed that the real problem for the tories at this stage was not so much their bleak exclusion as the variety of means available for ending it. Should they concentrate on appeasing the King and his ministers, with a coalition government as their ultimate aim? Or should they utilise the parliamentary leverage supplied by the dissident whigs, appeal to the ambitions of the Prince of Wales, and try to defeat the administration, with the prospect of replacing it *en bloc*? Less attractive but not yet implausible was the Jacobite option. When the earl of Mar remarked of the tories in 1716, 'I see no other they have to lay hold on, but the King' – meaning of course King James III – he could hardly have been more wrong, but English Jacobites did have a limited prospect of Swedish military assistance and the certainty of generous financial aid from Philip V of Spain. The tories' tragedy was that they lacked a unified leadership capable of identifying the most viable strategy and of persuading the party to pursue it in a consistent manner. As one journalist remarked in 1718, 'It would be endless to recount the many Advantages they have let slip...The Tories are the very Hannibals of their Age; they know how to hew out a Victory, but never could compleat their Conquest.'[37]

Both Bolingbroke and Oxford recognised that the tories would do better to wait on George I's exasperation with whig pretensions than become associated with either Walpolian or princely dissidence. They were unable to harmonise their advice or use their common percipience as a basis for reconciliation. In 1717 Lord Harcourt informed Bolingbroke that Bromley and Hanmer had convinced many tory M.P.s of the futility of Jacobite intrigue and urged him to consult with Oxford on how best to further this drift towards political respectability. Bolingbroke was adamant: 'I should make a wrong step in writing to that worthy person...That acquaintance is broke entirely.' He had in fact just been negotiating for his pardon, and ratting on Oxford was part of the deal. In 1719 Oxford was to respond to von Bernstorff's discreet suggestion that 'the King was against the peerage bill' by a careful set speech against the legislation. William Bromley lent these overtures to the Court his considerable support, but Sir Thomas Hanmer and his friends, who were attached to the Prince, and Wyndham's Jacobite coterie were much less responsive. Bolingbroke could appreciate the wisdom of Oxford's manoeuvres, but since he needed Stanhope's and Sunderland's support for his pardon, he was obliged to give the Peerage Bill his distant support.[38]

Rival strategies and a dissonant leadership made it easier for the Jacobite wing of the party to sabotage any tory *rapprochement* with the Hanoverian regime. As Atterbury argued, so long as the tories believed they had a prospect of political recovery by constitutional means, the Pretender would be ignored. Nothing, therefore, was to be left 'unattempted towards keeping every single Tory that may have his eyes on a place at Court from closing with any motion of that kind'.[39]

Between 1716 and 1720 different groups within the tory party explored different escape routes from proscription. Throughout the summer of 1716 the Swedish minister in London, Count Gyllenborg, discussed with some tory M.P.s (and, it would seem, some dissident whigs) the possibility of a Swedish invasion on behalf of the Pretender. Gyllenborg's close friend, Charles Caesar, together with Atterbury and the former Jacobite M.P. for Minehead, the Swedish-born Sir Jacob Bankes, duly raised and dispatched to Sweden the sum of £18 000. As some Hanoverian ministers suspected (though Gyllenborg and the English conspirators did not), the invasion project was largely bogus – a device whereby the Swedish minister *cum* adventurer Baron von Görtz could restock Charles XII's depleted wartime treasury and salvage his own career. Most tories were ignorant of the attempt and many believed, with some justice, that its subsequent exposure by the government was intended to provide George I with a pretext for intensifying Britain's naval involvement in the Baltic. Nonetheless, when Stanhope read out copies of Gyllenborg's treasonable correspondence to the Commons on 20 February 1717, it was the tory M.P. for Scarborough, John Hungerford, who rose and demanded war with Sweden.[40]

Gyllenborg had always been aware when wooing the tories that he had to contend with rival suitors. As he wrote to Baron Görtz in November 1716, 'If we do not take Advantage of their [the tories'] present Animosity, it will cool; for the Court, that is to say, the Party of the Prince, does all that is possible to gain them.' The King's departure to Hanover the previous July had allowed Prince George to adopt a more individualistic political stance. He was too cautious to accept the tory-sponsored Addresses from Gloucestershire, Oxfordshire, and Worcestershire extolling his 'graciousness to all Persons without Distinctions of Party', but he did welcome tories to Court and consult with the party through such flexible politicians as Lords Shrewsbury, Carleton, and Windsor.[41] The King's return to England effected neither a familial nor a whig reunion. In December, after a protracted campaign by Stanhope and Sunderland and a disagreement over foreign policy, Lord Townshend was removed from his post as Secretary of State and given that invariable sop to problematic ministers, the Lord Lieutenancy of Ireland. As so often happened, the device failed. On 6 April 1717 Townshend was dismissed. Robert Walpole and nine other office-holders resigned and took themselves and about fifty whig M.P.s into opposition. Six days later Friedrich Wilhelm von Schulenburg, half-brother to the King's mistress, took note of the tories' public assumption that their party would be invited to join the depleted administration.[42]

The ministry certainly needed to recruit new support. The duke of Argyll's dismissal from his court and army posts in March 1717 meant that many Scottish peers and M.P.s were no longer reliable. The Speaker, Spencer Compton, had gone into opposition in his capacity as Treasurer to the Prince of Wales, and by August a harassed government was discussing whether he should be replaced and forced to accept a peerage. In a division on the Army in December Stanhope's Commons majority fell to fourteen. In the Lords some normally compliant peers (such as Longueville) and some recent tory defectors (for example Carteret) began to waver in their voting behaviour.[43]

Sunderland, Stanhope, and the new Secretary at War, James Craggs the younger, all considered remedying their insecurity by a tory intake. They intensified their efforts to bring Bolingbroke home and his secretary, John Brinsden, was granted an interview with the King in October. George was still too hostile to Oxford to make a ministerial approach in that direction very profitable, but the Treasury did repay the £7500 owing to him since 1714. By way of Lord Carnarvon, Sunderland opened negotiations with Harcourt and Trevor. By November rumours of a tory accession to government had reached the European press as well as an obscure tory curate in Cumberland: 'Lord Trevor to come into the ministry', John Thomlinson noted in his diary; '[he] has declared he would never come in unless Lord Nottingham and Sir Thomas Hanmer came in too, that they might enter into a league, and stand or fall together.'[44]

It was not that easy. George had been antagonised by what he saw as Walpolian arrogance and insensitivity to his foreign policy needs. His immediate reaction to the schism, Schulenburg judged, was to lean 'plutôt aux Torys, qu'a des Gens si ingrats envers luy'. Lord Carnarvon agreed. The King had determined, he informed Bolingbroke in October, to bestow his favour 'on all (without distinction of Party) who will endeavour to deserve it'. But having experienced the limitations attendant on undiluted whiggery, George was scarcely going to opt for a purely tory and traditionally isolationist administration. What he really wanted, thought Schulenburg, was to cream off tories like Harcourt and Trevor while keeping their suspect party at bay:

Il faut que le gazettier d'Amsterdam n'ait pas un correspondant trop fidele icy, s'il en est informé qu'on songe a faire entrer au Ministere le Chevalier Hanmer et d'autres Torys...Ce n'est donc point qu'on songe a faire un Ministere melé de deux partys, on en est fort eloigné, on voudroit seulement detacher quelquesuns de Torys pour les rendre Whigs...Il y en a de tres capables parmy les Torys...je suis sur que le Roy les gouteroit et qu'ils le serviroient en gens d'honneur, mais Leur party n'est pas encore en credit.[45]

The truth lay somewhere between this Hanoverian appraisal and tory euphoria. Whatever his own party attitudes, George knew well enough that a handful of tory recruits would not on their own remedy his administration's fragile majority. Had Bolingbroke been restored and been able to re-establish his party following, or had Trevor or Harcourt been able to guarantee a contingent of tory votes, these politicians could have achieved both individual access to office and gradual tory acceptability by harnessing the party to governmental survival.

But there could be no prospect of tory assimilation into the administration once it became identified with legislative sympathy for Dissent. This was the obstacle which leading tories were unable to surmount in the two years after the whig schism, and on which Robert Walpole relied to guarantee his own and his followers' indispensability. Stanhope and, to a lesser degree, Sunderland were determined to repeal the Occasional Conformity and Schism Acts. Stanhope's long-term aim (and that of the King) was the abrogation of the Test Act. Bolingbroke recognised that such measures would force the majority of tories into opposition. As he warned Lord Stair, in a phrase which anticipates his future anti-party stance as well as its contortions when confronted with stubborn partisan sentiment, moves against the Church of England would alienate 'the honestest of the Torys, those who without being Jacobite are weak enough to imagine that there is any difference between them and the whigs'. In November 1717 Lord Trevor was granted an audience with the King and warned Sunderland to avoid 'all hot Courses, such as the Occasional Bill'. This intransigence, combined with disagreement over the extent and timing of tory promotions, caused the negotiations with the ministry to break down.[46]

Walpole was delighted. During the spring and summer of 1717 he had intrigued to get Oxford released from the Tower. (With Oxford at liberty it was much less likely that a restored Bolingbroke would be able to reunite the tory party.) Throughout 1718 he championed the integrity of the Anglican Church. He endeavoured, in short, to make himself sufficiently attractive as an ally to the tory party to prevent its aligning with the administration and so condemning him to prolonged unemployment. He sacrificed a few whig ideals but very little whig policy in the process. The tories were left in the lurch in their opposition to the Land Tax in December 1717 and in the vote on the Mutiny Act the following February. Walpole allowed them opposition whig support in their nomination of the High-Church Dr Snape as Commons' preacher for the Restoration Day sermon, in the vote to retain Parliament's commemoration of Charles I's execution, and in the motion of January 1718 to reduce the number of half-pay officers.[47]

Walpolian strategy was furthered by the Prince of Wales. In December 1717 he was expelled from St James' and sought refuge in the London house of the former tory M.P. for Taunton, Henry Portman. He was promptly visited by a group of Hanoverian tories including Archbishop Dawes, Hanmer, and Ralph Freman. They promised him tory support, discussed with him their future parliamentary strategy, and agreed to send out whips to every tory M.P. to attend in the new year. 'Unless I am mightily deceived', wrote Lord Finch, 'there is a firm bargain struck...to support each other & oppose publickly the ministry in every attempt they shall make upon ye Prince or in any of their Church bills.' He urged his father, Lord Nottingham, to align himself once and for all with his former party: 'The Torys must prevail and it is good to strike in quick.'[48] George I had already been warned by Bishop Nicolson of Carlisle that at least eighteen bishops, including Archbishop Wake, would oppose the repeal of the Occasional Conformity Act. The new year seemed to augur an insuperable conjunction between the tories, the dissident whigs, the Prince, and three-quarters of the episcopal bench. This, at least, was the opinion of the ministerialist Bishop Gibson: 'The Tories have gained such a considerable accession of strength and spirits ...and whether the next is to be a Whig or Tory Administration, or if Tory (as it certainly can be nothing else) whether the Archbishop or Bishop of Rochester is to be at the head of Church Affairs, Judge you!'[49]

Gibson's analysis was defective on two counts. Precisely because the Prince of Wales and the Walpole faction joined in opposing the repeal of the Occasional Conformity and Schism Acts in December 1718 and January 1719, the tory party was prevented from cementing an exclusive association with the Anglican hierarchy. Wake was forced to be anti-government; he was not, at this stage, forced to be anti-whig. Secondly, Gibson had underestimated whig solidarity and exaggerated the area of agreement between the Hanoverian heir and the tories. On 12 February 1718, on the third reading of the Mutiny and Desertion Bill, Walpole voted with the Court. Prince George, stricken by the death of his youngest son and submitting to the instructions of Walpole and Townshend, abstained from voting in the House of Lords.[50] The tory leaders had wanted mutineers facing the death sentence to be tried by civil rather than martial law and they had demanded that the Prince join them in rejecting the bill as it stood: 'all of them to a man declar'd they would give him up to the mercy of the ministry if he did not give them that proof of his regard to the liberties of the subject'. The tories were as good as their word. After the February division, the bulk of the party boycotted Leicester House. In March, when the Princess of Wales celebrated her birthday, no prominent tory came to pay his respects but Walpole and Townshend were there to supply the omission.[51]

This ineptitude owed as much to poor tory leadership as to persistent tory principles. Massive tory attendance in January 1718 and a 79 per cent tory turn-out for the debates on the Occasional Conformity and Schism Acts the following winter showed the party's receptivity to its leaders' instructions. For the latter emergency Shippen had simply shut himself in his London lodgings and prepared the requisite number of hand-written whips. What was lacking was continuous and unified direction. Early in 1719 the tory Bishop Smalridge of Bristol noted how, out of gratitude for the Prince's opposition to the recent concessions to Dissent, some tories had shown a willingness to re-establish contact with his Court: 'I find severall others would be glad to go, if those whom they us'd to follow, would shew 'em the Way; but they don't care to be singular.'[52] Nor could the party's spokesmen agree to respond to the various overtures made during this year by the earl of Sunderland via Lord Harcourt, or to the advances of his fellow Secretary of State, James Craggs: '[the tories] act in the same manner as former', wrote Auditor Harley to Oxford, '. . .leave every thing & drift, they hold the Ballance and are by turns courted by the parties of father and son'. Oxford did little to remedy his party's paralysis. His absence from London during the Peerage Bill crisis of December 1719 allowed Walpole to secure prime credit for its defeat.[53]

The tories' position was undeniably invidious. They could trust neither Stanhope and Sunderland, who were bound up with Dissent, nor Walpole, who had supervised the tory impeachments and was associated with Junto extremism. A tory alignment with the ministry in 1719 would have entailed tory support for the Peerage Bill, which was inimical to tory backbench opinion and almost certainly unwelcome to the King and the Prince. Too strident tory opposition to the Peerage Bill and a too blatant defeat of the ministry might precipitate Walpole's rehabilitation. The party's solution was to vote against the bill while refraining from speaking against it, thereby underlining its distinct quality within the opposition. Tory parliamentary silence unfortunately also suggested tory parliamentary impotence. Since Stanhope's administration needed an accession of strength in the Commons and since the tories had already rejected ministerial overtures, the way was made clear for the whig reunion in April 1720 and for Walpole's return to office as Paymaster General. 'The Tories have leisure to reflect on the prudence of their own conduct', wrote Dr Stratford to Lord Harley; '...they were not for taking any advantage against those that were in, lest [those] that were out should come in again...They may in vain perhaps wish again for such an opportunity as they have had and not used.'[54]

III

On 20 April 1720 that shrewd journal, the *Commentator*, speculated on how the tories would respond to their novel parliamentary isolation: 'I cannot but reflect, how unhappily the Tories have been carried... from one year to another, between the Two Extremes of the Jacobites on the one Hand, and the Whigs on the other.' Now that whiggish options had receded, was it not likely that the tories would revert 'to their first natural Opinion of trusting rather to a Jacobite than a Whig'? Bishop Atterbury, writing to the Pretender in May, was much less confident. The party had lost its balancing power in Parliament and was too demoralised and divided for any positive action: 'I think myself obliged to represent this melancholy truth thus plainly, that there may be no expectation of any thing from hence, which will certainly not happen.'[55] Yet it is at least arguable that the collapse that autumn of the South Sea scheme, with its attendant individual bankruptcies, widespread unemployment, and a nation-wide shortage of specie, provided the English Jacobites with their only opportunity to launch a rebellion with the likelihood of domestic support.[56]

Except of course that the South Sea Bubble by no means discredited only the whigs. The company had been a tory creation and one writer listed no fewer than twenty-eight tory peers and seventy tory M.P.s who had purchased South Sea stock on the third subscription in July 1720. These figures represent ministerial propaganda, but many tory politicians

had speculated heavily and a few of them corruptly. Six high-tory M.P.s
– Sir Coplestone Warwick Bampfylde, his brother, Sir John Bland, Sir
Thomas Sebright, Charles Longueville, and Sir William Carew – were
listed in the Commons' report as having accepted stock at a preferential
rate, these concessions being part of Sunderland's earlier attempts to buy
off individual tories. It seems strange, and contemporaries certainly found
it so, that crypto-Jacobites should have linked themselves to a company
which was guaranteed by and dependent upon a Hanoverian Parliament.
In October 1720 Atterbury was to suggest his colleagues' priorities by
warning a Stuart agent that many tory–Jacobites wanted to defer an
invasion until they had recovered their South Sea losses by a parliamentary
inquiry.[57]

When Parliament met in December the tories attended in force. If
only because of the party's own involvement in the speculation, their
attack was concentrated neither on what Lord North styled 'the fraudu-
lent and pernicious practice of stock jobbing', nor indeed on the South
Sea Directors; ministerial and court complicity in the scandal gave it all
the potential of a Watergate affair, and the tories were intent on using
it to subvert the administration. In this project they could rely (to a
limited degree) on independent whig support. The thirteen-man Committee of Inquiry, selected by ballot on 11 January 1721, contained five
Hanoverian tory M.P.s and six independent whigs. Events were to show
that some Country whigs would dilute their aversion to corruption if
the inquiries came too near to compromising the whig–Hanoverian
regime. On 28 February Sir Joseph Jekyll, Lord Molesworth, and Thomas
Brodrick (all members of the committee) deferred to royal instructions
and abstained from the vote on Charles Stanhope, the indisputably guilty
Secretary to the Treasury. Stanhope was acquitted by a majority of
three.[58]

Independent whig ambivalence, contingency, and Robert Walpole all
combined to defuse the immediate crisis. Death removed those politicians
whose real or supposed guilt was most likely to tarnish whig government
– Stanhope, James Craggs, and his father, the Postmaster General. The
Commons was thrown a minor victim and allowed to expel the Chancellor
of the Exchequer, John Aislabie, while Walpole gave his attention to
more important men. In lobbying whig M.P.s in readiness for 15 March,
when Sunderland's fate was to be decided, Walpole concentrated less on
vindicating him from South Sea culpability than on the inexpediency of
his disgrace: 'If you come into this vote against Lord Sunderland the
ministry are blown up, and must & necessarily will be succeeded by a
Tory one.'[59]

Sunderland was acquitted by 233 votes to 172. The fact that some tory M.P.s lent him their votes indicated that Walpole's partisan interpretation of the division had been something of an over-simplification. Atterbury had been in contact with the Court since 1718 and negotiating with Sunderland since 1720. By 1721, he was partly convinced that, in order to extricate himself from the ministerial and intra-party contest with Walpole, Sunderland was willing to call a general election at a time convenient to the tories. In the wake of the South Sea crisis and with some government influence on its side the party could hope to obtain a parliamentary majority and could then decide whether it also wanted a dynastic revolution.[60] Sunderland's other, more important, tory intermediary was Lord Harcourt. In 1720 Harcourt had been made Lord Privy Seal and given a pension. He had also obtained jobs for his tory relations and had been led to believe that these concessions were the first instalment of a mixed administration which would exclude Walpole. Sunderland assured Harcourt that in approaching the tories he had George I's backing, and as a token of his sincerity offered to promote Lord Trevor – an offer which Trevor refused.[61]

It is difficult to gauge Sunderland's intentions in these tory overtures; it is not even clear if he knew himself what he was doing. He had always been unstable, and the pressure of his possible impeachment and Walpole's bid for primacy had damaged his health and political sense. With Stanhope dead, he was the King's favourite amongst the English ministers (though – and this was crucial – his status was not guaranteed by any particular expertise in foreign policy), so his desire for a Stuart restoration in the current reign seems dubious. As he had some royal support for a mixed administration, it seems possible that this was his aim – provided that in pursuing it he did not drive his whig supporters into the arms of Walpole, now first Lord of the Treasury, Chancellor of the Exchequer, and taking his stand on the beauties of unadulterated whiggism.[62]

As far as the majority of his tory sympathisers were concerned, Sunderland's main attraction lay in the prospect of office he held out to them. Archibald Hutcheson knew well enough that Atterbury and his associates were involved in Jacobite intrigue and that their endeavours were born of political deprivation rather than devotion to the Stuarts. Tory admission to government would pre-empt these extremists and ensure tory loyalty for the future. 'Your Lordship, no doubt, has acquainted the King with your conversation of late with my-self and some others', Hutcheson wrote to Sunderland in July 1721, 'and I am persuaded, His Majesty will soon see, That many Persons who have been represented as Enemies, are far from being so; and will be found Good Englishmen and Loyal Subjects.' More significant than the enthusiasm of the peripheral Hutcheson was Sunderland's attempt in 1721 to get

Bolingbroke pardoned. Both the Minister and Lord Harcourt hoped to restore Bolingbroke not only to his English estates but also to high political office where he could serve as a counterweight to Walpole. By March the pardon clause making Bolingbroke eligible for state employment had been drafted and submitted to the Attorney-General, a former tory and a close friend of Harcourt, Sir Robert Raymond.[63]

A compact which involved Bolingbroke's reinstatement was bound to alienate the Harleyite group, and in July 1721 Lord Oxford refused to come to London for the crucial stage of the tory negotiations with Sunderland. 'The Projector hath neither will, capacity or strength to bring about what he pretends', he wrote to his son, 'and I hope nobody that is worth any thing will put themselves in his power.' Bromley was more receptive but, as he told one of Sunderland's tory advocates, the party needed results, not just glowing promises. Why, for instance, had the Minister not appointed a tory to one of the bishoprics which had recently fallen vacant? 'This is looked on as a demonstration of want of will & sincerity, more than of Power...I take his station to be less difficult than the like has been to others that have gone before him – nothing can make it difficult unless treading in crooked paths, when he might walk in straight.'[64]

As well as Harleyite incredulity, Sunderland had to contend with Walpole and Townshend, who were working to undermine his position with the King. After July his nerve seems to have broken at the prospect of alienating George by too blatant an insistence on tory advancement. By autumn both Sir William Wyndham and Bromley felt certain that no tory promotions would be made and that Parliament would be allowed to run its full course. When Hutcheson gave him a final chance to make good his former declarations and carried a Commons bill to cut electoral corruption, Sunderland had it quashed in the Lords and the tory peers' Protest at its defeat erased from the records of the House.[65]

Sunderland's recidivism threw the Jacobite–tories back on their own resources. In December 1721 Bishop Atterbury, Lords North, Strafford, and Arran, and the former Horsham M.P., Sir Henry Goring, dispatched a letter to the Pretender committing themselves to an armed rising in England.[66]

Without foreign aid the failure of the Atterbury plot was a foregone conclusion. The Jacobites had always had difficulty in mobilising effectual tory support for their schemes, but in 1722 even the Jacobite wing of the party was divided. Atterbury's intrigues with Sunderland had led to suspicions that he was a double agent, and his irascibility and occasional arrogance disgusted his less intelligent but aristocratic colleagues. 'He is so full of his own abillitys', grumbled Strafford to the Pretender, 'that if he can't have things go his own way, he would rather they did not go on att all.' James would have preferred Lord Oxford to supervise the conspiracy but Oxford was too old, too ill, and much too cautious to commit himself to treason.[67] Even more debilitating was the diffidence of some of the younger Jacobites. Wyndham had resisted Bolingbroke's pro-Hanoverian polemics for several years, but a visit to his former mentor in France in 1720 indicated and confirmed his drift towards the politics of respectability. Lord Gower also kept his distance from the plot, and so did Bathurst: 'I am at this time', he told Atterbury, 'inclin'd to think it ye wisest course to live quite still.' Orrery favoured a Stuart restoration in principle but argued that the plot was imprudent and that the tories would do much better to concentrate their resources on the impending election campaign.[68]

By February 1722 even Atterbury had belatedly lost faith in the project. Belatedly, because his abortive scheme was already being investigated by the British Post Office and had been betrayed throughout to the English Ambassador in Paris by the earl of Mar. Walpole's agents were also privy to the correspondence of Christopher Layer, a Norfolk Roman Catholic and romantic Jacobite, whose epistolary references to the proposed capture of the Tower of London and the poisoning of George I made exciting if insubstantial reading. By conflating these detailed inventions with the more authentic letters of Atterbury's circle the ministry obtained a cache of evidence which seemed to indicate a nation-wide and tory-inspired conspiracy.

Even without the Atterbury plot the prospects for a tory political recovery after 1722 would have been limited. The decision to allow Parliament to run its full seven years and the amount of whig money and organisation expended on the general election neutralised a great deal of the extra-parliamentary revulsion at the South Sea affair. The tories won 170 seats – a slightly higher figure than their pre-dissolution total. The tory leadership had also to accept the governmental implications of Sunderland's death in April 1722. 'Will it not establish ye Governour', William Bromley had remarked, employing one of his party's more polite but still indicative synonyms for Robert Walpole, '& make him absolute?' In the event it did, but in the summer of 1722 there was still some leeway at the centre of politics. In May a group of tories including Hutcheson, and two dissident whigs, Lords Cowper and Somerset, were approached by Sunderland's former allies, the ex-tory Lords Carteret and Carleton. They met several times to discuss an anti-Walpolian coalition. Whatever impact these congeries might have had (for George I was still unhappy with his first Minister) was pre-empted by Walpole's exposure of Atterbury's conspiracy.[69]

Irrespective of whether the tories let Atterbury sink or sought to defend him, the party was bound to be branded anew with crypto-Jacobitism. All that its leaders could do was endeavour to keep it united, sustain its morale, and outface suspicion. It was agreed to propose Hutcheson as chairman of the parliamentary committee which would reply to the King's opening speech, and to get one or more tories appointed to the committee investigating the plot. These initiatives proved abortive, but Lord Harley, Sir Thomas Hanmer, and Ralph Freman helped to draw up Addresses to the King condemning the conspiracy. Most tory M.P.s had been ignorant of the plot, and the fragmentary and eccentric nature of the evidence and the necessary reliance on the deciphering ability of Walpole's creatures did little to convince them of its authenticity. 'I can really apprehend this only as a Plot of Layer', wrote the Warwickshire M.P., Robert Digby,

...And two or three others of ye same rank, who perhaps in conversation with some of better quality might draw from them some hearty rash expressions...But as to ye real danger from this plot, I think there could be none to the nation, but of its being made an occasion by an artful Minister, of suspending its liberties & subjecting it to an increase of Forces.[70]

More influential tories, who knew that a plot had existed but had kept aloof from it, took care to emulate this tone of indignant incredulity. When Gower momentarily lost his nerve, Bathurst dispatched an acerbic letter ordering him to London and telling him to whip up every M.P. and peer he could influence. Tory absence at the opening of the session would be attributed to tory guilt: 'Give no room, My dear Lord, for any reflections to be made upon a character hitherto so unblameable.' As a boost to early attendance the tory leadership floated a rumour that the party would contest the Speakership – a tactic which proved remarkably successful, if exasperating to M.P.s like Sir Justinian Isham and Sir Nicholas Morice, who made a supreme effort to reach London in time only to be disillusioned on arrival.[71]

Initially high tory attendance was also prompted by the hope that many newly elected whig M.P.s would be less responsive than their predecessors to Walpole's direction. On 18 October 1722 over fifty whigs supported a tory motion that Habeas Corpus should be suspended for six months rather than for a year. The fact that the amendment was still defeated by 246 votes to 193, and twenty tories voted with the ministry out of fear of being linked with the conspirators, convinced many tory M.P.s of the futility of further effort. On 26 November a motion to double the tax obligations of Roman Catholics passed by sixteen votes, and as one tory Member complained, 'had not many of our friends been gone into ye Country...we had rejected it'. When it came to divisions more directly related to the plot, both Houses reverted to strict party voting. On 6 April 1723, when the Commons debated Atterbury's punishment, tory M.P.s demonstrated their solidarity and their certitude of defeat by walking out *en bloc*. On 15 May Atterbury's Bill of Pains and Penalties passed the Lords by eighty-three votes to forty-three, only three errant whigs joining in the minority.[72]

The extent of the tory party's decline by 1723 must have surprised even those politicians who had worked to achieve it. From 1714 to the South Sea crisis the whig party's attitude to its accession to power had been characterised by insecurity. One of the most potent ministerial arguments for the Peerage Bill had been that unless the whigs so guaranteed their majority in the Upper House, the next tory administration would stabilise the supremacy of its own peerage. Walpole's opposition to this legislation reflected his confidence that whig control could be consolidated without it, but his was a close-run victory. A succession of fortuitous deaths, and a conspiracy so conveniently timed that many tory M.P.s genuinely believed it to be a governmental ploy, contributed as much to Walpole's premiership as his skill or the acquiescence of George I. It was not until early in 1724 that Lord Stair felt able to cite, as a development of some novelty, that 'ye King's favour is entirely on ye side of Mr. W[alpole]'. Even after 1724, that favour never entirely excluded the prospect of tory admissions to the government.[73]

Sir Arthur Onslow's retrospective verdict on the Atterbury plot is well known – that it consolidated Walpole's position, and discouraged dissident whigs from lending the tories their support; but the second part of this assessment needs qualification. By 1722 two groups of potentially deviant whigs had emerged: careerists like Pulteney, Sandys, and Carteret, who were being edged out into the cold by Walpolian success, and independent whigs like Edward Wortley Montagu, Trenchard, Molesworth, and Sir Joseph Jekyll, who claimed that Sunderland and Walpole had debased whig principles in their conduct of government. The ultimate mutation of this latter category was the whig Jacobite. The marquess of Wharton, son of the Junto purist, and Viscount Rialton, grandson of the first earl of Godolphin, both argued in the 1720s that true whiggism must entail a rejection of the Hanoverian dynasty which had corrupted its party champions. 'The reasons which my Father gave for the supporting of the Hanover Succession', wrote Wharton, 'fall to the ground & those who follow the Maxims of the Old Whigs are obliged to resist such destructive Tyranny unless they forget their Principles.'[74]

More commonly, independent whigs argued that what was needed to redress this central corruption was co-operation between real whigs and non-Jacobite tories. In 1721 Bishop Gibson believed that the South Sea débâcle had already achieved or rather restored this kind of parliamentary alignment: 'In both Houses the Game is like to be much the same, as in the latter end of King William's Reign: that is a conjunction against the Court, of the Tories & lowest Whigs.' The Atterbury plot may have postponed Pulteney's rebellion for a few years; it did not persuade independent whigs like John Trenchard to acquiesce in Walpolian statecraft. In March 1723, at the height of Atterbury's trial, Trenchard denounced the conspiracy in the Commons, but in the same speech he also attacked ministerial suspension of Habeas Corpus. Since his 1722 parliamentary candidature had been championed by Sir Thomas Hanmer, Trenchard's realignment was already underway. And such contacts between tory politicians and dissident whigs were to increase, not because the former had lost their party identity, but because they were adjusting to the tactical demands of their party's minority status. Before 1723 a Hanoverian tory administration was a possibility; after that year the tories were far from being doomed to exclusion, but they were 'out of any Condition to aim at Places and Power, except as Auxiliaries'. Hence, argued the same mid-eighteenth-century historian, the revival of the 'Earl of Oxford's old Scheme, under the new Title of a Coalition of Parties'.[75]

As tories began to come to terms with the format of their future opposition activity, so their leadership was undergoing a sea-change into efficiency. In the years after his release from the Tower Oxford had rehearsed the political sin committed by Sir Robert Peel after 1847. He had neither given his followers a clear indication of what policy they should pursue, nor got sufficiently out of the way to allow a younger and more positive leader to emerge. A Stuart agent's report in 1722 indicates the extent of Oxford's deterioration and the persistence of his mesmerising intra-party status. 'Oxford is perfectly well in his intellectuals', wrote James Hamilton, 'his hearing is not so good as formerly, he has lost most of his teeth.' And with a certain sad obstinacy, Hamilton went on to quote as authoritative the bed-ridden tory peer's assessment of the current political situation. When in 1723 Walpole spurned the political advances of Gower, Bathurst, and, most particularly, Sir William Wyndham (who wanted limited tory, not just their own, access to government), he ensured that Oxford would have able and much more straightforwardly ambitious successors – successors, moreover, who had discarded their earlier belief that a Stuart restoration could salvage tory political fortunes.[76] Atterbury's plot was a disaster, but it did at least convince these three tories and the bulk of their party of the futility of Jacobite schemes and the relentless efficiency of Walpole's intelligence system. The summer of 1724 saw the death of the earl of Oxford and the arrival in England of Madame de Villette, who came to secure by bribery and the political leverage of Harcourt, Wyndham, and Bathurst the restoration of her husband, Viscount Bolingbroke.

The Twisted Threads of Party: 1725–41

The hybrid opposition which confronted Sir Robert Walpole after 1725 is one of the great set-pieces of eighteenth-century English history, and its tactics and press campaign have been chronicled many (some would say too many) times. Few tories would have been as reverential about the distinction of this period as some of its historians are. They had been opposing not only Walpole, but also the party and much of the governmental system he represented, since 1714. For many of them, parliamentary co-operation with the growing number of dissident whig peers and M.P.s was only a way of continuing the same battle by different means. '*They* vote with *You*', a government pamphleteer told William Pulteney in 1731, 'because *You* now proceed with Violence against a Person who is one of the greatest Enemys to Tory Principles ...they hate the *Whig* as much as *You* hate the Man.' In a pamphlet rejoinder Pulteney denied neither the binary composition of the opposition nor the implication that for him ousting Walpole was its prime purpose: 'The Whigs who oppose you, are neither govern'd by the Tories, nor are the Tories govern'd by them; but they act in Concert together (and may they long continue to do so!) because it is their united Opinion that you are a wicked, as well as a weak Minister.'[1] Disagreement on policy, if not an eventual betrayal of one party group by the other, was built into the coalition from the start. The dissident whigs had to oppose in such a way as to topple the King's Minister without endangering whig control; the tories naturally inclined towards a more extensive campaign both within and outside Westminster: unlike their allies they had nothing to lose.

In these circumstances it is remarkable that the joint opposition held together as well as it did; it is quite impossible to establish how exactly this feat was achieved. The anti-party polemics of the *Craftsman* and analogous publications must have helped, but it is of course no accident that the tory association with the so-called Patriot whigs has been examined primarily through their purported ideological conjunction.[2] The opposition's propaganda, its pamphlets and newspapers, have survived in bulk.

The major Patriot politicians – Daniel and William Pulteney, Samuel Sandys, Walter Plumer, Sir John Rushout, William Pitt, and Lord Carteret – have left hardly any opposition correspondence. Extant tory papers, sparse at the best of times, are particularly so for the 1730s. As a result too much emphasis has probably been placed on the political efficacy of the opposition's literati, and not enough on its organisation. 'The organisation of the malcontents was fundamentally an irregular succession of *ad hoc* arrangements, made and dissolved time after time', Archibald Foord once commented; 'The history of their career as a confederate Opposition is the record of their sporadic co-operative efforts in significant matters and at critical junctures.' Possibly so, but since government commentators were ignorant of the opposition's routine organisation and frequently exaggerated its disarray, we simply do not know.[3]

What is clear is that the period 1725–41 was not a unity in terms of either opposition efficiency or opposition effort. What tory politicians and the various groups of dissident whigs could achieve in the way of collaboration within Parliament and outside it was best demonstrated between 1730 and 1735. Before 1730 many tories believed (with some justice) that they had too much to hope for from the Court to make a confederate opposition either necessary or attractive. By 1735 the very success of the opposition's campaign, which had brought it within sight of political power, had also reminded its two main party groupings of their separate and conflicting interests.

I

On 23 January 1725 the new earl of Oxford and the late earl of Sunderland's son-in-law, Lord Morpeth, presented a petition to Parliament on behalf of the lunatic dowager duchess of Montagu. Anti-Walpolian by inheritance or marriage, both sponsors hoped for an inquiry into the Court of Chancery which would escalate into a full-scale exposure of ministerial graft. They were fobbed off with the impeachment of Lord Chancellor Macclesfield, which was no loss to Walpole, but the episode did resuscitate a standard formula for cross-party collusion. The parliamentary managers of Macclesfield's impeachment included four potential Patriot leaders, Phillips Gybbon, Samuel Sandys, Sir John Rushout, and Walter Plummer, as well as four tory M.P.s, Thomas Gore, Thomas Palmer, John Snell, and Thomas Lutwyche. And just as their joint participation in the Commission of Public Accounts had helped to blend tory M.P.s with Robert Harley's New Country whigs in the 1690s, so in the late 1720s and 1730s whig and tory dissidents were to use assaults on the old bugbear of state corruption and reformist parliamentary committees to consolidate and advertise their alliance. The tory James Oglethorpe's Gaols Committee of 1729 spawned an opposition pressure-group. The Committee on Charitable Corporations of 1732 was an opposition device from the start, taking in seven tories (three of them members of Edward Harley's Board), ten dissident whigs, and only four government M.P.s.[4]

In retrospect, therefore, the parliamentary session of 1725 was significant in the evolution of the opposition's platform; at the same time, it witnessed the emergence of two leading oppositionists. On 8 April William Pulteney, insufficiently employed as Cofferer of the Household, formalised his defection by an anti-Walpolian harangue. Twelve days later Lord Finch introduced a Commons bill restoring Bolingbroke to his English estates, though not to his seat in the House of Lords. Many tory M.P.s were absent from the subsequent debate, but only five voted against the motion. Of the tory peers, only the Jacobite earl of Scarsdale, and Oxford, for reasons of family piety, opposed. Other Harleyites, including Bingley and Dartmouth, as well as Lords Abingdon, Stawell, Berkshire, Leigh, and Cardigan, took care to deposit proxy votes with their tory colleagues to cast in Bolingbroke's favour.[5] This broadly based tory support was a response not so much to one man's rehabilitation as to what it might portend. Lord Finch was the uneasily whig son of the uneasily tory Lord Nottingham. Like his fellow defector, Lord Harcourt, Finch wanted a mixed administration to resolve his own partisan schizophrenia, and he regarded Bolingbroke's return as essential to its achievement. He was not alone in his diagnosis. When government M.P.s joined the tories in defeating an independent whig motion that Bolingbroke be barred from ever again holding office, it was, thought the whig M.P. for Guildford, 'a fair indication (as everybody thought) that he [Bolingbroke] was again to be brought into business, & why not, as well as Lord Harcourt...I take a motley ministry (very soon) for granted'.[6]

Bolingbroke's own hopes of a return to royal favour and employment proved abortive.[7] But the belief that was to be a Leicester House orthodoxy in the 1750s – that in the last two years of his reign George I contemplated adulterating single-party rule – may well have had some substance. In 1725 it was rumoured that Sir Thomas Hanmer would replace Pulteney as Cofferer, or be restored to the Speakership. Approaches were made to the able tory lawyer, Thomas Lutwyche; Ralph Freman and Lords Anglesey and Abingdon were seen to be regularly in attendance at Court; and in March 1726 Lord Trevor was made Lord Privy Seal. His appointment was widely interpreted as a royal attempt to offset and possibly dismantle Walpolian dominance. 'I myself should be glad to know whether it be any more, than [the King] listing against the Walpole Whigs', wrote Lord Poulet, 'or does the Court in finding the faults of other men, at last see their own in having set up so many party tyrants.' By November tory hopes were sufficiently high to drag the earl of Oxford from his obsessive antiquarianism and tempt him to London, where he joined Freman and Hanmer in their negotiations with the Court.[8]

Had George I lived longer, his great-grandson was told in 1755, 'we might have seen a coalited, that is a national party formed'. Justified or no, this expectation kept the bulk of tories from joining William Pulteney's early opposition gambits. Pulteney anyway had little at this stage to recommend him. He was notorious for his parliamentary prosecution of Bishop Atterbury and in 1725 he was credited with only seventeen followers.[9] There seemed little reason why a party with a technical Commons strength of over 150 should link itself to a few whig mavericks and so compromise its prospects in the current and, more important, the future reign. For if, after having seen whig assertions of tory crypto-Jacobitism reified in miniature in the '15 and in the 1717, 1719, and 1722 Jacobite plots, George I still wanted to offset Walpolian dominance with tory promotions, how much more might be expected from his heir, whose relationship with Walpole was distant, and whose acquaintance with tory politicians like Hanmer and Lord Bathurst, had been longstanding and friendly?[10] So the tories reasoned, and on 14 June 1727 Bathurst and three other tory politicians lent their signatures to the formal recognition of George II. In the following fortnight every tory M.P. and peer who was able, with only two known exceptions, advertised his 'disposition... to run into ye Court' by visiting St James' to compliment the new monarch. By the end of the month tory preparations for the general election were already underway, spurred on, as Lord Strafford informed one tory M.P., by 'The hopes given of impartiality in the King. The torys are resolved all over England to make their strongest efforts to get the majority in the next parliament.'[11]

They reckoned without the new Queen, the temperament of the new King, and the powerful vested interest which Walpolian whiggery had already become. As Princess of Wales, Caroline had been one of Lord Sunderland's fiercest opponents in his attempt in 1721 to institute a mixed administration – not surprisingly perhaps, since that Minister had once advocated her husband's transportation to the colonies. Bolingbroke's known intrigues with Sunderland must have contributed to his cold reception at Leicester House in 1725, and his friendship with the tory leader, Sir William Wyndham, may well have detracted from the party's acceptability in 1727. According to Archdeacon Coxe, Caroline represented to her husband 'the folly and hazard of dismissing a well established ministry and of forming a motley cabinet of Whigs and Tories'.[12] The emphasis on the settled nature of the administration was as likely to appeal as the proven ability of its leader. George II was shrewd; he was also middle-aged and fundamentally indolent. He may, as Lord Chancellor King believed, have 'formed a system both of men and things, and to make alterations in several offices', but he had no real desire to remodel his government, always providing that the existing one catered to his interests and prejudices. Walpole supplied George with a more than generous Civil List and agreed to promote some of his whig favourites; at the same time, he indicated very clearly the limits which a Hanoverian king had to accept unless he was prepared for a pitched battle with the whig elite.[13]

The King had promised Ralph Freman ministerial support if he stood again for Hertfordshire at the general election. Walpole reacted by urging the county's government employees as well as its leading dissenters to vote for the crypto-Jacobite candidate Charles Caesar. Freman had come first in the 1722 county poll and Caesar third; in 1727 their positions were reversed. 'If you should. . . say why did the Dissenters vote for Mr. Caesar last Election', a Hertfordshire nonconformist was to confide to a co-religionist, 'I answer it was to throw Mr. Freman out who they thought having more Influence in the House of Commons might do them more harm than he.' As a tory politician with royal favour, Freman might have done Walpole more harm also.[14]

George encountered more whig obstruction in local government. He had instructed Lord King to increase the number of tories on the Commissions of the Peace. Wyndham's conversion from Jacobitism was accordingly recognised by his restoration to Somerset's Bench. But when Lord Thanet and Sir Thomas Hanmer gave the Lord Chancellor lists of tory gentlemen they wanted included in the Westmorland and Suffolk Commissions, King immediately came up against these counties' Walpolian Lord Lieutenants. Lord Lonsdale deigned to accept Lord Thanet as a Westmorland J.P. but vetoed his nominees.[15] Hanmer's modest list of five Suffolk tories aroused the duke of Grafton to apoplectic fury. 'He went to the King, and complained to the King, who told me of it', wrote the Lord Chancellor; 'the Duke of Grafton assured him these men were Jesuits. . . [the King] told me that I must in this be guided by the Duke of Grafton, the Lord Lieutenant; so I did not put them in.' George II has been rescued from the description 'A King in Toils', but this episode at least is more suggestive of lazy royal capitulation to hectoring whig aristocrats than of royal independence succumbing to reasoned argument.[16]

Long before these minor setbacks, the retention of Walpole as first Minister had led many tories to discount the possibility of political change. In the 1727 election the party fielded about 184 candidates and only 122 of these were to win and retain their seats. The next three years saw the last bout of tory defections before Gower's departure in 1745. Lord Orrery and Charles Caesar lapsed from Jacobitism into reliance on ministerial funding. Thomas Winnington, M.P. for Droitwich and one of the most able products of the great Harley–Foley connection, went over in 1728; his friend Stephen Fox defected after 1730; and, having failed as a tory candidate at Hindon in 1727, Henry Fox entered Parliament as a whig in 1735. Five years earlier, Lord Bingley had accepted the Household Staff and its attendant duty of ministerial voting. Rebuked by his former colleagues, Bingley was unrepentant: the tory party, he told them, had become as ineffectual as 'a rope of sand'.[17]

During the first two years of George II's reign the party did little to belie Bingley's assessment. Disillusionment with the new King and depression at Walpole's effortless majorities led, inevitably, to parliamentary absenteeism. In the division on Britain's employment of Hessian troops on 14 February 1728, the opposition mustered only 84 votes to the ministry's 280. Allowing for the dissident whig contingent, at least fifty tories must have been absent. The Patriots were still limited in number and selective in their support. On 21 January 1729 Samuel Sandys and Robert Vyner joined the tories in criticising the Commons' Address to the King. William Pulteney, however, refused to vote with them, in case, he said, it was 'interpreted as a want of respect to his Majesty'. Having seen his party and its few whig auxiliaries defeated by 249 votes to 87, Wyndham went home to Somerset and, like many other tories, only returned to Westminster in March to support Watkin Williams Wynn's successful bill against electoral bribery.[18] Just eleven months later, Sandys got his first Place Bill through the Commons by 144 votes to 134; the opposition exposed the French refortification of Dunkirk in violation of the Treaty of Utrecht, and in the process was able to build up its voting support in the Commons to some 175 M.P.s.[19]

Describing the opposition's transformation-scene in 1730, Coxe identified Lord Bolingbroke as the responsible fairy godfather; Eveline Cruickshanks has opted instead for the Pretender. On 22 January N.S. James had written to the duke of Ormonde, urging that his 'friends' in England should be instructed to co-operate with the opposition whigs. Four days later he stressed the importance 'of supporting "any measures which tend to promote a misunderstanding between the English Government and any foreign power, but most especially France"'. In response to this, Cruickshanks argues, 'Wyndham inaugurated the coalition by unexpectedly producing evidence that Dunkirk harbour had been restored.'[20] But parliamentary coups are not so easily staged. As early as 1728 the earl of Oxford had hired a Captain Booth, resident in France, to supply him with newsletters on the state of the harbour and on Horatio Walpole's negotiations with Cardinal Fleury. In the autumn of 1729 Bolingbroke had visited France and ordered his factotum, Brinsden, to compile a special report on Dunkirk. Of course the Pretender's instructions helped to reconcile the few remaining Jacobite M.P.s to collaboration with whig dissidents – Shippen made a point that year of referring to William Pulteney as 'my new ally on the floor' – but the Dunkirk affair demonstrated that the anti-Walpolian confederation had come of age, it did not engender it.[21]

Much of the credit must go to Bolingbroke. His enforced private status under Walpole's government ensured his commitment to the opposition and meant that he had ample time as well as experience to devote towards its organisation: time to lobby the premier oppositionists into joint activity, and time to write for the *Craftsman*, which he and the two Pulteney brothers had instituted in 1726. Bolingbroke had always been adept at cross-party friendships, and his lapse from orthodox toryism enabled him to impress the quasi-republican and anti-clerical Daniel Pulteney; William Pulteney was never beguiled to the same degree. As far as his tory intimates were concerned, Bolingbroke claimed that Wyndham had been converted to the principle of coalition in 1726, and Lord Gower certainly supported Daniel Pulteney in his canvass of Preston in 1727.[22]

The advance from these individual recruits to general tory concurrence in a mixed opposition was made possible by Wyndham's consolidation of the leadership and by the realisation that Bolingbroke's strategy was, by 1730, the only option. This had not seemed to be the case in the early years of the new reign. The relationship between Walpole and his Secretary of State, Lord Townshend, had been patently deteriorating. The Secretary for Ireland, Lord Carteret, and even Speaker Onslow had been politically restive.[23] in April 1729 the hope that ministerial dissonance would lead to ministerial change reputedly led a group of tories to offer George an increased Civil List in return for a share of employment. William Pulteney's parliamentary deference to the King that same year was just as calculated. A reconstructed ministry might allow him and his friends political re-entry without their needing to resort to an association with the tories. Townshend's resignation in 1730 and a reallocation of offices which only confirmed Walpolian control compelled tories and dissident whigs into parliamentary conjunction.[24]

The exigencies of mutual need were sweetened by each party's increased desirability as a parliamentary ally. By 1730 the organisational efforts of the Loyal Brotherhood and the Harley Board had made tory M.P.s more capable of fulfilling their numerical potential in the House. Walpolian consolidation, events abroad, and the Gaols Committee had all helped to swell the whig dissidents to some fifty M.P.s.

The Treaty of Hanover of 1725 had failed to stabilise Britain's foreign policy and the Treaty of Seville, signed in November 1729, provoked criticism at home, especially amongst those merchants involved in Spanish colonial trade. Even before the treaty one tory M.P. judged that Walpole had 'disobliged ye merchants of all persuasions' by his rather cavalier response to a petition from the West Indian traders. Whig M.P.s representing the larger, mercantile constituencies found themselves under pressure to adopt a more critical line at Westminster: Abraham Elton, M.P. for Bristol, Micajah Perry, M.P. for London, and George Heathcote, M.P. for Hindon but a West Indian merchant himself, all drifted into opposition about this time.[25] The Gaols Committee, appointed on 25 February 1729, brought Elton and several other wavering or self-styled independent whigs – some of them Trustees of the colony of Georgia which was vulnerable to Spanish ambitions – into contact with hard-core oppositionists like William Pulteney, Rushout, Sandys, and Waller. The committee also made for increased whig–tory contact with twenty-one tory M.P. participants, including Wynn, Hynde Cotton, and Edward Harley, and Aldermen Child and Parsons. But its main achievement, as Lord Hardwicke noted in 1760, was that it gave rise to a distinct group of whigs ('the spawn of the Gaols Committee' as Edward Harley styled them in 1736) which bridged full-time dissidents, new recruits, and some of Walpole's less reliable supporters: men like Lord Egmont, John Laroche, and John Page.[26]

II

A mailing list for the *Craftsman*, compiled in September 1730 and seized by Walpole's agents, testifies to the opposition's newly forged vigour.[27] Fifty-eight whig and tory politicians were listed as subscribing regularly to this anti-party propaganda, in a way which only emphasised the reality of binary party distinctions. Eighteen tory M.P.s, Lords Bathurst, Gower, and Lichfield, and a close friend of Bolingbroke, Alderman Barber, undertook to purchase and distribute 315 copies of each issue; 315 other copies were allocated to opposition whigs. The breadth of tory involvement is impressive. Wyndham's purchase of forty copies – the highest individual subscription – was perhaps predictable, but high tories like

Watkin Williams Wynn, inarticulate county tories like Sir William Stapleton, M.P. for Oxfordshire, and the Harleyite reformist, Thomas Bramston, also contributed to the scheme.

The whig subscribers demonstrate the Patriots' still more variegated composition and some of the obstacles to their policy agreement with the tories. Daniel Pulteney, Lord Chetwynd, Sir Thomas Lee, John Aislabie, his son-in-law, Edmund Waller, and Lord Morpeth, had all been attached to the earl of Sunderland. Some of them, like Chetwynd and Aislabie, had been implicated in their master's South Sea culpability; others, like Morpeth and his father, Lord Carlisle, shared Sunderland's sympathy for Dissent. Sir Thomas Aston, M.P. for Liverpool, personified the tensions between independent and commercial whiggery and orthodox toryism. Happy enough to join tory M.P.s in reforming gaols and attacking the monopoly trading companies, Aston also wanted non-landed and non-Anglican men made eligible for Parliament. In 1733 he opposed the tory Henry Rolle's bill for higher landed qualifications for M.P.s; three years later he voted for the repeal of the Test Act. No less problematic were the disappointed and vindictive men: the former Lord of the Admiralty, Sir John Norris, and his son, the M.P. for Rye, dismissed for their opposition in the Dunkirk debates; Sir Thomas Saunderson, refused a peerage; and Lord Vane, vetoed as the ministerialist candidate for Kent in 1727. Recruits with such personal grievances were likely to be vigorous opponents, but also likely to be bought off. Admiral Norris returned to his place and docile voting in 1734; his son had succumbed to a customs appointment two years earlier.[28]

The motives of the leading Patriots were more complex than ministerial pamphleteers, with their endless jibes at frustrated ambition, allowed. Even at the height of the Atterbury crisis, Samuel Sandys, Phillips Gybbon, and another future Patriot, Walter Plumer, had been sufficiently purist in their whiggery to criticise Walpole's suspension of Habeas Corpus. Sandys, indeed, was always to maintain that it was Walpole's perversion of whiggism and not one-party whig government which he opposed. 'What ever my conduct in publick affairs may have been of late years', he wrote in 1742, 'it has never proceeded from any change of principles in me but from a real persuasion that things were not conducted for the good of the nation and many things contrary to the principles I was bred in and always professed – those of a whig.'[29] Pulteney's vulnerability to accusations of career opportunism (and reminders that in 1718 he had condemned Walpole's alignment with the tories) made him equally insistent on his whiggish credentials. His regular parliamentary paeans to 'the principle of Resistance' first exasperated and then bored his tory allies. His electoral recommendations were no less allusive. A candidate for the Provostship of King's College, Cambridge, competing in 1734 against both tory and ministerialist academics, was, Pulteney wrote, 'an honest whig and no courtier'; in 1739 he described a candidate for Cockermouth as 'a very good whig, but not of the modern stamp'. These genuflections to primitive whiggery reflect Pulteney's discomfort, his own and his Patriot associates' need to legitimise their collusion with the tories in opposition to a whig government, and their determination to do so in terms of conventional party dogma.[30]

Given this inbuilt partisan dissonance, the opposition was bound to require considerable organisation if it was to perform well. In the first half of the 1730s the parliamentary results of tory–Patriot consultation are evident enough. We know very little about how they were engineered. The opposition obviously took care to press for legislation which had a common Country appeal. So in February 1732 four tory M.P.s and two Patriots combined to draft and introduce a bill raising the landed qualifications of J.P.s; Sandys reported from the committee and the tory Thomas Bramston carried the successful bill to the Lords. The opposition's duality was also catered to in the set-piece motions which were launched at the start of every session so as to gauge numerical support. In January 1732 and in February 1733 the Patriot Lord Morpeth moved that the Army be reduced to 12 000 men. On the former occasion he was seconded by Watkin Williams Wynn, on the latter by Edward Harley. This system was still operative in January 1736. In a motion 'finely drawn up by Sir William Wyndham', Lord Cornbury, tory M.P. for Oxford University, proposed a further reduction of the Army, and was seconded by one of the Patriot's newest recruits, George Lyttelton.[31]

Wyndham's contribution to this last initiative is indicative. The opposition relied upon the activity and policy agreement of a fluctuating oligarchy. Tory and Patriot leaders would meet together, sometimes formally – as in the talks at Cassiobury House at Christmas 1732–3 between Gower, Wyndham, Pulteney, Bolingbroke, and 'friends' to settle 'the plan of opposition this session' – but more commonly on an *ad hoc* basis during the parliamentary session. Tactics having been decided, Wyndham and Pulteney were then responsible for mobilising their respective party followings. This meant that there was no back-up system if communication between the Patriot and tory chiefs broke down, and this deficiency was fundamental to the opposition's disarray after 1735. Only at the end of the decade was there a realisation that high-level dissension might be offset by more open organisation, by mass-meetings of Patriot and tory M.P.s and the founding of inter-party co-operation on negotiated consent.[32]

The Cassiobury talks had been held to concert the opposition's response to the expected Excise Bill. Much can be said in the way of financial justification for Walpole's scheme, but it was a major political error. Late in 1732 the Dissenting Deputies had seemed about to initiate a parliamentary campaign to repeal the Test Act. Had they done so, the coalition's carefully nurtured unison would have been unmade. Instead, the Excise Bill provided for opposition agreement, and allowed it to demonstrate and focus the press network and the mercantile and popular support which it had built up over the years.[33] Wyndham and Pulteney had already shown their ability to harmonise rhetoric against indirect taxation when Walpole reintroduced the Salt Tax in 1732. In the House of Lords the same measure had cut the Minister's majority from its customary fifty-plus to twenty-three. During the Excise debates in March and April 1733 opposition attendance in both Houses was high and steady. 105 of the 127 tory M.P.s were present to divide against the bill on 14 March; 102 attended two days later. By 5 April Walpole's Commons majority had slumped to seventeen.[34]

The opposition's contribution to the anti-Excise agitation outside Westminster (arguably a more extensive phenomenon than the Wilkite riots of 1768 and much more in need of examination) was considerable, but Patriot whig participation was necessarily restricted. Of the forty-nine constituencies which Langford has cited as instructing against the Excise Bill, twenty-four were represented by tory M.P.s. Three other boroughs – Taunton, Colchester, and Rochester – had their Instructions stage-managed by tory activists on their corporations. The unrepresented towns of Newbury and Birmingham instructed the tory M.P.s of Berkshire and Warwickshire respectively; Towcester and Daventry in Northamptonshire instructed under the cheerful supervision of Sir Justinian Isham. Patriot M.P.s – outnumbered by their tory allies by more than two to one, many of them suspicious of these genuflections to the popular will, and most of them ensconced in boroughs where public opinion was electorally irrelevant – accounted for just thirteen Instructions.[35] London's anti-Excise campaign, which indubitably influenced voting at Westminster, was dominated by tories. The campaign had been initiated in December 1732 by the tory Vintners' guild. The committee it set up included Robert Willimot and Robert Godschall, who were to contest the City as tories in 1734. In February 1733 the tory Lord Mayor, John Barber, promoted a resolution in the predominantly tory Common Council, instructing London's M.P.s to vote against the Excise Bill. On 17 February he met Wyndham and Shippen to discuss how best to co-ordinate grass-roots campaigning with the opposition's effort in Parliament. Three days later, he held a banquet at the tory Goldsmiths' Hall which eighteen tory and twelve Patriot politicians attended to advertise the rapport between metropolitan resistance and both components of the coalition.[36]

The rapport was imperfect. Pulteney had no love for Instructions, and his own pocket borough of Hedon seems not to have taken part in the campaign. He was nervous of Barber's Jacobitism and still more of the consequences of unchecked City activism. When Barber stood for London in 1734, Pulteney, who had been nominated for Middlesex, warned him by way of Lord Gower that he must not expect Patriot support in his canvass, and would be well advised to retire. Barber was not elected.[37] Wyndham's and Pulteney's differing attitudes to popular political participation were to prejudice their working relationship as well as the evolution of the opposition's extra-parliamentary strategy.

Walpole saved his majority and shelved the Excise scheme on 22 April 1733. Given the representative system, he could also be confident of a majority at the general election, but, on the basis of the local elections, only a reduced majority. In September Rochester chose a tory mayor despite the influence of the duke of Dorset and the Admiralty. A tory mayoral candidate was also successful at Taunton, where the dissenting interest usually guaranteed ministerial control. The King had already told Lord Hervey that if he were forced to change his administration he would rather risk a tory government than combine politicians from that party with the Patriots.[38] If the election was to witness a tory resurgence, the party might legitimately wonder whether its whig allies – Pulteney with his lauding of resistence, and Sandys with his reputed republicanism – were not something of a liability.

The general charge against us Tories, is, that we have ever been too strenuous, and too warm for the Royal Prerogative, too tender of the Person of the Prince, and too tenacious for supporting the Power of the Crown...Shall we unite with such Men, who are for stripping the Prince of that Balance of Power, absolutely necessary to be held in the Royal Hand, as a Security for the Protection of the Church and State, and the Suppression of – Republican Faction?

So argued a pamphlet published late in 1733 and aimed, it declared, at showing the tories 'True Friends to the present establishment, some of the capital Pillars of the Constitution, and worthy of Royal Trust & Confidence'. Both ministerial and Patriot whigs monitored these electoral and propaganda developments with a certain unease. Might not a united and seemingly buoyant tory party be able to challenge whig as well as Walpolian predominance? It was this partisan apprehension which lent piquancy to the Commons ballot on 24 April for a committee to inquire into the Customs.[39]

The opposition had pressed for this inquiry as a follow-up to the Excise Crisis, and further to suggest, even if it could not prove, ministerial corruption. Government and opposition each nominated twenty-one M.P.s, and Pulteney, predictably, arranged that the opposition list would consist only of Patriots. Wyndham promptly told him that unless eight tories were included he would not answer for his party's support. The evening before the ballot Walpole summoned a meeting of 262 whigs, including some M.P.s who had reneged on the Excise Bill. Drawing attention to the tory component of the opposition list, Sir Robert pointed the moral – or rather the moral he knew would be most persuasive: 'The contention of this ballot is in plain and intelligible language for dominion, for dominion between Whigs and Tories and the sole design of it is to feel the pulse of this Parliament whether they wish for a change or not.'[40] The subsequent ballot was to demonstrate two things. Agreement – however fragile – between Wyndham and Pulteney, and concessions to its two-party composition, had secured, as was invariably the case, an impressive opposition performance. Of the 209 tory and Patriot M.P.s present, only eighteen failed to vote for every name on the opposition list. Ministerial cohesion was still more impressive. As many whig M.P.s as Walpole had counted on voted for the government list, despite the opportunity to rat provided by a secret ballot: the list went through by a majority of eighty-five votes.[41]

The appeal to the ministerial whigs' sense of party identity had been a potent one. 'I thought', wrote that staunch and little-thinking whig, Colonel Charles Howard, 'The [opposition's] pushing things in the manner they had done of late, had this list succeeded, would have obliged the King to employ Torys instead of Whiggs.' Walpole's polemic was doubly insidious in that it preyed on Patriot insecurity. Hence in part the extreme reluctance with which Pulteney ordered his followers to support the March 1734 motion to repeal the Septennial Act – a tory-sponsored measure designed for tory electoral advantage. Only five dissident whig M.P.s spoke in favour of shorter Parliaments. The debate served instead as a show-piece for the newly confident tory elite. William Bromley moved and Sir John St Aubyn seconded repeal; they were followed by Shippen, Wyndham, Wynn, Cotton, Lord Noel Somerset, and Edward Harley. The motion failed by sixty-three votes, but the Patriots' grudging compliance enabled the opposition to end the parliamentary session on a popular note and appeal to the constituencies with its internal tensions decently overlaid.[42]

III

It was, ironically, the election which precipitated the opposition's dis-integration. Ironically, because its campaign had a central co-ordinator – Bolingbroke spent March and April at Wyndham's Somerset estate, 'rising early each morning and writing much' – and because in some con-stituencies an impressive degree of collaboration was achieved. In York-shire Lords Bruce and Strafford worked with the whig Lords Carlisle and Rockingham and succeeded in returning the tory, Sir Miles Stapylton, though not the dissident whig candidate. The predominantly tory gentry of Middlesex accepted Pulteney as a partner for the banker Sir Francis Child.[43] In Kent, Lord Vane and his tory partner Sir Edward Dering circularised whig and tory electoral patrons alike and adopted an avowedly Country platform: 'These are Candidates untainted in their principles, and uncorrupt in their practice, who have always shewn their inclination to maintain liberty and Property, their zeal in opposing that Badge of Slavery an Excise and the Instrument of Arbitrary power a standing Army.' Of the 4441 Kentish freeholders who are recorded in the poll book as having voted for Dering, 3993 split their votes between him and Vane; only twenty-six were sufficiently purist to plump for the tory alone.[44]

In other counties neither the electorate nor the elite was as amenable. The Patriot Lord Winchilsea had expressed hopes that 'instead of Courtiers' Leicestershire would return 'honest Country Gentlemen of both denominations without any idle distinctions of party'. Leicester-shire's gentry, accustomed to identifying whiggism with Dissent and the pretensions of the Rutland family, rejected such a novel analysis, and stolidly selected two candidates in their own image, the tories Ambrose Phillipps and Edward Smith. In Buckinghamshire, Edmund Waller, Patriot M.P. for Great Marlow, lent his electoral interest at Amersham to the tory Drake family, and, as he complained, antagonised 'the whigs both there and at Chesham and I shall not, I fear, have that interest amongst them as I used to have'. In return for this self-abnegation he expected the tories to agree to two Patriots, Sir William Stanhope and Sir Thomas Lee, being returned for the county. Not only were tory voters at Amersham reluctant to comply, but a group of Buckingham-shire freeholders also insisted that a local tory, Richard Lowndes, should contest the county. 'I declined as much as possible', wrote Lowndes, rather lamely, to one of the whig candidates, but 'they answered if I would not stand they would make me sit...My Friends tell me if so great a Number of my Countrymen do call me out and demand a Poll for me, I must on no account Refuse 'em.' Although some tories with interest in Buckinghamshire, Sir William Stapleton and Lord Lichfield among them, abided by the agreement with the Patriots, Lowndes was able to pick up 1314 votes – more than a quarter of them plumpers.[45]

And however much tories and Patriots co-operated in the election, the former party was bound to benefit most from the anti-Excise backlash. Over two hundred tory candidates stood, and the party cheerfully contested such whig strongholds as Sussex, Norwich, and Northumberland, failing only by some 350, 130, and 40 votes respectively. At Norfolk, Yorkshire, Hampshire, Leicestershire, Rutland, Cheshire, and Worcestershire the tories gained one seat; at Gloucestershire they gained two. Of the eleven borough seats the tories won from the government, all had more than 250 voters; eight had more than 500. The tories returned to Westminster with 150 M.P.s. Concentrated in the smaller boroughs where the Excise had minimal electoral effect and where the Treasury could facilitate their defeat, the Patriots returned from the election with their numbers diminished. Twenty-two had retired from their seats, not all of them voluntarily: Lord Mountrath had been dropped from Castle Rising because its patron was pro-administration. Ten Patriots had been defeated. Edward Vernon was beaten at Penryn through the exertions of Richard Edgcumbe, Walpole's new manager in Cornwall; Sir James and John Dalrymple and Thomas Erskine lost their small and susceptible Scottish burghs to stronger ministerialist candidates.[46]

Government journalists made it crystal-clear to the Patriots that they had been duped. What had their 'Servile Compliance in flattering the Tories' achieved, inquired the *Free Briton*, other than jeopardising 'the Whig-Interest'? 'Our Patriots boast, that...the Counties are with them', sneered the *London Journal* on the election results, 'that is, with the Tories, for *they* have not above Six.' The new electoral vocabulary abounded with opportunities for Patriot-baiting. The *Daily Gazetteer* reprinted the *London Evening Post*'s glowing report of the tory victory at Exeter's mayoral election: 'The Whigs have the Mortification to see, that as long as the Country Interest is joined by that of the City, their Endeavours will always have the same Cast', and commented,

This paragraph is worthy to be written in Letters of Gold for the Perusal of *all the Whigs* in the Kingdom. Here they are plainly and truly told, that the *Country Interest* is a Faction formed in Opposition to them, their *Principles and Interest*; that the Success of this *Country Interest* is always to be the Mortification of the *Whigs*.[47]

While the government's post-electoral propaganda corroded the opposition's sense of common purpose, the rigged election of Scotland's representative peers depleted its strength in the House of Lords. This was particularly damaging as harmony between the two components of the opposition was far more pronounced in the Upper House than in the Commons. The tory peers were comparatively few in number, distinctly limited in parliamentary talent, and usually willing to acquiesce in Patriot direction. Their complacency owed much to the tory origins or marital connections of many of the leading Patriot peers – Carteret, Bedford, Winchilsea, and Somerset. In the eighteen significant divisions which occurred in the Lords during the first four months of 1734, the ministry had seen its majority fall to an average of twenty-five; on five occasions it had fallen below twelve. This attrition reflected defections over the Excise Bill and the organisational efforts of the Rumpsteak Club which included some moderate tories as well as all the dissident whig peers.[48] By 1735 the club was in disarray. By 1735, too, Lord Islay had been able to use the Scottish elections to exclude two very able opposition spokesmen, Lords Marchmont and Stair, and to replace them and any other recalcitrant Scot with ministerial nominees. In the eighteen Lords divisions held in the first session of the new Parliament, Walpole secured a comfortable average majority of thirty-eight. Frustration at the ministry's apparent invulnerability in both Houses only exacerbated the opposition's dissolution: its leaders were 'tearing one another to pieces', Lord Hervey gloated early in 1735, 'dividing a reversion...which all of them covet and perhaps none of them will ever possess'.[49]

The rot had begun with Carteret. He had been repelled by the demotic jargon of the Excise campaign and by its gift to the opposition of the former Lord Steward of the Household, Lord Chesterfield – a showy, clever, and fundamentally lightweight politician, who seemed nonetheless to threaten Carteret's position as the Patriots' most notable spokesman in the Lords. In the spring of 1735 Wyndham summoned a meeting of Patriot and tory peers to put them on their guard against Carteret's manoeuvres. On his own, Wyndham could do little to avert the coalition's disjunction in the Commons. Pulteney was feeling the strain of his subsidies to the opposition's propaganda and intelligence network (one of the reasons, perhaps, why Bolingbroke had accepted French money for this purpose in 1733). The death in 1734 of his political secretary and man of business, the St Albans M.P. John Merrill, and his own neurosis only compounded Pulteney's post-electoral malaise: his sense of political futility and sensitivity to Patriot accusations that the coalition had paid dividends only to the tory party. In the summer of 1735 he made some half-hearted approaches to the ministry and spent most of 1736 in Holland, where Horatio Walpole was to encounter him, more 'dead-hearted than sick in body'.[50]

Bolingbroke was a more equivocal loss. The contortions of his earlier career had too often served to smear the opposition at Westminster and outside. During the election, 'No Bolingbroke, No Pretender' had been one of the most common counter-slogans to the ubiquitous 'No Excise'. Had Walpole been fully informed of Bolingbroke's French pension and his fatuous intrigues with the French Ambassador he could have played the Atterbury game again, and frightened many errant whigs back into orthodox voting. Bolingbroke's retirement to France in 1735 prevented such an exposure, but it also cost the coalition its busiest, if increasingly disillusioned, intermediary and the prime advocate of a common Country platform.[51]

Even if Pulteney and Bolingbroke had remained politically active and in England, it is doubtful whether they could have prevented Dissent from wrecking the opposition. Precisely because of their declamations against Walpole's adulteration of whiggism – and the minister's alliance with Bishop Gibson and frigidity towards nonconformist demands were part of that process – many Patriots were assertive in their anti-clericalism and commitment to a wider toleration. Some of them, like Lord Carlisle, had been 'ever a sure friend' to the Quakers; others had been in contact with the Dissenting Deputies since their inception in 1732. After 1734 the Patriots may also have felt – though with how much justification is not clear – that their association with the tories had alienated their dissenting constituents and contributed to their limited electoral achievement. The desire to redeem themselves (and perhaps to spite their more successful tory allies) did not affect all dissident whigs to the same degree. When Walter Plumer and Sir Wilfred Lawson moved to repeal the Test Act on 12 March 1736, one newspaper estimated that only twenty of their Patriot colleagues supported them.[52]

The Quaker Tithe and Mortmain Bills were however less extensive measures. Since they were aimed primarily at the Church of England's secular influence, they were also far more likely to attract ministerial and Patriot whig support. Sir William Wyndham tried hard to avert disaster. Knowing that it was the Tithe Bill's assault on the ecclesiastical courts which most aroused tory fury and Patriot complacency, he asked the bill's promoter, the ministerialist William Glanville, to include a clause safeguarding the courts' authority. Glanville's Quaker friends vetoed the amendment, and, with the tories almost isolated in opposition, the bill passed the Commons. In the House of Lords it was defeated; but it was only defeated because most of the ministerial whigs and fifteen bishops voted with the tory peers; the leading Patriots – Carteret, Chesterfield, Cobham, and Winchilsea – all voted in its support. Sir Joseph Jekyll's Mortmain Bill passed both Houses with all the ease of a measure backed by all sectors of the whig party.[53]

The events of 1736 revived tory political introversion. Some tories began to show renewed enthusiasm for the Pretender. Many more stayed away from Parliament or adopted an irresponsible if not virulent attitude towards their whig allies. Sir John Barnard's bill of 1737 to reduce the interest on the National Debt to 3 per cent won tory support as a blow to the City financiers and as a means to ease taxation. But when the bill was debated many tories were absent, and a few, like Edmund Lechmere, M.P. for Worcestershire, contributed to its defeat out of sheer perversity. 'On Friday the 3 per cent Bill will certainly be brought in', he had written to his wife, 'and I am in hopes now t'will not succeed, which will be a prodigious baulk to the worthy Patriots.'[54]

Even Wyndham was not immune to tory accidie. On 22 February 1737 Pulteney moved that Frederick, Prince of Wales, should receive an increased grant of £100 000 *per annum*. Forty-five tory M.P.s absented themselves from the division and the proposal was defeated by 234 votes to 204. It was not Jacobitism which had motivated the tory defaulters. Shippen had been only too happy to support Pulteney's initiative and divide the Hanoverian Royal Family. It was rather that they distrusted Frederick, and regarded the motion as an affront to the King. And for personal as well as tactical reasons, Wyndham for once was in no mind to lobby his M.P.s into obedience. Exasperated by Pulteney's instability, in poor health himself, and distracted by the illness of his daughter, the tory leader could be persuaded to attend the debate only by last-minute messages from his tory friends, and then only late in the afternoon.[55] Despite persistent nagging from Bolingbroke, Wyndham was not to be reconciled to collaboration with Frederick until the autumn of 1738, and for good reason. He must have remembered his friend Lord Bathurst's doting attendance on Prince George in the two years before his accession, and his and the tory party's disillusionment in 1727. ('Bathurst laments the truth the Psalmist sings', the opposition's pet poet, Alexander Pope, had written on that occasion, 'And finds that Princes are the Sons of Kings.') Not surprisingly the tory leader wanted some assurance that Frederick's opposition investment was a serious one and that his political attitudes differed from those of the current administration. In January 1738 he asked the Prince to order his servants in the Commons to support a reduction in the Army. Like his father twenty years before, Frederick refused to make concessions on the military. Tory isolationists reacted by converting the Army debate of 3 February into an indictment of the tergiversation practised by ministerial, Patriot, and Leicester House whigs alike. 'The Tories have always opposed this grievance', declared Shippen of standing armies, and, with an eye to Walpole, Pulteney, and the Prince in the gallery, 'Can some gentlemen, Sir, who affect to call themselves

Whigs, boast of such an uniformity of Conduct? Can they say that time and circumstances never influenced the measures they pursued? Or that when they were in posts, they always acted in consequence of the principles they professed when they were out?'[56]

This kind of partisan self-congratulation was palatable enough, but its logic left the tories stranded and out of power. Wyndham ultimately had to have recourse to the Prince, not only because of the M.P.s and borough patronage he could contribute to the opposition, but also because of his more specific advantages for the tory party. As Lord Hardwicke reasoned, once Frederick had committed himself to the opposition, the Patriots would be deterred from quitting their allies 'lest it should throw the successor wholly into the hands of the Tories, and make their cause desperate when he comes to the possession'. Bolingbroke's hope that Frederick would provide 'a centre of union' for the opposition, 'a superior authority amongst yourselves; under whose influence men of different characters, and different views will be brought to draw together', was less pertinent. Frederick was an empty space. Vacillating in his politics and resolution, and limited in intelligence, he supplied the premier oppositionists – Chesterfield, Cobham, Pulteney, and Wyndham – with yet another cause for contention as they all strove to dominate him. By late 1739 the tory leader was generally regarded as having emerged the victor.[57]

The Prince's uncertain allegiance was only one of several external factors which contributed more to the opposition's final and limited success than did its parliamentary campaign. Far more important were the outbreak of the war with Spain, and a slight but perceptible blurring of Walpole's, political grip and parliamentary vigilance.

The extent to which Walpole's decline was predetermined by 1734 should not be over-stressed. His majority had been reduced, but so too had the opposition's effectiveness. The death of Queen Caroline in 1737 did not in fact weaken the Minister at Court; it rather increased the King's dependence on him. Walpole's attraction for young and careerist whigs was of course likely to diminish with age, but as long as he retained royal favour and the loyalty of professional politicians like Hardwicke, Pelham, and Newcastle his appeal to the ambitious was still a potent one. The gradual erosion of his control may thus have owed as much to his own over-confidence and fatigue as to his administration's longevity and changing political circumstances. Between 1732 and 1735 he had parried the *Craftsman*'s attack by an expensive press campaign. When the opposition slumped, so too did Walpole's subsidies to the government press, and even after 1739 they never returned to the level of the early 1730s.[58] In 1737 and 1738 it was noted how ministerial nominees on several parliamentary committees were both lax in their attendance and allowed by the Minister to be so. The same period witnessed a decline in the parliamentary attendance of government peers. Attuned to success and having survived the Excise furore, the components of Old Corps whiggery relaxed; as they did so, the opposition began to recover momentum.[59]

Wyndham's association with the Prince had brought him into contact with two members of his household, George Lyttelton and William Pitt, as well as with their self-proclaimed mentor, Lord Cobham. Cobham's group corresponded with Lord Chesterfield and with the Scottish Patriots – Lords Stair and Marchmont and Marchmont's two sons, the M.P.s Lord Polwarth and Alexander Hume Campbell – all known to Boling-broke and consequently recommended to Wyndham's attention. Linked by friendship, and by suspicion of Pulteney and Carteret, this coterie was able to refurbish the opposition's organisation and supply it with a more appropriate rationale.[60] In correspondence and pamphlets, in the news-papers *Common Sense* and the *Champion*, the leaders of this 'New Opposition', as Pope was to describe it in 1738, '(or rather the old one reviv'd)', proclaimed their attachment to Broad-Bottom principles. The name was perhaps impolitic, but not the doctrine. In contrast with Bolingbroke's 'Country' analysis, the Broad-Bottom programme tacitly recognised the survival of binary party distinctions. Its exponents con-demned any individual or single party's admission to government, advocated a clean sweep of Walpolian men and measures, and insisted that both of the opposition's two main constituent groups be given a share of employments. Broad-Bottom has been described as 'anti-party', and so it was in that it postulated a comprehensive administration as the future ideal. Its immediate appeal in the late 1730s was that it promised to satisfy the separate ambitions of tories and Patriot whigs.[61]

Equipped with a revivified leadership and with the prospect that its participants' ambitions might be appeased, the opposition was able to appear united on the need for war with Spain. Initially the tory response had been variegated. The mercantile lobbies of London and Bristol had too much to gain from illicit colonial trade and too much to lose from Spanish privateering to allow their tory M.P.s to be pacific. In November 1739 Wiltshire, Gloucestershire, and Somerset tories were to assemble at a Steadfast Society meeting to raise money for the defence of Bristol's Merchant Venturers: '£5250 was subscribed in ¼ hour...Mr. Berkeley [to be elected tory M.P. for Gloucestershire in 1741] subscribed £500.' The tory M.P. for Cardiff, Herbert Mackworth, who sold his coal to London, welcomed the prospect of European war because his Newcastle upon Tyne competitors would have to run the gauntlet of enemy privateers on the long sail to Plymouth. The coal-owning and equally tory M.P. for Newcastle, Walter Blackett, was predictably more diffident. Some of the less interested and more conventional tories, like George Wrighte, M.P. for Leicester, could see no reason why Britain should be dragged into an expensive war for the vested interests of the whig-dominated South Sea Company. 'If we could obtain by peaceable means, the utmost we could expect by Force of Arms', he told the House in May 1738, when he opposed a bellicose motion from Pulteney, 'No Man of common Prudence, unless he had some other View than that of the Good of his Country, would advise us to provoke the Kingdom of Spain to a War.' By 8 March 1739 Wrighte, together with Blackett, Mackworth, and every other tory M.P. present (there were only fourteen missing, and two of these had taken care to pair with ministerial whigs), had been persuaded to vote against the ministry's Convention Treaty with Spain.[62]

The tories were joined by 102 whigs and together they reduced Walpole's majority to twenty-eight. The following day Wyndham, in what one M.P. considered 'the most solemn speech I ever heard in Parliament', announced that the opposition would secede from the Commons where 'the sentiments of the Majority were against the Sentiments of every other man in the nation; who must conclude that Majority to be a Faction under an undue Influence'. The idea of a secession was not new. The opposition had considered staging one in 1732; Wyndham and many other tory M.P.s had actually boycotted the House at the end of 1723 and through most of the 1724 session as a protest at Atterbury's exile.[63] The 1739 secession was intended to be a much more positive manoeuvre. Egmont told Lord Bathurst that the opposition was only letting Walpole off: 'The minority do in this like a greyhound that has coursed a hare till he is ready to chop her up, stops short, and lets her go'; but this presupposed that the erosion of the ministry would have continued and that opposition pressure could have been maintained. Walpole had certainly been damaged by the defection of the Prince and the duke of Argyll, but his position was still strong. In the Commons debate on the Army in February 1739 he had secured a majority of seventy – a slightly higher figure than in the equivalent division in 1735 and the same margin as he had obtained in the Army debate of 1732. The Convention vote had been a classic parliamentary emergency and the aftermaths of those comparable episodes, the Dunkirk and Excise crises, suggested that while the government would be able to recover much of its credibility and support, the opposition would see its adherents' morale and attendance wane.[64]

Seceding after defeat pre-empted individual absenteeism and was intended to jolt the extra-parliamentary nation: 'to destroy this fallacy, that the voice of the House of Commons is the sense of the nation'. How the opposition leaders expected the constituencies to react to this revelation is not clear. According to some ministerialists, they expected popular alienation from a manifestly unrepresentative Parliament to lead to revolution on behalf of the Pretender, or, more plausibly, the Prince of Wales, who had voted against the Convention in the House of Lords. It would seem more likely that they intended the constituencies to petition the King for a general election and that it was this design which made the secession such a fiasco.[65]

Whig and tory dissidents had frequently disagreed on the desirability of genuflections to extra-parliamentary opinion. In December 1731, when the *Craftsman*'s printer, Franklin, was on trial, Wyndham had been appalled by the tameness of most of the printer's opposition advisers:

Not one of his Councell had spirit enough to enter into the merits of the Cause (except Mr. Noel [tory M.P. for Stamford] who spoke extremely well) but bandied about the little shifts & quirks of the law. The determination of this cause must as stop [sic] to the liberty of the press as an act of parliament for that purpose could.

In 1737 Edward Harley noted how the 'Patriots in both Houses' had demanded harsh measures against the Porteous rioters in Edinburgh 'in hopes to ruin Sir R. Walpole with the Scotch'. The tories had opposed such repressive action even though they may have approved the ulterior motive. In 1738 Wyndham had vindicated and Pulteney had opposed the printing of parliamentary debates. In March 1739 Wyndham wanted the secession to be supplemented by a plethora of pamphlets, petitions, and Instructions, and this was precisely what ministerialists like Horatio Walpole predicted: 'inflammatory papers...dispersed all over the Kingdom'. By June the opposition had still to issue a manifesto. Pulteney had promised one of his very able pamphlets but failed to produce it: 'He could not take on himself', he told Lord Polwarth, 'to venture to give advice to the people what was proper...As to the Instructions themselves, he thought it were better quietly to return next year.'[66] By the time Wyndham himself had produced an apologia, his tone could only be defensive. About half of the 160-odd seceders had already returned to their parliamentary duty. This was partly because of the demands of local legislation, but primarily because the absentees had been allowed to appear as irresponsible truants. All that Wyndham could do was suggest that the opposition seek belatedly to legitimise its behaviour in print, and prepare for its return to Westminster by a succession of constituency Instructions. Pulteney promptly dissociated his own constituency of Middlessex and the Patriots from the campaign: if Wyndham wanted Instructions, he and the tories could organise them.[67]

On 1 October the London tories, followed by those of Bristol, Leicester, Nottingham, Salisbury, York, and Bridgwater (the latter borough represented by Wyndham's son), obediently submitted Instructions to their M.P.s. Wyndham told Pulteney that he regarded this as the first instalment of the election campaign, and that unless the Patriot leaders joined him in harrying Walpole he would initiate another secession '& by this means', reported a government whig, 'add fresh fuel to the fire they have already kindled & so by repeated clamours inflame the discontent against the administration & prepare the peoples' inclination for the next general election'.[68] Pulteney's response was scarcely reassuring. Disturbed by Wyndham's capture of the Prince of Wales, he inaugurated the new session by applauding the speech from the throne. 'The Tories are heartily angry with Mr. Pulteney', gloated one of Walpole's Welsh supporters; '. . . I hope he despises their anger as much as he dislikes their principles.' Pulteney had no intention of breaking with the opposition at this stage, only of reminding Wyndham of his indispensability to its success. By Christmas the two men had at least come to an understanding on the need to exploit foreign policy disagreements within the Cabinet by concentrating their attack on Walpole and not merely on the measures of his administration. How this was to be done was more difficult: 'Some were for always using the word Minister in the singular number in both Houses; & making it as familiar to name him there as in Print or in Private Conversation, & after laying that foundation to follow the precedent of the Duke of Buckingham's Case in King Charles the 1st reign and impeach him on Common Fame.' In view of what was to happen in February 1741, it is significant that early in 1740 both Wyndham and Pulteney argued that there could be no effective parliamentary indictment of Walpole 'without some particular charge'.[69]

Having reached this tenuous policy consensus, the leadership turned its attention to the opposition's morale and attendance, which had still to recover from the secession. On 1 February 1740 Pulteney moved for a Call of the House. The following day Wyndham held a meeting of oppositionists from both Houses at the Crown and Anchor Tavern. With the Patriot Lord Carlisle in the chair, Wyndham expounded on parliamentary and electoral strategy, asked for his audience's suggestions for future parliamentary initiatives, and appealed for full and regular attendance. The meeting was a seminal one in opposition organisation. Wyndham's death in June 1740 was to be a setback, for, as Chesterfield wrote, no other opposition politician commanded the same multilateral respect, but in December 1741 and early 1742 it was to be frequent assemblies of this kind, held at the Crown and Anchor or the Fountain Tavern, which helped to ensure opposition union in the final assault on

Walpole. By 1743 tory M.P.s and the remaining dissident whigs had formalised the device and over 120 of them were meeting regularly as 'The British Club' at the Thatched House Tavern.[70]

On 21 February 1741 the opposition acted on its decision to isolate Walpole. Pulteney moved for an Address to the King, asking that all papers on the Convention of Pardo be made available for parliamentary inspection. When Sir Robert rose to defend the treaty, Wyndham, who had seconded the motion, pounced: 'He could not apply this Question solely to himself without assuming the Supremacy of Power & owning that he did everything in the Ministry.' Walpole was not so easily caught and secured 249 votes to the opposition's 196. His destruction would clearly require a long campaign of continuous parliamentary pressure – the most difficult strategy for a composite opposition to implement. It was made more arduous by developments within the tory party. Its few Jacobite M.P.s had become progressively more disgruntled at Wyndham's attachment to the Prince of Wales and, at the same time, more optimistic that France would enter the war against Britain and support a Stuart invasion. Jacobite optimism seldom did any harm, but in 1740 the cause recruited a committed if elderly tory in Lord Barrymore, M.P. for Wigan. Early that same year an Irish Jacobite agent, Colonel Brett, arrived in England to sound out tory opinion. He found Shippen 'weak upon the prospect of real business' and Sir John Hynde Cotton doubting 'or seem[ing] to doubt of others', but he still felt able to assure the Pretender in March that his English supporters would join any French invasion on his behalf. Barrymore agreed to go to Paris to consult with Cardinal Fleury. Before he could do so, Wyndham himself had left for France, determined to see both Fleury and Bolingbroke and neutralise this Jacobite initiative before it could prejudice tory unity and compromise the constitutional opposition to Walpole.[71]

For the tories, their leader's death in June was a disaster. Despite Speaker Onslow's prediction, it is unlikely that Wyndham would have gone over to the whigs after Walpole's fall.[72] He was too much a product of the tory ambiance of Somerset and Christ Church, Oxford, and, more substantially, his influence in Parliament and over the Prince of Wales would have given him sufficient leverage to obtain high office without having to purchase it by defection. Once employed he could have pressed for concessions for the tories – much as his less gifted friend Lord Gower was to try to do before 1745. Wyndham's death meant that there was no tory leader available in 1742 who could counter Pulteney's intrigues on behalf of his Patriot cronies. More immediately, it meant that tory M.P.s were left exposed to Barrymore's lobbying, particularly as Barrymore's close friend, the semi-Jacobite Sir Watkin Williams Wynn, was now able to exert much greater influence within the tory party. Neither Wynn nor his ally Sir John Hynde Cotton possessed Wyndham's personal and political acceptability amongst the opposition whig elite, and in the autumn of 1740 the Patriot leaders tended to go their own way. They had a new, whig, and prestigious figurehead in the duke of Argyll, and with Wyndham dead the Prince of Wales was more than ever vacant and exploitable. It was this reduction of contact and policy discussion between the Patriot and tory dissidents which lay at the root of the abortive motion of February 1741.

On 13 February Sandys and his fellow Patriot Lord Limerick moved that the King be asked to remove Walpole. They were defeated by 290 votes to 106. Sixteen tories voted in Walpole's support and thirty-seven abstained; twenty-five dissident whigs also walked out before the division or voted with the majority.[73] Whig participation in this rebellion should be a warning against the frequent assumption that it was engineered by William Shippen. The most active Jacobite–tory M.P.s, Wynn and Barrymore, stayed on to vote against Walpole. It was rather the county tories who formed the bulk of what *Common Sense* called the 'Sneakers': Thomas Prowse, Wyndham's successor at Somerset, Edward Harley of Herefordshire, and the M.P.s for Warwickshire, Leicestershire, Worcestershire, and Norfolk. Like some of their equivalents amongst the Patriot defectors – for example Robert Vyner and George Bowes – these men objected to the motion because they considered it unjust; unlike the whig M.P.s, the tory dissidents were also concerned at the challenge to the royal prerogative; most of all, they were angry that the Patriot leadership should have resorted to such an extreme tactic without making any effort to sound out tory opinion. Since tory disarray over the motion was primarily a protest aimed at the Patriots, it did not cause a serious split within the party. Edward Harley's co-Member, Velters Cornewall, voted for Walpole's removal, but he was only mildly irritated by his colleague's high-minded abstention: 'Your neighbour who has been longer in Parliament & had been a eye witness to more of his [Walpole's] iniquitous doings had not any qualm about it & so voted with ye minority, which had been much larger but that Sandys & Lyttelton & Lord Limerick who headed ye affair, want popularity & kept it too secret.' He went on to instruct his friends in Herefordshire to quash any rumour of a split in the tory ranks at the forthcoming county election.[74]

While the tories were able to absorb this incident, their behaviour served as a warning to the Patriot leadership. 'Perhaps', wrote one pamphleteer, 'they were glad of an Opportunity to show the Whigs how little importance they were in the House...when they stood by themselves.' Such an object-lesson was scarcely conducive to goodwill or electoral co-operation. In 1741 there was an attempt to set up an opposition committee to supervise the election campaign, but party proprietorial sentiment was far more in evidence than in 1734. When the duke of Beaufort was asked for his interest on behalf of the opposition whig candidates at Weymouth and Melcombe Regis, he was quite unmoved by the argument that this was 'not a contest of party' but rather 'between the independent country interest and ministerial nomination'. He stolidly replied that he would lend his support only if one of the candidates selected was a tory.[75] Weymouth's patron, George Bubb Dodington, was just as partisan. Having been vetoed as a candidate for Wells by the Somerset tories, he came to an agreement with the government candidate at Bridgwater whereby they were both returned at the expense of the tory Sir Charles Wyndham. Lord Bruce again involved himself in the tory campaign in Yorkshire, only this time he complained to Lord Gower of the lack of co-operation he encountered from ostensibly Patriot peers like Lords Burlington and Leeds. Pulteney himself, despite his Yorkshire acreage and political status, refused to donate more than £50 to the opposition's county election fund. Lord Gower promptly wrote to him threatening the withdrawal of tory support at Middlesex. To Bruce, Gower outlined his own cautious attitude towards the coalition:

I agree with you in thinking that Any of our *Allies* that upon any pretence support a person in the Court Interest do exceedingly wrong & are no ways entitled to any assistance from our *friends*...but I cannot think we should look upon the misbehaviour of some particular persons as a breach of the Coalition. I have for some time thought...that some of our Allies act upon disinterested National principles & others only with self interested views, & am of opinion we should attach ourselves closely to the first & keep a watchful eye upon the last.[76]

Enough tory and Patriot politicians agreed with Gower's muted and realistic insistence on qualified co-operation between the two party groups to prevent a complete breakdown of joint electoral activity. The tory Charles Edwin stood for Westminster, first in partnership with Admiral Edward Vernon, and then with Viscount Perceval. Sir Charles Wyndham had planned to offer himself as a second tory candidate for the City, but to prevent such a public display of opposition disjunction the tory earl of Thanet offered to accommodate Wyndham in the seat he controlled at Appleby. Perceval and Edwin were eventually to win the City with the aid of a campaign fund raised by Patriots, by the Prince of Wales, and by a bevy of tory M.P.s including Velters Cornewall, Richard Lowndes, Richard Lyster and Sir Hugh Smithson.[77]

The general election returned 135 tories to Westminster. An unknown oppositionist calculated that Patriot and tory M.P.s together accounted for 266 Members, leaving Sir Robert with a majority of just twenty-six. This same obviously well-informed observer noted that there were eighteen ministerial whigs who had already wavered in their loyalty towards Walpole, and who were likely to defect if the opposition showed itself buoyant in the coming session.[78] Attendance on both sides turned out to be impressive. On the first day of the session 514 M.P.s appeared to take the oaths. Fifteen days later, on 16 December, 242 oppositionists, including all but eleven of the tory contingent, were present to vote for their candidate, Dr George Lee, as chairman of the Committee of Privileges and Elections. They won by a majority of four. 'This happy omen', carolled one of Shippen's friends, 'makes drooping Britain raise her head... & presages greater success.' He was right; but in view of the apparent chaos eleven months before, how had an opposition performance of this quality been engineered?[79]

Eveline Cruickshanks has given the credit to James Stuart. The opposition's new-found cohesion was supplied, she suggests, 'by a letter of 27 Sept. n.s. 1741 from the Pretender to Colonel William Cecil, his chief agent in England, strongly recommending "to all those with you who wish me well that they should pursue vigorous and unanimous measures in the next session of Parliament"'. This document had reportedly been obtained by Lord Chesterfield, and a hundred copies are said to have been distributed to sympathetic M.P.s in November 1741. There is little reason to doubt that some copies were so circulated; it is very likely that some tory–Jacobite and some Patriot–Jacobite M.P.s (like the Hon. James Erskine, M.P. for Stirling Burghs) were susceptible to their content. But, as with the Dunkirk crisis of 1730, it would be unwise to account for a complex and long-term political development by a single piece of Stuart evidence. The apparent atomisation of the opposition in the February 1741 motion almost certainly impressed Walpole too much. It was symptomatic of a prior deterioration in tory–Patriot communication rather than the precipitant of a coalition breakdown. And, as I have stressed, it had not been the Jacobites who had refused to vote with the Patriots for Walpole's removal but solid Hanoverian tories of some status and ability, who were likely to require rather more than a belated letter from the Pretender if they were to trust and work properly with their whig allies.[80]

Most of the work of repairing the opposition had in fact been completed by the time James' message arrived in England. Between July and October 1741 William Pulteney had journeyed through England and North Wales, organising a series of meetings in various country houses for local tories and opposition whigs. In October he and William Shippen had visited Sir Watkin Williams Wynn and other Welsh tory M.P.s in

Denbighshire; he had then gone on to hold a meeting of Lancashire oppositionists at the Liverpool house of Thomas Bootle, Chancellor to the Prince of Wales. At these meetings Pulteney urged the necessity of a final effort against Walpole, and he also assured the tory participants that the Minister's demise would be succeeded by political reform and the construction of a broadly based administration. The lesson of February 1741 had done its work, and the Patriots finally acknowledged that since many tories were as ambitious as they, their votes had to be purchased and not assumed: as Dodington wryly conceded, 'What man, or body of men, will act with another to be made professedly the scaffolding of his fortune, and then swept away with the rest of the rubbish?' It was largely due to Patriot assurances that they would not be so exploited, seconded as they were by the Prince of Wales, that the tories turned up to vote in such numbers and with such partisan unanimity in December 1741 and January 1742.[81]

On 4 February 1742 a jubilant Patriot M.P. reported Walpole's resignation and its immediate cause:

The Union of Parties has been more than the Work of Man...Those that were call'd Tories (for I thank God we are losing all Party Distinctions) have behav'd in a manner so noble, so just, that it must do them everlasting Honour. Their Country owes its safety...to their behaviour & I doubt not but they will meet with the Honour they deserve.[82]

Those M.P.s and peers who were not only called tories, but who also still regarded themselves as such, now awaited their reward.

Even in its own century, the tactics and duration of the anti-Walpolian confederation and the quality and rhetorical glamour of some of its exponents acquired an almost epic reputation. The Rockinghamite whigs consciously emulated much of its press strategy; they and their radical allies also assembled at the Thatched House Tavern; in 1772 various Rockinghamites advocated a secession in the manner of 1739, and in 1776-7 they implemented one. Yet what might equally have impressed the opponents of Lord North and Pitt the Younger was the confederation's demonstration of how difficult it was to overthrow, through formal or informal political means, an efficient administration possessed of royal support.

The crown can never fail of a majority in both houses of parliament; he makes them all in one house, and he chooses above half in the other. Four and twenty bishops and sixteen *Scotch* lords, is a terrible weight in one; forty-five from one country, besides the west of *England*, and all the government boroughs, is a dreadful number in the other. Were his majesty inclined

to-morrow to declare his body coachman his first minister, it would be just
as well...the coachman knows how to feed his cattle, and the other [Walpole]
feeds the beasts in service, and this is all the skill that is necessary in either
case.[83]

Much of this is hyperbole and the whole was composed in the bleak year
of 1735. Yet the fact that every eighteenth-century British administration
– provided that its leader was politically gifted, experienced, and acceptable to the monarch – survived until that leader was physically worn out
or dead suggests that William Pulteney's verdict was more than just
opposition spleen.

John Owen has stressed the considerable insecurity of Walpole's
parliamentary majority, pointing out that only 27 per cent of all M.P.s
were ministerial dependents and that the voting behaviour of even these
individuals could fluctuate, and arguing that the Minister could survive
only by retaining the allegiance of the 'independent' M.P.s. This de-
valuation of ministerial control is a useful corrective to the *Craftsman*'s
diatribes but is almost as misleading. Even if one accepts Owen's rather
narrow definition of what constitutes patronage, the ministry's ability
to influence 27 per cent of the Commons was no mean guarantee of its
stability, given that, as P. D. G. Thomas has remarked, an attendance
rate of three hundred M.P.s (54 per cent) was exceptional. Their peculiar
need to please their royal or ministerial paymaster by parliamentary
assiduity and, in some cases, their obligatory residence in London meant
that placemen in both Houses tended always to exert political weight
quite disproportionate to their number.[84]

And if not a many-splendoured thing, patronage took many forms.
The division list published by the opposition for the vote on the Convention in March 1739 is a partisan document but a fairly well-researched
one. It claimed that of the 260 M.P.s who voted with the ministry 184
were in direct or vicarious enjoyment of sinecures, places, or govern-
ment-bestowed privilege. Owen argues that such perks 'were the *result*
rather than the *cause* of...allegiance to the Administration; rewards
for past services, rather than bribes for future subservience'. Since the
continuity of individual need or ambition, and therefore of obligation
to the man or institution that can answer that need, is the *raison d'être*
of every patronage system, such a distinction is bogus. In 1733 Adolphus
Oughton, government M.P. for Coventry, was already a Colonel of
the Guards, but since he wanted further advancement either as Governor
of Minorca (which was not granted) or as Brigadier-General (which was
in 1735), his good conduct during the Excise Crisis was assured: 'on
m'a mis le marché en mains', he wrote, 'and if I do not vote for the
wine bill at least...I must renounce all hopes and thoughts of any

present or future recompense'. Patronage tended only to lose its efficacy when an administration seemed about to lose control of patronage: hence the defection or deliberate absenteeism of several army M.P.s and parliamentary placemen in December 1741 and January 1742. And as Owen makes clear, it was these betrayals and the earlier loss of the Cornish and Scottish boroughs controlled by Frederick and Argyll which finally cost Walpole his majority, *not* a mass exodus of 'independent' M.P.s to the opposition. Such an exodus would scarcely have been to the opposition's profit, since there were of course hardly any independent M.P.s in the Walpolian House of Commons.[85]

In 1741 Lord Egmont compiled a list of the M.P.s who had sat in the 1734–41 Parliament, classifying all but eight Members as being either for or against 'Court Measures'. He identified 372 M.P.s as being pro-administration during this period; in the case of 357 – all of them whig – this identification was correct. A few of these 357 were to go into opposition with Frederick or Argyll before the Parliament ended. But prior to their defection neither these M.P.s nor the majority of their associates seem to have been independent. Only forty-eight are known to have deviated from the ministerial line in the 1730s; only twelve are known to have done so on more than one occasion.[86] True, individual voting behaviour in most Commons divisions has gone unrecorded, but it is probable that the extant division lists and reports give an exaggerated impression of erratic voting amongst government whigs. Because of residual whig purism or fears of an electoral backlash, it was inevitable that some normally pliant M.P.s would leave the ministry over the more dramatic issues which were the stuff of newspaper reports and division lists – the Excise Bill, Place Bills and the repeal of the Test Act. Even that most obedient and pro-Walpolian of civil servants, the Lyme Regis M.P. John Scrope, broke with the government and voted for the repeal of the Test Act in 1736, having pledged himself to do so at his election two years earlier. But since most parliamentary business was not of this contentious variety, Scrope and his peers had usually little difficulty in reconciling conscience and convenience in the government's division lobby. Had this not been the case, Sir Robert Walpole would not have known which whig M.P.s to invite to his regular Cockpit meetings (nor would the bulk of them have attended), and he would not have been able to gauge his majority as confidently as he did in 1734. In twenty-one divisions held between January and April of that year he estimated that the ministry's highest turn-out was 294, its lowest 284: 'Majority at a medium about 87'.[87]

And as Walpole's frequent and successful appeals to whig proprietorial sentiment make clear, and as Edmund Burke recognised, in the first half of the eighteenth century patronage, as a cement of government, was supplemented by 'party attachments'. For one ministerialist like Oughton, kept in line by apprehension, there was another like that 'incorrigible whig', the M.P. for Aldeburgh, William Conolly. 'Neither the outcry against the excise, standing army etc., could change my thought', he wrote in 1734, 'without the hope of place or pension, which is attributed to be the only excuse of people's steadiness at this time.'[88] Conolly might not have been able to define his whiggism, but it meant that he was as responsive to Walpole's unimpeachably whig background as he was to the Minister's undeniably efficient government. Walpole flourished for so long not because he attracted the independent Members, but rather because so many M.P.s were clients of his administration, and/or attached to that conventional brand of whiggism which abhorred collusion with tories. Of course Walpole's remarkable parliamentary skills reinforced his position, but if his regime really had depended on his personal rapport with independent M.P.s the political situation after his fall would have been fluid in the extreme and probably fatal to Old Corps primacy. As it was, the Old Corps' retention of the King and of patronage, and its recourse to the standard tactic of appealing to whig identity and self-interest against tory pretensions, ensured tory desolation in 1742.

Their participation in the anti-Walpolian confederation, coinciding as it did with the peak of Sir William Wyndham's ability as a parliamentary leader, did much for the tories. Individual Patriots and their occasional whig extremism had been repugnant, but the possession of whig allies for over a decade had ensured that the party had a chance of a parliamentary majority or at the very least of giving the administration a run for its money. The need to co-ordinate its parliamentary activity with the Patriots had placed novel and constructive strains on tory organisation. By 1741 the party was producing not only bloc voting but also an attendance rate which could top 90 per cent. Coalition had not, however, bred tory–Patriot integration. Lord Gower had been constantly exposed both to Bolingbroke's polemics and to the tactical moderation of Wyndham, yet in 1741 he still instinctively distinguished between 'friends' like Lord Bruce, who happened to be a tory, and an 'ally' like Pulteney, who was not. Both the tories' enduring distinction and their alarming capacity for parliamentary efficiency encouraged the more careerist Patriots to come to terms with their fellow whigs in office in 1742.

The circumstances of their betrayal shaped the tories' political behaviour and attitudes for the next two decades. Disillusionment with junketings at Westminster tempted some tories into less conventional politics: a few placed renewed emphasis on intrigues with the Pretender;

many more experimented with extra-parliamentary agitation. To insure itself against another betrayal the party adopted a stance on subsequent political alliances which was at once carefully contractual and touchingly messianic. The reason why the anti-Walpolian confederation had failed, wrote the tory M.P. for Colchester, Charles Gray, was its 'defect of omitting previous settled terms', so that 'when the crisis came the Captain [Pulteney] was perverted, and the army instead of making any use of the Victory fell to scrambling for very paltry plunder'.[89] In their agreement with Henry Pelham in 1744-5 and with the Prince of Wales after 1747 the tories used their limited bargaining power to obtain paper guarantees – constitutional concessions and promises of office laid down in advance of their votes. The tories also looked for a politician who could lead them out of their wilderness and who would not be corrupted at the moment of victory: a search which was complicated by the fact that after Wyndham's death, this paragon had to be a whig, or a prospective or current Hanoverian monarch. It would have been no consolation, but it was true, that the tories' varied response to the events of 1742 – their limited Jacobitism, their increasing radicalism, and their political Messianism which was to embrace both William Pitt and George III – would make them a more formative component of later-eighteenth-century English politics than the Patriot leaders, who succumbed to stale if profitable douceurs.

Broad-Bottom Schemes and Princely Alliances: 1742–53

Because the ministerial reconstruction of 1742 in the end resulted in the primacy of Walpole's chosen successor, Henry Pelham, the political leeway made available by the Minister's fall and its popular impact have often been understated. The dismissive verdicts of bitter contemporaries ('Besides getting rid of this pacifick Whig Ministry', James Oglethorpe recalled in 1755, 'England got a number of Patriot Orators, and they got places') seem only to be confirmed by the meticulous accounts of modern scholars intent on explaining the Old Corps' longevity. The duke of Argyll, John Owen asserts, was the only major opposition whig to canvass tory promotions in 1742. The King himself remained stead-fastly opposed to this concession – which was really just as well, since the tory parliamentary party found the prospect of office 'uncongenial'. As the opposition had always been in general policy agreement with Walpole, royal intransigence, tory diffidence, and Patriot ambition combined to ensure that the only thing required to re-establish whig governmental supremacy in 1742 was a judicious reallocation of employments. When Lord Carteret was tactless enough to compromise this settlement by an over-enthusiastic pursuit of Hanoverian interests and monarchical favour, he too could be overborne in 1744 and, more successfully, in 1746, by yet more permutations in employments and a great deal of backstairs intrigue.[1] 'Consequently', wrote Archibald Foord, when he surveyed these high-political games of snakes and ladders and their reptilian and aspiring participants, the post-Walpolian malcontents 'made no contribution to the institutional development of parliamentary Opposition'.[2]

Yet it is arguable, and more than arguable, that the events of 1742 made for increased volatility at both the highest and the lowest political level. We do not know what sort of an administration George II initially envisaged as a replacement for Walpole. Since Egmont was informed on 15 February 1742 that the duke of Newcastle 'had prevailed with his Majesty, not to countenance the Tory Party in the least', and since in March, Walpole, now Lord Orford, still needed to spend three hours with the King before he could persuade him to omit Sir John Hynde Cotton from the new Admiralty Board, royal bias was clearly not a foregone conclusion. Once re-established in power, neither Pelham nor Newcastle showed their predecessor's aptitude or propensity for careful treatment of the monarch. Possibly in late 1743, certainly in late 1744 and early 1746, the Pelhams' lack of rapport with the Court led George II seriously to consider admitting tories to a mixed administration led by Lord Carteret.[3] These rebellions were short-lived, but in assessing the political hopes and fears of both whig and tory between 1742 and 1760, it should be remembered that throughout this period the Hanoverian Royal Family was often less than reliable as an Old Corps' adjunct. The Prince of Wales, William, duke of Cumberland, and Princess Amelia were all, at different times, at odds with the administration; Prince George, the future George III, was to be no less refractory when he came of age.

Less politically significant, but not insignificant, was the extra-parliamentary nation's reaction to 1742. In a private memorandum Viscount Perceval asserted that it was neither the Cabinet nor Parliament but 'The Opinion of the Nation that removed Sir Robert Walpole, for it was the Contagion of their Public Spirit which affected those in Public Stations & in great stations to contrive, & to attempt his fall...The force of this Power in the People is not sufficiently understood.' Perceval was abnormally exposed and sensitive to demotic pressure, but the demonstrations which surrounded Walpole's exit were violent and closely monitored by the opposition, particularly by its tory sector. Perceval's uncontested return for Westminster with the tory Charles Edwin on 31 December 1741 (both an ingredient and an indicator of imminent Walpolian collapse) had reportedly led to a procession of some 20 000 men and women, who marched four abreast down St James' Street and Pall Mall.[4] The news of the Minister's resignation ignited a wave of celebratory bonfires: tory mobs had grown 'desperately insolent', complained one dissenter, '...burning him in effigy'. The popular but normally responsible *London Magazine* urged the parliamentary committee appointed to inquire into Orford's conduct not to repeat the South Sea cover-up of 1721, but to execute the 'Beast bedeck'd with blue and green...the pond'rous, huge machine' who, living, besmirched the state.[5]

The more responsible constituency opinion which filtered back to tory M.P.s was both jubilant and expectant. Edward Southwell was informed that Bristol's Mercant Venturers expected a parliamentary trial at which Orford's governmental system would be formally condemned as a prelude to its dissolution. The tory M.P. for York was told by a squirearchical supporter, Bacon Moritt, that his party must seize the opportunity to secure Place Bills, triennial Parliaments, and an end to political discrimination in the localities. Evading proscription at the centre would not be enough. Tory spokesmen had said, time and time again, that their aim in opposing Walpole was to change measures, not just men. The party's populous constituencies now expected it to use what Sir John St Aubyn styled 'this interregnum of power' to effect the promised revolution in political life.[6]

Since the tories acknowledged the logic which was to inspire Henry Fox's caveat to Shelburne – 'It is the placeman, not the independent Lord, that can do his country good' – this public demand for change, as well as individual careerism, dictated that the party attempt to secure a quota of employments.[7] It was not the King, still less an outright Patriot veto, and least of all their own indifference which constituted the major obstacle to this ambition. The problem was rather the distinction and solidarity of the Old Corps and of the tories themselves.

As soon as Walpole resigned he joined Pelham, Hardwicke, and Newcastle in working to ensure that the administration remained substantially whig, that the number of New Whigs (that is, former Patriots) admitted to office was restricted, and that those Old Corps men displaced in their favour were suitably compensated. The Old Corps' sense of its own cohesive rectitude was further demonstrated in the New Whigs' political decline. 'Under you', Orford assured Pelham, 'all the independent Whigs will list and unite', whereas no politician would be able 'to secure a zealous and cordial union of the Whig party, if any body takes upon them the lead, that they know have been instruments, and active, in destroying the whig party for twenty years together.'[8] Neither William Pulteney, who in 1742 suppled into a peerage as earl of Bath, nor Carteret was able to live down his earlier and protracted parliamentary deviance and regain the trust of those conventional whig M.P.s for whom such conduct was anathema: hence, in large part, their comparative political insignificance by the end of the decade. William Pitt, one of the very few ex-Patriots whose career was to flourish in the 1750s, still found his progress badly hampered by lack of whig parliamentary support. In 1755 and the winter of 1756 he was forced to depend on tory auxiliaries; only after his coalition with Newcastle did he become *persona grata* to the bulk of ministerial whigs.

Tory solidarity in the 1740s was no less impressive, but while this quality made for the Old Corps' continued dominance, it only complicated its rivals' ambitions. Unlike their Patriot allies, the tories felt compelled to seek concessions as a party. This did not mean that they expected wholesale employment, but they did demand sufficient political weight and recognition to enable them to influence future policy and to extract further concessions for themselves and for their supporters in the constituencies. The tory M.P. for Newton, Legh Master, wrote in February 1742 that he could accept office only 'If the Administration was to be in the Hands of those with whom I had always voted'. One month later the Northamptonshire tory Sir Edmund Isham resigned his lucrative post as Advocate to the Admiralty (an exceptional perquisite for a lawyer M.P. of his bias) when he learnt that the King had negatived Cotton's appointment to the Admiralty Board. 'I heartily congratulate you upon your Glorious Resignation', wrote Isham's brother, an equally partisan Oxford don, 'and think you have shew'd a proper spirit.' There were two reasons why George II rejected Cotton. Orford had exerted all his cogency and personal force to extract the veto, and Cotton had insisted that his appointment usher in more extensive tory advancement.[9]

Even the tories' two noble apostates, Lords Bathurst and Gower, serve to demonstrate the resilience of party loyalties. In July 1742 Bathurst was made Captain of the Band of Gentlemen Pensioners – a prime court post worth £1000 *per annum* – and Gower replaced Lord Hervey as Lord Privy Seal. Bathurst did not succumb to whig ministerial compliance until 1743, and while his son, Henry Bathurst, defected with him, his brother, Benjamin, remained an ardent tory until death. Contrary to the assertions of many historians, Gower accepted his post in 1742 at the instigation of his premier party colleagues, who wanted an advocate at the centre.[10] In December 1742 both his brothers, Baptist and William Leveson-Gower, voted against the ministry's payment of Hanoverian troops; Gower himself opposed this outlay the following February. In December 1743 Gower resigned, Pelham having refused to recast either his domestic and foreign policy or the principle of tory proscription. Only in 1745, after failing in yet another attempt to secure major concessions for his party and having been supplemented as its premier peer by the duke of Beaufort, did Gower defect, thereby providing Samuel Johnson with a synonym for 'renegade' in the first and most partisan edition of his *Dictionary*.[11]

Had tory politicians not been so restrained by a sense of party responsibility, many more of them might have obtained office in the first half of the 1740s. In 1742 not only the Scottish dynast Argyll but also Lord Wilmington, the new *pro forma* First Lord of the Treasury, urged that the tories be rewarded for their part in Walpole's destruction. The Prince of Wales had contributed to this process by financing the early parliamentary attendance of some of the poorer or meaner tory M.P.s, and in March he told Pulteney that he must at least negotiate places for

Gower, Bathurst, and Cotton.[12] Pulteney submitted, but his subsequent argument to George II is perhaps more revealing about his own attitude towards the tory party than it is about the King's:

His Majesty by giving a few places at Court to some of the most considerable [tories], and by making others Lord Lieutenants of counties, and by some other marks of his royal favour taking off the heads and leaders of them, might draw the teeth of all the rest and they could never more unite in opposition to his government.[13]

Before 1746 it was this tactical acquiescence in limited and, it was hoped, disruptive tory advancement, not outright anti-toryism, which characterised most of the New Whigs and some of the Old Corps leaders. In October 1743 the new First Lord of the Treasury, Henry Pelham, told the Patriot Lord Chesterfield that he would employ a few tory politicians, 'but only upon a personal foot, and then even he would rather have 'em without their followers, than with, for fear of offending the old Whig Corps'. Fifteen months later Chesterfield himself, now Special Ambassador to the Hague, was to plead with Newcastle to pacify Gower and his immediate tory circle, 'which will at least break the Tory party, so as to make the other part of it absolutely inconsiderable'.[14]

Given their organisational and ideological distinction, the tories were bound to resist such a grudging and eschatological solution to their party's proscription. Only by recognising the complexity of the tories' post-1742 dilemma – their determination to secure more extensive concessions in terms of local and central office than whig ministerialists were prepared to allow, and their concurrent need to secure constitutional changes so as to appease their supporters – can the tories' fluctuating response to the major whig and royal allies available in this period – Pelham, Carteret, and the Prince of Wales – be properly understood.

I

In 1742 the tories betrayed their yearning for office first by their deliberate moderation, then, with the onset of disillusionment, by the violence of their parliamentary and extra-parliamentary reaction. Even before the Fountain Tavern meeting on 12 February, the admission to office of Carteret, Gybbon, Rushout, and Sandys, together with Pulteney's discreet consultations with Pelham (in progress before Walpole's fall), had prefigured tory betrayal. Sandys' personal apologia, 'The business of the Publick must go on; the King has removed the Chancellor of the Exchequer, and if somebody did not accept the office, His Majesty must employ the same person again, which he supposed they would not chuse', was plausible but disingenuous. Although he and the other 'scabby sheep in the flock', as Beaufort christened these New Whigs, claimed that they still favoured constitutional reform and some tory promotions, they had barely attempted to make their acceptance of office conditional on any such concessions. Nonetheless, at the great opposition meeting at the Fountain, the tory leaders present left the angry rhetoric to the dukes of Bedford and Argyll, the latter peer demanding that the coalition prolong its parliamentary campaign until it could enforce a mixed administration.[15]

It was this speech which won Argyll his short-term tory popularity. Other reasons have of course been suggested. It has been argued that Argyll's reappointment as Commander of the Army in February 1742 elicited tory support because the party expected him to 'act as the Monck of a second Stuart restoration'. Argyll's own politics were certainly unstable at this period, but if this was the tories' real expectation, they chose a strange way to show it.[16]

After much intrigue and at 2 o'clock in the morning of 17 February, Pulteney was able to assure the King that his heir had agreed to a reconciliation. This was a crucial stage of Orford's background strategy to detach the opposition's more powerful whig and royal adherents, but initially Frederick's submission was limited and conditional on Argyll's re-employment. With Wyndham dead and Gower still to be promoted, the tories had no politician at the centre to negotiate on their behalf. Hence, at a meeting of the 'heads of the denominations in the Opposition' held that evening at Dodington's house, all the tory leaders accepted Argyll's offer to return to his post and utilise its leverage to advance their promotion. He promised them that if he could not accomplish this, and 'also reduce every thing else in the administration of affairs to the public content', he would resign. 'Upon this', Beaufort later recorded, 'he was unanimously desired to undertake the Affair.' On 18 February, Beaufort, Wynn, Cotton, Gower, and Bathurst, together with almost every tory M.P. available, accompanied Argyll to St James', where the King received them with evident good grace. 'They endeavoured to wipe off the imputation of disaffection to the [Hanoverian] family; they made it difficult for the discontented whigs...to quit them; they shewed the King their attachment to the Prince...and they shewed the Prince that if he abandoned them, they could seek their protection from the King.'[17] So one ministerial whig evaluated the tory strategy. So, too, judging from the vigour of their retaliatory action, did those Old Corps and New Whigs who disrelished the tories' acquiring acceptability as a party group.

On 8 March George was persuaded to reject Cotton; two days later, Argyll resigned into an obscurity as futile as his brief return to office;

seven days later, Sandys moved successfully to close the parliamentary Committee on Elections. As he told Egmont, since December 1741 six out of seven tory election petitions had been successful; had he not intervened, 'several [more] tories would have come in'.[18] On 30 March Sandys and Pulteney, like all the other Patriot M.P.s who had accepted employment (and like some who had not), helped to defeat a tory motion to repeal the Septennial Act. On 6 April Carteret joined eighty other peers in rejecting a Place Bill: 'He had always spoke for it', noted Lord Oxford grimly, 'when he was out of place.'[19]

Until mid March the bulk of tories had taken care to display their parliamentary responsibility; now, the party resorted to a vituperative campaign against Orford. 'No wonder if the whole nation' hated the ex-Minister, Berkeley of Stratton told the Lords, 'I have felt the weight of his power with insult added to it.' 'All the titles, honours, pensions, places and other favours of the crown', Edward Digby complained, as he and his colleagues confronted the prospect of their continuing proscription, 'have for twenty years past been disposed of to none but such as voted in parliament, or at elections, according to the direction of the minister.' Before the Upper House resisted Orford's punishment, warned Cotton, it should remember the consequences of its obstruction of the national will in the 1640s. The tories acted, thought William Hay, as if 'resolved to push things to extremity'; and they did not confine their anger to Westminster.[20]

Between February and April 1742 thirty-four tory-represented constituencies, eleven Scottish burghs and counties responsive to Argyll's direction, and just two English Patriot constituencies submitted Instructions urging an inquiry into the late administration and substantial reform. In July and August Cotton ensured that eighteen more tory Instructions reached Westminster.[21] Opposition activists had by now learnt that for credibility's sake they must vary the wording of these ostensibly spontaneous protests, but in 1742 some constituencies seem genuinely to have spawned their own demands. Montgomeryshire, for example, asked its tory M.P. to work for the repeal of the Riot Act. The same reform was taken up by tory pamphleteers. *National Unanimity Recommended* linked a prospective tory administration with the repeal of the Riot, Black, and Smuggling Acts, and of a 'thousand coercive clauses in Acts relating to the Excise'. 'The Whigs have failed us constantly', argued another, purportedly plebeian, writer; '. . . if we must depend on any, let it be the Tories, who have not deceived us, and I believe never will deceive us.' Such proprietorial popularism was a vulnerable hostage to treacherous, high-level political fortune.[22]

For although the opposition remained numerically respectable (in

October 1742 Newcastle estimated its Commons strength at some 220 M.P.s, of whom 146 were tory), the next two sessions demonstrated that the tories had no prospect of influencing policy, or of reversing their own proscription by parliamentary means.[23] True, the tories retained some useful whig allies. Edmund Waller had refused a post on the Treasury Board: partly because he wanted better, partly because he wanted revenge on Orford, who had allowed his father-in-law, John Aislabie, to be expelled from Parliament in 1721. George Bubb Dodington had been left unemployed, and so had George Lyttelton and William Pitt – by the end of 1742 the only two of the Prince's followers still in opposition. With Pitt and Lyttelton went the three Grenville brothers; and in the next two years these five outdid their more diffident tory associates in anti-Hanoverian diatribes intended to attract notice, inflame public opinion, and widen ministerial divisions over foreign policy. Carteret's uneven diplomacy – the abortive Treaty of Hanau in July 1743, and his attempt to commit Britain to subsidising both Austria and Sardinia at the Treaty of Worms – also led some ex-Patriot M.P.s, such as Alexander Hume Campbell, to revert to opposition. Seventy whigs had voted against Britain's employment of Hanoverian troops in December 1742; eighty-eight did so in January 1744.[24] But neither this quota of whig talent, nor the tories' own dogged perseverance in opposition, could subvert an administration possessed of both patronage and the habitual obedience of Old Corps M.P.s. In thirty-two key divisions between November 1742 and the Broad-Bottom coalition agreement two years later, the opposition's average vote was 137 and the ministry secured an average majority of over sixty.[25]

It was to the high-level rivalry between Lord Carteret, Secretary of State for the North and prime royal favourite, and Henry Pelham, by December 1743 both Chancellor of the Exchequer and First Lord of the Treasury, that the opposition had to look for political gain. It was largely to facilitate negotiations with these ministerial prima donnas that late in 1743 Wynn, Cotton, Sir John Philipps, and three dissident whigs formed themselves into a central opposition committee.[26] Because their success was so contingent upon oligarchical manoeuvre, the chance of these politicians' reaching a settlement with the administration at all consonant either with tory backbencher sentiment, or with the expectations fostered in the tory constituencies, was dangerously small. This lacuna was to be fundamental to the tory party's contortions in the 1744–5 Broad-Bottom administration.

According to Lord Oxford, opposition consultations with the Pelhams had been in fitful progress since May 1743. Sir John Hynde Cotton and Lord Gower negotiated on behalf of the tories and they were joined by the ubiquitous Bolingbroke, who could not long survive without political intrigue, and by the opposition whigs Chesterfield, Cobham, Pitt, Lyttelton, and Waller. Because of the delicacy of their objective – the creation of a coalition which would exclude the royal favourite and the earl of Bath – these talks were exclusive. As late as September 1744 Sir Watkin Williams Wynn, the tory leader closest to mainline party opinion, was still under the impression that opposition was to continue unabated. Two months later and with George II's permission, Carteret, now earl Granville, informed Gower, Cobham, and Chesterfield 'that He would give them Carte Blanche & bring in all their friends if they & the Country party would join Him, & as a proof of his Intentions would turn out the Pelhams next day'. The opposition trio demurred, and thereby enforced Granville's resignation on 23 November, and the dismissal of thirteen of his own and Bath's whig followers.[27]

'We could have no Affections, no Attachments, to either of the Rivals for Power', argued a pamphleteer who must have been either a tory M.P. or supplied with information by leading tories to compose their apologia; '...We had but little Expectation of Good from one set of Men, and from the other none at all.' His commitment to intensive continental involvement and his own and his ally Lord Bath's vacillation in 1742 made Granville unacceptable; his parliamentary base was fragile in comparison with Old Corps strength: a junction with the Pelhams, the tories judged, was 'likely to be more permanent'. It was also expected to be profitable. Henry Pelham at least had averred his good intentions: 'That the long partiality in confining ye favour of ye Crown upon ye Whigs only was iniquitous & oppressive, & that if they would follow his advice, he and they together would establish ye Government, upon ye broad foundation of admitting equally all men into their share of power.'[28] On 22 December Gower regained the Privy Seal; Sir John Philipps and John Pitt, tory M.P. for Wareham, were appointed to the Board of Trade, and Cotton was made Treasurer of the Chamber.

These were not the only offers of advancement forthcoming. Lord Ailesbury was reportedly offered a dukedom and Wynn a peerage; Prowse was invited to accept a place on the Admiralty Board, Sir Edward Dering the post of Commissary General. Orford even told Sir Dudley Ryder that the Preston tory, Nicholas Fazakerley, 'was talk'd of to be made Chancellor' – information which may have had some small basis in fact, since weaning Fazakerley from toryism by way of that post had been canvassed in the 1730s.[29] With the exception of this last, rumoured promotion, these concessions were all of a piece: 'lucrative or honourable employments', as Hardwicke described them, which would attach the tories to the administration 'without letting any of them into places of great power at Court or of considerable influence in the Country'. Orford, whose shrewdness was unmarred by retirement, made a similar appraisal, without, however, succumbing to Hardwicke's complacency. The tories, he argued, would want a great deal more.[30]

Not that they were as unmoved by their leaders' prospects as has sometimes been maintained. Lord Barrymore, who only one year before had been the prime tory advocate of a Jacobite invasion, was now enchanted with Wynn's account of his party's governmental entente: 'I think after what has now been done, attendance is very unnecessary and we are for the future safe.' Safe, as far as Barrymore was concerned, from the need for conspiracy, and safe, in the opinion of the bulk of tory (and whig) M.P.s, from the need for parliamentary attendance in the short pre-Christmas session. The unanimity at Westminster in December 1744 struck observers as being almost uncanny: the only division – a procedural one – attracted just seventy-seven M.P.s. More naive tories continued to exude dazed euphoria into the new year. On 15 January 1745 another reputed Jacobite, Lord Orrery, described for his wife his progress in Hanoverian respectability. He had just been 'graciously received' at St James'; he was devoting the next day to Leicester House. 'I think the part we intend to act will be right, in case we keep to our present Resolutions. The Good of the Country is our first view, the next may be, if proper, Promotions.'[31]

Orrery's order of priorities is indicative, as is the steady scepticism displayed at this stage by astute tory politicians like Thomas Prowse. It was not so much that the posts on offer were peripheral – the tories knew their own enforced lack of administrative expertise better than anyone. But placebos to proscription unaccompanied by changes in governmental policy were not worth accepting. According to Edmund Waller, he, together with Cotton, Dodington, and Cobham, had insisted all along that any treaty with Pelham must provide for such changes. They had been overruled by Gower, Bedford, Chesterfield, Pitt, and Lyttelton, who had agreed to come in 'without any previous stipulations for the public'.[32] Whether this is true of Gower is not clear. He told an Oxford tory that Pelham had promised a speedy reduction in Britain's expenditure on the War of Austrian Succession, and Orford also believed that Gower had sought more extensive concessions. Certainly many tories thought that Gower had settled for too little. In 1742 the party had incited riots against Patriot M.P.s like Lord Baltimore who had accepted office and were seeking re-election. In 1745 the tories could not render the unpalatable cake of their parliamentary docility acceptable to their own constituents without the icing of 'some terms for the people'.[33]

Grub Street was quick to alert the party to its duty. The *Old England*

Journal warned that a broadly recruited administration *tout court* was an empty achievement: 'If the people are to be ridden, it is nothing to them whether they are bestrid by a narrow or a Broad bottom – the latter is generally most heavy.' A pamphlet entitled *Christmas Chat* depicted a new tory placeman standing for re-election and being cross-examined by his archetypal and appalled supporters – the huntsman, the parson, and the squire. How, this trio inquired, could the tory parliamentary party continue to function with its leaders silenced by employment? Their M.P. might believe he could reconcile reforming zeal with a government salary, but 'Supposing the few of your Party that are brought in, were to continue...honest and sincere...what can you do against numbers?' A pertinent query, repeated in a pamphlet aimed specifically at Sir Watkin Williams Wynn. The tory leadership had only repeated Pulteney's sell-out in 1742: 'Instead of coming in as Conquerors, you are received as Auxiliaries...You must serve upon their own Terms, or not at all.' Emotionally dependent on his reputation as the conscience of his party, Wynn shrivelled under this attack. By March 1745 Sir Dudley Ryder was noting his reversion to parliamentary opposition 'because of being abused in a late pamphlet'.[34]

The tory leadership was also arraigned by its parliamentary supporters. On 29 January 1745 Thomas Carew, himself under pressure from the Independent Electors of Westminster, moved for a bill for annual Parliaments, to determine, he declared, 'whether our new ministers and *quondam* patriots, did really stipulate any thing in favour of their country ...they seem to have stipulated nothing but places for themselves'. It is not known how many of the 113 votes that Carew secured were tory: he certainly obtained support from His Majesty's Minister of Trade, Sir John Philipps.[35]

The tories' demotic constraints were focused when London's Lord Mayor presented a bill to repeal sections of the 1725 City Election Act and so reduce aldermanic supervision of the relatively democratic and largely tory Common Council. Pelham's attack on this proposal on 12 February was an explicit rejection of a wider political nation, and an implicit condemnation of those politicians who curried extra-parliamentary favour. Such measures were touted by 'Popular leaders, whether Patrician or Plebeian, to arrive at the chief dignities and magistracies of the state'. The masses were bound to be 'fond of every regulation that gives them any share...in the government of their country', but it was 'plain from history, that no free state ever long endured, where the populace had any great share in the government'. The bill was lost by 117 votes to 90 with two tory M.P.s acting as tellers for the minority. Three days later several tory M.P.s, including Carew, Cotton, Phillips, Lord Noel

Somerset, and Wynn, joined three dissident whig politicians in patronising a mass-meeting of the Independent Electors of Westminster. Philipps led the toast to annual Parliaments, and 'twas said, there would be as much Heat, & Opposition the latter End of this Session of Parliament, as ever was known'.[36]

The tory elite had advertised its confinement by party sentiment and, of course, its political greed. If Pelham wanted to retain his tory allies (and they were only worth keeping as long as Bath, Cobham, and Granville and, indirectly, Granville's patron, the King, were unsettling his administration) he would clearly have to extend the terms of the coalition. It should also have been obvious to Gower that, unless he acted quickly, his party reputation would be permanently damaged. But ambition for his family, the distractions of his office, and the second-hand information he was fed by whig friends like Bedford and Chesterfield all militated against his partisan sensibility. He was encouraged to regard tory protests as the ephemera of his party's lunatic fringe – forgetting, perhaps, how after 1710 Bolingbroke had used ultra-tory sentiment to undermine the more moderate Oxford. In Gower's case, it was the bulk of tory M.P.s who now distrusted his leadership; moreover, in Lord Noel Somerset they also had an aggressive and aspiring spokesman. Early in 1745 Somerset, together with a chastened Sir Watkin Williams Wynn, compiled and submitted to Gower a nine-point programme of reform. They told him that 'unless something was done for the Constitution, it was in vain for the Ministers to expect their Assistance; and for fear of Mistakes, they put into his Hands their Propositions in Writing'.[37]

These so-called Broad-Bottom proposals anticipated the Carlton House declaration of 1747 in postulating a contractual basis for coalition. Like its successor, the 1745 document was a deliberate essay in moderation. No mention was made (at least in the initial version) of either annual or triennial Parliaments. The tories asked for a limitation, not for the abolition, of parliamentary placemen. They also acknowledged the realities of foreign policy. The army to be reduced, but only 'when the circumstances of affairs will permit'. The 16 000 Hanoverian troops in British pay were to be discontinued, but 'other troops if necessary be provided in their stead'. Customs and Excise officers were to be disfranchised, and an inquiry launched into the abortive British naval engagement at Toulon. The 1732 Act governing the landed qualifications of J.P.s was to be made more stringent, and this was to supplement what one critic described as the 'darling' measure of the tory activists: new Commissions of the Peace were demanded for 'Every County, and that all Gentlemen of Fortune be admitted without distinction'.[38]

What this meant in practice was that the number of tory Justices would have to be increased. There had been no extensive purge of tory J.P.s since 1723, but the whig predominance by then established had never been reversed. In some counties (like Glamorgan) tory J.P.s remained numerous; in others the local tory magnate, if his loyalty was above suspicion, could sometimes obtain preferential treatment. In 1738 Lord Oxford had used his friendship with Hardwicke to stave off a new Commission which would have given Herefordshire's tories even poorer representation than they currently enjoyed. But as Hardwicke's son, Philip Yorke, admitted, Oxford's success was exceptional: the tory manoeuvres of 1745, he wrote, were bound to prejudice the whigs 'with whom most of the commissions were filled up'. As Yorke also recognised, the tory initiative betokened more than a bucolic concentration on parity in local government. An increase in tory J.P.s would placate the party's gentry supporters, and facilitate a tory electoral revival.[39]

In 1742, when Bathurst had been appointed Captain of the Band of Gentlemen Pensioners, he had immediately sought to use this accession of court influence to obtain more tory J.P.s in Gloucestershire and Wiltshire. Local whigs had been no less prompt in alerting the government as to his motives. Lord Hertford warned Hardwicke that Bathurst's Wiltshire proposals would lead to a concentration of tory J.P.s in the Chippenham area, 'so that the design is to get a majority of their party there'. Sir John Dutton sent a similar analysis of Bathurst's machinations in Gloucestershire to the county's whig Lord Lieutenant: 'By [the] Commission as it now stands we have broke strongly into ye Tory interest about Cirencester & all that part of ye Country. His Lordship now wants to cure that inroad we have made there by adding some Friends of his own to turn the Ballance again on ye Tory Side.'[40] Justices had ample opportunities to persuade more compliant voters to poll, and just as many to deter the hostile from voting. The results of the 1734 and 1741 general elections had demonstrated that the electoral rewards attendant on tory popularity were bound to be limited: under the unreformed system, the party needed an increase in local patronage if it was to make more extensive electoral gains.

In the first four months of 1745 tory parliamentary conduct fluctuated in accordance with ministerial receptivity to the various Broad-Bottom proposals and to the J.P. issue in particular. On 23 January, when 28 000 troops were voted for Flanders with only a single negative, it was clear enough that tory compliance had been purchased. Six days later Carew and Sir Thomas Bramston were given leave to introduce a bill, drafted by Fazakerley, to enforce the Act on J.P. qualifications. Cotton and Wynn reciprocated by giving the ministry tory support in crucial divisions on 1, 16, 18, and 22 February.[41] But naturally the tories wanted more. Lord Gower had 'amicably adjusted' a new Commission for Shropshire, but apart from this he seems to have done nothing to advance his party's demand for a nation-wide remodelling of Commissions. On 20 March Somerset, now duke of Beaufort, presented Hardwicke with a list of six counties and a demand that they be given more tory J.P.s: 'The Lords and gentl[emen] with whom he had met or consulted, were uneasy that nothing was done in the affair of the justices of the peace...that they were very desiring that the coalition should take effect and continue, but were very apprehensive that it could not.' The next day Beaufort's threat was amplified, and his party status demonstrated, when the majority of tory M.P.s opposed a Commons vote of credit.[42]

At this stage the ministry could neither afford to dispense with tory support nor accede to Beaufort's demands without losing face and acknowledging Gower's displacement in the tory hierarchy. Its compromise solution was to spurn Beaufort's approach – 'Adieu coalition', commented Lord Orrery – whilst urging Gower to compile a similar scheme. On 7 April the King agreed to Gower's proposals for new Commissions for Bedfordshire, Cambridgeshire, Gloucestershire, Hampshire, Herefordshire, Oxfordshire, and the North Riding of Yorkshire. Between 17 May and 21 October the Lord Chancellor issued fiats for all these counties, in each case providing for a substantial increase in the number of tory landowners and clerics included.[43]

In view of the Young Pretender's invasion of Scotland in July, it is significant that the great majority of whig complaints at this accretion in tory local influence made no reference to the dangers of tory disaffection. Instead, the emphasis was that of Lord Doneraile, who had stigmatised Fazakerley's J.P. Bill as 'an attempt to give content to one party, at the expense of alarming the other'. Hardwicke received letter after disgruntled whig letter, all making the same turgid patronage calculation: concessions to the tories were bound to be detrimental to whig interests. 'I must beg leave to declare', wrote one typically self-righteous stalwart, '...that the general Notion which prevailed upon Lord Orford's going out, of uniting all Parties under the cant Term of Broad-Bottom, is to me absurd and ridiculous.'[44]

Broad-Bottom was not in fact an absurd governmental format, providing that it collocated the various whig groupings. What the 1745 experiment – and especially the J.P. furore – taught Pelham and his associates was that no broadly based whig administration could also contain the tories. The party was too distinct in its organisation and aspirations to be effectively incorporated, and whig backbenchers and grass-roots zealots were too conventionally partisan to tolerate its import. This was what

Chesterfield, now absent in the Hague, failed to understand when he warned Newcastle that the Old Corps should fear the pretensions of Cobham and William Pitt rather than the tories, 'whose inefficiency and insignificancy in business they well know'. Chesterfield's tactical appraisal was in prospect correct, but Newcastle's rejoinder was far more in line with prevailing whig sentiment:

What you say of the real jealousy that our old friends have conceived of Mr. Pitt and that set, may be true with regard to some few of the leading men in the House of Commons. But it was the dread and apprehension of taking in Tories that hurt us with our great friends in the House of Lords [the Lord Lieutenants] and the bulk of the party in the House of Commons. And it is those we must stick by; and it is those that have stuck by us.[45]

So in mid 1745 the Ministers temporised, implementing the new Commissions but minimising the concessions so as to placate whig opinion. Gower had asked for the Commissions to be issued before the end of the session – that is, by May – 'as a Specimen of what is intended, and that the rest be done whenever they are wanted before the next Session of Parliament'. Not only were the seven new fiats delayed, but in the final agreement Hardwicke also took care to erase this last time-clause. A succession of tory M.P.s, who had been led to expect new Commissions for counties other than those originally specified, consequently found that their demands met only with the Lord Chancellor's bland disregard. And even in the Commissions that were issued, 'violent party men' who met the property qualification were nonetheless vetoed for their bias.[46] The Lord Lieutenant of Yorkshire refused point-blank to accept Bacon Moritt as a J.P.: 'I do not know he has. . . any Qualification to recommend him but that of being a very busy Stirrer in all Opposition to the Whig Interest'; a similar negative, for similar reasons, was given to Dr Coningsby's pretensions to be a Herefordshire J.P. In Cambridgeshire, Lord Lieutenant Montfort and Hardwicke agreed 'not to add any [more] of our Friends to ye Commission & to use that as an Argument for not putting in more of Sir John [Hynde] Cotton's list'.[47]

Government prevarication on the J.P. issue ensured Gower's usurpation. Party purists had regarded him as the lost leader ever since March, when he had allowed his brother, Baptist Leveson-Gower, to replace Sir John Philipps at the Board of Trade. Philipps had resigned because of Pelham's dilatory response to the Broad-Bottom proposals, and Gower's appropriation of his place was, thought Dr William King, 'sufficient manifestation of his intentions, if there were wanting other proofs'. The tories seem in fact to have excluded Gower from their inner councils long before he decided finally to quit them, his 'defection' only occurring, like the departure of the premier opposition whigs, in the wake of the Jacobite invasion.[48]

Tory involvement in Charles Edward Stuart's attempted coup was, as we have seen, effectively nil. Indeed, as Sir Edmund Isham noted, George II acknowledged as much in his speeches to Parliament on 17 October 1745, and again on 12 August 1746 when he remarked that the rebellion's suppression had been 'universally seconded' by the nation. 'Even his M[ajest]y, in a Speech from the T[hro]ne', the Leicester House newspaper the *Remembrancer* was subsequently to argue on the tories' behalf, 'has most graciously condescended to acknowledge our services; as also to declare, That they should never be forgotten by him.' Forgotten or not, tory loyalty met with small reward.[49]

When Parliament reassembled in October the party almost fell over itself in punctilious displays of rectitude. Cotton, Philipps, Thomas Prowse, and six other tory M.P.s joined twenty whigs in the Commons committee which ordered the Young Pretender's proclamations to be burnt by the common hangman. But all this real or, in the case of a few individuals, affected probity was beside the point. In 1743 William Pitt had declared to the House his perfect alliance and friendship with Sir John Hynde Cotton; no ambitious whig dissident was likely to make such avowals after an invasion had reinforced stock equations of parliamentary opposition with disaffection. In the autumn of 1745 Pitt made tentative approaches to the ministry and in February 1746 his delegate, Lord Cobham, agreed with the Pelhams 'to come into us, and to bring in his Boys...exclusively (as he expressly said) of the Tories for whom he had nothing to say'.[50] One month later the future Secretary at War, Henry Fox, described what he rightly called a 'coalition dinner' which 'pass'd off very cheerfully, consisting of Pitt, Lyttelton, Barrington, and the two eldest Grenvilles, Pelham, Yonge, Winnington, Legge and me'. The constituents of Pelham's ideal polity – 'a thorough Whig Parliament all of a piece' – had finally, if only temporarily, been assembled.[51]

II

If by the end of 1746 the tories had been deprived of all their politically effective whig allies (one observer calculated that out of the 125 M.P.s still in opposition in 1747, 107 were tory), this did not mean that the party's cohesion and distinct identity had been shattered: rather the reverse.[52] On 11 April 1746, when the Hanoverian troops were ratified by 255 votes to 122, the tories made up 76 per cent of the minority. Forty-seven tory M.P.s betrayed their despondency by absenting themselves, and only eight gave their votes to the administration: Charles and

Thomas Gore, Baptist and William Leveson-Gower, John Pitt, William Levinz, Edward Southwell, and Sir Miles Stapylton. The first five had voted with the government since the November 1744 coalition agreement; to the other three one can add Henry Bankes, John Proby, and Sir Hugh Smithson, who were to leave their party before the 1747 election. But Archibald Foord's forty tories who followed Gower into ministerialdom did not exist. Three weeks after the Hanoverian division, twenty opposition peers, seventeen of them tory, issued a manifesto in the guise of a Protest on the war in Flanders. Having outlined their objections, the signatories demanded 'The re-establishment of peace, and of order, by wise oeconomy, and temperate reformation...and reviving in the nation a truly British and moral spirit. With all who will concur in such a conduct we will unite with affection. All other connections and views we disclaim and abhor.' 'I have [this] last Protest always at hand', wrote Sir Watkin Williams Wynn later that year, 'the last Article of which is my Creed in Politicks, to them I will adhere, to the Promoters of it I will Connect, without it, I will not even consult.'[53]

It was not tory distinction so much as tory morale which suffered from the Broad-Bottom experiment and the '45. The party had lost Lord Gower, and suspicions that Wynn and Cotton had also negotiated with no other end in view than their own advancement were voiced at both Cocoa Tree and constituency level. These aspersions only glanced off the surface of Cotton's thick political skin and he was soon cheerfully intriguing with Lord Granville and the Prince of Wales; Wynn was far more vulnerable. 'You must very well know...how we have been served by those we have consulted with', he wrote to Cotton in November 1746; 'I therefore dread all Consultations...being quite in a State of Despair of any good that can accrue from it. All over Staffordshire, Shropshire etc. in the parts I have been in ye Summer our former Consultations with [Pelham] have been talked of in so disagreeable a way that I am surfeited.' Wynn claimed that Beaufort had also succumbed to political introversion, and it is certainly true that the party activity and reputation of all three men never regained their pre-1746 level. Beaufort was increasingly beset with gout as well as disillusionment, and Wynn and Cotton suffered from their incrimination as Jacobite conspirators at Lord Lovat's trial in 1747.[54]

Tory apathy and the party's internal bickering contributed to a poor electoral performance in 1747. Of the 133 tory candidates who are known to have stood, 110 were returned. Five of these were subsequently expelled by a House of Commons 'seemingly inclined', as Thomas Carew wrote, 'to be perfectly unanimous, and for that purpose... getting rid of as many as they can of those who differ from the majority'.[55] It was a fitting epilogue to a grim campaign. Sir Charles Mordaunt's return for Warwickshire had eventually gone uncontested, but not before his parliamentary conduct in 1745 had been exposed to denigration by his tory neighbours. When Sir Roger Newdigate sought Sir Robert Grosvenor's tory interest in the Middlesex county contest, he was told that Grosvenor 'would promise no body till he saw their behaviour next session'. Grosvenor himself was beginning his family's long and unctuous pursuit of respectability and a peerage. At the 1747 Chester contest he discarded all partisan designations and stood 'neuter'.[56]

Predictably enough, the ministry attributed tory decline to tory treason: 'the eyes of people are much opened by rebellion', wrote Sir Dudley Ryder with much complacency. Since only sixty-five English constituencies were contested in 1747, few people were actually in a position to register their alienation from a disaffected toryism. In the Middlesex, Westminster, and London contests, tory defeat certainly owed something to their opponents' exploitation of those Jacobite trials which had been held in the capital. In Lancashire and Yorkshire too – both counties which had been directly imperilled by the invasion – some tory candidates received the attentions of anti-Jacobite mobs. But in most of the constituencies involved, such low-level protests naturally had little effect on the actual election result. Sir Richard Shuttleworth's coach was overturned by loyalist rioters, but he was still returned for Lancashire; Richard Barry, son of the Jacobite Lord Barrymore and himself a suspect, was still able to defeat two whig candidates at Wigan.[57] Far more damaging to the tories was the defection of some of their own electoral patrons and the loss of much of the opposition whig assistance on which they had previously been able to draw. In 1741 Lichfield, Newcastle under Lyme, and Staffordshire had given their six seats to tories; in 1747, after the revolution in Leveson-Gower allegiance, they gave the party only one. In 1741 the whig Eliot family had returned John Hynde Cotton, son of the tory leader, as one of St Germans' two opposition M.P.s. In 1747 the Eliots gave their electoral interest to the government, and the young Cotton became a victim twice over of his party's ostracism. Evicted from St Germans, he went and contested Bedford. But the duke of Bedford, who had returned two tories for this borough in 1741, was now First Lord of the Admiralty. In 1747 Bedford elected two whig M.P.s: not, one suspects, because of its voters' anti-Jacobitism, but rather, as contemporaries judged, as 'absolutely the Effect of the Duke's Influence & assiduity'.[58]

The tories had not, it is true, been deprived of all whig electoral aid. Since May 1746 those M.P.s attached to the Prince of Wales had tended to vote against Pelham's administration. On 4 June 1747, fourteen days before Parliament was dissolved, Frederick sanctioned the Carlton House declaration. This document promised the tories moderate constitutional reform: Place and Militia Bills, restrictions on the Civil List, and a £300 *per annum* landed qualification for J.P.s. It also urged them to 'coalise and unite' with the Prince, and made clear their incentive: 'His R.H. promises...totally to abolish for the future all Distinctions of Party...to take away all Proscription from any Set of men whatever, who are Friends to the Constitution.'[59]

It has sometimes been suggested that this initiative was designed to secure tory–Leicester House collaboration in the July elections. Sir Francis Dashwood, one of the three whig M.P.s present when Frederick issued his declaration, certainly assisted the tory Coningsby Sibthorp in his return for Lincoln. In the contested election at Hereford, Velters Cornewall placed his tory interest behind one of Frederick's associates, Daniel Leighton, and had his wife made woman of the bedchamber to the Princess as a reward.[60] But these were sporadic and individualised efforts. As Lord Oxford noted in his journal, the tory leaders did not agree to the terms of the Carlton House declaration until 6 February 1748; their reply was rightly characterised by Philip Yorke as 'respectful but cold'; and Frederick's own reaction, when Dashwood gave him this belated document two days later, scarcely suggests a fully fledged and current alliance: 'I told him it was a very Civil Paper, but what then?'[61] In the sense of what did the treaty mean to its tory participants, and what impact did it have on Pelham's ministry, the Prince's uncertainty has remained the historiographical norm. Yet in its inception at least, the tory–Leicester House agreement is remarkably well documented.

The prime tory agent in the negotiations had been Peniston Powney, M.P. for Berkshire and one of Frederick's creditors. By way of his brother, a Fellow of Balliol, Powney communicated with Dashwood, and with Dashwood's uncle Lord Westmorland – a one-time whig Jacobite turned Leicester House man, and soon to be made High Steward of Oxford University. Serious negotiations seem to have got underway only in October 1747. By then the tories had digested their electoral attrition; rumours of the Prince's reconciliation with the ministry had proved false; and Powney was dispatched to Leicester House to indicate tory interest if Frederick would add to his terms a promise to restore triennial Parliaments. Frederick refused, and it was only after some hectic intrigue and two tory conferences in London that Powney's brother was able to assure the Master of Balliol on 30 November that 'the Execution of the Scheme is defer'd till after Xmas, and there is a strong Probability that it will then take place... [the

Prince] expresses in the most pathetic Manner the thorough sense He has of the ill Treatment we have met with'. In the new year the duke of Beaufort was delayed in the country by gout, but in February 1748 the tory reply was finally drafted at his London residence in the presence of Lords Oxford and Lichfield, Sir Walter Bagot, Cotton, Fazakerley, and Prowse.[62]

The tories had kept their negotiations secret; the Prince made their agreement known. The copies of the Carlton House declaration which survive in the manuscript collections of whig V.I.P.s are as indicative as the consternation of a nondescript M.P. like Edward Bayntun Rolt: 'The Prince's proposal to the Tories', he noted in November, 'has given great offence to the Whiggs.' Frederick must have relished the fuss. Aware of his own reputation for inadequacy, jealous of the duke of Cumberland's military exploits (and furious at his support of the Pelhams' February 1746 coup), Frederick needed parliamentary auxiliaries to advertise his nuisance potential and attract ministerial notice. This personal need made him, as the tories recognised, an unstable political ally. By 1751 Frederick was defying the opposition strategy of his chief adviser, Lord Egmont, and lapping up the attentions of the duke of Newcastle and his Paymaster General, William Pitt.[63]

At first glance one might wonder why either Pitt or Newcastle bothered. After the 1747 election the Prince was credited with forty-eight supporters in the Commons, and in October 1748 Lord Dupplin calculated that there were only seventy-four dissident whigs of any description in the House. Neither these M.P.s nor the 110 or so tories attended in strength between 1748 and 1751. In the parliamentary divisions forced by the tory–Leicester House group in 1748, 1749, and 1750, the opposition's average vote was only eighty-six, and the ministry's average divisional majority actually rose over this period: fifty-six in 1748, sixty-four in 1749, and seventy-eight in 1750.[64] The Prince's counsels were divided, with Egmont, Dodington, and the Liskeard M.P., Dr George Lee, contending for primacy, and tory mistrust of the Prince and contempt for his personality were no less evident. 'I have talk'd the death of Fred[eric]k over with our friends', the wife of one of the Prince's premier tory advocates, the Suffolk M.P. Sir Cordell Firebrace, was to write in April 1751, 'and they all seem to like it.'[65] Why, then, did such a muted and shabby alliance arouse ministerial alarm and the interest of careerists like Pitt?

The obvious answer is of course that by 1750 George II was sixty-seven: puny as Frederick was, his future importance seemed both assured and imminent. But there was, perhaps, more to ministerial whig consternation than this. It is not easy to reconstruct high-political activity and opinion between the defeat of the Young Pretender in 1746 and the triumph of Pitt ten years later. Not only does John Owen's excellent narrative account terminate in 1746 and lack a sequel, but contemporary evidence is also confused and uneven. Only one complete Commons division list appears to have survived for the period 1747–56, and the bulk of the papers of the prime and most balanced whig Minister, Henry Pelham, have perished. The duke of Newcastle's archives are, by contrast, only too abundant, tempting their afficionados into confusing labyrinthine gossip, busy speculation, and the duke's wearisome anxieties with the real stuff of politics. What is certain is that if Henry Pelham could be panicked (as reportedly he was) into believing that a talented visionary like Lord Egmont would be his successor, and if that equally stolid and informed whig, Philip Yorke, could 'consider our government in a state very near anarchical', then ministerial security in this period must at times have seemed more precarious to its contemporaries than the parliamentary statistics would suggest.[66]

Ministerial difficulties were twofold. The duke of Bedford, who had been made Secretary of State for the North in 1748, was soon at odds with the Pelhams, and the interest which this potentially internecine dispute aroused can be seen in the attendance of nearly four hundred M.P.s at the division on the Bedford Turnpike Bill on 29 January 1750 – the 'Fullest House and greatest division of any day of the Session'. Bedford was intriguing with the duke of Cumberland and Princess Amelia, and the Pelhams were thus confronted with both a psychological and a substantive threat: the alienation of the bulk of the politically active House of Hanover.[67] By recruiting his ministry from a variety of whig and ex-tory sources, Pelham had already deprived himself of those appeals to Old Corps elitism and whig distinction which Walpole had deployed to such parliamentary effect. Now it seemed that the House of Hanover, the only traditional focus of partisan loyalty which Pelhamite whiggery retained, was beginning seriously to detach itself from its conventional champions. The Pelhams were paying the price of thinking proprietorial party attitudes redundant, and their response to Horace Walpole's pamphlet *Delenda est Oxonia* gives some indication of their vulnerability on this score: a vulnerability which gave the tories' princely alliance an impact quite disproportionate to its parliamentary strength.

In March 1749, after some quasi-Jacobite demonstrations in Oxford, the administration made plans for a visitation of the University. Horace Walpole, who had been writing against the government since 1747 (because, as he subsequently and significantly explained, the Pelhams had 'neglected the Whigs to court the Tories'), composed an ostensibly tory riposte. He reminded the government that one of the precipitants of the whigs' own Glorious Revolution had been James II's assault on the property of Oxford University, and that the proposed visitation, like recent political realignments, showed how bankrupt the conventional emphases of whig propaganda had become: Oxford men wished, he wrote, 'to have it reconciled to their apprehensions, how affection to the eldest son of the Elector of Hanover should be a mark of Jacobitism; how attachment to the House of Pelham is whiggism & loyalty'. Ministerial agents descended on Walpole's printer and seized the manuscript before its inconvenient historical parallels could be made public.[68]

Oxford affairs also showed how the ministry's ideological and royal predicament could be accompanied by tory benefit. On 13 April 1749 Dr William King, the once-Jacobite Principal of St Mary's Hall, delivered a Latin speech at the opening of the Radcliffe Camera, urging that Britain be restored to rightful kingship and political purity. This speech has usually been described as pro-Stuart in impetus, and some of its audience must indeed have interpreted it that way. But amongst the audience was not only the tory hierarchy – Beaufort, Oxford, and Wynn – but also Peniston Powney, link-man with the Prince of Wales, and several of Frederick's own associates – Westmorland, Dashwood, and Lord Chief Justice Sir John Willes.[69] For these men the speech was an invocation not to the Stuarts, but rather to the prospect of a renovated Hanoverian regime. By 1749 high tories like King had been informed of Charles Edward Stuart's deterioration into an avaricious and undignified sot: an impression not reversed by his visit to London in 1750. As a man, Frederick was unimpressive, but his potential kingship and the English upbringing of his sons could serve both to reanimate tory royalism, and to attract disillusioned crypto-Jacobites like the London M.P., George Heathcote, and Lord Orrery, who communicated with Frederick by way of Dr Lee. Frederick took care to foster this legitimist transference. He planned to renounce his claim to Hanover at his accession; he had successfully interceded for one of the rebel Scottish Lords after the '45; and he even employed Catherine Walkinshaw, the sister of the Young Pretender's mistress, as maid of honour to his own Princess.[70] So while ministerial whigs rehearsed the dilemma of the 1760s, and waited for the death of the monarch they had possessed for over twenty years and the hostility of his successor, the pro-Hanoverian bulk of the tory party and its crypto-Jacobite residue felt themselves to be regaining one of the fundamentals of their historical creed.

The Prince also offered immediate and practical advantages. It was primarily because of the celerity of his response that the ministry withdrew its threat of a visitation of Oxford. Defeated by Newcastle for the Chancellorship of Cambridge University, and spurred on by the consideration that Cambridge's High Steward was Newcastle's confidant, Lord Chancellor Hardwicke, Frederick took the other and more suspect English University under his wing. On 1 May 1749 116 Lords and Commoners, drawn mainly from the tory party but with the leading Leicester House men also in attendance, met at the tory St Albans Tavern. Their ostensible aim was to condemn the visitation. In fact, since the ministry's decision to withdraw was already known to the tory leadership, the real design was to advertise a potent association. 'We are much beholden to a great Person, for sending in All under his Influence to our assistance', wrote one tory participant, 'and as we suppose, it may now be found that some Fingers have been burnt; so we are in no pain lest our Adversarys should soon venture to rally.'[71]

Given the size of the tory contingent at the St Albans meeting, and its agreement with Frederick's representatives to oppose 'not only measures directly threatening the Universitys, but also any other Points which should appear to them destructive of the Publick Good', how extensive was the tory parliamentary party's commitment to Leicester House, and how was this commitment expressed in joint political activity?[72]

In the constituency analyses which Egmont compiled for the Prince between 1749 and 1751 only three tories are identified as hostile. One of these was Beaufort's brother-in-law, Norborne Berkeley. The others were George Pitt and George Chaffin, both M.P.s for Dorset and members of Lord Shaftesbury's Shaston Club, a constituency society which had attracted the firebrand Beckford brothers and which was attached, like Shaftesbury himself, to Egmont's rival George Bubb Dodington. Since Egmont lived to a considerable degree in his own political world his estimate is hardly conclusive, but we know from other sources that by 1750 the Prince had made contact with most sectors of the tory party. He met and consulted with its new generation of leaders – Prowse, Northey, and William Beckford. He had won support from the Jacobite fringe and from substantial county tories like Powney, Cornewall, and Sir Walter Bagot. He had penetrated the radical toryism of the metropolis by way of Dodington's links with the Independent Electors and his own subsidies to the Independents' candidate in the 1749 Westminster by-election. He also contributed money and his followers' votes to the tory George Cooke's return for Middlesex in 1750, thereby aiding the party's recovery from its 1747 débâcle in England's most politicised county.[73]

Mutual concern for metropolitan popularity also provided for parliamentary collaboration between tory and Leicester House M.P.s. In March 1750 eighteen tories and eleven of Frederick's supporters, including Egmont and Lee, dominated a parliamentary committee set up to improve poor relief and night-watch facilities in St Martin-in-the-Fields – one of Westminster's poorer and most opposition-orientated parishes. Tories participated too in those extra-parliamentary ventures, which were designed to promote Frederick's image as a humane and responsible prince. On 19 September 1750 Frederick, his Chancellor Thomas Bootle, and Dodington consulted with Sir Nathaniel Curzon, William Northey, and Velters Cornewall on ways to aid the white herring industry and so (the newspapers claimed) improve the domestic economy and employment opportunities. Their place of meeting was the King's Arms Tavern, the regular venue of the Leicester House socio-political King's Arms Club.[74]

There is no doubt that a few tories were attracted by the Prince's popularist gambits and vaunted reformism. The Colchester tory Charles Gray wanted Frederick's accession to be accompanied by parliamentary reform. John Morton, M.P. for Abingdon, urged the Prince's Clerk of the Household, Sir John Cust, to make 'Oeconomy' the fulcrum of his master's campaign – so that 'whatever we obtain must be a real good to ye people'. More generally, Frederick's hostility to the duke of Cumberland ensured that one of the persistent policy obstacles to an agreement between the tories and the Hanoverian heir – the former's desire to reduce the Army and the latter's determination to maintain it at full strength – was modified. In 1749 and 1750 both tory and Leicester House politicians combined in Commons motions to limit the military and the application of martial law.[75]

But when Peniston Powney compiled a party circular on 'reasons for the Tories coaliting with the Prince', he placed far more emphasis on future and substantial gains than on policy compatibility with Leicester House or the immediate benefits of coalition: 'It is necessary for him [Frederick] to have Assurances, whereby to form a future Administration; & if you decline taking part in that, you can be nothing but in Opposition in conjunction with the worse set of Men in the present Ministry.' By 1750 the main spokesman for principled tory isolationism, Sir Watkin Williams Wynn, was dead; the younger tory leaders and the veteran Sir John Hynde Cotton had always been in favour of the tories' pursuing office on terms. The party was uniquely exempt from the main disadvantage attendant on collusion with the reversionary interest. Whereas Dodington had to make his ill-fated decision in 1749 to give up Pelhamite employment and gamble on future glory under King Frederick, no such sacrifice was demanded of the tories. In

Powney's blunt paraphrase: 'The present Ministry & all its Connections hate you, & will proscribe you, as long as they are in power.'[76]

Frederick and most (though not all) of his advisers were far more sympathetic. By April 1750 Egmont and Frederick had agreed that the new reign would see Lord Oxford as Privy Seal; that Cotton would revert to his former office as Treasurer of the Chamber; and that Lords Harley and Guernsey and Sir Charles Mordaunt would be appointed to the Treasury Board. As the tory commitment to the Prince developed, so an increasing number of men had to be accommodated in Egmont's schemes for future promotions. Peniston Powney and Sir Cordell Firebrace were put down for the Admiralty; William Northey was allocated to the Board of Trade; while Thomas Prowse was to receive somewhat modest recompense as Surveyor General of the Woods.[77] The seductive power of even prospective employment can be traced in Nicholas Fazakerley's fluctuating response to the Prince's overtures. As late as January 1748 he had regarded the Carlton House proposals with suspicion: 'I don't at present', he told Prowse, 'think any thing so amiable in any of them as to have determin'd upon any measures to guide my own action.' Yet Fazakerley helped to draft the tory reply in February, and by April 1749 Egmont judged him 'very cordial' – his receptivity doubtless being heightened by the prospect of appointment as Master of the Rolls 'upon the change'.[78]

III

Frederick's death in March 1751 aborted these specific projects and seemed also to compromise the tories' more general ambition for a productive association with a Hanoverian king. Although the Princess Dowager had no love for the Pelhams, she disappointed tory optimists by deciding to entrust herself and her eldest son to the protection of their King. Dr George Lee, like Dodington and the bulk of the Leicester House contingent, also sought salvation in political orthodoxy. Since 1749 that most talented monitor of political flux, William Pitt, had paid tribute to improved tory prospects by renewing his contacts with the party's notables, as well as by forging his own links with the Prince. As soon as Frederick died, Pitt reneged on these opposition initiatives, and scuttled back for a time to the Pelhamite fold.[79]

Even before these individual manoeuvres had been finalised, attempts to prolong the tory–Leicester House conjunction by artificial means had proved impractical. On 25 March, five days after Frederick's death, George Cooke and William Northey instructed James Ralph to continue publishing the opposition journal the *Remembrancer*, and on 7 April

Lords Westmorland, Oxford, and Shaftesbury agreed to raise £200 to finance the paper. The independent whig earl Stanhope drew up a new opposition manifesto around which dissident politicians might coalesce.[80] This document is mildly interesting as political theory; it could hardly have been more inadequate as a blueprint for immediate political action. Sir Francis Dashwood noted that it was 'not approved by Torys', and Betty Kemp has attributed their disinclination to the manifesto's partisan bias:

> The Tories may well have disliked its philosophy of government, its assertion of natural rights, its hint of an association and such phrases as 'Delegation of Power from the People to their Representatives in Parliament'. These things, combined with a reverence for the principles of the Revolution and a conviction that the times were corrupt and the constitution in danger, were 'true Whiggism' rather than Toryism.

This observation itself is suspect, but the theoretical content of Stanhope's paper was scarcely the point at issue. No more in their association with Leicester House after 1747, than in their working alliance with the Patriots in the 1730s, had the tories been primarily concerned with an ideological *rapprochement* with the whigs. They had wanted rather to increase their parliamentary weight in the short term, and, in the case of the Carlton House agreement, to ensure the sympathetic attention of the future monarch. Neither Stanhope's manifesto, written, as Dodington was quick to notice, 'in terms...that imply an exclusion of coming into office', nor its sponsorship by a group of peripheral peers, had anything to offer a proscribed minority in Parliament.[81]

The end of 1751 and the next two years seemed to see the summer of Pelhamite whig content. Their opposition to the terms of the 1751 Regency Bill allowed tory M.P.s to advertise their monarchism, and the Jewish Naturalisation Bill provided scope for some intolerant Anglican oratory. But these episodes took place in a tactical vacuum and amidst general parliamentary absenteeism. When Sir James Dashwood opened the tory attack on the Jew Bill on 15 November 1753 – the first day of the session – the Commons was well-nigh empty: 'Sir James took notice of the thinness of the House and mov'd for a general call...to take ye repeal of ye Jew Bill into consideration.' More errant tory activists, such as Sir John Philipps and William Beckford, sought relief from parliamentary ennui in intrigues with the duke of Bedford and popularist *cum* republican campaigns against Princess Amelia as Ranger of Richmond Park. More sober tories, such as Thomas Prowse, acquiesced in Pelham's bland and efficient administration while keeping a close eye on William Pitt, immobilised as Paymaster General and at a distance from royal regard since 1746.[82]

An administration as broadly based and as colourless as Pelham's could prevent effective opposition from without; it was ill-equipped to satisfy its own more brilliant and idiosyncratic members. As Lord Hillsborough reminded that conventional (and therefore incredulous) intriguer, Bubb Dodington, a system in which 'Everybody of consequence ...had everything divided amongst them' catered only to the simpler varieties of greed: 'Pitt's passion was ambition, not avarice. That he was at a full stop as things were, and could have no hopes of going farther: he was once popular: if he could again make a disturbance, and get the country of his side, he might have hopes: now, and on this system, he could have none.' Neither Pitt, nor his rival Fox, nor the troublesome duke of Cumberland needed to look far for a potential source of disturbance. Since the Treaty of Aix-la-Chapelle in 1748, Pelham and Newcastle had monitored French expansion in North America, rightly regarding it as a continuation in the New World of France's manoeuvres in the Old. If a colonial war was to occur and escalate into a European conflict, it would strain the Pelhamite consensus and Newcastle's own abilities as Secretary of State, while supplying the ideal *point d'appui* for an aspiring politician.[83]

Any politician in revolt against the Old Corps was likely to require parliamentary fodder, which was all that the tories, with their membership reduced to one fifth of the House of Commons, could plausibly expect to be. But the Broad-Bottom experiment of 1744–5 and the Carlton House agreement had shown that the tories' remarkable cohesion exacted its own price. Rather as that other minority, the Foxite whigs, in their 1783–4 coalition with Lord North, were to suffer from the expectations aroused by Burke's prior insistence on party distinction and responsibility, so the tories had found it difficult to coalesce with Pelhamite whiggery or render such a liaison acceptable to their extra-parliamentary supporters. With only limited if disciplined voting power to offer, the tories, as Horatio Walpole diagnosed in October 1754, could settle for nothing less than an acknowledged patriot in return. It was fortunate indeed that the tory leaders' need to reconcile practical policy with their supporters' emotional protest, or, as one pamphleteer was later to describe their predicament, the need to 'recover your importance without giving up the absurdities of your ancestors', coincided for a time with the imperatives of Pitt's ambition.[84]

Acceptance and Dispersal? 1754 and Onwards

The death of Henry Pelham in March 1754 tends to invigorate political historians of the eighteenth century as much as the demise of Lord Palmerston does their nineteenth-century counterparts. Just as the consensual politics of the early 1860s supposedly gave way to a two-party competition for a Reform Act, so Pelham's complacent whig confederation and 'unexciting useful measures' are traditionally followed by the abrasive parliamentary rivalry of William Pitt and Henry Fox and the glamour and cupidity of empire. It was natural that contemporary historians should also have sought in the 1750s the genesis of the convulsions of George III's early reign. Predictably enough, they found it. Both John Almon and Horace Walpole claimed that the fragmentation of conventional whig and tory alignments in the 1760s – a fragmentation which gave the King much greater room for manoeuvre than hitherto – was already in process in the previous decade. Even in their own day, this thesis did not go unmodified. Walpole himself was later to date the abrogation of two-party distinctions from the Regency Crisis of 1765.[1] Yet it is his earlier argument, that some of the structural changes usually attributed to George III's accession began in fact ten years before, which has recently been disinterred and lent the cosmetic of fresh complexity.

J. C. D. Clark has asserted that the mid 1750s witnessed a revolution in political arguments and alignments which culminated in the Pitt–Newcastle coalition of 1757 – a governmental amalgam so multifarious that it absorbed and obliterated the three parliamentary categories of tory, ministerial whig, and opposition whig which had been the parliamentary norm since 1715.[2] From the 1740s onwards, Clark argues, the Old Corps' leaders had come to rely 'less and less on their whig purity for their hold over the King'. The duke of Newcastle, who became First Lord of the Treasury in 1754, 'was, and thought himself, essential for his administrative expertise...and for the numbers he could command in Commons divisions'. Consequently, government spokesmen in the early 1750s felt able to dispense with the usual rallying invocations of the Old Corps' elitist whig identity and the traditional identification of tory oppositionists with crypto-Jacobites. Indeed, Newcastle anticipated the manoeuvres of Lord Bute in considering a parliamentary juncture with the tories. This ministerial innovation meant that whereas earlier whig dissidents like William Pulteney had coalesced with tory M.P.s and denied their disaffection, in the 1750s errant and aspiring whigs like William Pitt were forced to challenge the administration's *sotto voce* presentation of Jacobitism, pose as the guardians of whig purity, and accuse Newcastle of implementing tory, in the sense of arbitrary, policies. Thus Newcastle's rehearsal of Butism was countered by Pitt employing what was to be a stock device of Rockingham whig propaganda in the 1760s and 1770s: the accusation that an unworthy whig administration was implementing a 'New Toryism'.[3]

According to this version, George III's reign not only witnessed a continuation of these ministerial and opposition whig polemics, but also confirmed rather than inaugurated the era of tory acceptance and therefore of tory dispersal. (For both the historians who date tory acceptance from 1760 and those who antedate it imply that toryism was bound to dissolve once the mould of proscription had been removed.) Since, according to Clark, post-1714 toryism derived its rationale and major ideological thrust from Jacobitism, the failure of the '45 was bound to weaken the party and make it receptive to accommodation with the administration. In the autumn of 1754 the tories reached an agreement with Newcastle and achieved 'a valuable working relationship' with the Minister which lasted until September 1755: a remarkable achievement, given that Parliament had been prorogued in April. Because of this governmental entente the tories initially held aloof from Pitt's concurrent opposition ventures, and it was this tory indifference and mistrust which underlay his parliamentary weakness in 1755–6. When the tories did agree to co-operate with Pitt, and to support the Devonshire–Pitt administration of 1756–7 and its Newcastle–Pitt successor, they found themselves upstaged – 'Left with no distinctive Patriot platform from which to attack a ministry whose Patriot status they admitted', and forced to acquiesce 'in a vicarious identification with a wartime regime in which the real losers were themselves'.[4]

All this is too neat. Historians have often exaggerated the novelty and impact of George III's political conduct (to say nothing of the novelty and extra-parliamentary impact of John Wilkes) by ignoring pre-1760 developments. But one is unlikely to redress excessive concentration on one decade of British political history by a myopic obsession with its predecessor. Signs of impending rot can certainly be detected in the high and low politics of the 1740s and 1750s. But the accession of a new King, the emergence of a new generation of leading politicians, and the domestic strains (still largely unexplored) of Britain's involvement in the Seven Years War were bound to ensure that the rate and extent of political change increased after 1760.

In the 1750s most of the major ministerial posts were filled by yesterday's men. When his brother died, the duke of Newcastle was sixty-one; Lord Chancellor Hardwicke was sixty-four; the duke of Argyll, who influenced the bulk of Scotland's M.P.s if not the disposal of its patronage, was seventy-two; and the King himself was seventy-three. George III was to ascend the throne at the age of twenty, determined never to allow ministers to 'trample' on him; George II was never entirely committed to Newcastle as first Minister, but he was usually prepared to trust and be guided by him. This qualified royal support, and all that it implied about the likely distribution of patronage, helped to ensure that the bulk of whig M.P.s and peers who had followed Walpole and Pelham also stuck by Newcastle. As Lord Waldegrave told the King when Newcastle was in temporary retirement in February 1757,

It was very apparent a great majority in both houses of parliament still considered him as their chief, and were ready to act under his direction. That some of these might possibly be attached to him by a principle of gratitude; but the greater number were his followers because they had reason to expect that he would soon be in a condition to reward their services.[5]

The greater number of Old Corps parliamentarians also followed Newcastle because he represented a variant of whiggism which had been dominant for over thirty years. This Old Corps image meant that, while Newcastle had some dealings with the tories ('but I do not think he ever liked it' wrote Richard Pares, and neither do I), he did not need, nor was he able, to indulge in an overt association with tory M.P.s. The tories' reputed crypto-Jacobitism was never the *primum mobile* of eighteenth-century whig prejudice. Consequently, when various ministerial spokesmen denied the reality of Jacobitism in 1754 (largely in order to protect William Murray, Newcastle's Attorney-General, from disingenuous aspersions on his Jacobite ancestry), their disclaimers could not and did not dispel that prejudice. Xenophobic whiggery was rather an instinctive emotion and a rational product of greed for patronage. In 1752, when Murray and Andrew Stone, Lord of Trade and Sub-Governor to the Prince of Wales, were accused of indoctrinating the Hanoverian heir with arbitrary and pro-tory notions, Lord Chesterfield had commented that 'No reasonable man' thought them guilty, 'But parties do not reason, and every Whig party man, which is nine in ten of the Whig party, is fully convinced.'[6] Newcastle's capacity to retain nine out of ten whig party men in the Commons constituted, as

Clark notes, one of his major recommendations to the King. It is thus convoluted in the extreme for Clark to quote as valid the duke of Grafton's judgement that Newcastle survived the parliamentary and ministerial crises of 1754–5 'because he was supported by the body of Whigs', and simultaneously to claim that Newcastle was able to adopt an a-party stance because of his administrative and parliamentary strength. Had this parliamentary strength not been based on habitual whig loyalty to Ministers in the Old Corps tradition as well as on royal favour, Newcastle would not have been able to prevent George II from appointing a Fox–Waldegrave administration in June 1757 by threatening a mass resignation of Old Corps ministers. When Newcastle tried this same blackmail device in 1762, it failed. Clearly whig political habits and expectations had changed in the interim.[7]

Partly they had changed because of mortality. In one of the most illuminating roll-calls in British historical writing, Sir Lewis Namier pointed out how the gerontocracy which had ruled England throughout the 1750s succumbed at last to the reaper in the 1760s, as did many middle-aged whig stalwarts.

The Duke of Argyll died in 1761, Lord Anson and Lord Melcombe (Dodington) in 1762, Lord Granville and Lord Egremont in 1763, Lord Hardwicke, Lord Bath, H. B. Legge, and the Duke of Devonshire in 1764, the Duke of Cumberland in 1765, Charles Townshend in 1767, the Duke of Newcastle in 1768, Lord Ligonier, Lord Granby…George Grenville, and Charles Yorke in 1770, the Duke of Bedford in 1771. When Lord North became First Lord of the Treasury, of those who had been leaders in 1760 and for many years before it, hardly any were alive, and, barring Chatham and Sandwich, none were any longer active in politics. It was in these ten years, 1760–70, that the real change supervened in the political personnel as well as in political ideas.[8]

And that change was marked because the prime governmental successors of these Old Corps old men were not just younger, but also of a different partisan background.

What was novel in high politics in the late 1740s and 1750s was not so much the emphases of parliamentary argument, as the number of up-and-coming politicians who were compelled into trumpeting whiggery because their own origins were tory. In 1754 the Secretary at War, Henry Fox, the Chancellor of the Exchequer, the Hon. Henry Legge, and the Paymaster General, William Pitt, were all sons of tory politicians; Viscount Dupplin, Lord of the Treasury, was a grandson of Robert Harley, earl of Oxford; William Murray, Attorney-General, was the son of a Jacobite peer. The fact that the Old Corps had drawn so heavily on alien recruits for its talent suggests that it was in demographic difficulties before the antics of George III; but again, this partial ex-tory influx also confirms that the 1750s was a transitional period. The new reign did not witness a New Toryism, but it was to be dominated by old tory families. Henry Pelham left no sons and the duke of Newcastle no progeny at all. The Yorkes and Walpoles were all dead or politically insignificant by 1770. After the deaths of the fourth duke of Devonshire in 1764 and the duke of Bedford seven years later, no Cavendish or Russell achieved major ministerial office until the next century. Not the scions of the great whig families, but another Pitt, another Fox, and Lord North, grandson of Robert Harley's Lord of Trade and Chancellor of Oxford University, were to predominate in late-eighteenth-century British politics.

And what of those tories who remained true blue? When the Leominster tory M.P., Chase Price, looked back in 1762, it was clear to him that their association with William Pitt and the political responsibility exacted by a national war had altered the tories' political stance. He also recognised that this modification had been partial. Proscription at the centre had not been removed. Neither Newcastle nor Pitt had wanted to employ tories *qua* tories, as distinct from insisting (as had been the practice since 1715) that tory politicians desirous of office should conform to the nuances of whiggery. George III's appointment of tory courtiers – a concession announced separately from his whig appointments – was thus an innovation of enormous symbolic importance: 'Behold then these guardians of the liberties and landed interest of Britain, these formidable & serious rivals & heterogeneous long-established faction, these plain *honest* country gentlemen at once incorporate in the vast Body at St. James.'[9] Price here was sacrificing exactitude to irony, because the tories derived their distinction from their ideology as well as from their exclusion. The Newcastle–Pitt administration had not been able to pre-empt the tory platform. Rather, in working out its response to a new type of whig minister of tory birth, the party was made to recognise that no administration could satisfy the peculiar blend of monarchical, Anglican, anti-executive, and radical attitudes which it had been able to nurture in the vacuum of political irresponsibility. Nor could any monarch. It was not only access to respectability and limited employment which compromised tory cohesion after 1760, but also the parliamentary, extra-parliamentary, and transatlantic developments of George III's early reign. The tory bloc at Westminster was bound to undergo considerable fragmentation in the 1760s and 1770s because, although most of its Members still thought and endeavoured to act like tories, they could no longer reconcile those potentially contradictory policy emphases which had characterised them under proscription.

I

The 1754 general election returned 110 tory M.P.s to Parliament – a total which includes Viscount Philip Wenman and Sir James Dashwood, victims of a double return for Oxfordshire. On 18 November eighty-eight tories attended for the first Commons division on this most contentious of election petitions. They were defeated by 267 votes to 97 and, as one tory observer noted, his party's nine whig auxiliaries were only '*silent* voters'. On 25 November William Pitt launched into a eulogy of the whig principles and nonconformist supporters of the petitioner for Berwick-on-Tweed, one John Wilkes. Two days later he attacked Oxford University, 'perpetually breeding up a race of Jacobites', and touched, none too lightly, on the supposed disaffection of Newcastle's prime spokesman in the Commons, William Murray. Not to be outdone in these genuflections to unsullied whiggery, Henry Fox inaugurated 1755 by moving to abolish Parliament's commemoration of Charles I's execution.[10]

Both whig and tory politicians recognised the purpose behind this theatre. Pitt and Fox had been immobilised in their respective state offices for ten years; with Newcastle stranded in the Lords, both men were in pursuit of the leadership of the Commons, and, like dissident whigs before them, they legitimised their truculence and ambition by claiming to be more whig than the whig premier. Their instinctive resort to this tactic and Murray's vulnerability to references to his unorthodox past demonstrate the political continuity of the 1750s and the duke of Newcastle's own confinement. Since Pelham's death he had been in sporadic consultation with Dr George Lee, who had maintained some of the tory contacts forged in the service of the late Prince of Wales. Early in December reports were current that Newcastle had been visited by yet another ex-Leicester House chieftain, Lord Egmont, who brought with him three tory M.P.s, including Thomas Prowse and Dashwood: 'to let him know that the body of tories would assist him in all points *not directly inconsistent with their political creed*'.[11]

Although there were rumours that this initiative would lead to limited tory employment, the safety clause and Dashwood's inclusion in the deputation indicate its limited nature and mainspring. John Bright's symbolic defeat at Manchester in 1857 is perhaps the only electoral shock at all comparable with the tories' loss of Oxfordshire in 1754–5. Much of the party's history, many of its ideologues, and the educational background of the majority of its Members were all bound up with this constituency. Hence the Treasury's allocation of the largest portion of secret service money expended on the general election to

Oxfordshire's conquest, and hence the tories' own costly investment in the election and their nation-wide subscription to fund the subsequent petition.[12] But financial ingenuity was futile unless the tories also acquired whig support in the Commons. Henry Fox had been responsible for encouraging the duke of Marlborough to challenge the tories' hold on the county and had subsequently made himself whig manager for the Oxfordshire petition; Pitt's provocative attack on Oxford University had similarly advertised his desire 'to court the whigs', not the tories, in his pursuit of political primacy. In 1754 the tories may, as Newcastle's spy reported, have preferred his administration to the pretensions of 'those who are only for themselves', but the duke's main attraction was that he was the party's only remaining option.[13]

For Newcastle, however, the tories would normally have been no option at all. His insecurity was of paranoiac proportions, but since he estimated that his Commons majority was over two hundred, what he needed was an adept politician to manage this whig miscellany, not the conditional co-operation of tory backbenchers. Just as the tories' approach to Newcastle had been primarily an *ad hoc* response to a particular emergency, so the party's only real appeal derived not from any major parliamentary reconfiguration, but from his predicament over the Mitchell election.[14]

In 1754 this Cornish borough had returned Robert Clive and John Stephenson – a one-time dissident whig who had assisted George Cooke in his tory canvass of Middlesex in 1750. The two unsuccessful Treasury candidates, Richard Hussey and Simon Luttrell, petitioned, but found themselves opposed by Henry Fox, by the M.P.s responsive to the direction of the dukes of Argyll and Bedford, and even by Newcastle's closest ally, Lord Hardwicke. Prowse and Northey saw their opportunity. They were not so unrealistic as to demand (as Horace Walpole claimed) that Fox and Pitt be displaced in their favour. But since the dispute seemed likely to escalate into 'A contest between the Duke of Newcastle and Mr. Fox, and if the former do carry it...all seem to think it will be by so small a majority as will prove fatal to the present premier', they offered the Minister their party's votes. And, as he complained to the whig M.P. for Chippenham, the Oxfordshire petition was 'the condition of their supporting him'.[15]

This arid and complicated gambit emphasises the tories' current desperation, and it could have no weight at all with Newcastle. His whips assured him, erroneously as it turned out, that sufficient whig M.P.s would vote for Luttrell and Hussey for him to be able to rebuff tory coercion. And even if Newcastle's anxieties had not been so appeased, the partisan spite which Foxite, Pittite, and Treasury M.P.s all demonstrated during the Oxfordshire election inquiry would have made it impossible for a whig Minister to yield on such a symbolic issue. The tory leaders also found their strategy obstructed by party sentiment, their supporters having little desire to salvage the politician who most personified Old Corps corruption. George Cooke and some of his tory friends felt morally obliged to vote for Stephenson. The tory M.P.s for Bedford and Brackley, Robert Henley Ongley and Marshe Dickinson, owed their seats to the duke of Bedford and tended to vote as he ordered unless issues of party principle intervened.[16] William Beckford and Sir John Philipps were under pressure from London and Bristol mercantile interests wanting a more aggressive foreign policy than that favoured by Newcastle. Both men urged their party to throw its weight behind Fox, and Fox's nephew later calculated that if all the tory M.P.s whose support Beckford and Philipps had promised had indeed voted for Clive and Stephenson, 'We should have carry'd it. . . by 17 or 18.'[17]

Given this disarray, what Northey and Prowse achieved was organisationally impressive if tactically futile. Throughout March 1755 they held a series of meetings at the Horn Tavern. Of the fifty-nine tory M.P.s who are known to have attended the final meeting on 24 March (and the scale of absenteeism bears ample testimony to the tories' lack of enthusiasm for either of the two ministerial contenders), forty-three agreed to vote for Luttrell and Hussey, five more (including Beckford) were persuaded to be absent from the division, and only eleven voted for Clive and Stephenson, who were unseated by 209 votes to 185. Newcastle had prolonged the Oxfordshire inquiry to keep tory hopes and the possibility of co-operation alive, but on 23 April three Commons divisions gave Oxfordshire's representation to the two whig candidates. The administration that day secured an average majority of 131 and its tellers included Pitt's brother-in-law, Sir George Lyttelton, and Fox's ally, Robert Nugent.[18]

Yet the tories were not as isolated or as ineffectual as the Oxfordshire and Mitchell fiascos suggested. Newcastle's foreign policy skills were considerable, but if he was not what Pitt so cruelly styled him – a child in a pushchair on the brink of a precipice – the precipice was nonetheless there and even a more sophisticated vehicle was in danger of toppling over. In July 1755 it was learnt that Admiral Boscawen's expedition to prevent three thousand French troops from reaching North America had failed in its objective, while seizing enough French ships on the way to constitute an act of war. Anglo-French conflict, which Newcastle had hoped to limit to the colonies, was now likely to involve the continent of Europe. The threat this was bound to pose

George II as Elector of Hanover was only accentuated when, in the same month, British negotiations with Austria broke down and Maria Theresa committed herself to France. Newcastle's response was a series of subsidy treaties with Russia and, more controversially, with various German states, including Ansbach, Wurzburg, and Hesse-Cassel. The prudence of this policy was debatable; as the administration foresaw, its domestic unpopularity was not. British money for 'German interests' and, after March 1756, for German troops brought into England, revived the xenophobia of the early 1740s and was denounced in some remarkably virulent, often anti-aristocratic, and occasionally republican prints and publications. The summer of 1755 also provided parliamentary opposition with a spokesman. As the tory pamphleteer John Shebbeare exulted, a new David had come forth, fit to challenge the ministerial Goliath.[19]

It might seem strange that Pitt's self-interested oppositionism should engage tory support. In 1745–6 he had deserted the opposition for the most suspect employment of them all. In 1749 he had wheedled his way back into tory circles only to ostracise them in 1751. In 1754 he had stigmatised the party as Jacobite and in September 1755 he assured Dodington (as opposition whigs always did assure their orthodox peers when compelled into alliance with the tories) that 'he would always act upon plain Whig principles'.[20] It could be argued of course that by 1755 repeated betrayals and their own parliamentary weakness meant that the tories would clutch at any straw without relying on it overmuch. But this would be too facile. Their response to the Broad-Bottom attempt of 1744–5 and to the negotiations with Newcastle over Oxfordshire and Mitchell showed that tory M.P.s could not bring themselves to act for very long or with much enthusiasm with any conventional Old Corps politician.

Pitt, with his earnest and idealistic political style (as distinct from his political practice), and with his capacity to sense his parliamentary and extra-parliamentary audience, had never been conventional. In 1755–6 he entranced most tory M.P.s, as he entranced for a time John Wilkes, Samuel Johnson, and the tory radicals of the Half Moon Club, because he articulated, often with genius, their multi-faceted and impotent distaste for all that seemed stale, cynical, and exclusive in British political life. The fact that his manner was unapproachable, that his political correspondence was almost frighteningly opaque, and that he was occasionally mad, only intensified his attraction: he became the impersonal if brilliant oracle which every alienated and incoherent tory M.P. could interpret as he chose. And Pitt seemed almost young. In 1755 he was forty-seven: of the same age-group as his fellow political climbers – Bute, Fox, Legge, Murray, and the Grenvilles – and only slightly older than the average tory M.P.[21] Both his comparative youth and his startling rhetoric reinforced his invocations of a national renaissance, as did his gift for telling and well-publicised gestures. His sturdy refusal to speculate with the balance of the public money entrusted to him as Paymaster General is now a textbook commonplace; at the time it was unparalleled and expensive. When Henry Fox took over the office in 1757, his tenure coincided with a war unprecedented in its cost. Nonetheless, his profits of some £23 000 *per annum*, maintained until his death in 1774, give some indication of what Pitt made sure Parliament and the public knew he had renounced.[22]

One of Pitt's more prosaic attractions for the tories also helps to explain how he re-established contact with the party in 1755. After Fox had been admitted to the Cabinet in December 1754 and made *de facto* ministerial spokesman in the Commons, Pitt became able and eager to respond to the overtures of Leicester House. The Princess Dowager disliked both Fox and Newcastle, and between May and September 1755 she and her new adviser, Lord Bute, formulated an opposition agreement with Pitt. The tories had their own contacts at Leicester House. Edmond Bramston, who had contested Maldon for them in 1747, was now a gentleman usher; the wife of the Herefordshire tory, Velters Cornewall, was a lady-in-waiting; most important, the favourite of the Princess, Lady Charlotte Edwin, was the wife of the tory M.P. for Glamorgan. The Elder like the Younger Pitt was not averse to his relations indulging in those high-level, petty intrigues which he himself affected to despise, and according to Dodington the female Grenvilles and Temples had long been 'making court' to Lady Edwin.[23] Once the tories learnt that Pitt had reached an understanding with the reversionary interest, he could be regarded not only as their sole and desirable high-political option, but also as some guarantee of their prospects in the future reign.

II

Late in September 1755 and evidently after much prior correspondence, Thomas Prowse wrote to Pitt urging a joint consultation on the first day of the parliamentary session, 'which seems to me to be decisive of the Fate of this Country'. On 13 November Pitt condemned the recent subsidy treaties and the tories supplied about seventy of the 105 votes cast in his favour. The 311 whig M.P.s who voted with the administration in this division, like the 289 whig M.P.s and sixty-three whig peers who reportedly attended its pre-sessional meetings, emphasise Pitt's crucial weakness at this stage: not, as Clark suggests, persistent tory mistrust, but rather a desperate lack of whig auxiliaries and – a related problem – the hostility of the King. Pitt worked hard to engage more whig support. He espoused issues like naval expansion and militia reform which had a primitive whig as well as a tory appeal. He tried to protect his own partisan reputation by dealing with his tory allies only through intermediaries: the Leicester House whig Thomas Potter, George Townshend, whig M.P. for Norfolk, whose oppositionism was rooted in dislike of the duke of Cumberland, and, after January 1756, William Beckford. But substantial whig support was to remain elusive until the second half of 1757.[24] Neither a gradually acquired parliamentary majority nor the royal favour which was to elevate his son, but war, metropolitan and provincial agitation, tory votes, and his own fervid determination were to give Pitt his short-lived primacy in 1756.

It was George Townshend who on 8 December 1755 moved for a Militia Bill. As had been the case with those earlier mixed opposition gambits, attacks on placemen and standing armies, a citizen militia could be justified by reference to the seventeenth-century worthies of both whiggism and toryism. Trenchard and Fletcher had praised the institution as the proper alternative to a standing army; Sir Thomas Clarges had celebrated its contribution to Monmouth's destruction in 1685. It was because of this binary attraction that Frederick had incorporated a promise to 'raise and establish a numerous militia' in his Carlton House declaration of 1747. Five years later the independent whig M.P. William Thornton had given the Prince's initiative posthumous endorsement by moving for militia reform and getting the Newcastle tory Sir Walter Blackett to second him.[25] When Townshend drafted his bill in 1755–6, he was equally careful to cater to tory susceptibilities. All officers had to possess landed qualifications and those above the rank of captain had to own land worth £300 *per annum* or be direct heirs to land worth twice as much. To safeguard against absentee monied men, two-thirds of a militia officer's land had to be in the country for which he was serving. Churchwardens were to be responsible for storing arms and considerable powers were entrusted to the Land Tax Commissioners. These latter officials were selected by the House of Commons, not by the King, so while the majority of Commissioners were probably whig, they did not outnumber their tory equivalents to the same degree as whig J.P.s did on the Commissions of the Peace.[26]

Townshend's main concession to the tories was his provision that, when a militia officer retired, any man prepared to take the oaths and equipped with the necessary landed qualifications would have a legal right to replace him. In the localities at least, the system whereby substantial posts were restricted to men of one party complexion was to be gradually undermined. Before the Militia Act finally passed the Lords in 1757, Hardwicke and Newcastle tacitly acknowledged its pro-tory tendencies by modifying some of its clauses. The churchwardens were omitted from the scheme; J.P.s, not the Land Tax Commissioners, were given the main task of local implementation; and the King was given one month's grace in which to veto any volunteer officer of whom he or his Ministers disapproved.[27]

As Pitt may have realised when he seconded Townshend's motion, given the climate of extra-parliamentary opinion in 1755, projects for a remodelled militia were likely to exceed the bounds of conventional high-political manoeuvre. Three years earlier the Society of Noblemen and Gentlemen for the Preservation of Game had been formed – the culmination of the spread of County Game Law associations. The society held regular meetings at the St Albans Tavern (not surprisingly, as some tory peers belonged to it) and, it was believed, planned to safe-guard game by making plebeian possession of fire-arms illegal. London's radical press interpreted this proposal as a preparatory move for an aristocratic coup – 'You'll find that the Association, / Pretended but to save the Game, / Is form'd to make you blind and lame' – alarmism which caught fire when Newcastle ordered his hired Hessian mercenaries to England in 1756. As John Shebbeare warned his readers, the Minister could 'retain these Hirelings in his Service, to subdue with more Certainty, and less danger, that People, which, though he has deprived them of Arms, he has not yet forgot to fear'.[28] As had been the case in Grub Street's campaign against the duke of Cumberland in the early 1750s, and in the propaganda spawned by the tories' legal action in 1754 against Princess Amelia for her closure of Richmond Park, this opposition to the Game Laws and their extension blended in 1755–6 with popular anti-German prejudice, and found sporadic expression in republican ephemera and slogans. It is doubtful whether these out-bursts were founded on any serious political intent, but they were none the less alarming for that. 'Hang Byng or take care of your King' was the popular chant which most appalled Newcastle after the Minorca crisis: understandably so, if one remembers that even the most violent Wilkite rioters rarely indulged in threats remotely as subversive.[29] By the mid 1760s a more popular monarch and the glow of recent patriotic achievement were available to mute the fury and extremism of the crowd. In the mid 1750s Britain's rulers seemed not only oppressive but also unappealing and inept.

In these circumstances any debate on arming the people was bound to be inflammatory. William Beckford's *Monitor* might present the militia as a school for the lower orders, inculcating self-discipline and love of country. Another tory publication might argue that those who wished to see the people 'sober, brave and free...and save you from the Expense of larger standing armies and higher taxes, these will wish to see you know how to handle a Firelock'. But as Harwicke warned the Lords, any insistence on the importance of popular initiative was likely to be democratic in its logic. It was indeed no accident that the debate on the citizens' right and obligation to bear arms was followed in the 1760s by demands for their analogous right to vote. In the 1750s some pamphleteers raised more dangerous spectres yet. 'Shall I hazard life for...imperious Lordlings?' inquired a writer in the *Universal Magazine* in August 1756. 'The late plan of a Militia bill would undoubtedly have been of infinite Service, in protecting us from our common Enemy', wrote another in 1757, 'But then, if weapons had been put into our Hands, could it be reasonably expected, that whilst we are labouring under such grievous Oppressions at Home, we should turn the Edge of our Swords against the External Foes of Britain, when we have internal Enemies, much more obnoxious to every free-born Englishman?'[30]

Both the demotic implications of Townshend's bill, and its provision that the militia should be funded by way of general taxation and not by an equitable tax on land, help to account for the tories' ambivalence towards the scheme. Only two tory M.P.s, William Northey and Richard Crowle, joined the parliamentary committee on the Militia Bill appointed on 21 January 1756. Four months later Lord Guernsey and Edward Kynaston, tory M.P.s for Maidstone and Montgomeryshire, both confessed to Edward Bayntun Rolt that their party was lukewarm on the issue 'tho' obliged to support it'. Desire for more power in the localities, traditional commitment to a militia, and novel commitment to Pitt all helped to preserve the tories' reluctant acquiescence. In December 1756, six months after the Lords had rejected Townshend's earlier bill, eight tory M.P.s were included on the second Militia Bill committee; seventeen tories joined the parliamentary committee to defend the new bill from further noble erosion in May 1757.[31] But in these early tory qualms, and in the nervousness of leading tories like Prowse after the Militia Act had been passed, one can surely see the beginnings of the process whereby some tory landowners reconsidered their relationship with popular causes.

Not that the cost or the recruitment pattern of the new militia turned out to be popular. Having reluctantly espoused the Militia Act, in 1757 some tories like Gabriel Hanger, M.P. for Maidstone, and the former

M.P. for Stockbridge, Sir Humphrey Monoux, found themselves under attack from anti-militia rioters: an experience which again confronted tory gentlemen with the tensions between their socio-economic status and their occasionally radical rhetoric. In 1761, when the Hexham militia rioters threatened the property of Sir Lancelot Allgood, a former tory M.P. for Northumberland, his wife was quick to remind him where his duty (and interest) lay; he had, after all, just been knighted by George III: 'Attempting the breach of one law is attempting the whole subversion of government which must not be submitted. Whilst the Gentlemen have the laws and force in their hands they must exert them to the support of their authority over the commonalty.'[32]

In 1756 and 1757, however, the tories, like Pitt himself, were obliged to combine traditional opposition methods with an extensive appeal to provincial, sometimes plebeian, opinion. Throughout 1756 the British position *vis-à-vis* French America and Germany visibly deteriorated. In mid July Newcastle received confirmation of Admiral Byng's failure to relieve the British garrison at Minorca and the fall of the island to the French. Irrespective of whether the fault lay with Byng or with his inadequate fleet and instructions, this disaster seemed to substantiate tory and Pittite arguments that subsidy treaties were a costly and futile distraction and that Britain must concentrate on and expand her naval power. The tory-dominated *London Evening News* and *Monitor* linked Minorca with a second British defeat at Oswego in America, demanded constitutional reform and a new militia, and urged the dismissal of the Fox–Newcastle administration. These papers also incited provincial Grand Juries to submit protests of their own; not accidentally, the provinces, as well as London's Common Council, complied.[33]

Between August and December nineteen boroughs and seventeen counties submitted Addresses to the King and/or Instructions to their M.P.s. They were as one in their insistence on an inquiry into the loss of Minorca and in their concern for militia reform; their additional demands were more varied, but usually characterised by what George Lyttelton indicatively styled 'a Jacobite spirit'. Oxford wanted a 'fair and equal land tax'. Salisbury, like many of the other constituencies, demanded free and triennial Parliaments. Nottingham wanted taxation reduced and – because of the recent bad harvest – government action against corn engrossers.[34] Given the provenance of these protests and the men who seem to have rigged them, their emphases were predictable. Twenty-four of the thirty-six constituencies involved had tory M.P.s; nor was this all. Lichfield and Wells had returned whig representatives in 1754, but their Instructions were the work of Staffordshire's tory gentry and a High-Church corporation respectively. Huntingdonshire had not returned a tory M.P. since 1722, but the Grand Jury which compiled its Instructions was a tory construct. Bedfordshire's Instructions to its whig M.P.s also derived from an *ad hoc* Grand Jury, directed by an interesting caucus of 'Jessop & Hill...ye two managing Torys of that Town [Bedford]', Thomas Potter, the Pittite M.P. for Aylesbury, John Wilkes, now High Steward of Buckinghamshire, and Henry Pye, tory M.P. for Berkshire.[35]

A public strategy had been enforced upon Pitt and his allies because Parliament was in recess from before the loss of Minorca to Newcastle's resignation. This fact alone makes it difficult to gauge the campaign's high-political impact, just as its partisan supervision makes it difficult and, indeed, inappropriate to estimate whether popular agitation over Minorca was real or only synthetic. *Pace* Samuel Johnson's aphorism, Pitt was not 'a Minister given by the people to the King': the people had no such positive power even if this had been their conscious intention.[36] But there seems little doubt that many literate and semi-literate sectors of English society were alienated from Newcastle's administration, and that their alienation helped to unsettle it. The complaints in the Instructions and Addresses of 1756 were reproduced throughout the country in newspapers, pamphlets, handbills, and ballads. As such, they lent coherence to the pre-existing and ill-defined hysteria which had been prompted by Britain's current localised food shortages, by her recent defeats, and by her apparent vulnerability to French invasion. Certainly Newcastle had decided to employ Pitt even before Fox made clear his own opinion of the government's future security by resigning in October. With Murray's elevation to the Upper House as Lord Mansfield in November, and Pitt's refusal to join any administration which also included Newcastle, the latter was left with little choice but to prove his indispensability by a temporary retirement.

In mid November Newcastle and Hardwicke resigned. They left – as Lord Granville jibed – 'with a majority in Parliament of 150', with the bulk of their secondary ministers still in office, and with the duke of Devonshire as new First Lord of the Treasury and guarantor of the Old Corps' continuing influence. They also left the new Secretary of State for the South, William Pitt, to deal with an international crisis and the inflated expectations he had encouraged of reform at home and recovery abroad, and to do so with no resources in the Commons other than his own small coterie of whigs, and the tories, who (Newcastle was informed) would assist Pitt 'as a body'.[37]

On 4 December 1756 Lords Lichfield and Windsor and eleven tory M.P.s including Northey, Sir Armine Wodehouse (co-Member with

George Townshend for Norfolk), and Sir John Philipps (who had jumped on the bandwagon just in time, severed his connections with Fox, and written his first letter to Pitt on 21 November) had all lent their signatures to a whip requesting every tory M.P. to attend for the opening of Parliament: 'As there is now a Prospect that Government will support Constitutional measures, this Country may still be saved unless betray'd by the Desertion of those who are freely entrusted with the care of its Liberties. We therefore beg leave to solicit the early and steady attendance of all our Friends which alone can evince the Reality of their Professions.' When the Commons reassembled ten days later, the tories were present in force and, remarked Henry Fox, had the debate on foreign policy come to a vote, 'The Ministers and Torys would have been on one side and the whole House besides on the other. It was as much mark'd. . .as a division could have mark'd it.'[38]

What most provoked whig gossip was not so much the existence of this juncture, but its lack of a conventional cement. Pitt assured Hardwicke, and Lord Barrington told Newcastle, that the tories had laid down no conditions for their votes. They had not stipulated a share of offices; how could they, with most Old Corps men still employed? Did the tories anticipate a renovated, patriot regime? Lord Lichfield had endorsed the party whip, but his own muddled doubts and aspirations seeped into his private correspondence: 'I propose being in town. . .to *see* what may happen from this Change of Hands. What are they about? – are we likely to have any *National* Good? If not, adieu to Old England.' Whig politicians were equally sceptical. Sir Edmund Thomas and Edward Bayntun Rolt, two M.P.s on the periphery of Leicester House and therefore moderately sympathetic to Pitt, neatly identified the Scylla and Charybdis of his tory voyage. As a power base, judged Sir Edmund, the tories were likely to be impracticable; 'any attention to them', thought Bayntun Rolt, 'will be intolerable to the whigs'.[39] Both men underestimated tory realism and Pitt's capacity for symbolic gesture.

Northey and Prowse had agreed with Pitt that however great their unpopularity Hessian troops must, in the short term, be retained. In 1756 as in 1701, tory M.P.s also accepted that French expansion must be halted and that this would be expensive. On 21 February and again on 7 and 10 March 1757, Pitt's tory allies grimly agreed to the huge parliamentary grants needed to revitalise Britain's war effort, finding some consolation in the fact that the largest sum voted was to be expended on the country's Navy.[40]

What did the tories get in return? Chiefly, perhaps, what the Pelhams, despite their smattering of tory appointments, had never seen the need to concede: ministerial receptivity to tory nuance. The King's speech on 2 December 1756 was, thought one tory auditor, 'in a style totally different from what he had been used to'. Not surprisingly, as Pitt's composition marked a break with the tradition of almost twenty years in which the oration had been the responsibility of Lord Hardwicke. The King's new ventriloquist was seen in his support of a militia, in his undertaking to reduce the price of grain, in his compliments to the public for their Instructions on Minorca, and in his explicitly British patriotism. France was 'the ancient Enemy', and it was on 'the Spirit and Zeal of my People', not on foreign or electoral troops, that the reluctant King undertook to rely. Throughout most of George II's reign no tory M.P. had formally approved the Royal Speech, and only William Beckford had done so in November 1754 when a tory–Newcastle entente is supposed to have been imminent. In December 1756 seven tory M.P.s joined the committee to draft the Commons' Address of Thanks to the King, and Pitt submitted the final version to Sir John Philipps for his and his party's approval.[41] In the parliamentary business of the spring of 1757 one sees the same ministerial concern for tory sensibilities. A committee was appointed – with Philipps reporting from it – to regulate corn prices and tighten laws against forestalling and engrossing. The Wine Licence Office was given a semblance of reform, and the British Fishery, the more equitable maintenance of turnpike roads, and the regulation of legal fees also came before the House under tory auspices and with the approval of Pitt. 'I think him', Velters Cornewall announced, 'the most uncorrupt, as well as the most popular minister we ever had.'[42]

That a war-time House of Commons gave time to such ameliorative committee activity bore witness to the unreality of Pitt's position. As two agonised meetings between George Townshend and some leading tories on 14 January and 1 February 1757 finally established, any full-scale debate on the iniquities of the late administration (the sort of exposure which tory constituencies had beeen led to expect) would re-unite Newcastle and Fox, and demonstrate that Pitt was governing from a Commons minority. Pitt did not lack for parliamentary talent. But some of his prime whig supporters, like his Chancellor of the Exchequer, Henry Legge, were uneasy at his 'visionary' reliance on tory co-operation, and this alliance also exacerbated his main deficiency: lack of numbers. In February Newcastle estimated that he could command 280 'sure' whig supporters. Not all of these were present on 3 May when the parliamentary committee on Minorca made its report but Pitt, who was now out of power, and his allies, who attended in strength, were still defeated by 147 votes to 91, and 195 to 115.[43]

Some grass-roots tories, like those attached to Bristol's Steadfast Society, had entertained hopes that a general election might be called to supply Pitt with an amenable Parliament: a foolish optimism which was repeated in the Foxite press so as to alarm whig opinion. 'Can another tory administration be thought eligible?' inquired the *Test* in April 1757, and, less hypothetically, was 'a feeble ministry link'd with an association of Tories' to govern 'a nation rent asunder by private cabals and party animosities?' But this was propaganda. Although Newcastle's recent biographer has attributed the duke's being 'the pivot upon which the political negotiations of the period revolved' primarily to the contemporary 'political world [being] deluded about the nature of political power', informed politicians had every reason to interpret his resignation in 1756 as a case of *reculer pour mieux sauter*.[44] George II disliked the Devonshire–Pitt administration, so there was no possibility of his calling a general election to supply it with a majority, as George III was to do to rescue Pitt the Younger in 1784. The Elder Pitt was not only deprived of royal favour and therefore of considerable patronage powers, but also in open alliance with the tory parliamentary party, so he could appeal neither to the self-interest nor to the partisan loyalty of those scores of Old Corps M.P.s who were determined to abide by Newcastle. But while George II could obstruct his administration and, in April 1757, enforce its resignation, this same Old Corps solidarity, together with Bute's insistence on Pitt's reinstatement, prevented him from appointing a replacement government led by Henry Fox. After some abortive consultations in May, negotiations began in June to construct the most complex and inclusive coalition of them all. The kingdom was to have both Newcastle's power and Pitt's glory joined in its service, and, like extras on the film-set of an epic, the tory leaders too were soon in busy attendance at Newcastle House.[45]

And the tories did not confine themselves to ministerial congeries. As Paul Langford has shown, the bestowal of gold boxes on Pitt and Legge in the summer of 1757 was largely tory-inspired. (Contemporaries were equally perceptive: the *Test* claimed that the whole campaign was coordinated by the Cocoa Tree and Half Moon Clubs.) The tory corporations of Bedford, Chester, Exeter, and Salisbury; the borough of Boston, represented by the tory Charles Amcotts; Newcastle upon Tyne, at the instigation of the tory Lord Windsor; Worcester and Tewkesbury, at the suggestion of their tory Recorders, Lord Ward and Robert Harley; all these, together with four other boroughs and the City of London (where James Hodges, the tory bookseller and Half Moon habitué, was the agitator responsible), presented their freedoms to Pitt and Legge.[46]

These *cachets* were accompanied by inflated tributes to Pitt's integrity and constitutional zeal, intended, Langford argues, to confirm Pitt's patriot status, assist his re-employment, *and* regulate his future conduct. Pitt's return to power in collusion with 'His Grace and his corruption' (and His Grace's Euro-centric foreign policy) therefore placed his tory allies in an invidious and compromising position. This, of course, is what scornful whig and purist tory critics maintained at the time. In November 1756 the *Monitor* had sworn vengeance on Pitt and his supporters if they 'Should [ever] veer about, and without blushing become the accomplices of the very criminals they had avowed to bring to justice; and only make use of popularity, to be wafted into a situation, where they may with impunity rivet that yoke, which they stood engaged to...break.' Early in 1759 the newspaper fulfilled its threat, lambasted Pitt, and adapted one of Swift's verses to stigmatise the tories' capitulation:

> So have I seen the Tory Race
> Long in the Pouts for want of Place,
> Never in humour, never well,
> Wishing for what they dar'd not tell,
> Their Heads with Country-Notions fraught,
> Notions in Town not worth a groat;
> These Tenets all reluctant quit,
> And step by step at last submit
> To Reason, Eloquence and PITT.[47]

But it is surely arguable that both the contemporary dithyrambic descriptions of tory enthusiasm for Pitt in 1756, and contemporary and more recent claims that this association corroded the tories' identity thereafter, exaggerate the party's naivety and, by this stage, its political prospects. The tories retained considerable solidarity and were not devoid of talent, but their minority status, lack of administrative experience, and introverted partisan attitudes were bound to limit their expectations. In November 1756 euphoria at Newcastle's imminent resignation might lead the *Monitor*'s director, William Beckford, to urge on Pitt the indispensability of 'a new system', but a letter to a tory friend one month later shows that he recognised the chasm between what the tories would have liked Pitt to accomplish and what his parliamentary prospects were bound in fact to be. 'I wish he may be able to do as much good as he seems inclined to do for the country', wrote Beckford, 'but I am afraid the old Pack of Black tans [the Old Corps whig M.P.s] will not follow the right scent.' Once Pitt had come to the necessary terms with the Black and Tans' prime representative, Beckford made his own necessary adjustments and continued to support him, despite the jibes of his dissident journalists.[48] Recognising that a coalition including Pitt would be more advantageous to them than its only alternatives – unadulterated Pelhamite or Foxite supremacy – other leading tories followed suit. On 23 June 1757 a weary William Northey confided to a fellow West Country M.P. that 'he owned himself inclined to embark with the Court'. Since Northey was not yet forty this was only prudent. Too much tory sulking at the Newcastle–Pitt coalition would have been gratuitous as well as unrealistic. George II was old; his successor was inexperienced and unpredictable. Political reconfiguration in the new reign was likely; the death of one of the coalition's (and the Old Corps') main props, a certainty. So the majority of tory M.P.s, like the majority of whigs, bided their time. Horace Walpole's jibe in 1759, 'One may describe the House of Commons like the price of stocks: Debates nothing done: Votes under par: Patriots, no price: Oratory, books shut', was a comment not on the achievement of bland, high-political unanimity, but on a short-term political truce produced by war and evanescent circumstance.[49]

III

Three other factors provided for tory acquiescence in government at the end of George II's reign, though not yet for tory dispersal. Pitt's successful conduct of the war, thought Chase Price, was crucial. 'Triumph & victory', he grumbled, 'the embroidery of the war cover'd everything, they [the tories]...pass'd the most amazing votes with implicit obedience & the publick treasure was dispos'd of with as much inattention as it was supplied with credulity.' This assessment was too sour. Acquiring and consolidating overseas territory and markets was consonant both with old-style tory enthusiasm for a patriotic war, and with the party's new investment in constituencies and towns like Bristol, London, Newcastle, and Birmingham, which were increasingly dependent on Atlantic, West Indian, and Indian trade. Initially, too, the tories were pleased at Pitt's concentration on naval warfare: a concentration which even excused one of his early failures – the abortive expedition against Rochefort late in 1757.[50] A change occurred, but not a complete one, in April 1758, when Pitt determined on intensive subsidies for Prussia. Two months later he agreed to send British troops into Germany – a strategy he had vetoed the previous August. Prussian subsidies provoked some tory unease and Sir John Philipps, disappointed in a recent attempt to repeal the Septennial Act, threatened to lead a Commons revolt. The subsequent anxiety of Thomas Prowse and William Northey exemplifies the familiar dilemma of the mid-century tory leadership, torn between the conflicting demands of an indispensable whig ally and its own indignant backbenchers. As Thomas Potter explained to Pitt,

If a Division is made they are in Pain how to act. To divide against you is to act against their Opinion & destroys the idea they wish to inculcate that the *Body* of the Country Party are hearty in their Confidence & Support. To divide with you & to be left without followers...would ruin their future Influence with the Party, it would ruin their own Credit in their respective Counties.[51]

In the event, tensions were eased by an emergency meeting at the Cocoa Tree and a high-level dinner party on 15 April between Philipps, Lord Temple, George and James Grenville, and Pitt's most committed tory ally, William Beckford. Four days later the Commons accepted the Convention signed between Prussia and Britain without a division. The decision to send British troops to Prussia's aid was less easily swallowed, not least because it precipitated the final breakdown of relations between Pitt and Leicester House. Thereafter, self-interested concentration on the prospective reign was bound to lead some tory M.P.s to distance themselves from the current war policy. Again, however, a rift between the party and Pitt was avoided, partly because of the immense admiration which many tories nurtured for Frederick of Prussia as the epitome of a patriot king – a compliment which tory writers like Shebbeare stressed to the disadvantage of George II. Thomas Prowse and William Northey also worked hard lobbying their parliamentary following on Pitt's behalf, and on 23 November ten tories, including Sir Richard Grosvenor, Beckford, Philipps, Newdigate, and Mordaunt, joined the parliamentary committee which ratified the Royal Speech and its bellicose content.[52] Not till 1759 did tory enthusiasm perceptibly wane. The *annus mirabilis* was expensive; peace seemed as far away as ever; and Prowse took advantage of his ill-health and the Somerset militia to extricate himself from the strains of playing dragoman. William Northey, already under tory newspaper and pamphlet attack for his excessive compliance in government, was also reported to have retired from Parliament by March 1759, and to be 'out of countenance when pressed on his power with the tories'.[53]

In terms of constitutional concessions – always at a discount during war – Pitt dealt out some calculated but peripheral douceurs. On 20 February 1758, when Philipps and the Flint M.P., Sir John Glynne, moved to repeal the Septennial Act, Pitt took care to be absent while allowing the Grenvilles and Thomas Potter to join their fellow whigs in defeating the motion. This was the background to a lengthy rebuke by William Blackstone to Sir Roger Newdigate: a reminder, yet again, that vaunted tory reformism brought constituency pressures as well as constituency applause in its wake:

I cannot think all patriot schemes & publick spirited Measures are to be dropped, merely to support a Minister who has yet given you nothing but fine Words...if he means well let him join the Country Gentlemen in all proper measures...in ye restoration of triennial, or at least quinquennial Parliaments; in a better Place bill; in a Freeholder's bill; in reducing not increasing the number & influence of the Army...Posterity will be amazed at ye Conduct of ye Country Gentlemen; if, after having insisted on certain constitutional points for an Opposition of 40 years, they should at last join a Minister (as much dipped in iniquity as his Brethren) without any one stipulation & should linger away two sessions of Parliament without so much as trying the sincerity of their New Ally...or attempting any one beneficial Alteration to satisfy the expectations of their constituents.[54]

Blackstone's verdict was sufficiently representative to prevent tory sympathisers from confusing concessionary whiggism with their constitutional ideal; initial tory enthusiasm for George III was to reflect how far tory desire for political change as well as tory political ambition had been left unfulfilled. But as the duke of Devonshire remarked, Pitt was prepared to give way in the odd 'point of no consequence' to make government run more smoothly. Later in 1758 Philipps was allowed to pass the Freeholder Qualification Bill for which Blackstone so yearned. Two years later, Philipps and Beckford were permitted to pass an Act tightening the laws on landed qualifications for M.P.s and the London tories were given greater control over the City's trained bands.[55]

Tory M.P.s and their more important or importunate supporters were also inveigled by their controlled admission to the peripheries of state acceptance. When Sir Richard Grosvenor and Norborne Berkeley were allowed to second the Commons' Address to the King in 1758 and 1759, they were breaking with post-1714 precedent, advancing their careers, and assisting Pitt by suggesting that tories as well as whigs concurred in his measures. One wonders how much of Blackstone's constitutional ire survived his appointment as Professor of Common Law at Oxford, publicised some eight months after his outburst to Newdigate, or how restive Sir John Glynne remained when his son was promoted Lieutenant of a light infantry regiment in 1759.[56] Similarly, if one examines Sir John Philipps' index of letters, there is a remarkable contrast between his almost exclusively partisan pre-1756 correspondence and its conventionality and catholicity thereafter. 'To James West Esq., with a memorial to the Duke of Newcastle on behalf of Mr. Henry Garnett'; 'To Lord Anson on behalf of Captain Thomas Smith': these, and the references to Philipps' many other begging letters, illustrate the process whereby this restless spirit was transformed into the elder tory statesman and Privy Councillor of George III's reign.[57]

Prime local government posts remained whig-dominated, but in some counties the implementation of the Militia Act did help to reintegrate the tory landed gentry with their whig peers. In 1759 Lord Poulet, Lord Lieutenant of Somerset, claimed that his county's militia had 'In a great measure destroyed all distinction of Partys...for none who voluntarily inlists in His Majesty's service...can go any longer under any other denomination than friends to this Government, & Gentlemen now associate & act together who were very shy lately & scarce knew one another before.' Poulet was a well-meaning man and a former tory himself, so his invocations of the militia as a party solvent may be too roseate. Indeed, the papers of Hardwicke and Newcastle are full of complaints – some of them well documented – that in the Bedfordshire, Cambridgeshire, Devon, Essex, Gloucestershire, Kent, Lincolnshire, and Surrey militias understandable whig reluctance to expend time and money on exercising unco-operative civilians had led to a tory majority in the officer ranks. Tory landowners had been subjected to a long period of rationing in local influence, and these positions had the savour of novelty as well as of electoral and patronage benefit. Thomas Prowse doubted the constitutional and social wisdom of the Militia Act, but he still accepted a Major's commission in Somerset's militia and exploited it for all it was worth. When Poulet showed him a list of proposed Deputy Lieutenants for Somerset (and it is significant that a tory M.P. was now consulted), Prowse reminded him that he 'had omitted some principle Gentlemen, to wit Thomas Carew, John Hippisley Coxe, Will Helyar, Will Piers, Sir Richard Warwick Bampfylde'. All of these men were of course tory, and all, with Pitt's blessing, were subsequently appointed.[58]

IV

However shambolic George III's coronation was in general, its symbolism was at least appropriate for its tory participants. At the ceremony the second sword of state was entrusted to the earl of Suffolk, future Deputy Earl Marshal and Privy Councillor, while the earl of Northampton, soon to be made Ambassador to Venice, bore the ivory sceptre with the dove. Tory readmission to the less central government offices and the party's reconciliation with the Hanoverian dynasty would seem to have been neatly prefigured. Whig contemporaries were to view these developments with a mixture of alarm and complacency. 'It may be worthy of our prudence to reflect', wrote one pamphleteer, 'whether the Tories, by their duty and observance, by their zeal and attachment to his person and government, may not fix themselves so firmly in the affection of our young monarch, as not easily to be removed.' The assertion implied here, that George III would woo old tories in order to promote a new, pro-executive toryism, was to be a stock theme of whig and opposition propagandists in the 1760s and after. Yet when news of the new King's early concessions to tory politicians, reached the London-based author William Mason, his verdict was rather different: 'I am glad at heart to find this annihilation of Toryism.' It is this latter assessment which most modern scholarship would endorse: that having been weaned from unthinking opposition by Pitt, tory politicians were robbed of their remaining distinction by George III's accession and the end of proscription. Like the tories at the coronation ceremony, such a finale is much too tidy.[59]

Tory promotions were limited. At the instigation of both Pitt and Bute – the former supporting the principle, the latter determining most of the beneficiaries – George appointed Lichfield, Oxford, and Bruce lords of the bedchamber, and Northey, George Pitt, and Norborne Berkeley grooms of the bedchamber.[60] Sir Richard Grosvenor and Sir Nathaniel Curzon were made English peers, and Bute went on to ensure that Sir William Courtenay and George Fox-Lane were ennobled in 1762. A few more promotions were used to win able tory M.P.s over from Pitt. John Morton had been wooed by Newcastle in 1756, and made a K.C. by Pitt and Bute in 1758. In 1762 he was appointed Chief Justice of Chester, and in the crucial division on the legality of General Warrants in February 1764, Morton, like all but one of the tory lawyer M.P.s, aligned with the administration.[61] But neither the scale nor the specific impact of these tory douceurs should be exaggerated. Of the 113 M.P.s whom Namier listed as being tory in 1761, only twenty-seven were offered government places or honours by post-1760 administrations. Only four of these 113 went on to achieve careers of some political distinction. Norborne Berkeley made a remarkably good Governor of Virginia; William Dowdeswell and William Meredith became Rockingham politicians of status; while in more radical style, William Beckford continued to lend *élan* and inspiration to the business of opposition.[62]

The divergent careers of these men demonstrate that the tories' initially euphoric reception of George III did not go unmodified. Certainly it was sweet and novel to have a king who declared himself both a Briton and an Anglican. George's reply in 1760 to the compliments of his whig erastian chaplain, Dr Thomas Wilson, 'I desire *those Gentlemen* may be told, that I come here to praise God, & not to hear my own praises', was widely circulated by tory correspondents, as was his reputed commitment to electoral purity. ('Nothing, I say, my L[or]d', he was supposed to have told the duke of Newcastle when he inquired how much secret service money should be allocated to the general election, 'I desire to be tried by my country.') And of course the reversal of proscription signified far more than a quota of employments. What most moved the mediocre Lord Bruce in 1761 was not so much his court promotion as the royal regard it implied: 'His Majesty would not be offended if he did not accept it; tho' he wished he might, as a testimony of his good opinion, & good will to the Party his Lordship had ever adhered to.' Similarly, while Sir Armine Wodehouse never gained a government post, his avowal to George Townshend in 1767 that the tories were bound to revere Lord Bute 'for taking from 'em that brand which has been upon 'em the two last reigns...excluding ...their families from the minutest degree of attention' bears witness to his party's satisfaction at regaining free access to the Court, to royal and ministerial levees, and to the myriad varieties of patronage.[63]

To a limited degree the tories' sense of obligation to George III and his Ministers, combined with their ingrained royalism, was bound to have a centrifugal effect on their parliamentary representatives in the 1760s. A certain policy schizophrenia had been present in toryism since its parliamentary genesis. Charles II's most fervent supporters had wedded monarchism to a deep suspicion of executive interference in the Church and the localities. To this potential complication, late-seventeenth- and eighteenth-century tory politicians had added another: the tension between the social conservatism attendant on their landed status and the sometimes subversive implications of their increasing popular appeal. Proscription had allowed these potentially divergent attitudes and their tory champions to hold together, but even under the Newcastle–Pitt coalition there had been signs of impending schism. In 1758 William Beckford and the metropolitan tories of the Half Moon Club had been the most enthusiastic supporters of Pitt's proposal to extend Habeas Corpus to men pressed for the Army. But having passed the Commons, Pitt's bill had met with opposition not only from the leading Old Corps peers, but also from the tory Lords. Hardwicke had reinterpreted the bill as an assault on the royal prerogative and the social order. 'Liberty without Law', he warned, would 'destroy all authority, both public and private'. Both emphases told. The tory Lords Lichfield, Aylesford, and Ward advised Pitt's prime representative in the Upper House, Lord Temple, 'that they hoped he would not divide the House, for that if he did they must either go away, or if they stayed they must vote against the bill'.[64]

These internal tory tensions were bound to escalate in the 1760s. Although after 1762 most tory M.P.s supported the administration of George Grenville – the most austere and overtly principled of the cousin-hood and Sir William Wyndham's son-in-law – over forty tory M.P.s voted against him on General Warrants. Thomas Prowse could only be thankful that he was absent from the House during this crisis, because while he considered Wilkes 'an impudent worthless fellow', he could not support 'dismantling the fences of their liberties' in order to punish him.[65] Torn like Prowse between loyal stolidity and libertarianism, both the two Harley and the two Beckford brothers discovered that their common toryism was no longer an adequate cement, and found them-selves in different division lobbies. During the Middlesex election crisis of 1767–8 the agony of some tories, devoted to their King but also attuned to their party's mid-century championship of wider electoral rights, was acute: 'My mind is distressed to give a vote', wailed Herbert Mackworth, as he divided for Wilkes in 1769, '...I shall go against his Majesty's ministers, but my principle is to support them.' Relief came with the 1770s. The tory lineage of Lord North, the dwindling of Wilkes, the dissenters' renewed assaults on the Test Act and the Thirty-Nine Articles, and the rebellion in America, which tory polemi-cists interpreted as a violation of non-resistance and as an exemplification 'of the principles of the Independents in Oliver's time', all assisted in the process whereby most tories reconciled ministerialdom with their party's historical loyalties.[66] Indeed, it has been argued that the American crisis revivified English tory arguments almost as much as it cast self-proclaimed whigs into ideological disarray – which perhaps suggests that if ever 'The Rise of Party' after 1760 is to be written the continuity of tory doctrines, as well as the evolution of a new and more capacious whig ideology, will have to be a predominant theme.

Growing tory inclination towards government was naturally fostered by increased whig oppositionism. Lord Macaulay's 'wonderful metamor-phosis', whereby whig and tory 'changed their very nature and essence' in reciprocal relation to each other, was again in progress, but in the opposite direction to its mid-eighteenth-century operation. After the General Warrants crisis a few dissident or disappointed tories like Humphry Sturt and Sir Edward Dering attached themselves to Wild-man's Club, but most tories could not stomach collusion with Newcastle, any more than Newcastle's ally, the duke of Cumberland, could stomach tory auxiliaries. Even with these old men off the political stage and the Old Corps reduced to modest proportions under the marquess of Rock-ingham, the majority of tories still baulked at its occasional anti-clericalism, its aristocratic bias, and its vaunted if ill-defined whiggery.[67]

When Sir William Dolben, M.P. for Oxford University, attacked Edmund Burke's 1781 bill regulating the Civil List, he demonstrated the radicalism which could be latent even in the most loyalist toryism, but also its incompatibility with the Rockingham norm. If, Dolben argued, Burke's legislation was intended

To destroy the influence by which Members were returned to that House, it did not go far enough, for it ought also to have destroyed the influence of the aristocracy and of wealthy individuals as well as the influence of the Crown; and he said he should have no objection to a general and fair plan of reform that went to the reduction of influence on both sides.

One of the obstacles to late-eighteenth-century political reform was perhaps this inbuilt dissonance between some self-proclaimed whig and some self-proclaimed tory proponents of change. Certainly Dolben left the cause of parliamentary reform increasingly alone, and concentrated on that more apolitical 'crying evil', the slave trade.[68]

And with the exception of humanitarian reformers like Dolben, and the predominantly West Country and metropolitan tories who attached themselves to Rockingham and later to Fox, self-interest ensured that most tory landowners had little inclination towards social or political alterations. In a passage which could be a commentary on Norman Ravitch's thesis of an 'aristocratic resurgence' in late-eighteenth-century Britain, Lord Shelburne detected one of the long-term consequences of tory readmission to court society, to political respectability, and to local parity in 1760: 'the alienation of all the landed interest from the ancient plan of freedom'.

Every landed Man setting up a little Tyranny...with Magistracy, and oppressive Laws...Thus employed the country gentlemen were willing, instead of controlling the abuse of Power, to take their Choice with that Government under which their own peculiar Tyrannies were maintained.[69]

Whatever George III's disruptive effect on the rarified worlds of Whitehall and Westminster, by finally reversing tory proscription he sedated and beguiled what had been the least stable sector in that much wider, more influential, and most durable political world: Britain's landed elite.

Conclusion

'Men are all Tories by nature', wrote Dr Arnold in 1836, 'when they are tolerably well off.'[1] The central problem of this book has been why it was that political adversity and neglect were unable to extirpate the mid-eighteenth-century tory party and its extra-parliamentary support. At Westminster diminishing tory numbers were partly offset by improved organisation. Traditional but still relevant political and religious attitudes sustained tory politicians quite as much as did their cultural debt to Oxford, and their families' extensive inter-marriage. Outside Westminster the counties and large boroughs supplied the party with a limited but irreducible electoral base – general election after general election demonstrating that, throughout this period, one-party whig government had been superimposed on a two-party, predominantly tory, state. Among the enfranchised and the unenfranchised, tory strength owed much to the influence of landlord and parson, but it also derived from the party's ideological overlap with inchoate popular prejudice and sentiment. Tory rhetoricians and publicists could address themselves to the growing aversion to the weight of indirect taxation and to the whig officials it salaried; they could apply to a popular Anglicanism which had little to do with church attendance; or they could exploit an unruly nationalism capable of overriding social divisions. All these appeals were fully in accord with the party's seventeenth-century emphases.

The fact and the circumstances of tory survival bring into question the convention whereby eighteenth-century English history is divided into three hermetically sealed periods. Pre-1715 English society is scrutinised primarily for signs of whig and tory strife; the middle decades of the century are discussed mainly in terms of political stability and the dichotomy between Court and Country; while the post-1760 era is examined for royal whimsy, and for the emergence of radical protest and of homogeneous, unapologetic party (courtesy of Edmund Burke and the Rockingham whigs). Certainly the tempo of political activity and its means of expression within and outside Westminster changed during the century, but such an approach can obscure some important continuities.

Most whig politicians did not feel assured of their ministerial supremacy until 1722. Even after that date there were various junctures when a mixed administration taking in tories seemed a possibility, and when the monarch appeared sympathetic towards such a construct. The sporadic prospect of evading proscription under a Hanoverian king ensured that Jacobitism, which had rarely been ideologically attractive, was also never more than a tactical side-show for the vast majority of tory M.P.s and peers. Instead, they accepted the inevitability of opposition to successive whig administrations, in alliance with successive whig rebels. Such mongrel conjunctions were ineluctable expedients; they were never able to effect a durable reconfiguration of parliamentary alignments in which considerations of whig and tory would be rendered nugatory. Professor Elton's verdict on early Stuart Parliaments may be transposed, without undue violence, to their Walpolian and Pelhamite successors: 'Court and Country are useful concepts in defining certain attitudes and occasional positions, as well as offering political poles for ambition and opinion to gather round. But they were not movements or parties, not entities by means of which the political battles were fought.'[2]

If the mid eighteenth century was usually politically quiescent, it was primarily because England's formal political life, like her economy and her social organisation, was stable and predominantly traditional from the late seventeenth century to the first half of the nineteenth. Tory proscription was anomalous. It prejudiced the solidarity and the essential conservatism of the nation's landed elite, and to this extent George III's accession, which brought tory readmission to the hierarchies of Court, civil service, and county, was indeed significant. But the new reign did not transform toryism or all of its parliamentary adherents. It was the persistence of conventional tory attitudes towards the Crown and non-resistance, towards the Church of England, and towards the claims of large electorates and urban opinion which ensured tory confusion and dispersal in the face of the domestic and American crises of the 1760s and 1770s.

In other ways, too, 1760 is an uncertain watershed. By the 1750s Old Corps dominance as Edward Gibbon described it – the Pelhams 'fixed on the old basis of the Whig aristocracy' – was near to bankruptcy in terms of personnel and talent.[3] George III did not so much annihilate this particular whig nucleus as curtail its death agony and, in 1762, kick its corpse.

If it is simplistic to date the dissolution of Pelhamite *Realpolitik* from

1760, it is no less inappropriate to commence the account of eighteenth-century radicalism (however one interprets that difficult term) with the career of John Wilkes. In some of their propaganda and symbolism, in many of their reform proposals and electoral initiatives, in their encouragement of and co-operation with extra-parliamentary lobbies and voter societies, mid-century tory M.P.s pioneered or fostered much of the content and many of the methods of subsequent protest. The accession of George III did not inaugurate radicalism: it effected a change in its quality and personnel. And the virulence lavished on tories who reverted after 1760 to the socio-political complacency which befitted their income bears witness to their earlier acceptance as the advocates of the excluded. Thomas Spence, the Newcastle schoolmaster who urged the forcible nationalisation of land as the pre-requisite of political change, was accustomed to reprove any backsliding artisan agitator by calling him 'a Sir Walter Blackett' – the Newcastle tory M.P. whose oppositionism had lasted only as long as his proscription.[4]

The tories were indeed superseded; but within Westminster as without, they were emulated in eclipse. Later in the eighteenth century, the marquess of Rockingham's followers achieved fame because, as Disraeli explained, Burke was able to restore the 'moral existence' of whiggery which had languished under the Pelhams. Yet, as I have sought to show, Burke's insistence that his connection was ideologically homogeneous, that it should seek government concessions only as a group, and that it should prefer minority status and the political wilderness to collusion with 'those who contradict the very fundamental principles on which their party is formed', was by no means novel. Nor, as the tory experience showed, were these canons of conduct a guarantee of speedy political success.[5] At the same time, however, such a strategy could create an easily recognised, self-conscious, and durable political group. This, too, Burke might have learnt from those tories who had defied the whig oligarchy. For they had, after all, been there before him.

Appendix

Both the tables below raise the vexed question of how one determines tory strength in the eight Parliaments elected between 1715 and 1761. Some historians would argue that it is impossible and invidious to distinguish between mid-century tory and non-tory opposition M.P.s. One can only answer that most informed contemporaries could and did make that very distinction. Certainly a few M.P.s, especially in the 1750s, pose problems: the Abingdon M.P. John Morton for instance, and (an example which Sir Lewis Namier and John Brooke cherished and returned to again and again) Sir William Maynard, a reputed Essex tory who was returned for that county in 1759 under whig auspices. Since Morton championed the cause of the tory candidates for Oxfordshire in 1754 (something which no recognised whig M.P. is known to have done), since he corresponded with tory notables, and since his voters lauded his commitment to the Anglican Church, I classify him as a tory. Maynard and men of his ilk have been omitted from these tables, and it needs to be emphasised that such hybrids achieved contemporary notoriety precisely because they were exceptional. For the rest, I have drawn on tory correspondence, on the membership lists of the various tory societies, and on the parliamentary lists described by David Clayton and Clyve Jones (eds.), *A Register of Parliamentary Lists 1660–1761* (Leicester, 1979), 103–18. As yet no lists have been found for the 1722 Parliament, but a tory friend informed Lord Gower in May 1722 that 'by a modest computation' there would be 'about a hundred and seventy Tories' in the new House: a calculation which accords with my own researches.

Table 1 shows the voting behaviour and attendance rate of tory M.P.s in seventeen Commons divisions between 1716 and 1755. Many of these divisions spawned several division lists, each of them slightly different. The lists on which my own calculations are based are specified in the notes to the Appendix. Rival lists and their variations are described in Sedgwick, 1, 81–105, 126–31.

Table 2 is in two sections. Table 2(a) shows the total number of tory M.P.s returned at each of the eight general elections of this period, how many of them underwent contested elections, and the number returned for county and for borough constituencies. The total number returned at each election includes tory M.P.s subsequently unseated by a whig petition; similarly, it excludes those six tory M.P.s who were defeated in 1741 but whose subsequent petitions benefited from the brief interregnum in Old

Corps dominance in 1742. Table 2(b) concentrates on those tory M.P.s who were returned to English borough constituencies, and tabulates them according to the size of the electorate involved. Five categories have been adopted: under 100 voters, 100–250 voters, 250–500 voters, 500–1000 voters, and over 1000 voters. The two University constituencies have been counted as boroughs, and all estimates of numbers of voters are based on Sedgwick, 1, 190–370, and Namier & Brooke, 1, 204–458.

Table 1: *Evidence from division lists of Tory M.P.s' attendance rate and voting behaviour*

Date and subject of Division	Tory M.P.s entitled to sit	Tory M.P.s voting for	Tory M.P.s voting against	Tory M.P.s absent	Tory absentees as percentage of Tory M.P.s entitled to sit
April 1716 Septennial Bill[1]	196	8	147	41	21
January 1719 Repeal of Occasional Conformity and Schism Acts[2]	179	0	141	38	21
December 1719 Peerage Bill[3]	176	5	129	42	24
23 April 1729 Civil List arrears[4]	123	1	45	77	63
4 February 1730 Hessian troops[5]	120	0	87	33	28
26 January 1732 Army estimates[6]	126	0	94	32	25
14 March 1733 Excise Bill[7]	127	0	105	22	18
13 March 1734 Repeal of Septennial Act[8]	127	107	0	20	16
8 March 1739 Convention Treaty[9]	144	0	130	14	10
21 November 1739 Navigation Address[10]	141	–	–	36	25
29 January 1740 Place Bill[11]	143	114	0	29	21
18 November 1740 Amendment to Address[12]	140	–	–	47	33
16 December 1741 Chairman of elections[13]	134	123	0	11	8
10 December 1742 Hanoverian troops[14]	149	4	125	20	13
18 January 1744 Hanoverian troops[15]	147	1	138	8	5
11 April 1746 Hanoverian troops[16]	140	3	93	44	34
24 March 1755 Sitting M.P.s for Mitchell[17]	109	21	53	35	34

Average absentee rate 24%

Table 2: *Tory electoral performance 1715–61*

(a)

General Election	Tory M.P.s returned	Tory M.P.s returned after contest	Tory M.P.s returned for counties	Tory M.P.s returned for boroughs
1715	220*	99	63	161
1722	169*	103	60	116
1727	129*	58	44	88
1734	150*	59	51	101
1741	135	27	56	79
1747	110*	22	47	65
1754	110*	25	44	67
1761	112	25	47	65

*Four tories in 1715, seven in 1722, three in 1727, two in 1734 and 1747, and one tory in 1754 were returned for two constituencies.

(b)

	Tory M.P.s returned by English boroughs with				
General Election	under 100 voters	100–250 voters	250–500 voters	500–1000 voters	over 1000 voters
1715	54	19	35	19	25
1722	27	16	26	19	21
1727	19	11	21	14	18
1734	20	12	24	19	22
1741	15	7	11	18	24
1747	16	8	10	8	19
1754	9	8	6	5	25
1761	13	8	5	10	25

Manuscript Sources

INSTITUTIONAL LIBRARIES AND RECORD OFFICES

All Souls College, Oxford
Appeals 525–61

Balliol College, Oxford
Leigh MSS.

Bank of England
Morice MSS.
Stock Ledger Books (Records section, Roehampton)

Berkshire R.O.
Craven MSS.
Hartley–Russell MSS.

Bodleian Library, Oxford
Ballard MSS.
Carte MSS.
Dashwood MSS.
North MSS.
Microfilm 740
MS. Add. A269
MS. Eng. Letters c. 144
MS. Eng. Misc. b. 48

Bristol City Reference Library
Southwell MSS.

Bristol City R.O.
Ashton Court MSS.

Bristol University Library
Edward Bayntun Rolt's diary (microfilm; restricted access)

British Library
Add. MSS.

6043	Secker Papers
9120–232	Coxe Papers (used selectively)
22218–48	Strafford Papers
27732–5	Essex Papers
32686–3053	Newcastle Papers (used selectively)
35337	Philip Yorke's parliamentary journal
35351–882	Hardwicke Papers (used selectively)
41348–57	Martin Papers
46400	Puleston Papers
46966–7159	Egmont Papers (used selectively)
49360 and M/602	Minute books of the Loyal Brotherhood
51375–445	Holland Papers (used selectively)

Egerton MSS.
  1719, 2540, 2618
Lansdowne MSS.
  852, 1017
Stowe MSS.
  180, 227–32, 247–56, 354
Loan 29: Portland Papers
Loan 57: Bathurst Papers
Blenheim Papers

Buckinghamshire R.O.
Claydon House MSS.
Hampden MSS.
Lee MSS.

Cambridgeshire R.O.
Cotton MSS.

Cambridge University Library
Cholmondeley Houghton MSS.
Edward Harley's parliamentary journal, 1734–51

Chester City R.O.
Cotton of Combemere MSS.
Grosvenor MSS.

Christ Church, Oxford
Evelyn MSS.
Wake MSS.

Cornwall R.O.
Buller MSS.
Carew MSS.

Coventry City R.O.
Item 36/3

Cumbria R.O.
Lonsdale MSS.

Devonshire R.O.
Courtenay MSS.
Rolle MSS.
Seymour of Berry Pomeroy MSS.

Dorset R.O.
Fox-Strangways MSS.

Essex R.O.
Mildmay MSS.
Gray and Round MSS.
Conyers MSS.
Q/SO 8

Exeter College, Oxford
Bray MSS.

Glamorgan R.O.
Kemys–Tynte MSS.

Gloucestershire R.O.
Dutton MSS.
Rooke MSS.

Greater London R.O.
CR 136/MX/FP2

Guildford Muniment Room
Brodrick MSS.

Herefordshire R.O.
Brydges MSS.
Cornewall MSS.
Foley MSS.
Harley MSS.

Hertfordshire R.O.
Delmé Radcliffe MSS.
Panshanger MSS.

History of Parliament Trust, Institute of Historical Research, University of London
Bute transcripts
Ryder transcripts

House of Lords R.O.
Proxy Books 1714–60
Historical Collection 82

Huntington Library, San Marino
Loudoun MSS.
Stowe MSS.

John Rylands Library, Manchester
Bromley–Davenport MSS.
Crawford MSS.
Legh of Lyme MSS.

Kendal R.O.
Levens MSS.

Kent R.O.
De L'Isle MSS.
Sackville MSS.

Leeds City Archives Office
Newby Hall MSS.
Temple Newsam MSS.
Vyner MSS.

Leicestershire R.O.
Braye MSS.
Finch MSS.
Halford MSS.

National Library of Wales
Bettisfield MSS.
Chirk Castle MSS.
Penrice and Margam MSS.
Picton Castle MSS.
Wynnstay MSS.
MS. 1089B
MS. 1352B

Northamptonshire R.O.
Cartwright MSS.
Isham MSS.
Langham (Cottesbrooke) MSS.

Oxfordshire R.O.
Dillon MSS.

Penzance Private Library
Borlase MSS.

Public Record Office, London
State Papers Domestic, Series 35 and 36
C234/1–90 Lord Chancellor's Warrants
C108/231
Chatham MSS.
Granville MSS.
Shaftesbury MSS.

Salop R.O.
Attingham MSS.
Forester MSS.
Longnor MSS.

Somerset R.O.
Carew MSS.

Staffordshire R.O.
Anson MSS.
Dartmouth MSS.
Leveson-Gower MSS.

Trinity College, Dublin
King MSS.

Tullie House, Carlisle
Ware Transcripts

Warwickshire R.O.
Mordaunt MSS.
Newdigate MSS.

West Sussex R.O.
Goodwood MSS.

Wiltshire R.O.
Savernake MSS.

Worcestershire R.O.
Lechmere MSS.
Pakington MSS.

Bedford Estates Office, London
Bedford MSS. (used selectively)

Bristol, Society of Merchant Venturers
Minutes of the Steadfast Society

Castle Ashby, Northampton
Compton MSS.

Chatsworth House, Derbyshire
Finch–Halifax MSS.
Devonshire MSS.

Clifton, Bristol
Leigh MSS. in the possession of Mrs Gwen Beachcroft

Rousham, Oxfordshire
Caesar Letter books

Walton Hall, Warwickshire
Prowse Memoranda

Windsor Castle, Royal Archives
Bootle MSS.
Georgian MSS.
Stuart MSS.

Notes

The place of publication is London unless otherwise stated. Unless otherwise indicated, all dates before 1752 are given in the Old Style of the Julian calendar, except that the new year has been taken as beginning on 1 January and not 25 March. When quoting manuscripts in the text I have modernised spelling, extended abbreviations, and altered punctuation whenever the sense has seemed to demand it. In the text and in the notes I have referred to individuals by the titles which they held at the time. The following abbreviations are used:

Add. MS.	Additional Manuscript
B.I.H.R.	*Bulletin of the Institute of Historical Research*
B.L.	British Library, British Museum
Chandler	Richard Chandler, *The History and Proceedings of the House of Commons* (14 vols., 1742–4)
C.J.	*House of Commons Journals*
C.U.L.	Cambridge University Library
E.H.R.	*English Historical Review*
Hay's Journal	William Hay's Journal, Northamptonshire R.O., MS., 4 vols. L(c) 1732–5
H.J.	*Historical Journal*
H.L.R.O.	House of Lords Record Office
H.L.S.M.	Henry E. Huntington Library, San Marino, California
H.M.C.	Reports of the Royal Commission on Historical Manuscripts
L.J.	*House of Lords Journals*
Namier & Brooke	Sir Lewis Namier and John Brooke, *The History of Parliament: the House of Commons 1754–90* (3 vols., 1964)
N.L.W.	National Library of Wales
Parl. Hist.	W. Cobbett, *The Parliamentary History of England from the Earliest Period to 1803* (36 vols., 1816)
P.&P.	*Past & Present*
P.R.O.	Public Record Office
R.A.	Royal Archives, Windsor Castle
R.O.	Record Office
Sedgwick	Romney Sedgwick, *The History of Parliament: the House of Commons 1715–54* (2 vols., 1970)
T.R.H.S.	*Transactions of the Royal Historical Society*
V.C.H.	*Victoria County History*

CHAPTER I

1. In a review of a new edition of *Sybil*, introduced by R. A. Butler, *Times Literary Supplement*, No. 433, 18 April 1980. Keith Feiling, *The Second Tory Party 1714–1832* (1938), a book greatly inferior to his *A History of the Tory Party 1640–1714* (Oxford, 1924), which nevertheless also implied that the tories' political collapse at Anne's death was inevitable and irreversible.

2. Sir William Holdsworth, *A History of English Law* (12 vols., 1938), x, 56. See J. H. Plumb's refutation of Macaulay's squirearchical caricature, in 'Nobility and Gentry in the Early Eighteenth Century', *History Today*, v (1955), 816–17.

3. Daniel A. Baugh, 'The Social Basis of Stability', in Baugh (ed.), *Aristocratic Government and Society in Eighteenth-Century England* (New York, 1975), 14–17, 23.

4. J. H. Plumb, *The Growth of Political Stability in England 1675–1725* (1967); Geoffrey Holmes, *British Politics in the Age of Anne* (1967); W. A. Speck, *Tory & Whig: the Struggle in the Constituencies 1701–15* (1970). This concentration on the violence of late Stuart party conflict was of course in part a reaction to Robert Walcott's sceptical and often anachronistic treatment of party divisions in *English Politics in the Early Eighteenth Century* (1956).

5. Plumb, *Political Stability*, 29, 71. See also Geoffrey Holmes, *The Electorate and the National Will in the First Age of Party* (Kendal, 1976).

6. Basil Williams, *The Whig Supremacy 1714–60* (2nd edn, 1962), 1.

7. Plumb, *Political Stability*, 172.

8. H. J. Habakkuk, 'English Landownership, 1680–1740', *Economic History Review*, x (1940), 2–17, and 'Marriage Settlements in the Eighteenth Century', *T.R.H.S.*, 4th ser., xxxii (1950), 15–30; see also his 'The Rise and Fall of English Landed Families, 1600–1800', *T.R.H.S.*, 5th ser., xxix (1979), 187–207, and xxx (1980), 199–221. Plumb, *Political Stability*, 9–10, 168n.

9. C. Clay, 'Marriage, Inheritance, and the Rise of Large Estates in England, 1660–1815', and 'The Price of Freehold Land in the Later Seventeenth and Eighteenth Centuries', *Economic History Review*, xxi (1968), 503–18, and xxvii (1974), 173–89; see also B. A. Holderness, 'The English Land Market in the Eighteenth Century: the Case of Lincolnshire', *Economic History Review*, xxvii (1974), 557–76. Average family size amongst the English peerage fell from 5.04 for those born between 1600 and 1624 to 3.83 for those born a century later. A similar decline seems to have occurred amongst the gentry over the same period. See T. H. Hollingsworth, 'The Demography of the British Peerage', *Population Studies*, xviii (1964–5), suppl., and L. Bonfield, 'Marriage Settlements and the "Rise of the Great Estates": the Demographic Aspect', *Economic History Review*, xxxii (1979), 483–93. For two local studies which modify Habakkuk's thesis, see J. V. Beckett, 'Landownership in Cumbria, c. 1680–1740' (unpub. Ph.D. dissertation, Lancaster University, 1975); J. O. Martin, 'The Landed Estate in Glamorgan, c. 1660–1760' (unpub. Ph.D. dissertation, Cambridge University, 1978).

10. Habakkuk, 'English Landownership', 4–5, 12–13; A. M. Mimardière, 'The Warwickshire Gentry, 1660–1730' (unpub. M.A. dissertation, Birmingham University, 1963). Sedgwick, i, 544; ii, 146, 359, 361–2, 482, 553.

11. Sedgwick, ii, 395. For Beckford, see Richard Sheridan, 'Planter and Historian: the Career of William Beckford of Jamaica and England, 1744–99', *Jamaica*

Historical Review, IV (1964), 38–45. I am most grateful to Dr Christopher Clay of Bristol University for information on the Wiltshire land market, and on tory landowners in general.

12. Sedgwick, I, 460, 519, 583; II, 57, 81–2, 128, 202, 222, 243, 318, 517, 536. Cf. John Owen, *The Rise of the Pelhams* (1957), 67–9.

13. Information on the earl of Salisbury from Dr Christopher Clay. For the Grosvenors, see G. E. Mingay, *English Landed Society in the Eighteenth Century* (1963), 58. On Foley, see H. J. Habakkuk, 'England's Nobility', in Baugh (ed.), *Aristocratic Government*, 103.

14. For the Wards, see T. J. Raybould, *The Economic Emergence of the Black Country: a Study of the Dudley Estates* (Newton Abbot, 1973), and M. B. Rowlands, 'Industry and Social Change in Staffordshire, 1660–1760', *Transactions of the Lichfield and South Staffordshire Archaeological and Historical Society*, VII (1965–6), 49. For Newdigate, see John Money, *Experience and Identity: Birmingham and the West Midlands 1760–1800* (Manchester, 1977), 2; for the Parsons–Cotton link, see Sedgwick, I, 586; II, 326.

15. Information on James Sharp from Dr Nicholas Rogers. Peter Mathias, 'Dr Johnson and the Business World', *The Transformation of England: Essays in the Economic and Social History of England in the Eighteenth Century* (1979), 295–317.

16. N. C. Hunt, 'A Consideration of the Relationship between some Religious and Economic Organisations and the Government, especially from 1730–42' (Ph.D. dissertation, Cambridge University, 1951), Appendices J and L; Bank Stock Ledgers, 1715–60, Bank of England (Records Section, Roehampton).

17. D. M. Joslin, 'London Private Bankers, 1720–85', *Economic History Review*, VII (1954), 171–2, 176–7. See the list of accounts in F. G. Hilton Price, *The Marygold by Temple Bar* (1902), 46–69.

18. *Commentator*, No. 47, 13 June 1720. P. G. M. Dickson, *The Financial Revolution in England: a Study in the Development of Public Credit 1688–1756* (1967), 109, 168n.

19. For the thesis that tories were the victims of a cash-orientated society, see Isaac Kramnick, *Bolingbroke and his Circle: the Politics of Nostalgia in the Age of Walpole* (1968).

20. And it has been argued that English instability in the 1640s, 1650s, and 1680s, was only part of a European trend; see Geoffrey Parker and Lesley M. Smith (eds.), *The General Crisis of the Seventeenth Century* (1978), and Andrew Lossky, 'The General European Crisis of the 1680s', *European Studies Review*, X (1980), 177–97.

21. For the English Civil War as accident not epic, see Conrad Russell, 'Parliamentary History in Perspective, 1604–29', *History*, LXI (1976), 1–27, and *Parliaments and English Politics 1621–29* (Oxford, 1979).

22. Lawrence Stone, *The Causes of the English Revolution 1529–1642* (1972), 78, where Behrens is also quoted.

23. Philip C. Yorke, *The Life and Correspondence of Philip Yorke, Earl of Hardwicke* (3 vols., Cambridge, 1913), III, 34, and see D. T. Witcombe, *Charles II and the Cavalier House of Commons 1663–74* (Manchester, 1966), 119. On the Game Act, see C. Kirby, 'The English Game Law System', *American Historical Review*, XXXVIII (1932–3), 241.

24. See the information given in Lawrence Stone, 'The Size and Composition of the Oxford Student Body 1580–1910', in Stone (ed.), *The University in Society* (2 vols., 1975), I, 19, 21–46. Obviously these figures are marred by changes in

social categorisation over time, but the decline in plebeian students they show is beyond doubt.

25. See Howard Tomlinson, 'Financial and Administrative Developments in England, 1660–88', in J. R. Jones (ed.), *The Restored Monarchy 1660–88* (1979), 94–117; Plumb, *Political Stability*, 1–65.

26. Quoted in J. A. W. Gunn, *Factions no More: Attitudes to Party in Government and Opposition in Eighteenth Century England* (1971), 54. See also Gary Stuart de Krey's remarks on how acute party tensions in London in the 1690s were contained within a framework of consensus among the City's elite, 'Trade, Religion and Politics in London in the Reign of William III' (unpub. Ph.D. dissertation, Princeton University, 1978), 418.

27. See S. B. Baxter, *William III* (1966), and E. L. Ellis, 'William III and the Politicians', in Geoffrey Holmes (ed.), *Britain after the Glorious Revolution 1689–1714* (1969), 115–34. For the rehabilitation of the last and best Stuart monarch, see Edward Gregg, *Queen Anne* (1980).

28. The issues which divided whig and tory are discussed most fully by Holmes, *British Politics*, 51–182. It is their destabilising effect on political society, *not* the existence of these issues, which I am questioning.

29. Holmes, *British Politics*, 107n.

30. Geoffrey Holmes, *The Trial of Dr. Sacheverell* (1973), and 'The Sacheverell Riots', *P.&P.*, LXXII (1976), 55–85. For an interesting and dissentient view of this crisis, see Mary Ransome, 'Church and Dissent in the Election of 1710', *E.H.R.*, LVI (1941), 76–89.

31. J. J. Cartwright, *The Wentworth Papers 1705–39* (1883), 389–90.

32. Quoted in Colin Brooks, 'Taxation, Finance and Public Opinion, 1688–1714' (unpub. Ph.D. dissertation, Cambridge University, 1971), 202.

33. W. A. Speck, 'Conflict in Society', in Holmes (ed.), *Britain after the Glorious Revolution*, 135–54 at 152.

34. See Brooks, 'Taxation, Finance and Public Opinion', *passim*, and his 'Public Finance and Political Stability: the Administration of the Land Tax, 1688–1720', *H.J.*, XVII (1974), 281–300.

35. Dickson, *Financial Revolution*, 27–8.

36. *Ibid.* 10; Speck, 'Conflict in Society', 148–52, 154 n. 40.

37. Archibald Hutcheson, 'Some Considerations relating to the Payment of the Publick Debts', *A Collection of Treatises* (1721), 19. For tory financiers under Charles II, and William III, see De Krey, 'Trade, Religion and Politics', 29–30, 54. Edward Hughes, *Studies in Administration and Finance 1558–1825* (Manchester, 1934), 164–6. Harley's financial policy is analysed in B. W. Hill, 'The Change of Government and the "Loss of the City", 1710–11', *Economic History Review*, XXIV (1971), 395–413.

38. Lawrence Stone, 'Social Mobility in England 1500–1700', *P.&P.*, XXXIII (1966), 16–55; Plumb, *Political Stability*, 152–3.

39. See Geoffrey Holmes, 'Post-Revolution Britain and the Historian', in Holmes (ed.), *Britain after the Glorious Revolution*, 15–18; Plumb, *Political Stability*, 121; J. A. Downie, *Robert Harley and the Press: Propaganda and Public Opinion in the Age of Swift and Defoe* (Cambridge, 1979).

40. Plumb, *Political Stability*, 155; Brooks, 'Taxation, Finance and Public Opinion', 137n.

41. Walter Bagehot, *Biographical Studies*, ed. R. H. Hutton (1907), 182.

42. Holmes, *British Politics*, 219.

43. J. H. Plumb, 'The Growth of the Electorate in England from 1600–1715', *P.&P.*, XLV (1969), 90–116; Holmes, *The Electorate and the National Will*, 23;

Derek Hirst, *The Representative of the People? Voters and Voting in England under the Early Stuarts* (Cambridge, 1975), 105, Ch. 2 *passim*.

44. Works which stress the independence of the Augustan voter include Speck, *Tory & Whig*; Speck and W. A. Gray, 'Computer Analysis of Poll Books: an Initial Report', *B.I.H.R.* XLIII (1970), 105–12; and Speck, Gray, and R. Hopkinson, 'Computer Analysis of Poll Books: a Further Report', *B.I.H.R.*, XLVIII (1975), 64–90. For growing electoral costs after 1688 and for the potential for landlord control in the Augustan electoral system, see Plumb, *Political Stability*, 87–94, and John Cannon, *Parliamentary Reform 1640–1832* (Cambridge, 1973), 24–46.

45. Holmes, *The Electorate and the National Will, passim*; see the breakdown of England's electorate in the 1713 and 1715 elections in Sedgwick, I, 79.

46. Norma Landau, 'Independence, Deference and Voter Participation: the Behaviour of the Electorate in Early-Eighteenth-Century Kent', *H.J.*, XXII (1979), 561–84. Plumb, *Political Stability*, 44–6.

47. Downie, *Robert Harley and the Press*, 133, 138; Plumb, *Political Stability*, 46n; Eric Pawson, *The Early Industrial Revolution* (1979), 193, 214.

48. See Hill, 'The Change of Government', 404, and Gregg, *Queen Anne*, 297–329.

49. I discuss the 1722 election in more detail above, 121–2. In addition to the 127 contests listed by Cannon, *Parliamentary Reform*, 278–89, Aylesbury and Tiverton (and, I would imagine, many other boroughs still to be studied) went to the polls.

50. Mathias, 'Taxation and Industrialization in Britain, 1700–1870', *Transformation of England*, 118; Plumb, *Political Stability*, xvi.

51. C. B. Macpherson, *The Political Theory of Possessive Individualism* (Oxford, 1962), 160–93.

52. See Poulet's report on the Somerset gentry in 1759, P.R.O., 30/8/53, Pt 1, fols. 115–16. The extent of social discrimination at the centre may be judged from a parliamentary incident on 5 February 1755. The tories won a Commons division that evening because most ministerialist M.P.s had been invited to a masquerade at Court: 'This success (immaterial as it is) was wholly owing to ye Masquerade, to which *very few* Country Gentlemen were invited' – John Dobson (secretary to the tory M.P. for Warwickshire) to John Mordaunt, 6 February 1755, Warwickshire R.O., CR 1368, V/10. Oxford to William Brydges, 21 January 1748, Herefordshire R.O., A81/31.

53. W. C. Lukis (ed.), *The Family Memoirs of the Rev. William Stukeley, M.D. and the Antiquarian and other Correspondence*, Publications of the Surtees Society, LXXIII (1882), 498.

54. Lord Chesterfield quoted by Edward Hughes, 'The Professions in the Eighteenth Century', in Baugh (ed.), *Aristocratic Government*, 188; Selwyn to Sir John Dutton, 25 July 1739, Gloucestershire R.O., D678 57D/198. Paul Lucas, 'A Collective Biography of Students and Barristers of Lincoln's Inn, 1680–1804: a Study in the "Aristocratic Resurgence" of the Eighteenth Century', *Journal of Modern History*, XLVI (1974), 227–61.

55. David Spring, 'Ralph Sneyd: Tory Country Gentleman', *Bulletin of the John Rylands Library*, XXXVIII (1956), 555; John Brewer, *Party Ideology and Popular Politics at the Accession of George III* (Cambridge, 1976), 18.

56. J. H. Plumb, 'Political Man', in James L. Clifford (ed.), *Man versus Society in Eighteenth Century Britain* (Cambridge, 1968), 1–21.

CHAPTER 2

1. Walpole's comment is quoted in John Brewer, *Party Ideology and Popular Politics at the Accession of George III* (Cambridge, 1976), 41. This version of toryism can be found in John Owen, *The Rise of the Pelhams* (1957), 66–76; J. H. Plumb, *The Growth of Political Stability in England 1675–1725* (1967), 159–86, and Sir Lewis Namier, 'Country Gentlemen in Parliament, 1750–84', *Crossroads of Power: Essays on Eighteenth Century England* (1962), 30–45, to name only the more notable accounts.

2. Eveline Cruickshanks, *Political Untouchables: the Tories and the '45* (1979), and see her essay and influence in Sedgwick, I, ix, 62–78. While I disagree with Dr Cruickshanks' conclusions, I wish to record my gratitude for all the assistance she has given me on this topic. Paul Fritz, *The English Ministers and Jacobitism between the Rebellions of 1715 and 1745* (Toronto, 1975). The best account of Jacobitism is now Bruce Lenman's *The Jacobite Risings in Britain 1689–1746* (1980).

3. J. C. D. Clark, 'The Decline of Party, 1740–60', *E.H.R.*, XCIII (1978), 499–527, and see his 'A General Theory of Party, Opposition and Government, 1688–1832', *H.J.*, XXIII (1980), 295–326.

4. *Parl. Hist.*, VII, 7. *Warning to the Whigs and to the Well-Affected Tories* (1744), 25.

5. *H.M.C. Mar and Kellie*, 505. For Lord Anglesey in 1714 see C. S. King, *A Great Archbishop of Dublin: William King 1650–1729* (1906), 164.

6. *To the Right Honourable the Earl of Oxford upon his Not Appearing at St. James's* (1727); for Oxford's approach to the Court in 1731, see B.L. Add. MS. 4163, fol. 279, and for the tories' in 1742, see Hay's Journal, IV.

7. For tory assimilation of the Revolution of 1688, see J. P. Kenyon, *Revolution Principles: the Politics of Party 1689–1720* (Cambridge, 1977), and M. A. Goldie, 'Tory Political Thought 1689–1714' (unpub. Ph.D. dissertation, Cambridge University, 1978). The Jacobite intrigues of Oxford and Bolingbroke may be traced most conveniently in J. H. and Margaret Shennan, 'The Protestant Succession in English Politics, April 1713–September 1715', in Ragnhild Hatton and J. S. Bromley (eds.), *William III and Louis XIV: Essays 1680–1720 by and for Mark A. Thomson* (Liverpool, 1968), 252–70. For an interesting but not entirely convincing piece of revisionism, see G. E. Gregg, 'The Protestant Succession in International Politics, 1710–16' (unpub. Ph.D. dissertation, London University, 1972).

8. *H.M.C. Stuart*, VII, 239. I have been assisted in my assessment of post-1714 Jacobite propaganda by the researches of Mr Paul Chapman of Gonville and Caius College, Cambridge.

9. This paragraph owes much to an unpublished essay by Mark Goldie, 'The Nonjurors, Episcopacy, and the Origins of the Convocation Controversy'. For nonjuring dissonance after 1716 see William Coxe, *Memoirs of the Life and Administration of Sir Robert Walpole, Earl of Orford* (3 vols., 1798), II, 97–8. For Charles Leslie and the ministry, see B.L. Add. MS. 47029, fol. 48.

10. R. J. Goulden, 'Vox Populi, Vox Dei: Charles Delafaye's Paperchase', *The Book Collector*, XXVIII (1979), 368–90. For a Stuart approach to William Pulteney and his opposition whig colleagues, see G. H. Jones, *The Main Stream of Jacobitism* (Cambridge, Mass., 1954), 181–2; for contract theory in Jacobite journals, *Mist's Weekly Journal*, 11 September 1725, and *Fog's Weekly Journal*, 10 February 1732.

11. *Copies of some Letters from Mr. Hutcheson to the Late Earl of Sunderland* (1722), 7–8.
12. D. N. Smith (ed.), *The Letters of Thomas Burnet to George Duckett 1712–22* (Oxford, 1914), 93; *Some Thoughts of an Honest Tory in the Country upon the Late Disposition of some People to Revolt* (1716), 30; *Remarks and Collections of Thomas Hearne*, Oxford Historical Society (11 vols., Oxford, 1885–1921), v, 121.
13. Elizabeth Handasyde, *Granville the Polite: the Life of George Granville, Lord Lansdowne, 1666–1735* (1933), 139–50; Gregg, 'Protestant Succession', 271–83; Sedgwick, 1, 62.
14. *H.M.C. Eleventh Report*, App., iv, Townshend MSS., 171. For Jacobite activity amongst the Somerset gentry in 1715, see Lady Llanover (ed.), *The Autobiography and Correspondence of Mary Granville, Mrs. Delany* (3 vols., 1861), 1, 14, 17.
15. Sir Nicholas Morice to Humphry Morice, 7 October 1715, and Walter Moyle to Humphry Morice, 25 and 26 September 1715, Bank of England, COU/B151/1, fol. 200 and COU/B151/11, fols. 333–5. Carteret to ?, 25 September 1715, B.L. Stowe MS. 228, fol. 126; Carteret had gone over to the whigs before Anne's death. Vyvyan also protested his innocence: see B.L. Add. MS. 38507, fol. 176.
16. *The Note Book of Sir Walter Calverley, Bart*, Publications of the Surtees Society, 11 (1886), 140–1; Sedgwick, 1, 465.
17. Sir William Pole to Humphry Morice, 13 November 1715, Bank of England, COU/B151/11, fols. 357–8; Lady Verney (ed.), *Verney Letters of the Eighteenth Century from the MSS. at Claydon House* (2 vols., 1930), 11, 26.
18. William Coxe, *Memoirs of Horatio, Lord Walpole* (1802), 290 (my italics). Robert Walpole's insinuation was described by Lord Perceval to C. Dering in February 1716, B.L. Add. MS. 47088, fols. 50–1.
19. Cruickshanks, *Political Untouchables*, 46, 60, 81. The 1744 Loyal Addresses are listed in the *London Gazette*, between 21/25 February and 1/5 May 1744.
20. Lord Sempill to James, 21 June 1745, R.A. SP 265/207.
21. Anthony Aufrere (ed.), *The Lockhart Papers* (2 vols., 1817), 11, 348–9. For Cecil's duplicity see Sedgwick, 1, 113–14.
22. *Hearne's Collections*, x, 471.
23. Carte's meeting with Walpole is described by Cruickshanks, *Political Untouchables*, 23–4, and see B.L. Add. MS. 34522, fol. 7. Dr Cruickshanks and I differ in our opinion of St Aubyn's bias; I burden the reader with my precise reasons for thinking him non-Jacobite primarily to indicate how complex is the task of individual labelling:
    1. He was offered a place on the Admiralty Board in 1742.
    2. He was a member of Edward Harley's non-Jacobite tory Board.
    3. In the ballot to select a committee to inquire into Orford's conduct in March 1742, all 518 M.P.s present voted for St Aubyn; Jacobite-tories such as Wynn and Cotton received fewer than 258 votes. St Aubyn had been on both the court and the opposition lists for the ballot – a clear indication of his reputed moderation.
    4. A series of letters from St Aubyn to William Borlase in Penzance Private Library. Many of these do indeed refer, as Cruickshanks notes (*Political Untouchables*, 54–5), to the pilchard fisheries. A letter of 21 June 1744 is however concerned with securing Penzance's coastal defences. St Aubyn writes of this 'Critical Season, when we are meditating how to guard against a Foreign and Common Enemy' and of the need to avoid 'Popular

discontent at Home, so easy to be rais'd but God knows so difficult to be appeas'd' (Borlase Letter Book 1, fol. 79). Given that the immediate danger of a French landing had receded, this does not read to me like the letter of a man desirous of such an invasion, nor of a man who wants to raise local tin-miners against the government; this latter strategy was what Carte attributed to St Aubyn (see R.A. SP 216/111D).

24. *Commentator*, 22 January 1720.

25. *Parl. Hist.*, VIII, 118–19. For Layer's confession, see *A Report from the Committee . . . to Examine Christopher Layer, and others* (1722), 53; his 'Norfolk List' has been printed by Fritz, *English Ministers and Jacobitism*, 143–6.

26. William Morice to Atterbury, 26 September 1728, C.U.L., C(H) Correspondence 1542, see also 1605. G. V. Bennett, *The Tory Crisis in Church and State 1688–1730: the Career of Francis Atterbury, Bishop of Rochester* (Oxford, 1975), 209, 239.

27. For the Remitters, see Lord Fitzmaurice, *Life of William, Earl of Shelburne, afterwards First Marquess of Lansdowne* (2 vols., 1875), I, 49. The discrepancy between Wynn's promises and his monetary contributions can be traced in Sedgwick, II, 543–5; A. Lang, *Pickle the Spy* (1897), 103; and the *Westminster Journal*, 12 October 1745. For some interesting Jacobite comments on tory meanness, see *A Letter from a Gentleman in Town to his Friend in the Country recommending the Necessity of Frugality* (1750), 8, 11.

28. J. P. Jenkins, 'A Social and Political History of the Glamorgan Gentry c. 1650–1770' (unpub. Ph.D. dissertation, Cambridge University, 1978), 235–45. For Wynn's influence in North Wales, see A. L. Cust, *Chronicles of Erthig on the Dyke* (2 vols., 1914), I, 229–33. For the third duke of Beaufort, see B.L. Add. MS. 47000, fol. 125.

29. Jenkins, 'Glamorgan Gentry', 237, 250; F. Jones, 'The Society of Sea Sergeants', *Transactions of the Honourable Society of Cymmrodorion* (1967), 57–91; J. P. Jenkins, 'Jacobites and Freemasons in Eighteenth-Century Wales', *The Welsh History Review*, IX (1979), 391–406. It is possible of course that masonic activity was sometimes a cover for crypto-Jacobite endeavour. For the European dimension of this connection see J. M. Roberts, *The Mythology of the Secret Societies* (1972).

30. The 1721 list is printed in Sedgwick, I, 109–13. It includes the Nottinghamshire tory M.P., William Levinz, who had subscribed £100 towards the cost of raising a county regiment during the 1715 invasion, and Sir Justinian Isham, M.P. for Northamptonshire, whose correspondence is full of hostile references to the Pretender. Philip Jenkins has suggested to me that the Welsh portion of the list may have been compiled by Robert Mansel and be more accurate than the rest.

31. Cruickshanks, *Political Untouchables*, 14–51.

32. 'List of lords and country gentlemen in each county given to Butler in 1743', printed *ibid.* 115–47. R. Fitzroy Bell (ed.), *Memorials of John Murray of Broughton*, Publications of the Scottish Historical Society, XXVII (Edinburgh, 1898), 49n. For Saxe's opinion of Butler's reports, see J. Colin, *Louis XV et les Jacobites. Le Projet de débarquement en Angleterre de 1743–44* (Paris, 1901), 118.

33. Cruickshanks has identified *le Sieur Pitt*, listed in 1743 as a potential Jacobite in Wiltshire, as William Pitt, who was then M.P. for Old Sarum, *Political Untouchables*, 121, 137. As John Cannon has reminded me, the spy's reference to 'great wealth' points more to William's brother and Old Sarum's patron,

Thomas Pitt. The government M.P.s listed were Sir Richard Corbet, Thomas Gage, William Mitchell, Robert Neale, and Henry Penton.

34. *Political Untouchables*, 70–1, and see also 45. Although mid-eighteenth-century tory family papers are sparse, the Grosvenor, Mackworth, Cornewall, Cave, Cartwright, and Isham MSS. survive in part, and contain several references to tory-Hanoverianism in this period. The Pakington MSS. at Worcestershire R.O. are a likely example of deliberate post-1715 destruction, but the Titus Oates-like argument that no evidence presupposes guilt is fraught with danger. Non-Jacobite oppositionists like William Pulteney and Lord Carteret also seem to have destroyed their political correspondence.

35. Thomas Carte to O'Brien, 4 May 1738, R.A. SP 206/106; Sedgwick, II, 279–80.

36. Atterbury to James, 20 August 1727, R.A. SP 109/87; Sedgwick, II, 340.

37. Cruickshanks, *Political Untouchables*, 53–4.

38. Bolingbroke to Marchmont, n.d., B.L. Add. MS. 37994, fol. 52.

39. *Parl. Hist.*, XIII, 886.

40. W. E. H. Lecky, *A History of England in the Eighteenth Century* (8 vols., 1878–90), I, 317.

41. James Hewitt and James Birch to Grafton, 22 October 1745; and Thomas Archer to James Birch, 25 October 1745, Coventry City R.O., 36/3, fols. 6, 7.

42. For Oxfordshire in 1745, see R. J. Robson, *The Oxfordshire Election of 1754* (Oxford, 1949), 1–10, and A. N. Newman (ed.), 'Leicester House Politics, 1750–60', *Camden Miscellany*, XXIII (1969), 149–50.

43. Draft letter by Sir Roger Newdigate, November 1745, Warwickshire R.O., CR 136 B1861; Rupert C. Jarvis, *Collected Papers on the Jacobite Risings* (2 vols., Manchester, 1971–2), I, 234, II, 228, 313.

44. Copy of a report from the Shropshire whigs sent by Lord Herbert to the duke of Devonshire, 10 October 1745, Chatsworth House, Devonshire MSS., Box 5, 320.5; C. Collyer, 'Yorkshire and the Forty-Five', *Yorkshire Archaeological Journal*, XXXVIII (1952), 71–95.

45. For the plan for a Jacobite landing in Essex, see Cruickshanks, *Political Untouchables*, 43. The behaviour of the county's tory M.P.s in 1745 can be reconstructed from Essex R.O., Order Book, 8 October 1745, Q/SO 8, and list of subscriptions, L/S 1/1.

46. Information on the stock-holdings of tory M.P.s has been derived from the Stock Ledger Books, Bank of England (Records Section, Roehampton).

47. David N. MacKay (ed.), *The Trial of Simon, Lord Lovat of the '45* (Edinburgh, 1911), 127; Sedgwick, I, 75.

48. Charles Noel Somerset, who became fourth duke of Beaufort in 1745, was head of the Remitters. For Wynn's activities in 1745, see Stephen W. Baskerville, 'The Management of the Tory Interest in Lancashire and Cheshire, 1714–47' (unpub. D.Phil. dissertation, Oxford University, 1976), 263. Cruickshanks, *Political Untouchables*, 86.

49. B. W. Hill, 'The Career of Robert Harley, Earl of Oxford, from 1702 to 1714' (unpub. Ph.D. dissertation, Cambridge University, 1961), 361.

50. J. H. Glover (ed.), *The Stuart Papers, printed from the Originals* (1847), 16; Bennett, *Tory Crisis*, 175, 289, 292, 303.

51. See for example the tory motion that Catholics above a certain age should be exempted from the special oaths introduced after the Atterbury plot, *C.J.*, XX, 286. For the 1722 Lancashire contest, see Baskerville, 'Tory Interest', 305–6; for Norfolk in 1734, see W. C. Lukis (ed.), *The Family Memoirs of the Rev. William Stukeley, M.D. and the Antiquarian and other Correspondence*, Publications of the Surtees Society, LXXIII (1882), 274. For tory claims of a

ministerial alliance with the Catholics in the 1734 general election, see Chandler, VIII, 177–8.

52. For Sir John Williams' initiative, see C. L. S. Linnell (ed.), *The Diaries of Thomas Wilson, D.D., 1731–7 and 1750* (1964), 178; for Sir John Bland, see *H.M.C. Egmont*, I, 229–30, 262. For conversions to Catholicism in Yorkshire in the 1730s see J. C. H. Aveling, *The Handle and the Axe: the Catholic Recusants in England from Reformation to Emancipation* (1976), 265.

53. *A True Copy of the Letter from Birmingham* (1751) is a typical example of Jacobite exploitation of the Young Pretender's sex appeal: see R.A. Unbound Stuart Papers, Box 6/82. The reality of popular Jacobitism, as distinct from High-Church and popular tory demonstrations, receives some attention in Nicholas Rogers, 'Popular Disaffection in London during the Forty-Five', *London Journal*, I (1975), 5–27 and 'Popular Protest in Early Hanoverian London', *P.&P.*, LXXIX (1978), 70–100. Sir Charles Petrie's 'The Jacobite Activities in South and West England in the Summer of 1715', *T.R.H.S.*, XVIII (1935), 85–106, is in fact a survey of High-Church riots and popular frustration in the wake of whig dismantling of the tory administration.

54. Philip Hardwicke (ed.), *Miscellaneous State Papers from 1501 to 1726* (2 vols., 1778), II, 548–9; *Manchester Magazine*, No. 492, 29 July 1746.

55. See W. A. Speck, *Tory & Whig: The Struggle in the Constituencies 1701–15* (1970), 114 and 'The General Election of 1715', *E.H.R.*, XC (1975), 507–22. For an assessment of the impact of the '45 on the 1747 election see above, 252–3.

56. Whig broadside, 19 June 1747; and William Bowes to Sir William Robinson, 27 June 1747, Leeds City Archives Office, NH 2506, 2875/25.

57. B.L. Add. MS. 6043, fol. 110, and Archbishop Secker's autobiography, fol. 29; information from Professor R. W. Greaves. See Hay's Journal, IV.

58. Sir Dudley Ryder's notebook for 1748, History of Parliament Trust, Ryder transcripts, document 35(1); *Parl. Hist.*, XI, 1285.

59. John Owen, *The Rise of the Pelhams* (1957), 3, 75.

60. Sedgwick, I, 80–1, lists forty-five tories as having defected between 1715 and 1754. The evidence for long-term defection seems to me to be unclear for Jacob des Bouverie (who accepted a title in 1747 but told his tory friends he had 'nothing but what he paid for and therefore shall not look upon himself under the least obligation', Somerset R.O., DD/TB/Box 16 FT 18), John Comyns, Sir Robert Gordon, James Grahme, John Hardres, Clement Kent, Thomas Lewis, Sir William Milner, George Pitt, Robert Pitt, John Proby, Sir Edward Williams, and Sir Robert Worsley. On the basis of MS. evidence I would list George Compton, M.P. for Northampton, and Charles Cotes, M.P. for Tamworth, as tories who went over to the government in 1742.

61. For St Aubyn, see 'Manuscript Collections at Castle Horneck 1720–72', *The Quarterly Review*, CXXXIX (1875), 379. John Cannon and W. A. Speck, 'Re-Election on Taking Office, 1706–90', *B.I.H.R.*, LI (1978), 206–9.

62. Velters Cornewall to William Brydges, 1 April 1742, Herefordshire R.O., A81/31.

63. A. N. Newman, 'Elections in Kent and its Parliamentary Representation 1715–1754' (unpub. D.Phil. dissertation, Oxford University, 1957), 129.

64. Bennett, *Tory Crisis*, 229; Archibald Hutcheson to Lord Cowper, 28 April 1722, Hertfordshire R.O., D/EP F55.

65. Master is quoted by Baskerville, 'Tory Interest', 315–16; Namier, 'Country Gentlemen', 42.

66. Sir Nicholas Morice to Humphry Morice, 10 December 1721 and 9 February

1722, Bank of England, COU/B151/1, fols. 224, 231. Owen, *Rise of the Pelhams*, 73, and see his similarly limited appraisal of patronage in 'Political Patronage in Eighteenth Century England', in P. Fritz and D. Williams (eds.), *The Triumph of Culture: Eighteenth Century Perspectives* (Toronto, 1972), 369–87.

67. Lord Orrery to James Stuart, 30 June 1727, R.A. SP 107/150. For Beaumont, see P. Roebuck, 'The County Squirearchy and the Fight for Place', *Yorkshire Archaeological Journal*, XLVI (1974), 103–9.

68. See Ragnhild Hatton, 'In search of an Elusive Ruler', in Friedrich Engel-Janosi, Grete Klingenstein, and Heinrich Lutz (eds.), *Fürst, Bürger, Mensch* (Vienna, 1975), 11–41 and her *George I Elector and King* (1978). John Owen, 'George II Reconsidered', in Anne Whiteman, J. S. Bromley, and P. G. M. Dickson (eds.), *Statesmen, Scholars and Merchants: Essays in Eighteenth-Century History presented to Dame Lucy Sutherland* (Oxford, 1973), 113–34.

69. B. W. Hill, *The Growth of Parliamentary Parties 1689–1742* (1976), 205, 209: for one such panic see Romney Sedgwick (ed.), *Some Materials towards Memoirs of the Reign of King George II, by John, Lord Hervey* (3 vols., 1931), III, 682.

70. For high-level whig Jacobitism see Sedgwick, I, 108–9, II, 67; Archibald S. Foord, *His Majesty's Opposition 1714–1830* (Oxford, 1964), 65n, 74, 126n; Lewis Melville, *The Life and Writings of Philip, Duke of Wharton* (1913); and E. Gregg, 'Marlborough in Exile, 1712–14', *H.J.*, XV (1972), 593–618.

71. [Bernard Mandeville], *The Mischiefs that Ought Justly To Be Apprehended from a Whig-Government* (1714), 39. Sir Henry Bunbury (ed.), *The Correspondence of Sir Thomas Hanmer, Bart., with a Memoir of his Life* (1838), 67.

72. William Coxe, *Memoirs of the Administration of the Rt. Hon. Henry Pelham* (2 vols., 1829), I, 35.

CHAPTER 3

1. The Carew deposit is at Somerset R.O. (DD/TB); Newdigate's papers are at Warwickshire R.O. (CR 136); and the Oxford family papers are B.L. Loan 29; the Portland MSS. at Nottingham University Library; C.U.L., Add. 6851; and Harley of Brampton Bryan MSS. at Herefordshire R.O.

2. Geoffrey Holmes, *British Politics in the Age of Anne* (1967), 247–321, and his 'Post-Revolution Britain and the Historian' and 'Harley, St John and the Death of the Tory Party', in Holmes (ed.), *Britain after the Glorious Revolution 1689–1714* (1969), 17, 216–37.

3. Keith Feiling, *A History of the Tory Party 1640–1714* (Oxford, 1924), 481; L. K. J. Glassey, 'The Commission of the Peace 1675–1720' (D.Phil. dissertation, Oxford University, 1972), 327. The literature on the internal tensions of the Oxford administration is extensive; three contemporary or near-contemporary assessments are a useful starting-point. For a Jacobite analysis, see Anthony Aufrere (ed.), *The Lockhart Papers* (2 vols., 1817), I, 345–477; Jonathan Swift, *An Inquiry into the Behaviour of the Queen's Last Ministry*, ed. I. Ehrenpreis (Bloomington, Ind., 1956), is more sympathetic to Oxford; *Memoirs of the Life and Ministerial Conduct... of the Late Lord Visc. Bolingbroke* (1752), 250–88, is an excellent summary and fair to both of the main proponents.

4. Holmes, *British Politics*, 279–83. For a conservative list of whimsical tories, see Eveline G. Cruickshanks, 'The Tories and the Succession to the Crown in the 1714 Parliament', *B.I.H.R.*, XLVI (1973), 184–5. 'Whimsical' is to be preferred to 'Hanoverian' as a description of this pressure-group, since what distinguished it was not acquiescence in the Act of Settlement, but a willingness to vote with

the whigs on matters impinging on the Succession – something which pro-Hanoverian but orthodox tory M.P.s like Sir Justinian Isham and Sir Thomas Cave would never have considered doing.

5. Henry Horwitz, *Revolution Politicks: the Career of Daniel Finch, 2nd earl of Nottingham, 1647–1730* (Cambridge, 1968), 249–57. H.L.R.O., Proxy Book 7.

6. This is my own estimate based on the divisions recorded in *C.J.*, xviii, 26–303.

7. For these Commons divisions see Appendix, Table 1. For the Lords division on the Occasional Conformity Act, see B.L. Add. MS. 47028, fols. 264–5. In 1716 Lord Carnarvon wrote that on average twenty-three tory Lords attended; a figure confirmed by the journals, H.L.S.M., ST 57, vol. xii, fol. 291.

8. George Clarke to Charlett, 30 January 1718, Bodleian Library, MS. Ballard 20, fol. 59. B.L. Add. MS. 47088, fol. 71; *C.J.*, xviii, 651.

9. A. N. Newman, 'Proceedings in the House of Commons, March–June 1714', *B.I.H.R.*, xxxiv (1961), 213. See the government agent's reports on Wyndham's excursions early in 1719, which may be have been connected with the Spanish-Jacobite plot of that year, though this was never proved, B.L. Stowe MS. 247, fols. 98–119.

10. *Remarks and Collections of Thomas Hearne*, Oxford Historical Society (11 vols., Oxford, 1885–1921), v, 281; *H.M.C. Portland*, vii, 228. The hostility of many of Bolingbroke's tory friends after 1715 emerges from Paul Baratier (ed.), *Lettres inédites de Bolingbroke à Lord Stair 1716–20* (Paris, 1939), 25–46.

11. Thomas Cave to Lord Verney, 11 June 1715, Buckinghamshire R.O., Claydon House MSS. (microfilm); *L.J.*, xx, 97, 111, 171.

12. Auditor Harley to Oxford, 17 December 1720, B.L. Loan 29/95; *H.M.C. Portland*, v, 613, vii, 246. No tory candidates were put up for the 1717 and 1718 by-elections in Cambridgeshire where Lord Harley had his estate at Wimpole, nor for the 1717 Herefordshire by-election.

13. Mrs Caesar's diary, 1 May 1723, Bodleian Library, MS. Film 740; *H.M.C. Portland*, v, 579; *Episcopal Opinions on the Test and Corporation Acts* (1790), 27.

14. Oxford to Dartmouth, 23 November 1719, Staffordshire R.O., D/1778/I/ii/538.

15. Thomas Brodrick to Lord Midleton, 26 April 1716, Guildford Muniment Room, Brodrick MSS., iii, fol. 370. For Anglesey's reputation for declamatory politics see Archbishop Wake's notes for 12 July 1715, Christ Church, Oxford, Arch. W. Epist. 19., fol. 4.

16. B.L. Add. MS. 47029, fol. 136; Stephen W. Baskerville, 'The Management of the Tory Interest in Lancashire and Cheshire, 1714–47' (unpub. D.Phil. dissertation, Oxford University, 1976), 110; *Parl. Hist.*, vii, 599.

17. Sir Charles Petrie, 'The Jacobite Activities in South and West England in the Summer of 1715', *T.R.H.S.*, xviii (1935), 85–106, at 102; Sedgwick, ii, 422; Oxford to Lord Harley, 27 September 1722, B.L. Loan 29/97.

18. *Parl. Hist.*, vii, 477–8. See also Shippen's deflation of Wyndham on 26 February 1733 after the tory leader had concluded an impassioned speech vindicating himself and his followers from Jacobitism: 'Mr. Speaker', interjected Shippen, 'I believe I have no occasion to make any professions of what I am' (*Parl. Hist.*, viii, 1222).

19. He drew up whips to tory M.P.s in readiness for the Occasional Conformity debates in 1718–19 (Baskerville, 'Tory Interest', 111). *H.M.C. Egmont*, iii, 331. See the indicatively indulgent description of Shippen supplied by Walpole's biographer, J. H. Plumb, *Sir Robert Walpole* (2 vols., 1956, 1960), ii, 183–4.

20. Holmes, *British Politics*, 277–8; J. J. Cartwright, *The Wentworth Papers 1705–39* (1883), 429; *H.M.C. Portland*, v, 570.

21. Robert Digby to Lord Digby, 18 October 1722, Digby Transcripts, fol. 48. These transcripts of papers which originally belonged to Ms Fiona Digby are in the possession of Dr Howard Erskine-Hill of Pembroke College, Cambridge. I am most grateful to him for allowing me access to them.

22. Feiling, *History of the Tory Party*, 471–7; H.M.C. *Portland*, v, 625; see also 582, 600, VII, 228.

23. H.M.C. *Portland*, VII, 309.

24. The other six tory bishops were Atterbury of Rochester, Bisse of Hereford, Dawes of York, Gastrell of Chester, Robinson of London, and Smalridge of Bristol: some of these had been whimsical in their voting behaviour in 1714. Bishop Trelawney of Winchester was politically ambidextrous and usually deposited his proxy with Atterbury after 1718. For the whig proposal to dismantle the episcopal Bench, see Bodleian Library, MS. Carte 266, fol. 25. Tory ministerial control in Scotland had been weakened even before 1714: see P. W. J. Riley, *The English Ministers and Scotland 1707–27* (1964), 233–61.

25. B.L. Add. MS. 47028, fols. 264–5; P.R.O., SP 35/17/101. Lords Harcourt, Carleton, Hunsdon, and Rochester were also lost to the tories by 1722. Lord Carteret had gone over to the whigs before George I's accession, as had James Brydges, who was made earl of Carnarvon in 1715. The alignments of two formerly tory Lords are unclear: Portmore was resworn to the Privy Council in 1721 but seems also to have been a Jacobite conspirator; Lexington was appointed Ambassador Plenipotentiary to the Southern Peace Conference in 1718 but voted against the repeal of the Occasional Conformity Act in 1719.

26. Sedgwick, II, 206–7; H.L.R.O., Proxy Book 15, entry for 14 January 1740.

27. Lord Mansel's draft letter, N.L.W., P & W L1029. House of Lords divisions for this period have been analysed and tabulated on microfiche by J. C. Sainty and D. Dewar, *Divisions in the House of Lords: an Analytical List 1685 to 1857* (1976).

28. C. B. Realey, *The Early Opposition to Sir Robert Walpole, 1720–27* (Philadelphia, 1931), 81. Calculations based on Sainty and Dewar, *Divisions*, entries between 1721 and 1723. See the advertisement in the *Freeholder's Journal*, No. 27, 27 June 1722: 'The last five PROTESTS are to be had single at 2d each, to compleat those Protests which Gentlemen bought of the first edition.'

29. Bathurst to Cowper, 20 June 1721, Hertfordshire R.O., D/EP F53. It has been suggested that Cowper's strategy was in fact counter-productive, Plumb, *Walpole*, I, 370–1.

30. These weekly meetings were cited as evidence of Jacobite plotting at the Atterbury inquiry, *Parl. Hist.*, VIII, 206. Whatever Cowper's own bias, the participation of the resolutely Hanoverian Archbishop Dawes suggests that he at least regarded the cabal as a component of constitutional opposition. For one of the cabal's whipping lists, see P.R.O., SP 35/40/423.

31. Aylesford to Dartmouth, n.d., Staffordshire R.O., D/1778/v/1079; James Hamilton to Edgar, 5 March 1729, R.A. SP 125/115A, 126/20.

32. *Parl. Hist.*, XII, 642; Bruce to Dartmouth, n.d., Staffordshire R.O., D/1778/v/ 795. For whips to other members of the tory peerage see B.L. Loan 29/36 and Cartwright, *Wentworth Papers*, 501.

33. *L.J.*, XXV, 594–5.

34. Bingley to Henry Weston, 14 May 1725, and Weston to Dartmouth, 17 May 1725, Staffordshire R.O., D/1778/v/587–8.

35. H.M.C. *Portland*, VII, 425. *Parl. Hist.*, VIII, 1209; William Coxe, *Memoirs of the Life and Administration of Sir Robert Walpole, Earl of Orford* (3 vols., 1798), I, 412; H.M.C. *Fourteenth Report*, App., IX, 467–8.

36. N. C. Hunt, 'A Consideration of the Relationship between some Religious and Economic Organisations and the Government, especially from 1730–42' (Ph.D. dissertation, Cambridge University, 1951), 187; *Parl. Hist.*, x, 800–12.

37. Wyndham to Gower, 22 July 1719 and 6 January 1724, Staffordshire R.O., D868/6/38b, 40b. Sedgwick, II, 87–8, 210–13. For one of Proby's hurried whips to the two Northamptonshire tory M.P.s, see Northamptonshire R.O., IL 4075.

38. William King, *Political and Literary Anecdotes of his own Times* (2nd edn, 1819), 45.

39. Sedgwick, I, 445–7; Cardigan to Gower, 13 February 1720 and 3 February 1723, Staffordshire R.O., D/868/7/12b, 15a. Sainty and Dewar, *Divisions*, microfiche entries 1715–43.

40. Cartwright, *Wentworth Papers*, 507; Sir John Dutton to Lord Berkeley, 15 September 1733, and Berkeley's reply, 18 September 1733, Gloucestershire R.O., D678 57D. For Bolingbroke and the opposition in the late 1720s and 1730s, see H. T. Dickinson, *Bolingbroke* (1970), 184–276. Wyndham made use of the tirade of Marius – a standard component of Bolingbroke's classical repertoire – in a speech on royal control of the Army on 3 February 1734.

41. H. Penruddocke Wyndham (ed.), *The Diary of the late George Bubb Dodington ... with an Appendix* (1784), 443–4; Edward Harley's parliamentary journal, C.U.L., Add. 6851, fol. 72.

42. Digby to John Ward, 6 March 1742, John Rylands Library, Manchester, Bromley–Davenport MSS. Coxe, *Memoirs of Sir Robert Walpole*, III, 575.

43. William King (ed.), *Memoirs of Sarah, Duchess of Marlborough* (1930), 306; William Coxe, *Memoirs of Horatio, Lord Walpole* (1802), 276. For whig opinions of Cotton, see B.L. Add. MS. 47089, fols. 2, 5 (from back of volume) and John Campbell to Pryse Campbell, 18 November 1742, N.L.W., 1352B, fol. 64.

44. For Cotton's attitude in 1745 see 'Some Memorandums concerning Mr. Prowse' in the possession of Sir Richard Hamilton, Walton Hall, fol. 46. A copy of this whip dated 31 December 1745 is in N.L.W., Add. 1089B: it confirms that the tories continued to employ party whips even when deprived of the stimulus of opposition whig allies.

45. Lord Mahon, *History of England from the Peace of Utrecht to the Peace of Versailles 1713–83* (3rd edn, 7 vols., 1853–4), III, lxxviii. George Harris, *The Life of Lord Chancellor Hardwicke* (3 vols., 1847), II, 287.

46. For Prowse's career see 'Some Memorandums', Walton Hall; Namier & Brooke, III, 213, 336; W. S. Lewis *et al.* (eds.), *Horace Walpole's Correspondence with Sir Horace Mann, IV*, The Yale Edition of Horace Walpole's Correspondence (New Haven, 1937–), xx, 32; B.L. Add. MS. 41355, fol. 28.

47. Printed in Lewis Namier, *England in the Age of the American Revolution* (2nd edn, 1974), 298–9.

48. Mahon, *History of England*, II, xxiii; R.A. SP 81/145.

49. Viscount Cornbury to the Vice-Chancellor of Oxford, 13 March 1736, All Souls College, Oxford, MS. 534; Newdigate's diary, 29 February 1756, Warwickshire R.O., CR 136/A 586. William Blackstone, *Considerations on the Question, whether Tenants by copy of Court Roll ... are Freeholders qualified to Vote in Elections for Knights of the Shire* (1758); for Philipps' bill see *C.J.*, xxviii, 120.

50. For tory entertainments in Oxford see Theophilus Leigh to the dowager duchess of Chandos, 22 August 1748, Balliol College, Oxford, MS. 403, and 'The Opening of the Radcliffe Library in 1749', *Bodleian Quarterly Record*, I (1915), 165–72. Ann J. Kettle, 'Lichfield Races', *Lichfield & South Staffordshire*

Archaeological & Historical Society, vi (1964–6), 39–41; *Worcester Journal*, No. 2039, 18 August 1748.

51. W. F. Lord, 'The Development of Political Parties during the Reign of Queen Anne', *T.R.H.S.*, xiv (1900), 117. For tory clubs before 1714 see H. T. Dickinson, 'The October Club', *Huntington Library Quarterly*, xxxiii (1969–70), 155–173, and David Allen, 'Political Clubs in Restoration London', *H.J.*, xix (1976), 574–80.

52. For a more detailed account of these two societies and lists of their known members see Linda Colley, 'The Loyal Brotherhood and the Cocoa Tree: the London Organisation of the Tory Party 1727–60', *H.J.*, xx (1977), 77–95. The Board's minute books for 1709–13 and 1748–60 are in B.L. Add. MS. 49360 and M/602; for 1735–41 and 1771–1833 in Greater London R.O., A/BLB/1–2.

53. Nathaniel Mist to Rome, 13 March 1733, R.A. SP 160/21. Theophilus Leigh to the dowager duchess of Chandos, 5 May 1749, Balliol College, Oxford, MS. 403. That the two tory Boards co-operated for common tory ends is suggested by the earl of Oxford's presence and speech at the 1749 meeting.

54. See the mailing lists for the *Craftsman* in C.U.L., C(H) P74/72.

55. Edward Harley to his wife, 18 February 1731, B.L. Loan 29/116. Harley's political morality emerges very clearly from his parliamentary journal, C.U.L., Add. 6851. I have been rightly taken to task by Eveline Cruickshanks for not supplying evidence of Harley's Hanoverianism and whig friendships (*Political Untouchables: the Tories and the '45* (1979), 75): I rest my case on Oxford to William Brydges, 21 January 1748, Herefordshire R.O., A81/32; B.L. Add. MS. 35588, fols. 264, 284; and the *London Gazette*, No. 8313, 24/27 March 1744.

56. Sedgwick, i, 482–3, 493, ii, 111. See Bromley's speech on Septennial Act repeal, *Gentleman's Magazine*, iv (1734), 232.

57. Newdigate's canvassing diary, Greater London R.O., Acc/1085/FP/2 (unfol). Isham's diary, Northamptonshire R.O., IL 2686, fol. 148.

58. Archibald S. Foord, *His Majesty's Opposition 1714–1830* (Oxford, 1964), 20–1 (quoting Namier).

59. William Maitland, *The History of London from its Foundation to the Present Time* (2 vols., 1756), i, 631. Feiling, *History of the Tory Party*, 205, 377. The February 1742 meeting is most famously described in Viscount Perceval's *Faction detected by the Evidence of Facts: containing an Impartial View of Parties at Home, and Affairs Abroad* (2nd edn, 1743), 45–8.

60. *A Letter to the Author of The Case Fairly Stated, from an Old Whig* (1745), 37–8. Lord Hartington to Devonshire, 23 December 1743, Chatsworth House, Devonshire MSS., Box 3, 260.27; see also John Owen, *The Rise of the Pelhams* (1957), 199n.

61. Henry Shiffner to H. F. Luttrell, 14 December 1754, Somerset R.O., Luttrell MS. 43, bundle 6. For the Cocoa Tree, see Bryant Lillywhite, *London Coffee Houses* (1963), 163; for its use as shorthand for the tory parliamentary party see Colley, 'The Loyal Brotherhood and the Cocoa Tree', 88; *H.M.C. Twelfth Report*, App., v, 268; and Robert Phillimore (ed.), *Memoirs and Correspondence of George, Lord Lyttelton* (2 vols., 1845), ii, 584–5.

62. James Bonnell to Thomas Hill, 18 November 1749, Salop R.O., Attingham MSS., Box 24 (unsorted).

63. Shiffner to Luttrell, 26 November and 14 December 1754, Somerset R.O., Luttrell MS. 43, bundle 6; John Dobson to John Mordaunt, 19 November 1754, Warwickshire R.O., CR 1368, Box 6.

64. Thomas Potter to William Pitt, 'Monday Night', P.R.O., 30/8/53, Pt 1, fol. 98.

65. Atterbury to Gower, 10 October 1718, and Bathurst to Gower, 5 October 1722, Staffordshire R.O., D/868/7/6b, 18a.

66. J. P. Jenkins, 'A Social and Political History of the Glamorgan Gentry c. 1650–1770' (unpub. Ph.D. dissertation, Cambridge University, 1978), 278; Beaufort to Brudenell Rooke, 20 March 1755, Gloucestershire R.O., D1833 F1.

67. Prowse to Tynte, Christmas Day 1744, Glamorgan R.O., D/DKT/1/47. For Wynn's local whipping see Barrymore to Francis Price, 2 February 1742, N.L.W., Puleston MS. 22, fol. 102, and Owen, *Rise of the Pelhams*, 28. Verses on Wynn's integrity were dispersed in London in 1742, *Parl. Hist.*, xii, 434; after his death, the Montgomeryshire tory Edward Kynaston composed an equally extravagant tribute for the local and London press; see *Worcester Journal*, No. 2099, 12 October 1749.

68. Cornewall to William Brydges, 6 December 1740, Herefordshire R.O., A81/31. For his electoral activities in 1747 see his letters to the Prince of Wales, Buckinghamshire R.O., D/LE/K1/2–3.

69. Namier & Brooke, iii; Isham's diary, Northamptonshire R.O., IL 2686; *C.J.*, xx, 369–442.

70. *Whitehall Evening Post*, 22 March 1722; Southwell to Smith, 20 February 1742, Bristol City Reference Library, Southwell Papers, vii (unpaginated); *Supplement to the Freeholder's Journal*, No. 8, 16 March 1722.

71. Calculations based on *C.J.*, xviii, xix. 108 tory M.P.s acted as teller in the 1715–22 Parliament and the following did so on more than five occasions: G. Baker, B. Bathurst, Sir G. Beaumont, Sir J. Bland, Sir H. Bunbury, S. Calmady, Sir W. Carew, J. Conyers, T. Conyers, C. Corrance, Sir J. H. Cotton, Sir T. Crosse, M. G. Drake, F. Drewe, R. Freman, J. Herne, W. Heysham, E. Jefferies, Sir A. Kaye, G. Lawson, W. Newland, D. North, T. Palmer, E. Rolt, T. Rowney, Sir T. S. Sebright, W. Shippen, Sir R. Shuttleworth, J. Snell, T. Strangways, T. Vernon, Sir G. Warburton, Hon. D. Windsor, W. Wrightson, Sir W. Wyndham. I would list William Bromley, Lord Guernsey, Sir Thomas Hanmer, John Hungerford, Archibald Hutcheson, Thomas Lutwyche, and Sir William Whitlock as active tory parliamentarians who confined themselves to speaking or to taking a leading part in committees.

72. J. Carswell and L. A. Dralle (eds.), *The Political Journal of George Bubb Dodington* (Oxford, 1965), 107–8.

73. Sir Nicholas Morice to Humphry Morice, 10 March 1719 and 8 September 1722, Bank of England, COU/B151/1, fols. 208, 250. Sedley's quip as related by Archbishop King to Edward Southwell, 24 March 1722, Trinity College, Dublin, MS. 2534, fols. 88–9.

74. *A Hint upon Instructions from the Electors to their Representatives in Parliament, with Remarks upon a Letter Publish'd in the LONDON EVENING POST on Tuesday the 5th Instant and Re-Publish'd on the 9th in the same Paper* (1742), 13, 18. Isham's diary, Northamptonshire R.O., IL 2686.

75. Cowper to George I (draft), Hertfordshire R.O., D/EP F133; Baskerville, 'Tory Interest', 92; Lady Verney (ed.), *Verney Letters of the Eighteenth Century from the MSS. at Claydon House* (2 vols., 1930), ii, 31.

76. G. H. Rose (ed.), *A Selection from the Papers of the Earls of Marchmont illustrative of Events from 1685–1750* (3 vols., 1831), ii, 56; *H.M.C. Fifteenth Report*, App., vi, 144–5.

77. B.L. Add. MS. 29597, fol. 29. See Appendix, Table 1.

78. E.g. Lewis *et al.* (eds.), *Walpole's Correspondence with Mann*, II, xviii, 383, III, xix, 33; Horace Walpole, *Memoirs of the Last Ten Years of the Reign of George*

the Second (2 vols., 1822), I, 79, and see his *A Second and Third Letter to the Whigs by the Author of the First* (1748), 83.

79. Barrymore to Price, 7 February 1738, N.L.W., Puleston MS. 22, fol. 36; *H.M.C. Fifteenth Report*, App., VII, 319.

80. Philip Yorke, *The Life and Correspondence of Philip Yorke, Earl of Hardwicke* (3 vols., Cambridge, 1913), I, 252–3. For tory dissension over the broad wheels debate see Prowse to William Gore, 25 February 1755, Somerset R.O., DD/GB 148/215, and John Dobson to John Mordaunt, 22 February 1755, Warwickshire R.O., CR 1368, Box V/12.

81. Cornewall to William Brydges, 25 February 1744, Herefordshire R.O., A81/32.

82. Disregard of eighteenth-century party nomenclature can play havoc with historical explanation. Peter D. G. Thomas quotes the duke of Newcastle's objection to Thomas Prowse as Speaker in 1760, 'I find a Tory will not go down well', and adds the information that Prowse had been active in the 'Country' interest. Had this been all, Newcastle would not have been worried. (*The House of Commons in the Eighteenth Century* (Oxford, 1971), 308–9.) For Bagot, see Namier & Brooke, II, 39.

83. Sir Robert Wilmot to the duke of Devonshire, 12 January 1742, Chatsworth House, Devonshire MSS., Box 3, 290.0.

84. Printed in Thomas, *House of Commons*, 114. For examples of concerted tory walk-outs see Lewis *et al.* (eds.), *Walpole's Correspondence with Mann, II*, XVIII, 383; Welbore Ellis to the duke of Devonshire, 12 December 1745, Chatsworth House, Devonshire MSS., Box 5, 335.0; Sir Roger Newdigate's diary for 29 March 1756, Warwickshire R.O., CR 136/B2549/11.

85. *Supplement to the Freeholder's Journal*, No. 8, 16 March 1722; Sir Lewis Namier, 'Monarchy and the Party System', *Crossroads of Power: Essays on Eighteenth Century England* (1962), 214; for Vaughan, see Sedgwick, II, 493.

86. Edward Southwell to Brickdale, 15 February 1742, Bristol City Reference Library, Southwell Papers, VI (unfol.). For Southwell's peculiar electoral constraints see above 166.

CHAPTER 4

1. Henry Berkeley to Richard Neville Aldworth, 30 November 1740, Essex R.O., D/DM A7–8. John Owen, *The Rise of the Pelhams* (1957), 69; B. D. Hayes, 'Politics in Norfolk 1750–1832' (unpub. Ph.D. dissertation, Cambridge University, 1958), 38; E. G. Forrester, *Northamptonshire County Elections and Electioneering 1695–1832* (Oxford, 1941), 36. See also Namier & Brooke, I, 185; David Thomson, 'The Conception of Political Party in England in the Period 1740 to 1783' (unpub. Ph.D. dissertation, Cambridge University, 1938), 78; John Brewer, *Party Ideology and Popular Politics at the Accession of George III* (Cambridge, 1976), 42–3.

2. These are my own calculations based on the information given in Sedgwick, I, II, and Namier & Brooke, II, III. More indirect marital connections between tory families especially in Cornwall, Devon, Cheshire, Leicestershire, and the Welsh counties were numerous

3. *Notes & Queries*, 2nd ser., X (1860), 366. See also W. R. Ward, *Georgian Oxford: University Politics in the Eighteenth Century* (Oxford, 1958).

4. P. J. Wallis, *The Social Index: a New Technique for Measuring Social Trends*, Project for Historical Bibliography 184 (Newcastle, 1978), 39–41.

5. J. P. Jenkins, 'A Social and Political History of the Glamorgan Gentry c. 1650–1770' (unpub. Ph.D. dissertation, Cambridge University, 1978), 418n. John

Nichols, *Literary Anecdotes of the Eighteenth Century* (9 vols., 1812–15), I, 119.
For the party controversy on Clarendon's *History*, see J. P. W. Rogers, 'The
Whig Controversialist as Dunce: a Study of the Literary Fortunes and Mis-
fortunes of John Oldmixon 1673–1742' (unpub. Ph.D. dissertation, Cambridge
University, 1968), 329–79.

6. Lord Dartmouth, 'Memorandums that I wrote on Bishop Burnett's History of
   his own Time', Staffordshire R.O., D(W) 1778 v 760. *H.M.C. Portland*, v, 637.
   Roger North, *Examen, or, an Inquiry into the Credit and Veracity of a
   Pretended Complete History* (1740).

7. List of subscribers to Carte's *History*, Bodleian Library, MS. Carte 175, fol. 105.
   On Carte and the vitality of party debate in the localities, see R. W. Greaves,
   'Fathers and Heretics in Eighteenth-Century Leicester', in Anne Whiteman,
   J. S. Bromley and P. G. M. Dickson (eds.), *Statesmen, Scholars and Merchants:
   Essays in Eighteenth-Century History presented to Dame Lucy Sutherland*
   (Oxford, 1973), 65–80. *The Case of the Royal Martyr* was reviewed in the
   Critical Review, VI (1758), 293. David Hume, *Essays, Moral, Political, and
   Literary*, ed. T. H. Green and T. H. Grose (2 vols., 1875), I, 469.

8. *Parl. Hist.*, XIV, 446. J. G. A. Pocock, 'Machiavelli, Harrington and English
   Political Ideologies in the Eighteenth Century', *Politics, Language and Time:
   Essays on Political Thought and History* (1972), 122. For Shippen's speech in
   1717, see *Three Speeches against continuing the Army* (1718), 13.

9. F. G. Stephens and E. Hawkins, *Catalogue of Prints and Drawings in the
   British Museum* (5 vols., 1870–1935), III.i, 87; for Lord Oxford's comments, see
   B.L. Loan 29/339, fol. 181.

10. Richard Blacow to Thomas Bray, 28 January 1755, Exeter College, Oxford,
    Bray MSS., transcripts in the possession of the History of Oxford University
    project. See also Helen Randall's survey, 'The Rise and Fall of Martyrology:
    Sermons on Charles I', *Huntington Library Quarterly*, X (1946–7), 135–67.

11. *The Church of England Man's Memorial; or the History of Comprehension and
    Toleration* (1718), 10. Lansdowne's speech became a best-selling pamphlet and
    was reprinted in 1790, *Episcopal Opinions on the Test and Corporation Acts*
    (1790), 30.

12. Sir Roger Newdigate's diary, 21 February 1757; Warwickshire R.O., CR 136/A
    (588); John Dobson to John Mordaunt, 20 November 1753, *ibid.* CR 1368
    Box 5/5/7; for William Northey's speech, see *Parl. Hist.*, XV, 147–8.

13. Quoted in Thomson, 'Political Party', 81. See J. G. A. Pocock, *The Machia-
    vellian Moment: Florentine Political Thought and the Atlantic Republican
    Tradition* (Princeton, 1975); H. T. Dickinson, *Liberty and Property: Political
    Ideology in Eighteenth Century Britain* (1977) and *Bolingbroke* (1970); Isaac
    Kramnick, *Bolingbroke and his Circle: the Politics of Nostalgia in the Age of
    Walpole* (1968); Augus McInnes, 'The Poiltical Ideas of Robert Harley', *History*,
    L (1965), 309–22.

14. Quentin Skinner, 'The Principles and Practice of Opposition: the Case of
    Bolingbroke versus Walpole', in Neil McKendrick (ed.), *Historical Perspectives:
    Studies in English Thought and Society in honour of J. H. Plumb* (1974), 93–
    128. I am not sure that the wickedness of formed opposition was as much of a
    problem in political thought and action as Walpolian pamphleteers suggested.
    Some tory polemicists certainly advocated the constitutional desirability of a
    permanent, party-based opposition; see *The Sentiments of a Tory* (1741) and
    the writings of Edward Spelman, great-great-grandson of the tory-royalist
    historian Sir Henry Spelman; P. Campbell, 'An Early Defence of Party',
    Political Studies, III (1955), 166–7.

15. *Parl. Hist.*, x, 380–3, 387–9, 424–5, 550. For whig–tory attacks on the Army in the late seventeenth century, see Lois Schwoerer, *'No Standing Armies!' The Antiarmy Ideology in Seventeenth-Century England* (Baltimore, 1974).

16. Charles D'Avenant, *Essay upon the Probable Methods of making a People Gainers in the Ballance of Trade* (1699); W. A. Speck and J. A. Downie (eds.), ' "Plaine English to All Who Are Honest or Would Be So if They Knew How", a Tract by Robert Harley', *Literature and History*, III (1976), 100–10; Chandler, VI, 177.

17. Mark Goldie, 'The Nonjurors, Episcopacy, and the Origins of the Convocation Controversy' (in preparation); J. R. Jones, *Country and Court: England 1658–1714* (1978), 227. For Atterbury's defence of Convocation's autonomy see G. V. Bennett, *The Tory Crisis in Church and State 1688–1730: the Career of Francis Atterbury, Bishop of Rochester* (Oxford, 1975), 44–160, and Isaac Kramnick, 'Augustan Politics and English Historiography: the Debate on the English Past, 1730–35', *History and Theory*, III (1976), 47.

18. *An Expostulatory Epistle to the Welch Knight* (1745), 31.

19. Samuel Johnson, *Political Writings*, ed. D. J. Greene, The Yale Edition of the Works of Samuel Johnson (10 vols., New Haven, 1958–77), x, 127–8. For a classic exposition of the tories' stance on foreign policy, see Velters Cornewall's Commons speech of 1748, *Parl. Hist.*, XIV, 158–64.

20. *The Honest Grief of a Tory, expressed in a Genuine Letter from a Burgess of ——, in Wiltshire, to the Author of The Monitor, February 17, 1759* (1759), 12–24. William Blackstone to Newdigate, 27 February 1758, Warwickshire R.O., CR 136 B. 1494.

21. These are my own calculations based on the list in Sedgwick, I, 87–8. I have excluded Sir Cecil Bishopp, Hon. George Compton, William Noel, and Samuel Ongley, as in 1734 these men were tory not Patriot M.P.s.

22. For the Patriots' reaction in 1734, see *Parl. Hist.*, IX, 395; for the attempt to repeal the Septennial Act in 1742, see John Campbell to Pryse Campbell, 1 April 1742, N.L.W., MS. 1352B, fol. 54.

23. Sir Roger Newdigate's diary, 20 February 1758, Warwickshire R.O., CR 136/A (589).

24. J. B. Owen, 'The Survival of Country Attitudes in the Eighteenth-Century House of Commons', in J. S. Bromley and E. H. Kossman (eds.), *Britain and the Netherlands* (5 vols., The Hague, 1960–75), IV, 42–69.

25. For Sir Joseph Jekyll, see C. L. S. Linnell (ed.), *The Diaries of Thomas Wilson, D.D., 1731–7 and 1750* (1964), 156–7, and Sedgwick, II, 174–5; John Sambroke to Forester, 16 September 1733, Salop R.O., Forester MSS., Box 335. Vyner's opinion of the *Craftsman* is quoted in Sedgwick, II, 501.

26. *Memoirs of the Life and Ministerial Conduct . . . of the Late Lord Visc. Bolingbroke* (1752), 337–8.

27. *Gentleman's Magazine*, XIII (1743), 181; *The Sentiments of a Tory*, 7.

28. Horace Walpole (ed.), *The Works of the Right Honourable Sir Charles Hanbury Williams* (3 vols., 1822), I, 65–6.

29. Hutcheson to Trenchard, 21 December 1721 (copy), Bodleian Library, MS. Carte 230, fol. 203. Compare [Hutcheson], *A Speech made in the House of Commons April 24 1716* (1722), 8, 14, with the 1675 tract quoted in Pocock, 'Machiavelli, Harrington and English Political Ideologies', 126.

30. Hutcheson to Cowper, 20 April 1722, Hertfordshire R.O., D/EP F55; P.R.O., SP 35/31/85.

31. Mrs Caesar's diary, Bodleian Library, MS. Film 740; Hutcheson to the earl of Sunderland, 11 April 1722, printed in *Three Treatises* (1722–3), III, 23.

32. For Cato's anti-clericalism see R. N. Stromberg, *Religious Liberalism in Eighteenth-Century England* (Oxford, 1954), 132–3. *Applebee's Original Weekly Journal*, 13 January 1722. On tory, whig, and occasional Jacobite exploitation of the charity schools see M. G. Jones, *The Charity School Movement* (2nd edn, 1964), 110–30.

33. See Bernard Mandeville, *The Fable of the Bees: or, Private Vices, Publick Benefits*, ed. F. B. Kaye (2 vols., Oxford, 1924), I, 253ff and lxx and 296–7n; *Parl. Hist.*, XII, 66. For tory criticism of Jenyns, see Basil Willey, *The Eighteenth Century Background* (1940), 48–51.

34. Baron Price's sermon is summarised in Mary Clement (ed.), *Correspondence and Minutes of the S.P.C.K. relating to Wales* (Cardiff, 1952), 117, and see *ibid.* 72, 81, 87 for tory concern in the Welsh charity schools. The *London Evening Post* extract is printed in W. S. Lewis and R. M. Williams, *Private Charity in England 1747–57* (New Haven, 1938), 20–1.

35. 'Diary of Thomas Smith, Esq. of Shaw House', *Wiltshire Archaeological and Natural History Magazine*, XI (1869), 105. Auditor Harley to Edward Harley, 3 May 1734, B.L. Loan 29/96. For the charges against Gordon and Trenchard, see W. A. Speck, 'Bernard Mandeville and the Middlesex Grand Jury', *Eighteenth Century Studies*, II (1978), 362–74.

36. P. de Rapin-Thoyras, *Dissertation sur les Whigs & les Torys* (translated by Mr Ozell) (1717), 68–9; Samuel Squire, *An Historical Essay upon the Ballance of Civil Power in England* (1748), 74.

37. [Fielding], *A Dialogue between a Gentleman of London Agent for Two Court Candidates and an Honest Alderman of the Country Party* (1747), 8–9; for Hynde Cotton, see Jenkins, 'Glamorgan Gentry', 277n; for Somerset, see *Parl. Hist.*, X, 391.

38. See *The Conduct of the Opposition and the Tendency of Modern Patriotism* (1734), 38, for whig comments on the persistence of tory concern for the prerogative. For the 1726 bill, see Chandler, VI, 366; for Oxford's opposition to the Peerage Bill, see *Parl. Hist.*, VII, 590.

39. *The Loyal or Revolutional Tory being some Reflections on the Principles and Conduct of the Tories*, (1733).

40. *Parl. Hist.*, IX, 470. *H.M.C. Mar and Kellie*, 536.

41. Chandler, VIII, 113–20.

42. *The Sentiments of a Tory*, 9–12.

43. [Horace Walpole], *Three Letters to the Whigs occasion'd by a Letter to the Tories* (3rd edn, 1748), 11; political notes by Viscount Perceval, n.d., B.L. Add. MS. 47096 (unfol.).

44. Batista Angeloni [John Shebbeare], *Letters on the English Nation* (1755), 25. *Remembrancer*, Nos. 2, 12 December 1747; 5, 9 January 1748; and 9, 11, and 12, 6, 20, and 27 February 1748. The Carlton House declaration was publicised by the London press in 1761 and the earl of Hardwicke asserted that it was the blueprint for George III's assault on the Old Corps; see Brewer, *Party Ideology*, 47, 280.

45. On this propaganda gambit and its efficacy see B. W. Hill, 'Executive Monarchy and the Challenge of Parties, 1689–1832: Two Concepts of Government and Two Historiographical Interpretations', *H.J.*, XIII (1970), 391–3, and Brewer, *Party Ideology*, 47–54.

46. Keith Feiling, *The Second Tory Party 1714–1832* (1938), 9–10; for Bishop Gibson's argument, see *The Lord Bishop of London's Caveat against aspersing Princes and their Administration applied to William Pulteney Esq; and the Lord Viscount Bolingbroke . . .* (1731), 21.

47. Edward Carpenter, *Thomas Sherlock 1678–1761* (1936), 24–35. Cf. Mary Bateson, 'Clerical Preferment under the Duke of Newcastle', *E.H.R.*, VII (1892), 685–96.

48. George Horne's commonplace book, C.U.L., Add. 8134; A. Kuhn, 'Glory or Gravity: Hutchinson vs Newton', *Journal of the History of Ideas*, XXII (1961), 303–22. For whig-latitudinarian annexation of Newtonianism see M. C. Jacob, *The Newtonians and the English Revolution, 1679–1720* (Hassocks, 1976), and Geoffrey Holmes' review, which makes some useful corrections, in the *British Journal for the History of Science*, XI (1978), 164–71.

49. Ward, *Georgian Oxford*, 205–6; W. K. Lowther Clarke, *Eighteenth Century Piety* (1944), 101–17.

50. B.L. Loan 29/350, fol. 38; Linnell, *Thomas Wilson*, 126. See also Jonathan Swift's poem *On Seeing a Worthy Prelate Go out of Church in the Time of Divine Service to Wait on his Grace the D[uke] of D[evonshire]* (1732): 'To the Court it was fitter to pay his Devotion/Since God had no Hand in his Lordship's Promotion.'

51. On Wake, the tories, and Convocation, see Norman Sykes, *William Wake, Archbishop of Canterbury 1657–1737* (2 vols., Cambridge, 1957), I, 141–5, and Archbishop King to Wake, 25 May 1717, Trinity College Dublin, MS. 750/6, fol. 220.

52. Henry Horwitz, *Parliament, Policy and Politics in the Reign of William III* (Manchester, 1977), 293–8; *H.M.C. Egmont*, I, 153; *C.J.*, XXII, 37, 119; Harley's parliamentary journal, C.U.L., Add. 6851, fol. 62.

53. An important if unremarked component of practical tory-Anglicanism was individual tories' commitment to church-building. Thomas Prowse had the church at Wicken in Northamptonshire built at his own expense, and William Beckford established his tory credentials in Wiltshire by paying for the new church at Fonthill Gifford in 1749. Prowse memoranda at Walton Hall and *V.C.H. Wiltshire*, III, 50.

54. *The Clergyman's Intelligencer* (1745). As the compiler noted, 'a Book of this kind can never be entirely free from Error, because many Livings are constantly changing their Patrons'. Hay's Journal, II.

55. G. Eland, 'The Shardeloes Muniments', *Records of Buckinghamshire*, XIV (1941–6), 348; Nichols, *Literary Anecdotes*, I, 437, 485.

56. For the tories' initiative in 1714, see Edward Hughes, *Studies in Administration and Finance 1558–1825* (Manchester, 1934), 218, and for the 1717 committee, *C.J.*, XVIII, 589. This estimate of vacant livings (and many other references to clerical poverty and disarray) can be found in *The Church of England's Complaints to the Parliament and Clergy* (1737), 11.

57. 'An Abstract of the Several Publick Charities given by Edward Colston', Bristol City Reference Library, Bristol Collection 507; *Parl. Hist.*, XIV, 199.

58. Christopher Hodgson, *An Account of the Augmentation of Small Livings by the Governors of the Bounty of Queen Anne . . .* (1826), 91–2, 132–60. Several whig politicians also participated in the scheme, e.g. the duke of Devonshire, Lord Parker, and Lord King; but they were in the minority. See also G. F. A. Best, *Temporal Pillars; Queen Anne's Bounty, the Ecclesiastical Commissioners, and the Church of England* (Cambridge, 1964), and A. Savidge, *The Foundation and Early Years of Queen Anne's Bounty* (1955).

59. [Arnall], *Animadversions on a Reverend Prelate's Remarks upon the Bill now depending in Parliament entitled a Bill to Prevent Suits for Tythes* (1731), 23–4.

60. Butler cited A. R. Humphreys, 'Literature and Religion in Eighteenth Century England', *Journal of Ecclesiastical History*, III (1952), 175. For the anti-clerical

explosion in the 1730s see Norman Sykes, *Edmund Gibson, Bishop of London, 1669–1748* (1926), 158n, and Duncan Forbes, *Hume's Philosophical Politics* (Cambridge, 1975), 215–16.

61. Harley's parliamentary journal, C.U.L., Add. 6851, fols. 57–8. Chandler, vi, 337.

62. *Parl. Hist.*, ix, 1111; Jones, *The Charity School Movement*, 55n.

63. Egmont's diary, B.L. Add. MS. 47066, fol. 57. The 1736 clerical petitions are listed in *The Political State of Great Britain*, lii (1736), 439–45. For how these petitions were managed by the tory parsons, see C. D. Linnell (ed.), *The Diary of Benjamin Rogers, Rector of Carlton, 1720–71*, Publications of the Bedfordshire Historical Record Society, xxx (1950), 68.

64. Thus Sykes writes of Bishop Gibson's failure as deriving from 'his attempt to create the hybrid phenomenon of a High-Church Whig...They [the whigs] were the representatives of the principle of the supremacy of the laity against the pretensions of the independence of the spiritual society' (*Edmund Gibson*, 181–2). For a tory view of the necessary autonomy of the Church – as a complement not as a threat to civil authority – see Sir John St Aubyn's speech on the Quaker Tithe Bill, *Gentleman's Magazine*, vi (1736), 367.

65. See 'A List of Members who Voted for and against a Bill for repealing the Acts of Occasional Conformity and Schism', Chandler, viii, Appendix. Those whigs who opposed Guernsey's motion are asterisked. *Parl. Hist.*, vii, 893; Sykes, *William Wake*, ii, 135–40.

66. Wynn to Sir William Williams, 28 March 1736, N.L.W., Wynnstay MSS., C 97.

67. *A Letter to Sir W[illia]m W[yndha]m, upon the Intended Application to Parliament for repealing the Corporation and Test Acts. By a Modern Tory* (1736). For the *Craftsman* and the dissenters see N. C. Hunt, *Two Early Political Associations: the Quakers and the Dissenting Deputies in the Age of Sir Robert Walpole* (Oxford, 1961), 208–10.

68. Hunt, *Two Early Political Associations*, 186–90.

69. J. E. Thorold Rogers (ed.), *A Complete Collection of the Protests of the Lords* (3 vols., Oxford, 1875), i, 278–9; for St Aubyn's attitude to the Quaker Tithe Bill, see the *Gentleman's Magazine*, vi (1736), 365.

70. *Parl. Hist.*, xv, 139. For the Jew Bill see T. W. Perry, *Public Opinion, Propaganda, and Politics in Eighteenth-Century England: a Study of the Jew Bill of 1753* (Cambridge, Mass., 1962).

71. A. Keith Walker, *William Law: his Life and Thought* (1973), 13–29.

72. [Samuel Wesley], *The Parish Priest. A Poem upon a Clergyman Lately Deceased* (1731). For Samuel's tory friendships see T. E. Brigden, 'Samuel Wesley Junior, and his Circle, 1690–1739', *Proceedings of the Wesley Historical Society*, xi (1918), 97–102, 121–9, 145–53.

73. John Telford (ed.), *The Letters of the Rev. John Wesley, A.M.* (8 vols., 1931), ii, 56; Nichols, *Literary Anecdotes*, v, 241.

74. Jenkins, 'Glamorgan Gentry', 286–7. For the Philipps–Methodist connection see Thomas Shankland, 'Sir John Philipps of Picton, the Society for Promoting Christian Knowledge and the Charity-School Movement in Wales, 1699–1737', *Transactions of the Honourable Society of Cymmrodorion* (1904–5), 174–216.

75. G. C. B. Davies, *The Early Cornish Evangelicals 1735–60* (1951), 30; Telford (ed.), *Letters of Wesley*, iii, 21; Edwin Sidney, *The Life of the Rev. Rowland Hill, A.M.* (1834) and *The Life of Sir Richard Hill, Bart.* (1839); Nehemiah Curnock (ed.), *The Journal of the Rev. John Wesley, A.M.* (8 vols., 1913), iv, 343.

76. Daniel Benham, *Memoirs of James Hutton comprising the Annals of his Life and Connection with the United Brethren* (1856), 8, 24, 207–10.

77. Hume, *Essays*, 133–43. Hume was unlucky with Jacobitism: in the same piece he argued that in Scotland 'the Jacobite party is almost entirely vanished from among us', a comment withdrawn from the post-1745 edition (Forbes, *Hume's Philosophical Politics*, 94).

78. E.g. in Edmund Bohun's usefully titled pamphlet *The Doctrine of Non-Resistance and Passive Obedience no way concerned in the Controversies now depending between the Williamites and Jacobites* (1689), and see M. A. Goldie, 'Tory Political Thought 1689–1714' (unpub. Ph.D. dissertation, Cambridge University, 1978), *passim*. George Berkeley, *Advice to the Tories who Have Taken the Oaths* (1715).

79. H. T. Dickinson, *Bolingbroke* (1970), 262; Dartmouth's 'Memorandums', Staffordshire R.O., D(W) 1778 v 760, fol. 396, and see also fol. 745.

80. *Gentleman's Magazine*, xx (1750) lists 430 books and pamphlets between January and November: the 132 religious publications form by far the largest category. In Henry Fielding's *Joseph Andrews* (1742), Book I, Ch. 17, the bookseller tells Parson Adams that there are too many sermons printed for him to stock: 'The trade is so vastly stocked with them, that really, unless they come out with the name of Whitfield or Wesley, or some other such great man, as a bishop...I don't care to touch.' The bookseller's qualification is interesting: 'unless now it was a sermon preached on the 30th of January'.

81. *The Honest Electors, or, The Courtiers Sent Back with their Bribes: a New Ballad Opera* (1733), 13–14: this was apparently staged in Villiers Street.

82. List of toasts c. 1762, Oxfordshire R.O., DIL XXV/49b; Kuhn, 'Glory or Gravity', 320.

CHAPTER 5

1. See Lewis Namier, *The Structure of Politics at the Accession of George III* (2nd edn, 1970), 64–74, 83–104, 299–401. On the pre-1715 electorate, see Geoffrey Holmes, *British Politics in the Age of Anne* (1967), 312–21 and *The Electorate and the National Will in the First Age of Party* (Kendal, 1976); J. H. Plumb, 'The Growth of the Electorate in England from 1600–1715', *P.&P.*, xlv (1969), 90–116; and W. A. Speck, *Tory & Whig: the Struggle in the Constituencies 1701–15* (1970), *passim*. Three articles which attempt to bridge this gap are Norma Landau, 'Independence, Deference and Voter Participation: the Behaviour of the Electorate in Early-Eighteenth-Century Kent', *H.J.*, xxii (1979), 561–84; F. O'Gorman, 'Fifty Years after Namier: the Eighteenth Century in British Historical Writing', *The Eighteenth Century: Theory and Interpretation*, xx (1979), 99–120, esp. 111–19; and J. A. Phillips, 'The Structure of Electoral Politics in Unreformed England', *Journal of British Studies*, xix (1979), 78–100.

2. This estimate of borough contests in Anne's reign is based on John Cannon, *Parliamentary Reform 1640–1832* (Cambridge, 1973), 280–9; Phillips, 'Structure of Electoral Politics', 80 (Table 1).

3. It has yet to be established whether septennial elections *invariably* cost their practitioners more than did the rash of contested elections between 1694 and 1716; see Speck, *Tory & Whig*, 46, 97.

4. I have adopted Phillips' regional definitions, which are based on Namier's ('Structure of Electoral Politics', 84n). My estimate of contested borough elections 1701–13 and 1715–47 is based on Cannon, *Parliamentary Reform*,

280–9; in addition to those listed, there were contests at Harwich in 1715, and at Aylesbury and Tiverton in 1722.

5. This table is taken from the more extended analysis in Sedgwick, i, 79. In the remaining English region, the South-East – Essex, Hertfordshire, Kent, Middlesex, Suffolk, Surrey, and Sussex – the tories won thirty seats in 1715 and fifteen in 1761.

6. *Freeholder's Journal*, No. 21, 23 May 1722.

7. Sir John Barlow to Sir John Pakington, 22 February 1721, Worcestershire R.O., Acc. 4657, vol. III. John Cannon, 'The Parliamentary Representation of the City of Gloucester 1727–90', *Transactions of the Bristol and Gloucestershire Archaeological Society*, LXXVIII (1959), 137–52. This estimate of tory candidacy in 1715 and 1722 is my own based on information in Sedgwick, i, 189–404.

8. For constituency complaints against compromised county elections in 1722, see the *Whitehall Evening Post*, No. 526, 23 January 1722 ('Bucks. Freeholder'), and the *London Journal*, 27 January 1722. For Leicestershire, see Sedgwick, i, 275 and *C.J.*, xx, 39.

9. *H.M.C. Portland*, VII, 316; J. H. Moses, 'Elections and Electioneering in the Constituencies of Nottinghamshire, 1702–1832' (unpub. Ph.D. dissertation, Nottingham University, 1965), 121. This analysis of Hart's support is based on *The List of the Votes of the Freeholders and Freemen of the City and County of Bristol, 1722* (Bristol, 1722, repr. 1899).

10. This estimate of whig and tory poll figures and borough and county performance in 1722 is based on Sedgwick, i, 189–370. William Bromley to Sir Justinian Isham, 30 April 1726, Northamptonshire R.O., IL 1877.

11. List of 'Persons preferred ... since the year 1701', in the Bagot MSS., Kendal R.O., Box B. For the administration's limited employment of secret service money at general elections, see Namier, *Structure of Politics*, 196–211. This estimate of government patronage is that of Phillips, 'Structure of Electoral Politics', 80 (Table 1).

12. Namier, *Structure of Politics*, 88. For the 1727 Christchurch election, see Sedgwick, i, 250.

13. Peter Davenant to Sir Robert Salusbury Cotton, 4 March 1734, Chester City R.O., CR 72/6, fol. 48. I am grateful to Dr John Morrill for drawing my attention to these papers. For Kent, see Landau, 'Independence, Deference and Voter Participation', 565. For government influence in a seaside borough, see Sylvia McIntyre, 'The Scarborough Corporation Quarrel, 1736–60', *Northern History*, XIV (1978), 208–26.

14. Sedgwick, i, 225, 251–2, 432; also for Henry Bankes, see Namier, *Structure of Politics*, 44. For Warwick, see Thomas Newsham to ?, 17 May 1740, P.R.O., C108/231, and Sedgwick, i, 341.

15. Levi Fox (ed.), *Correspondence of the Reverend Joseph Greene, Parson, Schoolmaster and Antiquary, 1712–90* (1965), 160. Even some opposition whigs would oppose tory election petitions; see Hay's Journal, i, 25 March 1735. For Hutcheson's proposal, see A. N. Newman (ed.), *The Parliamentary Diary of Sir Edward Knatchbull 1722–30*, Camden 3rd ser., XCIV (1963), 3.

16. For Boston and Banbury, see Sedgwick, i, 277, 303. Sir William Wyndham to Lord Gower, 5 March 1722, Staffordshire R.O., D/868/6/39c; Sedgwick, i, 316–17.

17. For patronage boroughs in this period, see Namier, *Structure of Politics*, 144–8, and Cannon, *Parliamentary Reform*, 50n.

18. See Appendix, Table 2.

19. For the two Shrewsbury party clubs, see Sir Nathaniel Curzon to Thomas Hill,

6 September 1749, and Richard Corbet to Thomas Hill, 2 June 1750, Salop R.O., Attingham MSS., 112/24. Cf. Namier, *Structure of Politics*, 267, for the whig Lord Powis' surprise when the tory gentry attended the Shropshire whigs' race-meeting in 1760. I believe that W. A. Speck has exaggerated the socio-political consensus within the mid-eighteenth-century landed elite; see *Tory & Whig*, 97, and *Stability and Strife: England 1714–60* (1977), 3–4.

20. Sedgwick, II, 323. For the London Shropshire Club, see *V.C.H. Shropshire*, III, 259.

21. On the 1754 Hertfordshire contest see Namier & Brooke, I, 306; *Felix Farley's Bristol Journal*, 9/16 February 1754; and the notes on the Royston Club in the *Gentleman's Magazine*, LIII (1783), Pt II, 813–16.

22. Newdigate's diary, 12 October 1753, Warwickshire R.O., CR 136A (584). For the 1731–4 Berkshire agreement, see Berkshire R.O., D/EHy 04.

23. Wrightson Mundy to Sir Thomas Cave, 26 June 1747, Leicestershire R.O., 23 D 57/3127.

24. Richard Hopton to William Brydges, 30 December 1740, and Velters Cornewall to William Brydges, 20 January 1741, Herefordshire R.O., A81/31–2. This analysis of the 1741 Hereford result is based on *An Alphabetical Copy of the Poll taken at the City of Hereford* (Gloucester, 1741). For the early whig use of the 'honest interest', see Holmes, *British Politics*, 17, 460. Cf. Lord Gower's recommendation of the tory Sir Rowland Lee to the borough of Lichfield in 1733, as being 'able to support the honest interest against all opponents', Ann J. Kettle, 'The Struggle for the Lichfield Interest 1747–68', in M. W. Greenslade (ed.), *Essays in Staffordshire History* (1970), 115.

25. Viscount Lonsdale to Sir James Lowther, 20 October 1721, Cumbria R.O., D/Lons Checklist 16/11. E. G. Forrester, *Northamptonshire County Elections and Electioneering 1695–1832* (Oxford, 1941), 13.

26. These calculations are based on *A Copy of the Poll ... for the County of Hereford* (Gloucester, 1754). Cf. Hayes, 'Politics in Norfolk', 42. For a useful discussion of deference in eighteenth- and nineteenth-century English politics, see J. G. A. Pocock, 'The Classical Theory of Deference', *American History Review*, LXXXI (1976), 516–23, and David Spring, 'Walter Bagehot and Deference', *ibid.* 524–31.

27. Forrester, *Northamptonshire County Elections*, 69–70. R. A. Kelch, *Newcastle: a Duke without Money* (1974), and E. Johnson, 'The Bedford Connection: the Fourth Duke of Bedford's Political Influence between 1732 and 1771' (unpub. Ph.D. dissertation, Cambridge University, 1980).

28. C. Collyer, 'The Yorkshire Election of 1734', *Proceedings of the Leeds Philosophical and Literary Society*, VII (1952–5), 71, 82. For the 1747 tory subscription in Staffordshire, see *Staffordshire County Council Education Department Local History Source Book*, No. 5, 8. On Bagot's reputed meanness (the freeholders asked his agents 'if they brought with them the key of the small beer cellar'), see Staffordshire R.O., D603/39.

29. See Namier's excellent if one-dimensional account of the English county M.P., *Structure of Politics*, 64–73. Tory maintenance of basic electoral machinery in mid-century Cornwall can be traced in the Buller and Carew MSS. at Cornwall R.O. consulted by kind permission of Colonel Sir J. G. Carew Pole.

30. Wrightson Mundy to Sir Thomas Cave, 15 January 1741, Leicestershire R.O., 23 D 57/3030; for the 1727 Shropshire campaign, see *V.C.H. Shropshire*, III, 259.

31. Ministerial agent's report on Queensborough's electorate, 1750, Sedgwick, I, 267.

William Maisterson to Sir Robert Salusbury Cotton, 14 January 1734, Chester City R.O., CR 72/6.

32. Namier, *Structure of Politics*, 95; *Newcastle General Magazine*, 1 January 1753, 51; John Sykes, *Memoirs of the Public Life of Sir Walter Blackett, Bt.* (Newcastle, 1819), xv, xxix.

33. These calculations are based on the 1741 Worcestershire poll book at the Institute of Historical Research, University of London.

34. Reverend Giles Nanfan to Lord Bellamont, 16 May 1741, Worcestershire R.O., Acc. 5117, Box 51.

35. These estimates are based on the 1715 Evans List which is printed in part in E. D. Bebb, *Nonconformity and Social and Economic Life 1660–1800* (1935), 182–3. Some of its figures are certainly wrong: it allocated 1118 dissenting freeholders to Devon – almost one third of that county's electorate – but the mid-century consensus was that dissenters formed one sixth of Devon's county voters.

36. *Jackson's Oxford Journal*, No. 47, 23 March 1754; *Worcester Weekly Journal*, No. 2295, 26 July 1753. See also G. A. Cranfield, 'The *London Evening-Post* and the Jew Bill of 1753', *H.J.*, VIII (1965), 16–30.

37. MS. notes in the 1754 Abingdon poll book at the Institute of Historical Research; for the clerical vote in the 1754 Bristol contest, see *The Bristol Poll-book* (Bristol, 1754), 3–6.

38. For Massingberd, see Sedgwick, I, 276; Talbot's monthly dinners are noted in 'Diary of Thomas Smith, Esq., of Shaw House', *Wiltshire Archaeological and Natural History Magazine*, XI (1869), 212.

39. Thomas Carte to ?, 8 February 1744 (intercepted letter), B.L. Add. MS. 32702, fol. 51; for Robertshaw's activities, see G. Eland, 'The Shardeloes Muniments', *Records of Buckinghamshire*, XIV (1941–6), 293.

40. Theophilus Blackall to Theophilus Fortescue, 6 October and 29 November 1740, Devonshire R.O., 1262M/Bundle 3. The Devon tories had to call on Fortescue because, as Blackall remarked, their current M.P., Henry Rolle, 'hath thrown himself into the hands of the Whiggs . . . there's no doubt but that he'll have all the Dissenters of his side'.

41. On Clavering's behaviour in 1730, see B.L. Add. MS. 9200, fol. 142; bishop of Peterborough to Sir Justinian Isham, 12 January 1734, Northamptonshire R.O., IL 2887.

42. For clerical defection in Hereford, see Velters Cornewall to William Brydges, 20 February 1741, Herefordshire R.O., A81/31, and *An Alphabetical Copy of the Poll taken at the City of Hereford*, and the broadsheets bound with it in the Hereford Public Library copy (Xerox copy at the Institute of Historical Research). For Wells, see Namier & Brooke, I, 333–4.

43. For ministerial influence and the Sussex clergy, see R. L. Hess, 'The Sackville Family and Sussex Politics: the Campaign for the By-Election, 1741', *Sussex Archaeological Collections*, XCIX (1961), 20–37, and the 1741 Sussex whig verses in Kent R.O., U269 O116. This analysis of clerical behaviour in Cheshire is based on Appendix Aii of Baskerville, 'Tory Interest', 345–60, and the information on patrons supplied by *The Clergyman's Intelligencer* (1745).

44. See Derek Fraser's account of how urban and 'national' politics interlinked in fact and in voters' minds in the mid nineteenth century, *Urban Politics in Victorian England* (Leicester, 1976), 9–30. Fielding, *The History of Tom Jones*, Book IV, Ch. 7.

45. D. S. O'Sullivan, 'Politics in Norwich, 1701–1835' (unpub. M.Phil. dissertation, University of East Anglia, 1975), 16, 36, 57, 67–70. M. M. Rowe and A. M.

Jackson, *Exeter Freemen, 1266–1967*, Devon and Cornwall Record Society (Exeter, 1973), xxviii–xxix.

46. Newsletter for 3 April 1722, B.L. Add. MS. 47077, fol. 18; *V.C.H. Shropshire*, III, 131.

47. On the 1716 Vestry Bill, see Norman Sykes, *William Wake, Archbishop of Canterbury 1657–1737* (2 vols., Cambridge, 1957), II, 112–13, and S. and B. Webb, *The Parish and the County* (1906, repr. 1963), 252–3.

48. Thomas Carew to Sir Charles Kemys Tynte, 21 January 1765, Somerset R.O., DD/TB/Box 17 OB5. For Beckford's initiative, see Sidney and Beatrice Webb, *The Manor and the Borough* (2 vols., 1908, repr. 1963), II, 456–9.

49. William Noel as quoted in 'The Historical Part of the Stamford Election', C.U.L., C(H) P68/11, fol. 3; Donald Ginter, *Whig Organisation in the General Election of 1790* (Berkeley and Los Angeles, 1967), xvii–xx; Lord Strafford to Sir Justinian Isham, 29 June 1727, Northamptonshire R.O., IC 2967.

50. For Winnington, see Sedgwick, II, 550–1, and for Walpole's support of his uncle Horatio, see J. H. Plumb, *The Growth of Political Stability in England 1675–1725* (1967), 75n. Sir William Morice to Humphry Morice, 10 October 1721, Bank of England, COU/B151/1, fols. 224–5.

51. John Campbell to Pryse Campbell, 10 December 1742, N.L.W., MS. 1352B, fol. 88. For the tories' rescue of Lutwyche in 1722, see Sir William Wyndham to Lord Gower, 17 January 1722, Staffordshire R.O., D/868/7/39b. Before 1715 the party had shown only a limited ability to provide 'reserve' constituencies for its talent; see Holmes, *British Politics*, 318–19.

52. For Hanoverian–Jacobite divisions in Cambridgeshire, see Sedgwick, I, 200–1, and Thomas Bacon to Lord Oxford, 15 August 1727, B.L. Loan 29/89. The 1722 London contest has been analysed in terms of tory versus dissident whig in W. A. Speck and W. A. Gray, 'Londoners at the Polls under Anne and George I', *Guildhall Studies in London History*, I (1975), 253–62; this was not how contemporaries saw it, see *H.M.C. Tenth Report*, App., IV, 344, and Thomas Carte's notes on the contest, Bodleian Library, MS. Carte 239, fol. 481. For the deterioration in the 'pure' tory vote in London after 1722, see Nicholas Rogers, 'Resistance to Oligarchy: the City Opposition to Walpole and his Successors, 1725–47', in John Stevenson (ed.), *London in the Age of Reform* (Oxford, 1977), 2–3. For the 1761 Canterbury contest, see Namier, *Structure of Politics*, 99–102.

53. Lord Cardigan to Sir Justinian Isham, 27 March 1722, Northamptonshire R.O., IC 2966; see the MS. poll book for the 1734 Northampton election at Castle Ashby, Compton MS. 1057.

54. For Southampton see Sedgwick, I, 254. *A List of all the Honorary and Gratis Freeman ... of the City of Worcester* (n.d.), Herefordshire R.O., Foley MSS.

55. For the financing of the 1754 Oxfordshire contest, see R. J. Robson, *The Oxfordshire Election of 1754* (Oxford, 1949), 158–9, and a copy of a subscription list which includes tory contributors from Northamptonshire, Monmouth, Cornwall, and Westmorland, B.L. Add. MS. 33055, fol. 81. For rumours in 1750 of a tory central fund, see *Berrow's Weekly Worcester Journal*, No. 2115, 1 February 1750, and W. S. Lewis *et al.* (eds.), *Horace Walpole's Correspondence with Sir Horace Mann*, IV, The Yale Edition of Horace Walpole's Correspondence (New Haven, 1937–), xx, 131.

56. Sir Edmund Isham to Sir Thomas Cave, 16 March 1762, Leicestershire R.O., 23 D 57/3177, and see letters 2894, 2938 and 3069 for the 1715 and 1741 subscriptions. On Flint boroughs, see Stephen W. Baskerville, 'The Manage-

ment of the Tory Interest in Lancashire and Cheshire, 1714–47' (unpub. D.Phil. dissertation, Oxford University, 1976), 241, and Sedgwick, I, 377.

57. R. W. Greaves, 'A Scheme for the Counties', *E.H.R.*, XLVIII (1933), 630–8. This document has caused some confusion, one copy of it being bound among the Stuart papers for 1739, R.A. SP 216/109–12. However its reference to the inception of Bristol's Steadfast Society in 1737 as being 'about 7 years ago' confirms Greaves' argument that it was composed in the early 1740s.

58. I am grateful to Mr J. N. W. Chambers, Honorary Secretary of the Bull Club, for information on this society. It is noteworthy that in 1855 its members decided 'that the Bull Club do represent Political Principles, and that those Principles are essentially of a Conservative character', *Rules and Regulations*, 14. For the Charter Club, see Essex R.O., D/DR B1 and D/Y 2/2, and A. F. J. Brown, *Colchester in the Eighteenth Century* (Colchester, 1969), 12–20.

59. *General Advertiser*, 16 May 1747. See also I. G. Doolittle, 'The Half Moon Tavern, Cheapside, and City Politics', *Transactions of the London and Middlesex Archaeological Society*, XXVIII (1977), 328–32. *V.C.H. Warwickshire*, VIII, 274, and 'Notes from the Minute Book of the Birmingham Bean Club, 1754–1836', Birmingham City Reference Library, 131399. In the 1760s tory disjunction at the centre also affected the Bean Club's partisan unity; see John Money, *Experience and Identity: Birmingham and the West Midlands 1760–1800* (Manchester, 1977), 99–102. For eighteenth-century electoral activity in Coventry, see T. W. Whitley, *The Parliamentary Representation of the City of Coventry* (Coventry, 1894), 141–65.

60. Sedgwick, I, 244–5. The minutes of the Steadfast Society on which this paragraph and the next are based are held by the Society of Merchant Venturers, Bristol. I have used the Book of Rules and Orders, I.

61. Nicholas Miller to Jarrit Smith, 5 March 1768, Bristol City R.O., AC/JS 90 (5)a; cf. Namier & Brooke, I, 284. Calculations of St Michael's voting in 1722 and 1754 are based on the respective Bristol poll books.

62. For Hart's plight, see James Pearce to Humphry Morice, 9 September 1727, Bank of England, COU/B151/III, fol. 581.

63. Josiah Tucker to Forster, 5 June 1754, B.L. Add. MS. 11275, fol. 134. Newcastle's spy believed that the sum involved was £1200; see B.L. Add. MS. 32736, fol. 139.

64. The next two paragraphs, on the 1745 Glamorgan by-election, are based on Glamorgan R.O., D/DKT/1/18–56; I am grateful to Dr D. Rees for lending me his microfilm of this correspondence.

65. J. P. Jenkins, 'A Social and Political History of the Glamorgan Gentry c. 1650–1770' (unpub. Ph.D. dissertation, Cambridge University, 1978), 272; Sedgwick, II, 247.

66. For whig constituency organisation in the 1780s and 1790s, see Ginter, *Whig Organisation*, *passim*, and D. R. McAdams, 'Electioneering Techniques in Populous Constituencies, 1784–96', *Studies in Burke and his Time*, XIV (1972), 26–8.

67. For Wynn's speech in 1734, see *Parl. Hist.*, IX, 430; Cannon, 'Parliamentary Representation of Gloucester', 139; Namier, *Structure of Politics*, 83.

68. Phillips, 'Structure of Electoral Politics', 76.

69. Sedgwick, II, 141–2.

70. Johnson, 'The Bedford Connection', 169; this estimate of Bristol tory support (probably coloured by whig bias) is in *An Alphabetical List of the Freeholders and Burgesses of the Several Parishes of the City and County of Bristol* (1734),

B.L. 291.b.24; Nicholas Rogers, 'Aristocratic Clientage, Trade and Independency: Popular Politics in Pre-Radical Westminster', *P.&P.*, LXI (1973), 78–81.

71. Namier & Brooke, I, 306; John Cannon, 'Short Guide to Records; Poll Books', *History*, XLVII (1962), 168.

72. These are my own estimates, based on information in Sedgwick and Namier & Brooke.

73. J. M. Norris, 'Samuel Garbett and the Early Development of Industrial Lobbying in Great Britain', *Economic History Review*, X (1957), 451; and M. W. Mc-Cahill, 'Peers, Patronage, and the Industrial Revolution 1760–1800', *Journal of British Studies*, XVI (1976), 84–107.

CHAPTER 6

1. *T[ren]t [ha]m and V[an]d [epu]t. A Collection of the Advertisements and Handbills ... Published on both Sides during the Election for the City and Liberty of Westminster* (Dublin, 1749), 21; for Pulteney's comment, see *The Lives of Dr. Edward Pocock by Leonard Twells; of Dr. Zachary Pearce and of Dr. Thomas Newton by Themselves and of the Rev. Philip Skelton by Mr. Burdy* (2 vols., 1816), II, 60–2; [George Lyttelton], *A Letter to the Tories* (1747), 14; *A Full & True Account of the Strange & Miraculous Conversion of All the Tories in Great Britain by the Preaching of Caleb D'Anvers* (1734), 25.

2. John Almon, *A Review of the Reign of George II* (2nd edn, 1762), 8–9. Cf. G. A. Cranfield, *The Development of the Provincial Newspaper, 1700–60* (Oxford, 1962), 130.

3. Christopher Hill, *Reformation to Industrial Revolution: a Social and Economic History of Britain 1530–1780* (1967), 157; Isaac Kramnick, *Bolingbroke and his Circle: the Politics of Nostalgia in the Age of Walpole* (1968); Robert W. Malcolmson, *Popular Recreations in English Society 1700–1850* (Cambridge, 1973), 98, 158–62; E. P. Thompson, 'The Moral Economy of the English Crowd', *P.&P.*, L (1971), 76–136; 'Patrician Society, Plebeian Culture?', *Journal of Social History*, VII (1974), 382–405; 'Eighteenth-Century English Society: Class Struggle without Class?', *Social History*, III (1978), 133–65; and *Whigs and Hunters: the Origins of the Black Act* (1975, rev. edn, Harmondsworth, 1977), e.g. 216.

4. Oliver Goldsmith, *The Traveller* (1764), quoted in Kramnick, *Bolingbroke and his Circle*, 80.

5. *Parl. Hist.*, XII, 1188; Douglas Hay, 'Poaching and the Game Laws on Cannock Chase', in Hay, Peter Linebaugh and E. P. Thompson (eds.), *Albion's Fatal Tree: Crime and Society in Eighteenth-Century England* (1975), 189–254; Joanna Martin, 'Private Enterprise versus Manorial Rights: Mineral Property Disputes in Mid-Eighteenth-Century Glamorgan', *Welsh History Review*, IX (1978), 155–75.

6. Chandos to Herbert Westfaling, 22 July 1727, H.L.S.M., ST 57, vol. XXX, fol. 150.

7. W. M. Myddelton, *Chirk Castle Accounts, A.D. 1605–1753* (2 vols., 1908–31), II, 447.

8. E. P. Thompson, 'Time, Work-Discipline, and Industrial Capitalism', *P.&P.*, XXXVIII (1967), 81–2; M. W. Flinn, *Men of Iron: the Crowleys in the Early Iron Industry* (Edinburgh, 1962), 59, 63, 71, 225–32. For a useful discussion of the ambiguity contained in paternalism, see Elizabeth Fox-Genovese, 'The Many Faces of the Moral Economy: a Contribution to a Debate', *P.&P.*, LVIII

(1973), 161–8; the point is of course recognised by Thompson, 'Class Struggle', 133–8.

9. Peter Linebaugh, 'The Tyburn Riot against the Surgeons', Hay *et al.* (eds.), *Albion's Fatal Tree*, 117; for an account of the 1724 Lords debate, see W. C. Lukis (ed.), *The Family Memoirs of the Rev. William Stukeley, M.D. and the Antiquarian and other Correspondence*, Publications of the Surtees Society, LXXIII (1882), 73–4.

10. *C.J.*, XIX, 40, 126–36, XX, 246; Thompson, 'Class Struggle', 145–6.

11. Sheila Lambert (ed.), *House of Commons Sessional Papers of the Eighteenth Century* (147 vols., Wilmington, 1975–6), I, 37–8. See John Styles, 'Criminal Records', *H.J.*, XX (1977), 977–81, for some perceptive comments on the Black Act and its whig perpetrators.

12. Sedgwick, I, 451; L. K. J. Glassey, 'The Commission of the Peace 1675–1720' (D.Phil. dissertation, Oxford University, 1972), 370; Malcolmson, *Popular Recreations*, 67–8; *H.M.C. Verulam*, 117.

13. For the 1715 motion, see *C.J.*, XVIII, 227; for Bathurst's speech in 1741, see *Parl. Hist.*, XII, 93. A £300 Land Tax qualification for J.P.s was the first clause of the Carlton House declaration of 1747: see E. N. Williams, *The Eighteenth-Century Constitution 1688–1815* (Cambridge, 1960), 180. For the Riot Act as viewed from below see Nicholas Rogers, 'Popular Protest in Early Hanoverian London', *P.&P.*, LXXIX (1978), 74–5; for the whig authorities' sometimes humane and often diffident implementation of the Act, see Tony Hayter, *The Army & the Crowd in Mid-Georgian England* (1978), 9–15.

14. John Chamberlayne, *Magnae Britanniae Notitia* (1755).

15. For the 1732 Boothall meeting, see *Gloucestershire Notes & Queries*, III (1887), 283. J. de L. Mann, *The Cloth Industry in the West of England from 1640 to 1880* (Oxford, 1971), 104–18; and 'Clothiers and Weavers in Wiltshire during the Eighteenth Century', in L. S. Pressnell (ed.), *Studies in the Industrial Revolution* (1960), 66–96. [William Temple], *The Case As It Now Stands between the Clothiers, Weavers, and other Manufacturers, with regard to the Late Riot in the County of Wilts.* (1739), 29, 34.

16. Thompson, 'Class Struggle', 142; Duncan Forbes, *Hume's Philosophical Politics* (Cambridge, 1975), 94, 176.

17. R. L. Schuyler, *Josiah Tucker: a Selection from his Economic and Political Writings* (New York, 1931), 262–3. Cf. Thompson, 'Class Struggle', 162–5.

18. For the tory initiative in 1701, see W. A. Speck, *Tory & Whig: the Struggle in the Constituencies 1701–15* (1970), 15. Langham's campaign is described in Gary Stuart de Krey, 'Trade, Religion, and Politics in London in the Reign of William III' (unpub. Ph.D. dissertation, Princeton University, 1978), 260–9, 310.

19. For this view of the eighteenth-century Church, see Thompson, 'Patrician Society, Plebeian Culture?', 390–4.

20. E. J. Evans, 'Some Reasons for the Growth of English Rural Anti-Clericalism c.1750–c.1830', *P.&P.*, LXVI (1975), 86–8, 101. For the 1722 Reading rebellion see *H.M.C. Portland*, VII, 317, and Thompson, *Whigs and Hunters*, 101.

21. D. G. D. Isaac, 'A Study of Popular Disturbances in Britain 1714–54' (unpub. Ph.D. dissertation, Edinburgh University, 1953), 214–15; C. D. Linnell (ed.), *The Diary of Benjamin Rogers, Rector of Carlton, 1720–71*, Publications of the Bedfordshire Historical Society, XXX (1950), *passim*; John Walsh, 'Methodism and the Mob in the Eighteenth Century', in G. J. Cuming and Derek Baker (eds.), *Popular Belief and Practice* (Cambridge, 1972), 213–28.

22. On church attendance, see R. Currie, A. Gilbert, and L. Horsley, *Churches and*

Churchgoers, Patterns of Church Growth in the British Isles since 1700 (Oxford, 1977), 22, but see also the rather different findings of R. J. Pope, 'The Eighteenth Century Church in Wirral' (unpub. M.A. dissertation, University of Wales, 1971).

23. M. H. Smith, 'Conflict and Society in Late Eighteenth Century Birmingham' (unpub. Ph.D. dissertation, Cambridge University, 1978), 6–7; H. E. Chetwynd-Stapylton, *The Stapeltons of Yorkshire* (1897), 301; H. McLachlan, 'Diary of a Leeds Layman 1733–68', *Transactions of the Unitarian Historical Society*, IV (1927–30), 239.

24. *Manchester Politics: a Dialogue between Mr. True Blew and Mr. Whig-Love* (1748), 4; *Manchester Vindicated: being a Compleat Collection of the Papers Lately Published in defence of that Town* (1749), viii–ix.

25. Tory election verses 1733, Chester City R.O., Grosvenor MSS., Folder B. *The Bristol Contest: being a Collection of All the Papers published by both Parties, on the Election* (Bristol, 1754), 13; *On the Hon. Mr. Southwell's getting the Election* (broadsheet, Bristol, 1739).

26. For the whig-sponsored Naturalisation Bills, see Geoffrey Holmes, *British Politics in the Age of Anne* (1967), 105–6; *C.J.*, xxv, 195, 258, 269, 275, 295, 306, 313, 334. For the grass-roots opposition to them, see Perry, *Public Opinion, Propaganda, and Politics in Eighteenth-Century England: a Study of the Jew Bill of 1753* (Cambridge, Mass., 1962), 24–40. Extracts from the 1748 pamphlet (and connected ephemera) are printed in E. S. Furniss, *The Position of the Laborer in a System of Nationalism: a Study in the Labor Theories of the Later English Mercantilists* (Boston, N.Y., 1920), 142–3, 181.

27. *Worcester Journal*, No. 2038, 11 August 1748; Mann, *Cloth Industry*, 110–11, and 'Clothiers and Weavers', 68; W. E. Minchinton, 'The Petition of the Weavers and Clothiers of Gloucestershire in 1756', *Transactions of the Bristol and Gloucestershire Archaeological Society*, LXXIII (1954), 216–27.

28. D. S. O'Sullivan, 'Politics in Norwich, 1701–1835' (unpub. M.Phil. dissertation, University of East Anglia, 1975), 94–8.

29. Graham Midgley, *The Life of Orator Henley* (Oxford, 1973), 236; for bourgeois Anglicanism in Norwich, see O'Sullivan, 'Politics in Norwich', 87; Carew's Address to 'The Gentlemen, Clergy & Freeholders of the County of Cornwall', 19 March 1744, Cornwall R.O., BO/23/63.

30. Peter Mathias and Patrick O'Brien, 'Taxation in Britain and France, 1715–1810. A Comparison of the Social and Economic Incidence of Taxes collected by the Central Government', *Journal of European Economic History*, V (1976), 606; see also D. N. McCloskey's rejoinder, *ibid.* VII (1978), 209–10.

31. [John Shebbeare], *A Third Letter to the People of England* (3rd edn, 1756), 46–7. For Massie see William Kennedy, *English Taxation 1640–1799: an Essay on Policy and Opinion* (1913, repr. 1964), 107n, and Peter Mathias, 'The Social Structure in the Eighteenth Century', *The Transformation of England: Essays in the Economic and Social History of England in the Eighteenth Century* (1979), 171–4. Walpole's memorandum of 1733 is printed in Edward Hughes, *Studies in Administration and Finance 1558–1825* (Manchester, 1934), 302.

32. Verse xv of the virulent *Britannia Excisa* (1733); Hughes, *Studies in Administration*, 119–22. For the belief that economic self-interest should have entailed tory and 'Country Gentleman' approval of the Excise Bill, see Paul Langford, *The Excise Crisis* (Oxford, 1975), 26–43, and J. B. Owen, 'The Survival of Country Attitudes in the Eighteenth-Century House of Commons', in J. S. Bromley and E. H. Kossman (eds.), *Britain and the Netherlands* (5 vols., The Hague, 1960–75), IV, 51. As Walpole found out, men respond to ideologies and

traditional prejudices as well as to crude economic determinism. See J. H. Plumb, *Sir Robert Walpole* (2 vols., 1956, 1960), II, 235–9, where the Excise Bill's wider significance is excellently described.

33. Kennedy, *English Taxation*, 78; Brooks, 'Taxation, Finance and Public Opinion, 1688–1714' (unpub. Ph.D. dissertation, Cambridge University, 1971), 340; J. H. Plumb, *The Growth of Political Stability in England 1675–1725* (1967), 149, 155. For Cooke's intervention see Lord Ilchester, *Henry Fox, First Lord Holland, his Family and Relations* (2 vols., 1920), I, 309.

34. Brooks, 'Public Finance and Political Stability: the Administration of the Land Tax, 1688–1720', *H.J.*, XVII (1974), 283. Hughes, *Studies in Administration*, 315. For Dowdeswell's speech, see Namier & Brooke, II, 333. I am grateful to Professor John Brewer for much useful information on taxation and debt in the eighteenth century.

35. Kramnick, *Bolingbroke and his Circle*, 55; *Parl. Hist.*, VIII, 953.

36. Kennedy, *English Taxation*, 106–10.

37. Harley's journal, 30 March 1737, C.U.L., Add. 6851, fol. 86; C. L. S. Linnell (ed.), *The Diaries of Thomas Wilson, D.D., 1731–7 and 1750* (1964), 195–200. Extracts from 'The Essay on Riots' appeared in the *Gentleman's Magazine*, IX (1739), 7–10. De Krey, 'Trade, Religion and Politics', 29; O'Sullivan, 'Politics in Norwich', 43–52.

38. *A Late Discourse between Mr. —— a Rich Man in the Opposition, and his Workman Thomas, a Weaver, together with his Neighbour John* [1747], Coventry Reference Library, C & W (M) 6261.

39. *Worcester Journal*, No. 2038, 11 August 1748; Tindal's comment is printed in *Parl. Hist.*, XIV, 572–4. Two Jacobite agent-provocateurs were reportedly present at the 1747 Lichfield riots and some tory M.P.s certainly were; both groups were exploiting popular anti-aristocratic sentiment for their different partisan purposes. See Ann J. Kettle, 'The Struggle for the Lichfield Interest 1747–68', in M. W. Greenslade (ed.), *Essays in Staffordshire History* (1970), 115–35, and 'Lichfield Races', *Transactions of the Lichfield and South Staffordshire Archaeological and Historical Society*, VI (1964–5), 40–1; cf. Eveline Cruickshanks, *Political Untouchables: the Tories and the '45* (1979), 107.

40. *Freeholder's Journal*, 4 and 25 April and 23 May 1722; F. C. Morgan, 'The Hereford Election Skits of 1741', *Transactions of the Woolhope Naturalists' Field Club*, XXXI (1942–5), 98–100; *Jackson's Oxford Journal*, 20 April 1754. Just as 'Wilkes and Liberty' in 1775 was insufficient for the voters of Cricklade, so the tory anti-bribery platform had its failures. Sir John Kaye's address to the York voters in 1734 'that if they would choose him, he would do the city all the service he could; but... would spend no money... did not at all please', Sedgwick, II, 184. Cf. John Cannon, *Parliamentary Reform, 1640–1832* (Cambridge, 1973), 68.

41. For the 1742 Derby by-election see L. Eardley-Simpson, *Derby and the Forty-Five* (1933), 18; information for the 1748 contest taken from the *Worcester Journal*, No. 2058, 29 December 1748; and the Derby poll book for 1748 at the Institute of Historical Research, University of London.

42. Lewis Namier, *The Structure of Politics at the Accession of George III* (2nd edn, 1970), 82–3.

43. Wesley is quoted in Hughes, *Studies in Administration*, 253n; for the 1731 and 1733 tory bills, see *C.J.*, XXI, 823, 836, 867; XXII, 39, 84; William Albert, 'Popular Opposition to Turnpike Trusts in Early Eighteenth-Century England', *Journal of Transport History*, V (1979), 1–17.

44. For Winford, see William Brome to Oxford, 12 October 1733, B.L. Loan 29/30.

Chandos to Captain Oakeley, 12 July 1727, and to William Brydges, 8 August 1727, H.L.S.M., ST 57, vol. xxx, fols. 124–5, 187. See Egmont's comments on Hereford in A. N. Newman (ed.), 'Leicester House Politics, 1750–60', *Camden Miscellany*, xxiii (1969), 138.

45. Newcastle under Lyme broadsheet, dated 18 April 1734, in my possession; *V.C.H. Stafford*, viii, 43; Stephen W. Baskerville, 'The Management of the Tory Interest in Lancashire and Cheshire, 1714–47' (unpub. D.Phil. dissertation, Oxford University, 1976), 183–200; *V.C.H. Cheshire*, ii, 133.

46. This account is taken from Richard Parkinson (ed.), *The Private Journal and Literary Remains of John Byrom*, I.ii, Chetham Society, xxxiv (1855), 440–90; *C.J.*, xxi, 697.

47. For the Independent Electors see Perceval's draft history, B.L. Add. MS. 47159, fol. 117, and Nicholas Rogers, 'Aristocratic Clientage, Trade and Independency: Popular Politics in Pre-Radical Westminster', *P.&P.*, lxi (1973), 75, 94–104. I believe that Dr Rogers has underestimated the tory content of metropolitan politics; see the interesting broadsheet printed in Henry Paton (ed.), *The Lyon in Mourning*, Scottish Historical Society (3 vols., Edinburgh, 1895), ii, 368–9.

48. [Perceval] *Faction detected by the evidence of Facts: containing an Impartial View of Parties at Home, and Affairs Abroad* (2nd edn, 1743), 51; *A Key to the Present Session . . . Certain Important Hints deliver'd to an Assembly of Independents* (1742), 35. For tory reform proposals in 1742–3 see Archibald S. Foord, *His Majesty's Opposition 1714–1830* (Oxford, 1964), 234–5.

49. Newman (ed.), 'Leicester House Politics, 1750–60', 188. For the Independents' involvement in the 1747 Middlesex contest, see Sir Roger Newdigate's canvassing diary, Greater London R.O., Acc/1085/FP/2; for their working relationship with the Cocoa Tree, James Bonnell to Thomas Hill, 22 October 1747, Salop R.O., Attingham MSS., Box 24.

50. The description of Samuel Johns is in Thomas Robinson to duke of Richmond, 30 December 1749, West Sussex R.O., Goodwood MS. 51, fol. 72; *Reasons humbly proposed by Several Inhabitants of the City and Liberty of Westminster, against the Coal-Jobb Bill* (n.d. [1746]). For Johns' and the tories' parliamentary activity in response to the bill, see *C.J.*, xxv, 128, 148. John Cust to Perceval, 7 June 1746, B.L. Add. MS. 47012B.

51. See Carew's papers, Somerset R.O., DD/TB/Box 16/FT 15. For Wilkes' acquaintance with the Independents, see the *North Briton*, No. 17, 21 May 1763.

52. Sir John Barlow to Sir John Pakington, 22 February 1721, Worcestershire R.O., Acc. 4657, vol. iii. Archibald Hutcheson advocated pledges in the *Freeholder's Journal*, No. 10, 21 March 1722. See Betty Kemp, 'Patriotism, Pledges and the People', in Martin Gilbert (ed.), *Century of Conflict* (1966), 40–3.

53. Edward Southwell's memoranda for 11 October 1739, Bristol City Reference Library, Southwell Papers, v.

54. Southwell to Robert Smith, 15 February 1741, Bristol City Reference Library, Southwell Papers, vi. For Burke's 1774 address to the Bristol electors see B. W. Hill (ed.), *Edmund Burke on Government, Politics and Society* (1975), 156–8. Cf. John Brewer, *Party Ideology and Popular Politics at the Accession of George III* (Cambridge, 1976), 236–7.

55. 'Lord Perceval's Answer to a Deputation of the Independent Inhabitants of Westminster' (MS. copy), West Sussex R.O., Goodwood MS. 109, fol. 890. On seventeenth- and eighteenth-century whig reactions to Instructions, see Lucy S. Sutherland, 'Edmund Burke and the Relations between Members of Parliament and their Constituents', *Studies in Burke and his Time*, x (1968), 1005–21.

56. Minutes of the Steadfast Society, Bristol Society of Merchant Venturers, Book 1, fol. 13. For Carew on Instructions, see *Parl. Hist.*, XII, 1060; for Cornewall, see the *Gentleman's Magazine*, XXVII (1757), 343–4.
57. Perry, *Public Opinion*, 115.
58. Thomas Carew to his constituents, 22 April 1742 (draft), Somerset R.O., DD/TB OB8.
59. *H.M.C. Report on the Records of the City of Exeter*, 245–6.
60. *The Livery-Man: or Plain Thoughts on Publick Affairs* (1740), 7, 56. *Considerations on the Addresses lately presented to His Majesty, on Occasion of the Loss of Minorca* (1756), 11.
61. *A Collection of Advertisements, Letters and Papers, and some of the Facts, relating to the Last Elections at Westminster and Hastings* (1722), 54; *Copies of some Letters from Mr. Hutcheson to the Late Earl of Sunderland* (1722), 12.
62. Bolingbroke's reform essay is reprinted in the *Gentleman's Magazine*, IV (1734), 381. Paul Langford has argued that Bolingbroke was unwilling to see his projected reform implemented. This is to take at face value his ironic conclusion: 'I would not be understood as if I design'd to propose any such Alteration at present ... It would now be called a Design to remove *Foundations*, to subvert the *Constitution* ... as we have lately seen in some Attempts to secure the ... *Independency of Parliaments*.' Bolingbroke was parodying ministerial arguments against the tory motion to repeal the Septennial Act in March 1734: since such a respectable motion had failed, there was clearly no chance for far-reaching electoral reform. Langford, *Excise Crisis*, 164–5. For Almon in 1768, see Cannon, *Parliamentary Reform*, 54–5.
63. The *Westminster Journal* extract is reprinted in the *Gentleman's Magazine*, XVII (1747), 329–31; Marie Peters, 'The "Monitor" on the Constitution, 1755–65: New Light on the Ideological Origins of English Radicalism', *E.H.R.*, LXXXVI (1971), 706–27; *Jopson's Coventry Mercury*, Nos. 925 and 929, 26 March and 23 April 1759.
64. *Parl. Hist.*, XV, 440; Brewer, *Party Ideology*, 180; Cannon, *Parliamentary Reform*, 52.
65. *H.M.C. Eleventh Report*, App., IV, 371.
66. Charles Gray, *Considerations on Several Proposals Lately Made for the Better Maintenance of the Poor* (1752), 20–3. See also Gray's letter to Egmont in 1749, suggesting a similar reform of corporation boroughs, Newman (ed.), 'Leicester House Politics, 1750–60', 181.
67. A. A. Brockett, 'Nonconformity in Devon in the Eighteenth Century', *Report and Transactions of the Devonshire Association*, XC (1958), 31–59, and 'The Political and Social Influence of the Exeter Dissenters and some Notable Families', *ibid.* XCIII (1961), 184–93.
68. *The Works of the Rev. John Wesley* (14 vols., 1872), XI, 196–8.
69. Schuyler, *Josiah Tucker*, 22; *The Bristol Riot* (1714), 5–6.
70. John Sykes, *Memoirs of the Public Life of Sir Walter Blackett, Bt.* (Newcastle, 1819), xxix. For Wilkes and Shebbeare see John Almon, *Biographical, Literary and Political Anecdotes of Several of the Most Eminent Persons of the Present Age* (3 vols., 1797), I, 373; *History of the Four Last Elections for the County of Suffolk* (1772), 15.
71. W. J. Smith (ed.), *The Grenville Papers: being the Correspondence of Richard Grenville Earl Temple K.G., and the Right Hon. George Grenville* (4 vols., 1852), II, 7. For Wilkes and the Minorca campaign, see Royston to Hardwicke, 24 August 1756, B.L. Add. MS. 35351, fol. 343.
72. Nicholas Rogers, 'London Politics from Walpole to Pitt: Patriotism and

Independency in an Era of Commercial Imperialism, 1738–63' (unpub. D.Phil. dissertation, Toronto University, 1974), 480, and 'Aristocratic Clientage, Trade and Independency', 77. Murray was defended at the King's Bench by the barrister and erstwhile tory M.P. Sir John Philipps. Philipps' speech was published by William Owen, who argued that 'the Case of Mr. Murray [was] in some Sense the Case and Concern of every Man in Great Britain'. The similarity with Wilkes' description of the significance of his own case to Chief-Justice Pratt in 1762 may not be accidental: William Owen was charged with libel in 1752, was tried by Pratt, and went on to act as printer for Wilkes. See *The Argument of Sir John Philipps, Bart* (1751), iv; Cannon, *Parliamentary Reform*, 58–9. For Wilkite songs and colours, see John Brewer, 'Political Argument and Propaganda in England, 1760–70' (Ph.D. dissertation, Cambridge University, 1973), 21, 156.

73. Lord Fitzmaurice, *Life of William, Earl of Shelburne, afterwards First Marquess of Lansdowne* (2 vols., 1875), I, 49.

74. William Bromley to Oxford, 20 March 1733, enclosing a transcript of Parson's speech taken down *verbatim*, B.L. Loan 29/36 (unsorted). One realises from this extract just how much has been lost by the parliamentary reporters' 'refinement' of speeches.

75. J. G. A. Pocock, 'Virtue and Commerce in the Eighteenth Century', *Journal of Interdisciplinary History*, III (1972), 122–4.

CHAPTER 7

1. Quoted in Eveline G. Cruickshanks, 'The Tories and the Succession to the Crown in the 1714 Parliament', *B.I.H.R.*, XLVI (1973), 179, and see 176.

2. For two detailed if rather different accounts of whig and tory behaviour at the end of Anne's reign, see B. W. Hill, 'The Career of Robert Harley, Earl of Oxford, from 1702 to 1714' (unpub. Ph.D. dissertation, Cambridge University, 1961), 332–70, and Edward Gregg, *Queen Anne* (1980), 330–96. For Marlborough's invasion plans, see Ragnhild Hatton, *George I, Elector and King* (1978), 107.

3. P. W. J. Riley *The English Ministers and Scotland 1707–27* (1964), 296; Gregg, *Queen Anne*, 380–5.

4. John Dunton, *Neck or Nothing* (1714), 8, and cf. *Impeachment or no Impeachment* (1714), 19. See J. A. Downie, *Robert Harley and the Press: Propaganda and Public Opinion in the Age of Swift and Defoe* (Cambridge, 1979), 172–80, for the two parties' propaganda battle at the end of Anne's reign.

5. For Anne's belated decision to modify her administration, see Philip Roberts (ed.), *The Diary of Sir David Hamilton 1709–14* (Oxford, 1975), 66. For Bolingbroke's behaviour at Anne's death, see Elizabeth Handasyde, *Granville the Polite: the Life of George Granville, Lord Lansdowne, 1666–1735* (1933), 138; for Harcourt's behaviour, see Gregg, *Queen Anne*, 393.

6. Schütz to Nottingham, 22/11 May 1714, Leicestershire R.O., DG 7 Box 4950, Bundle 24. For a report on Bromley's loyalty to Hanover, see James Macpherson (ed.), *Original Papers; containing the Secret History of Great Britain from the Restoration, to the Accession of the House of Hannover* (2 vols., 1775), II, 552; see 556, 560–1, 576, 604, for other whig-derived verdicts on tory loyalty. For tory complaints that the Oxford administration was inadequately represented at Hanover, see *ibid.* 549 and G. E. Gregg, 'The Protestant Succession in International Politics, 1710–16' (unpub. Ph.D. dissertation, London University, 1972), 67, 75.

7. Lord Wharncliffe (ed.), *The Letters and Works of Lady Mary Wortley Montagu* (2 vols., 1887), I, 15. Ragnhild Hatton, *Diplomatic Relations between Great Britain and the Dutch Republic 1714–21* (1950), 54–6. Craggs' letter to Robethon is printed in Macpherson (ed.), *Original Papers*, II, 645.

8. Hatton, *George I*, 119–28. For Oxford's reaction to the Hanoverian announcement in December 1711, see Gregg, *Queen Anne*, 346.

9. For George's North German concerns, see Hatton, *George I*, 84–5, 184–92. Tory writers naturally stressed the disadvantages of Hanoverian confinement to one party, e.g. *The Whigs Address to His Majesty* (1715): 'We who all Monarchy despise / Hope to find favour in your eyes; / Think you a Protestant so hearty / As not to disoblige our Party / . . . Grant this request, your cause we'll own, / And ease the Burthen of the Crown; / Make it the easiest e'er was worn, / You'll scarce know you've any on.' Such caveats were not disinterested, but Lord Chesterfield's advice to Newcastle in 1745 on coercing Granville and through him George II; 'It is surely time to show [him] . . . that, as you can do what you will there [i.e. in the House of Commons] you will do what he won't like', confirms their accuracy. See Richard Pares, *King George III and the Politicians* (Oxford, 1953), 94–5.

10. 'Memorandums of Things which I have Heard in Private from Archbishop Potter's own Mouth, as certain Truths by Dr. Chapman', *Christian Remembrancer*, III (1821), 338; see also Halifax to Cowper, 5 May 1715, Hertfordshire R.O., D/EP F55.

11. Friedrich Wilhelm von der Schulenburg to Friedrich Wilhelm von Görtz, 30 November N.s. 1717. Schulenburg's letters, which are invaluable as a source for British high politics 1717–19, are in the Gräflich Görtzisches Archiv, Hesse Staatsarchiv, Darmstadt, Section 121/6. I am most grateful to Professor Ragnhild Hatton for supplying me with copies of these papers and for her advice on this chapter in general.

12. Poulet to Dartmouth, 20 October 1715, Staffordshire R.O., D/1778/I/ii/487; Hatton, *George I*, 123.

13. Edward Nicholas to Lord Guernsey, 3 September 1714, John Bland to Aylesford, 27 October 1714, and Richard Shuttleworth to Heneage Finch, 12 October 1714, Chatsworth House, Finch Halifax MSS., Box 3, Letters 101, 106, 118.

14. Anglesey cited in *The Works of Lord Bolingbroke* (4 vols., 1844), I, 131; Aylesford to Nottingham, n.d., Lord Townshend to Aylesford, 20 August 1715, Chatsworth House, Finch Halifax MSS., Box 3, Letter 152, Box 4, Bundle 12; Musgrave to James Grahme, 4 December 1714, Kendal R.O., Bagot MSS., Box D.

15. Brydges to Hammond, 7 December 1714, H.L.S.M., ST 57/11, fols. 157–8; J. J. Cartwright, *The Wentworth Papers 1705–39* (1883), 429.

16. For some evidence that George I may not have been apprised of all the tory purges that were carried on in his name, see J. Nichols (ed.), *The Epistolary Correspondence of the Right Reverend Francis Atterbury, Bishop of Rochester* (4 vols., 1783), II, 47n. For removals from the judiciary, see John Oldmixon, *The History of England, during the Reigns of King William and Queen Mary, Queen Anne, King George I* (1735), 576, 582; for the Court, J. M. Beattie, *The English Court in the Reign of George I* (Cambridge, 1967), 177–9; for the Army, Charles Dalton, *George the First's Army 1714–27* (2 vols., 1910–12), I, 183–217, II, 117–25.

17. Tory removals as well as tory survivals within the lower administrative ranks may be traced in J. C. Sainty, *Treasury Officials 1660–1870* (1972); *Officials of the Secretaries of State 1660–1832* (1973); *Officials of the Board of Trade*

1660–1870 (1974); and *Admiralty Officials 1660–1870* (1975), and J. M. Collinge, *Navy Board Officials 1660–1832* (1978). For the revenue departments see Edward Hughes, *Studies in Administration and Finance 1588–1825* (Manchester, 1934), 271–7.

18. Sir William Pole to Morice, 13 November 1715, Bank of England, COU/B151/11, fol. 357; Lady Cowper's diary, 12 February 1715, Hertfordshire R.O., D/EP F205, fol. 28; Hatton, *George I*, 148–9; B.L. Add. MS. 47088, fol. 12.

19. G. M. Trevelyan, *England under Queen Anne: the Peace and the Protestant Succession* (1934), 319; L. K. J. Glassey, 'The Commission of the Peace 1675–1720' (D.Phil. dissertation, Oxford University, 1972), 350–85.

20. Cowper's memorandum, Hertfordshire R.O., D/EP F152; Glassey, 'Commission of the Peace', 357–8.

21. For one version of the Aldworth duel, see Thomas Peach to Cave, 19 February 1715, Leicestershire R.O., 23 D 57/2927; Cartwright, *Wentworth Papers*, 421. Second earl of Oxford's notes on Bolingbroke, B.L. Loan 29/21 (unfol.). For Newcastle's activities in 1715 see James L. Fitts, 'Newcastle's Mob', *Albion*, v (1973), 41–9.

22. *Some Thoughts of an Honest Tory in the Country upon the Late Disposition of some People to Revolt* (1716), 19. Wyndham's 1714 rebuke to Lansdowne (who had wanted to stage a restoration as soon as Anne died) is printed in Handasyde, *Granville the Polite*, 137.

23. *H.M.C. Portland*, VII, 200; Lord Harley's commonplace book for 16 and 18 August 1714, B.L. Loan 29/337; Oxford to Dartmouth, 'Friday night', *H.M.C. Dartmouth*, I, 321.

24. *The Secret History of the White Staff*, Pts I, II (1714). Oxford denied responsibility for its publication: see Henry L. Snyder, 'The Last Days of Queen Anne: the Account of Sir John Evelyn Examined', *Huntington Library Quarterly*, XXXIV (1971), 265n.

25. A. M. Ross, 'The Correspondence of Dr John Arbuthnot' (unpub. Ph.D. dissertation, Cambridge University, 1956), 349. For Oxford's relationship with and reputation at the Hanoverian Court, see Gregg, 'Protestant Succession', 61–256; B. W. Hill, 'Oxford, Bolingbroke, and the Peace of Utrecht', *H.J.*, XVI (1973), 241–63; Derek McKay, 'Bolingbroke, Oxford and the Defence of the Utrecht Settlement in Southern Europe', *E.H.R.*, LXXXVI (1971), 264–84.

26. Brydges to Bolingbroke, 23 September 1714, and see also Brydges to Lord Stanhope, 6 October 1714, H.L.S.M., ST 57/10, fols. 263–4, ST 57/11, fol. 33. H. N. Fieldhouse, 'Bolingbroke and the d'Iberville Correspondence', *E.H.R.*, LII (1937), 673–5.

27. For reports of meetings among the premier tory peers, see *The Political State of Great Britain*, IX (1715), 50; [Francis Atterbury], *English Advice to the Freeholders of England* (1714), 15, 20. Viscount Perceval thought this pamphlet crucial: 'It was not till now, that the King withdrew the favourable opinions he had of the Torys' (B.L. Add. MS. 47087, fol. 90). Given Atterbury's appeal to royal self-interest, one wonders which whig minister drew the King's attention to the piece and how much of it he was able to read.

28. W. A. Speck, 'The General Election of 1715', *E.H.R.*, XC (1975), 507–22.

29. Thomas Carte to Samuel Carte, 13 September 1714, Bodleian Library, MS. Carte 244, fol. 165. The other tory county losses were Sussex (two seats), Gloucestershire, Carmarthenshire, Pembrokeshire, and Radnorshire (one seat each). In Staffordshire and Cambridgeshire high/Jacobite tory candidates were defeated by whimsical tories. In Kent twenty-one tory J.P.s who had voted in 1713 abstained in 1715; see Norma Landau, 'Independence, Deference and

Voter Participation: the Behaviour of the Electorate in Early-Eighteenth-Century Kent', *H.J.*, XXII (1979), 570.

30. The tories' other large borough losses were two seats at London, Norwich, and Nottingham, and one seat at Canterbury, Liverpool, Westminster, and York. The tories won both seats at Hereford in 1715 as against one in 1713.

31. On the Scottish elections in 1715 see Lord Montrose to Nottingham, 19 February 1715, B.L. Add. MS. 29589, fol. 466.

32. Lord Wharton to Lord Coningsby, 17 March 1715, B.L. Add. MS. 57861, fol. 178; Oldmixon, *History*, 592. See the ballad 'On the Proclamation' (1715), B.L. Lansdowne MS. 852, fol. 161.

33. For the argument that the 1715 rebellion was to be attributed to plans laid by Oxford's administration, see *The Speech of Mr. Lechmere previous to the Impeachment of the Seven Lords* (1716), 2. The loyal initiative of Freman and Guernsey was recorded by Oldmixon, *History*, 603.

34. Moyle to Humphry Morice, 26 March 1715, Bank of England, COU/B151/11, fols. 331–2; Thomas Brodrick to Lord Midleton, 25 February and 19 April 1716, Guildford Muniment Room, Brodrick MSS., III, fols. 312, 368.

35. Anthony Corbière to Walpole, 3 July and 3 August 1716; transcripts of the Walpole (Wolterton) MSS. kindly lent me by Professor J. H. Plumb; W. A. Speck, 'The Whig Schism under George I', *Huntington Library Quarterly*, XL (1977), 171–9.

36. Strafford to his agent?, 22 November 1719, B.L. Add. MS. 22248, fols. 91–2. For defections among the tory peers in this period, see above, 61–2. George Bruere, Sir Roger Bradshaigh, Sir Richard Child, Thomas Crosse, Charles Eversfield, John Hardres, John Trevanion, Sir Edward Williams, and possibly Sir Robert Worsley can be classed as men elected as tories who defected between 1715 and 1722.

37. *Entertainer*, No. 43, 27 August 1718. For Lord Mar's analysis of tory options in 1716, see *H.M.C. Stuart*, II, 127. Spain supplied the Jacobites with the equivalent of £43 500 between 1715 and 1716; see Hatton, *George I*, 350 n. 12.

38. Walter Sichel, *Bolingbroke and his Times* (2 vols., 1901–2), II, 481; H. T. Dickinson, *Bolingbroke* (1970), 147–51. For Oxford's approaches to the Court in 1719 see *H.M.C. Portland*, V, 582, VII, 266; cf. Hatton, *George I*, 244, 360. For Bolingbroke's approval of the Peerage Bill, see Paul Baratier (ed.), *Lettres inédites de Bolingbroke à Lord Stair 1716–20* (Paris, 1939), 86.

39. J. H. Glover (ed.), *The Stuart Papers, printed from the Originals* (1847), 13.

40. For the Swedish plot, see C. J. Nordmann, *La Crise du nord au début XVIIIe siècle* (Paris, 1962), 69–205; J. J. Murray, *George I, the Baltic and the Whig Split of 1717* (1969), 243–349; Gregg, 'Protestant Succession', 272; and Paul Fritz, *The English Ministers and Jacobitism between the Rebellions of 1715 and 1745* (Toronto, 1975), 28–50, who also gives an account of the Spanish plot of 1719.

41. *Letters which Passed between Count Gyllenborg, the Baron Görtz, Sparre, and Others; relating to the Design of Raising a Rebellion in His Majesty's Dominions to be Supported by a Force from Sweden* (1717), 8; William Coxe, *Memoirs of the Life and Administration of Sir Robert Walpole, earl of Orford* (3 vols., 1798), II, 75–8.

42. J. H. Plumb, *Sir Robert Walpole* (2 vols., 1956, 1960), I, 240–5.

43. The ministry's difficulties emerge clearly from Schulenburg's reports to Görtz: see his letters of 23 April, 9 and 23 July, 17 August, and 26 November N.S. 1717, Görtz Archive. See also Atterbury's report to Mar, 14 December 1717, Glover (ed.), *The Stuart Papers*, 13–14.

44. 'Diary of Rev. John Thomlinson', *Six North Country Diaries*, Publications of the Surtees Society, CXVIII (1910), 93. Trevor was expected to be made Lord President; see J. M. Croker (ed.), *Letters to and from Henrietta, Countess of Suffolk and her Second Husband the Hon. George Berkeley from 1712 to 1767* (2 vol., 1824), I, 19. The Treasury repayment of Oxford was noted by Roger Millart to Sir Justinian Isham, 20 August 1717, Northamptonshire R.O., IC 2142. For a Harleyite view of the Court's approaches to Bolingbroke, see *H.M.C. Portland*, VII, 228.

45. Schulenburg to Görtz, 18 June and 30 November N.S 1717, Görtz Archive; Carnarvon to Bolingbroke, 5 October 1717, H.L.S.M., ST 57/13, fols. 58, 93.

46. Bolingbroke to Stair, 17 December 1717; he repeated the warning on 19 January 1718; Baratier (ed.), *Lettres inédites*, 46, 57. For Trevor's negotiations with the Court, see Carnarvon to Harcourt, 3 November 1717 and January 1718, H.L.S.M., ST 57/13, fols. 78, 92.

47. For Walpole's sporadic collaboration with the tories at this time see Plumb, *Walpole*, I, 249–72.

48. Lord Finch to Nottingham, 26 and 31 December 1717 and 12 January 1718, Leicestershire R.O., DG 7 Box 4951, bundle 25. For the tories' approach to the Prince, see Schulenburg to Görtz, 4 January N.S., 1718, Görtz Archive.

49. Gibson to Nicolson, 28 November 1717, Bodleian Library, MS. Add. A269, fol. 71; Bishop Nicolson's diary, 18 March 1717, Tullie House, Carlisle, Ware Transcripts.

50. Schulenburg to Görtz, 10 March 1718, Görtz Archive.

51. Cathcart to Lord Loudoun, 22 February and 4 March 1718, H.L.S.M., LO 7945, 7930.

52. Smalridge to Dr Charlett, 12 January 1719, Bodleian Library, MS. Ballard 7, fol. 68; Stephen W. Baskerville, 'The Management of the Tory Interest in Lancashire and Cheshire, 1714–47' (unpub. D.Phil. dissertation, Oxford University, 1976), 111. For high-tory attendance in January 1718 including fifty Members 'qui n'ont pas mis le pied dans la maison tant que le Roy est sur le Trone', see Schulenburg to Görtz, 28 January 1718, Görtz Archive.

53. For one of Craggs' tory initiatives see Sedgwick, I, 529 (under Sir William Carew); Auditor Harley to Oxford, 3 March 1719/20, B.L. Loan 29/143; for Oxford and the Peerage Bill, see *H.M.C. Portland*, VII, 265–6.

54. *H.M.C. Portland*, VII, 273–4.

55. Atterbury to James Stuart, 6 May 1720, R.A. SP 46/110; *Commentator*, No. 35, 29 April 1720.

56. For the South Sea Company and its collapse see P. G. M. Dickson, *The Financial Revolution in England: a Study in the Development of Public Credit 1688–1756* (1967), 90–156; W. R. Scott, *The Constitution and Finance of English, Scottish and Irish Joint-Stock Companies to 1720* (3 vols., Cambridge, 1911), III, 296–352; John Carswell, *The South Sea Bubble* (1960), 115–249.

57. This estimate of tory South Sea stock purchasers is based on *Index Rerum et Vocabulorem for the use of Freeholders of Counties and Freemen of Corporations* (1722); for the Commons report on holders of illicit stock, see *C.J.*, XIX, 441, 570. Atterbury to General Dillon, 22 October 1720, R.A. SP 49/78.

58. *C.J.*, XIX, 399. The tories on the Committee of Inquiry were Archibald Hutcheson, Edward Jefferies, General Charles Ross, Thomas Strangways, and the Hon. Dixie Windsor. Mountwood to Samuel Carte, 2 March 1721, Bodleian Library, MS. Carte 239, but see *H.M.C. Various Collections*, VIII, 300, where the whig M.P. for Great Bedwyn, William Sloper, is listed as a committee defector rather than Brodrick.

59. Brodrick to Lord Midleton, 16 March 1721, *Guildford Muniment Room*, Brodrick MSS., iv, fol. 430; Plumb, *Walpole*, i, 329–58.

60. R.A. SP 53/13. For Atterbury's intrigues with Sunderland see G. V. Bennett, *The Tory Crisis in Church and State 1688–1730: the Career of Francis Atterbury, Bishop of Rochester* (Oxford, 1975), 225–31; Sedgwick, i, 108–9.

61. *H.M.C. Portland*, v, 614–15. For Harcourt's role as intermediary between the tories and Sunderland see *ibid.* vii, 307, and John Evelyn's diary for 21 August and 8 September 1721, Christ Church, Oxford, Evelyn MSS.

62. For a conservative assessment of Sunderland's relationship with George I, see Hatton, *George I*, 210, 354 n. 94.

63. *Copies of some Letters from Mr. Hutcheson to the Late Earl of Sunderland* (1722), 16; Henry L. Snyder, 'The Pardon of Lord Bolingbroke', *H.J.*, xiv (1971), 227–40.

64. Bromley to James Grahme, 1 September 1721, Kendal R.O., Bagot MSS., Box B; Oxford to Lord Harley, 14 July 1721, B.L. Loan 29/96.

65. For a whig view of Sunderland's difficulties with the King see G. Webb (ed.), *The Complete Works of Sir John Vanbrugh* (4 vols., 1927–8), iv, 142–3. For Hutcheson's Election Bill, see *C.J.*, xix, 697–738. The expunged protest is in B.L. Blenheim Papers, D I. 38b.

66. In general I have followed the account of the Atterbury plot given by G. V. Bennett, *Tory Crisis*, 223–75, and 'Jacobitism and the Rise of Walpole', in Neil McKendrick (ed.), *Historical Perspectives: Studies in English Thought and Society in honour of J. H. Plumb* (1974), 70–92.

67. Strafford to James Stuart, 18 May 1722, R.A. SP 59/118A; Lord Mahon, *History of England from the Peace of Utrecht to the Peace of Versailles 1713–1783* (3rd edn, 7 vols., 1853–4), ii, App., xix–xx; Harold Williams (ed.), *Correspondence of Jonathan Swift* (5 vols., Oxford, 1963–5), ii, 383. Fritz is entirely wrong to claim, in *English Ministers and Jacobitism*, 44, that Lord Oxford was the leader of a 'set' of English Jacobites which included Poulet, Foley, Dartmouth, Bingley, and Auditor Harley. Oxford certainly maintained a desultory and opaque correspondence with Rome after 1717; there is no evidence that he was a committed activist, whereas there is considerable evidence for his approaches to George I. The 'set' which Fritz describes consists merely of Oxford's chief friends and relations, for whose Jacobitism there is even less evidence.

68. R.A. SP 48/69; Bathurst to Atterbury, 18 September 1721, P.R.O., SP 35/28/57a; Bennett, *Tory Crisis*, 233.

69. Bromley to James Grahme, 22 April 1722, Kendal R.O., Bagot MSS., Box B; Hutcheson to Cowper, 25 April, and Strafford to Cowper, 28 April 1722, Hertfordshire R.O., D/EP F55; *H.M.C. Fifteenth Report*, App., vii, 226–7.

70. Robert Digby to Lord Digby, 7 March 1723, Digby Transcripts (see above, Ch. 3, n. 21), fols. 61–2. For Hanmer, Harley, and Freman during this crisis, see *C.J.*, xx, 12, 167–8.

71. Bathurst to Lord Gower, 5 October 1722, Staffordshire R.O., D/868/7, fol. 18a; Sir Justinian Isham to his son, 9 October 1722, Northamptonshire R.O., IC 1845.

72. Robert Digby to Lord Digby, 18 October and 27 November 1722, Digby Transcripts, fols. 47–8, 50; Bennett, *Tory Crisis*, 265–6, 272.

73. Stair to Lord Loudoun, 2 January 1724, H.L.S.M., LO 7628; J. M. Graham, *Annals and Correspondence of the Viscount and the First and Second Earls of Stair* (2 vols., Edinburgh, 1875), ii, 341.

74. 'His Grace the Duke of Wharton's Reasons for Leaving his Native Country &

Espousing the Cause of his Royal Master King James 3 in a Letter to his Friends in G. Britain & Ireland', Bodleian Library, Eng. Hist. Misc. c. 374, fol. 25. For Rialton see Sedgwick, II, 66–7. Onslow's assessment of the Atterbury crisis is in *H.M.C. Fourteenth Report*, App., IX, 462–5.

75. *Memoirs of the Life and Ministerial Conduct . . . of the late Lord Visc. Bolingbroke* (1752), 337; Gibson to Nicolson, 11 November 1721, Bodleian Library, MS. Add. A269, fol. 101; for Trenchard in 1723, see Robert Digby to Lord Digby, 12 March 1723, Digby Transcripts, fol. 66.

76. James Hamilton to James Stuart, 20 November 1722, R.A. SP 63/33; Coxe, *Memoirs of Sir Robert Walpole*, II, 264–5.

CHAPTER 8

1. *A Letter to Mr. P[ulteney] in which the Controversy betwixt the Friends of the Present Administration and Him Is Fairly Stated* (1731), 10; [W. Pulteney], *An Answer to One Part of a Late Infamous Libel . . . in which the Character and Conduct of Mr. P[ulteney] Is Fully Vindicated* (1731), 17.

2. E.g. Isaac Kramnick, *Bolingbroke and his Circle: the Politics of Nostalgia in the Age of Walpole* (1968); H. T. Dickinson, *Bolingbroke* (1970), 184–276; Bertrand A. Goldgar, *Walpole and the Wits: the Relation of Politics to Literature, 1722–42* (Lincoln, Neb., 1976); M. M. Goldsmith, 'Faction Detected: Ideological Consequences of Robert Walpole's Decline and Fall', *History*, LXIV (1979), 1–19.

3. Archibald S. Foord, *His Majesty's Opposition 1714–1830* (Oxford, 1964), 167–8. Compare Sir Thomas Robinson's report of a 'general conclusive meeting' at the Patriot duke of Queensborough's house on 9 February 1735, 'when all the Minority Lords were summoned, but not one of the Tories attended', with an opposition account of the same meeting, which shows that Lords Berkshire, Scarsdale, Denbigh, Bathurst, and Gower were not only present but also spoke. *H.M.C. Fifteenth Report*, App., VI, 148, and G. H. Rose (ed.), *A Selection from the Papers of the Earls of Marchmont illustrative of Events from 1685–1750* (3 vols., 1831), II, 64–5.

4. *C.J.*, XXI, 795–6. For the Macclesfield affair, see *C.J.*, XX, 379–80, 408; cf. J. A. Downie, 'The Commission of Public Accounts and the Formation of the Country Party', *E.H.R.*, XCI (1976), 33–51. For the Gaols Committee, see *C.J.*, XXI, 237–8, and Lewis Namier, *England in the Age of the American Revolution* (2nd edn, 1974), 188.

5. Dickinson, *Bolingbroke*, 177–8; Lord Weston to Dartmouth, 13 May [1725], Staffordshire R.O., D/1778/v/580a.

6. Thomas Brodrick to Lord Midleton, 24 April and 4 and 6 May 1725, Guildford Muniment Room, Brodrick MSS., vol. VI, fols. 207, 222–3. Harcourt's wider expectations from the April 1725 motion emerge from Mrs Charles Caesar's diary. After Bolingbroke had committed himself to the opposition, she wrote of the 'Disappointment I knew he [Harcourt] had Met with in Lord Bolingbroke. He not Answering the Purpose for which he had long labour'd to bring him Home' (Bodleian Library, MS. Film 740).

7. Conflicting versions of Bolingbroke's approach to the Court in 1725 can be found in 'Horace Walpole's Marginal Notes written in Dr Maty's Miscellaneous Works and Memoirs of the Earl of Chesterfield', *Miscellanies of the Philobiblon Society*, X (1866–7), 12–15, and William Coxe, *Memoirs of the Life and Administration of Sir Robert Walpole, Earl of Orford* (3 vols., 1798), II, 340–5.

8. For contemporaries' anticipation of 'Changes amongst the Great' in 1725, see

G. Webb (ed.), *The Complete Works of Sir John Vanbrugh* (4 vols., 1927–8), IV, 172; *H.M.C. Various Collections*, VIII, 390; *H.M.C. Portland*, VII, 399, 401, 407, 411; J. H. Glover (ed.), *The Stuart Papers, printed from the Originals* (1847), 179. Poulet to Dartmouth, 11 November 1726, Staffordshire R.O., D/1778/v/592; Lord Oxford to Dr William Stratford, n.d., B.L. Loan 29/171.

9. For the Leicester House tradition that George I wanted a mixed administration, see James Lee McKelvey, *George III and Lord Bute: the Leicester House Years* (Durham, N.C., 1973), 85–6. Pulteney's followers in 1727 are listed in Sedgwick, I, 86.

10. For Walpole's difficulties with Prince George, and his improved relationship with the King by 1725, see J. H. Plumb, *Sir Robert Walpole* (2 vols., 1956, 1960), II, 162–4, and Ragnhild Hatton, *George I Elector and King* (1978), 256–60.

11. Strafford to Sir Justinian Isham, 29 June 1727, Northamptonshire R.O., IC 2967. For the tories' enthusiasm for George II, see Lord Orrery to James Stuart, 30 June 1727, R.A. SP 107/150; *C.J.*, XXI, 3.

12. Coxe, *Memoirs of Sir Robert Walpole*, I, 283. For the mutual aversion between Sunderland and Leicester House, see R.A. Georgian Add. MS. 28/74, and Hatton, *George I*, 214, 355 n. 8. The Prince's indifference to Bolingbroke is described by William Bromley to James Grahme, 18 July 1725, Kendal R.O., Bagot MSS., Box B.

13. Lord King, 'Notes of Domestic and Foreign Affairs', *The Life of John Locke, with Extracts from his Correspondence* (2 vols., 1830), II, 47; Plumb, *Walpole*, II, 165–72.

14. *H.M.C. Egmont*, II, 164–5; transcript of a letter (1734) from the Hertfordshire dissenter, Robert Berry, to William Wilshere, kindly lent me by Mr Lionel Mumby.

15. L. K. J. Glassey, 'The Commission of the Peace 1675–1720' (D. Phil. dissertation, Oxford University, 1972), 387; Lord King to Lord Lonsdale, 18 July 1730, and Lonsdale to King, 3 August 1730, Cumbria R.O., D/Lons Checklist 16/22–3.

16. King, *Life of Locke*, II, 49–50. See John Owen's skilful rescue operation on George II, 'George II Reconsidered', in Anne Whiteman, J. S. Bromley, and P. G. M. Dickson (eds.), *Statesmen, Scholars and Merchants: Essays in Eighteenth-Century History presented to Dame Lucy Sutherland* (Oxford, 1973), 113–34.

17. Mrs Caesar's diary, Bodleian Library, MS. Film 740. This is my own conservative estimate of the tory candidature in 1727, based on information in Sedgwick, I, 189–381.

18. *Parl. Hist.*, VIII, 642; Pulteney cited by Thomas Winnington to Lord Hervey, 24 March 1729, Dorset R.O., D124, Box 240 (unsorted): I am indebted to Dr W. A. Speck for this reference, *H.M.C. Fifteenth Report*, App., VI, 57.

19. Viscount Perceval's journal for 16 and 27 February 1730, B.L. Add. MS. 47060, fols. 25, 38.

20. Cruickshanks in Sedgwick, I, 67–8; cf. Coxe, *Memoirs of Sir Robert Walpole*, I, 320. For Anglo-French relations in this period, see A. M. Wilson, *French Foreign Policy during the Administration of Fleury, 1726–43* (Cambridge, Mass., 1936); G. C. Gibbs, 'Britain and the Alliance of Hanover, April 1725–February 1726', and 'Parliament and Foreign Policy in the Age of Stanhope and Walpole', in R. Mitchison (ed.), *Essays in Eighteenth Century History from the English Historical Review* (1966), 260–86, 326–45.

21. Dickinson, *Bolingbroke*, 225–8; Booth's reports are in B.L. Loan 29/38. For Shippen, see *Parl. Hist.*, VIII, 778–9.

22. M. Wyndham (ed.), *Chronicles of the Eighteenth Century* (2 vols., 1924), I, 77.

For tory assistance of Daniel Pulteney in 1727, see Stephen W. Baskerville, 'The Management of the Tory Interest in Lancashire and Cheshire, 1714–47' (unpub. D.Phil. dissertation, Oxford University, 1976), 161.

23. Plumb, *Walpole*, II, 195–202. Sedgwick, I, 95, finds Speaker Onslow not guilty of opposition tendencies in the late 1720s, but see King, *Life of Locke*, II, 51, and the *Craftsman* mailing list for 1730, C.U.L., C(H) MS. P 74/72.

24. For tory hopes of employment in 1729, see *H.M.C. Fifteenth Report*, App., VI, 62, and *Parl. Hist.*, VIII, 703. William Pulteney's ambitions in 1729 were avowedly more extensive; see Sedgwick, II, 375.

25. John Ivory Talbot to Lord Bruce, 13 March 1729, Wiltshire R.O., Savernake MSS. (unsorted); Sedgwick, II, 11–12, 121–2, 341–2.

26. Edward Harley's parliamentary journal for 8 March 1736, C.U.L., Add. 6851, fol. 55.

27. C.U.L., C(H) MS. P 74/72. For the *Craftsman*, see M. Harris, 'The London Newspaper Press, 1725–46' (unpub. Ph.D. dissertation, London University, 1974), and S. R. Varey, 'The Craftsman 1726–52: An Historical and Critical Account' (unpub. Ph.D. dissertation, Cambridge University, 1976).

28. Information derived from Sedgwick, I, 409–11, 424–5, 546–7; II, 153, 205, 298–9, 372–4, 505–6.

29. Sandys to Sir John Dutton, 28 March 1742, Gloucestershire R.O., D 678 57D/186; Sandys' diary, 14 October 1722, Bodleian Library, MS. D. D. Dashwood (Bucks), D 1/2, fol. 9.

30. For Pulteney's oratory on the theme of 'resistance', see George Harbin to Thomas Carew, 24 February and 3 March 1737, Somerset R.O., DD/TB/Box FT 18; Pulteney to the duchess of Marlborough, 22 November 1734, B.L. Blenheim Papers, E 38; Pulteney to the duke of Somerset, 29 July 1739, Devonshire R.O., 1392 M/L 1837/2.

31. *C.J.*, XXI, 803, 818, 831, 848, 850, 856; Harley's journal, C.U.L., Add. 6851, fols. 30–1.

32. For the Cassiobury meeting, see Henry Pelham to Lord Essex, 5 January 1733, B.L. Add. MS. 27732, fol. 80.

33. For the Excise Bill, see Paul Langford, *The Excise Crisis* (Oxford, 1975); Plumb, *Walpole*, II, 233–83; Basil Williams, 'The Duke of Newcastle and the Elections of 1734', *E.H.R.*, XII (1897), 448–88; E. R. Turner, 'The Excise Scheme of 1733', *E.H.R.*, XLII (1927), 34–55.

34. J. C. Sainty and D. Dewar, *Divisions in the House of Lords: an Analytical List 1685 to 1857* (1976), microfiche entries for 1732. For the source of these estimates of tory attendance during the Excise debates, see Appendix, Table 1.

35. Langford lists forty-eight constituencies and six unrepresented towns as instructing against the Excise Bill, *Excise Crisis*, 172.

36. London's anti-Excise campaign is described *ibid.* 46–93 *passim*, and see Nicholas Rogers, 'Resistance to Oligarchy: the City Opposition to Walpole and his Successors, 1725–47', in John Stevenson (ed.), *London in the Age of Reform* (Oxford, 1977), 1–29. For the Goldsmiths' Hall banquet, see Nathaniel Mist to Rome, 13 March 1733, R.A. SP 160/21.

37. Mrs Caesar's diary, Bodleian Library, MS. Film 740; Langford, *Excise Crisis*, 52n.

38. For the Rochester election, see Dr Curteis to the duke of Dorset, 21 September 1733, Kent R.O., U269 C148/8; for Taunton, see *The Downfall of Bribery: the Honest Men of Taunton* (1733); George II cited in B. W. Hill, *The Growth of Parliamentary Parties 1689–1742* (1976), 205.

39. *The Loyal or Revolutionary Tory* (1733), 60–1. For an example of government

whig nervousness at the apparent tory resurgence, see Baron Scrope to Sir John Dutton, 28 July 1733, Gloucestershire R.O., D 678/ 57D/188.

40. Romney Sedgwick (ed.), *Some Materials towards Memoirs of the Reign of King George II, by John, Lord Hervey* (3 vols., 1931), I, 181. For Wyndham and the Customs ballot, see Perceval's diary, 25 April 1733, B.L. Add. MS. 47062, fol. 66. The rival lists for the ballot are in *H.M.C. Fifteenth Report*, App., VI, 112. The eight tory M.P.s were Sir Francis Child, Hon. George Compton, Sir John Hynde Cotton, Edward Harley, William Noel, Sir Thomas Sebright, and Wyndham himself. Walpole was being deliberately alarmist when he claimed at the 23 April meeting that half of the opposition's nominees were tory.

41. Coxe, *Memoirs of Sir Robert Walpole*, III, 134.

42. Colonel Howard cited in *H.M.C. Fifteenth Report*, App., VI, 113. For the debate on the repeal of the Septennial Act, see *Parl. Hist.*, IX, 392–478, and *The Fitness of Repealing the Septennial Act* (1740).

43. H. A. Wyndham, *A Family History, 1688–1837: the Wyndhams of Somerset, Sussex and Wiltshire* (1950), 89; C. Collyer, 'The Yorkshire Election of 1734', *Proceedings of the Leeds Philosophical and Literary Society*, VII (1952–5), 53–82.

44. Electoral manifesto, Kent R.O., U269 C148. The poll book for this county contest was consulted at the Institute of Historical Research: I have omitted the out-voters from the analysis.

45. Lord Winchilsea to Lord Bruce, 9 October 1733, Wiltshire R.O., Savernake MSS. (unsorted). For correspondence on the 1734 Buckinghamshire election, see Buckinghamshire R.O., D/LE/A/2/2, D/LE/A/2/5, D/LE/A/3/1/D: the MS. poll book for the county election is D/MH 40/2.

46. I estimate that the opposition's post-electoral strength was 227 M.P.s. For the Patriot whigs who retired or were defeated in 1734, see Sedgwick, I, 87–8.

47. These newspaper extracts are printed in the *Gentleman's Magazine*, IV (1734), 242, 370; V (1735), 586. See also the *London Journal* of 6 July 1734: 'near four fifths of the minority are determined tories . . . there is near one third more in Number than were chosen into the Old House'.

48. Calculations on Walpolian strength in the House of Lords in 1734–5 are based on the relevant microfiche entries in Sainty and Dewar, *Divisions*. On the Rumpsteak Club, compare Egmont's assertion 'They will not suffer a Tory to be of it', 26 January 1734, B.L. Add. MS. 47064, fol. 6b, with the list of members given in Rose, *Selection from the Marchmont Papers*, II, 19–20.

49. Lord Ilchester (ed.), *Lord Hervey and his Friends, 1726–38* (1950), 219–20. The rigged election of the Scottish representative peers and its aftermath can be traced in Rose, *Selection from the Marchmont Papers*, II, 50–65.

50. Coxe, *Memoirs of Sir Robert Walpole*, I, 321. For Cartaret and the opposition in 1735, see *H.M.C. Polwarth*, V, 97. Dr Thomas Newton, dean of St Paul's and a rather biased friend of Pulteney, claimed that apart from the Patriot leader few politicians supported the opposition's campaign 'with so much as a subscription of five guineas', *The Lives of Dr. Edward Pocock by Leonard Twells; of Dr. Zachary Pearce, and of Dr. Thomas Newton by Themselves and of the Rev. Philip Skelton by Mr. Burdy* (2 vols., 1816), II, 138. For Bolingbroke and the French government, see Paul Vaucher, *La Crise du Ministère Walpole en 1733–34* (Paris, 1924), 36–65.

51. Dickinson, *Bolingbroke*, 240–5; Coxe, *Memoirs of Sir Robert Walpole*, III, 137–41. For an example of anti-Bolingbroke electoral slogans, see Sir Basil Dixwell to the duke of Dorset, 6 November 1733, Kent R.O., U269 C148/54.

52. *Daily Gazetteer*, No. 276, 15 May 1736. In the Kent and Liverpool elections of

1734 some dissenters had supported the Patriot–tory candidates, but their behaviour was exceptional: see William Glanville to the duke of Dorset, 6 November 1733, Kent R.O., U269 C148/29, and Baskerville, 'Tory Interest', 302–4. For the Patriots and nonconformity, see *The Life of Thomas Story, abridged by John Kendall, revised by William Alexander* (2 vols., 1832), II, 218–20, 325, and N. C. Hunt, *Two Early Political Associations: the Quakers and the Dissenting Deputies in the Age of Sir Robert Walpole* (Oxford, 1961), 77–83, 130–62.

53. Hunt, *Two Early Political Associations*, 87–91. The House of Lords division list on the Quaker Tithe Bill is given in *An Account of the Proceedings and Debates on the Tithe Bill* (1737). Lord Bathurst was the only tory peer to vote in its support, and as he explained, his reasons were distinctive: 'In order to put the Proceedings of our Ecclesiastical Courts upon a better Foot; and at the same time to consider, whether any Thing can be done to satisfy the Quakers, without doing an Injury to the Clergy, I am for...committing the Bill', *ibid.*, 52.

54. Lechmere to his wife, 19 April 1737, Worcestershire R.O., Acc 5117, Box 64 iii.

55. For tory conduct in this debate, see George Harbin to Thomas Carew, 24 February and 3 March 1737, Somerset R.O., DD/TB/Box FT 18. In the House of Lords, Oxford, Northampton, and Strafford voted against an increased grant for the Prince, and Foley and Windsor abstained (*H.M.C. Fifteenth Report*, App., VI, 161–2).

56. *Parl. Hist.*, x, 380–3. For Bathurst and Prince George, see *Mist's Weekly Journal*, 14 August 1725, and Mrs Caesar's diary, Bodleian Library, MS. Film 740. Wyndham's ultimatum to the Prince is described by Egmont in his journal, 26 January 1738, B.L. Add. MS. 47068, fol. 49b.

57. Philip C. Yorke, *The Life and Correspondence of Philip Yorke, Earl of Hardwicke* (3 vols., Cambridge, 1913), I, 175; Coxe, *Memoirs of Sir Robert Walpole*, III, 506. For Wyndham's capture of the Prince see Hay's Journal, III, IV. By autumn 1739 Hay was describing Wyndham as the 'Conductor' of the Prince's party.

58. Walpole's subsidies to the government press between 1731 and 1741 can be gauged from the estimates of the 1742 Committee of Inquiry, and from the annual payments of secret service money to the Treasury's intermediary with the press, Thomas Lowther; see *C.J.*, XXIV, 316–17, 329–30. For Britain's relations with Spain, see J. O. McLachlan, *Trade and Peace with Old Spain, 1667–1750* (Cambridge, 1940), and H. W. V. Temperley, 'The Causes of the War of Jenkins' Ear, 1739', *T.R.H.S.*, 3rd ser., III (1909), 197–236.

59. The ministry's neglect and consequent tory capture of various parliamentary committees was noted by Egmont in 1737, B.L. Add. MS. 47067, fol. 47, and by Thomas Carte in 1738, R.A. SP 206/106. Cf. the pro-Walpolian assessment of the Rev. Henry Etough, in John Owen, *The Rise of the Pelhams* (1957), 8–9. In 1741 the duke of Newcastle estimated that the ministerial contingent in the Lords stood at 111, the opposition's at 61; yet ministerial attendance was sporadic and Walpole's average Lords majority in 1741–2 was less than 25. B.L. Add. MS. 33034, fols. 1–3; Sainty and Dewar, *Divisions*, microfiche entries for 1741 and January 1742.

60. The activities and ideas of this modified opposition coterie are best followed in Rose, *Selection from the Marchmont Papers*, II, 90–250. Wyndham's attitude to the Prince is discussed in Alexander Pope's letter to George Lyttelton, 1 November 1738, in George Sherbury (ed.), *The Correspondence of Alexander Pope* (5 vols., Oxford, 1956), IV, 42–3.

61. Horace Walpole summed up Broad-Bottom's ambivalence very well when he wrote in 1742 of 'The Tories ... if Tories there are, for now one hears of nothing but the Broad Bottom; it is the reigning cant word, and means, the taking all parties and people, indifferently, into the ministry. The Whigs are the dupes of this, and those in the Opposition, affirm that Tories no longer exist. Notwithstanding this, they will not come into the new ministry, unless what were always reckoned Tories are admitted.' W. S. Lewis *et al.* (eds.), *Horace Walpole's Correspondence with Sir Horace Mann, I*, The Yale Edition of Horace Walpole's Correspondence (New Haven, 1937–), xvii, 336–7; cf. John Brewer, *Party Ideology and Popular Politics at the Accession of George III* (Cambridge, 1976), 67–8.

62. For the Steadfast Society meeting, see Edward Southwell's memoranda, 7 November 1739, Bristol City Reference Library, Southwell Papers, v (unfol.); for Mackworth, see J. P. Jenkins, 'A Social and Political History of the Glamorgan Gentry c. 1650–1770' (unpub. Ph.D. dissertation, Cambridge University, 1978), 115–16; for Wrighte, see Chandler, ix, 10. The division list on the Convention is printed in the *Gentleman's Magazine*, ix (1739), 304–10. The Hon. Bussy Mansel paired with the Hon. Charles Fane and Charles Pelham paired with Edward Ashe.

63. Hay's Journal, iii. For the opposition's plans to secede in 1732, see *H.M.C. Egmont Diary*, i, 268. Walpole made a contemptuous reference to the secession after Atterbury's trial in his reply to Wyndham's declaration of intent, *Parl. Hist.*, x, 1323–4.

64. *H.M.C. Egmont Diary*, iii, 33, 41.

65. Rose, *Selection from the Marchmont Papers*, ii, 125. Horatio Walpole to Robert Trevor, 8/19 May 1739, *H.M.C. Fourteenth Report*, App., ix, 30.

66. Rose, *Selection from the Marchmont Papers*, ii, 143–4. Sir William Wyndham to the duke of Somerset, 4 December 1731, Devonshire R.O., 1392 M/L18 31/5; Edward Harley's notes on the Porteous affair, C.U.L., Add. 6851, fols. 95–6.

67. Coxe, *Memoirs of Sir Robert Walpole*, iii, 523–4.

68. Pratt to Richard Neville Aldworth, 10 December 1739, Essex R.O., D/DM A7–8. Some of the Instructions are reported in the *Gentleman's Magazine*, ix (1739), 548, 637–8, 650.

69. Hay's Journal, iii. For Pulteney's support of the royal speech, see John Campbell to Pryse Campbell, 22 November 1739, N.L.W., MS. 1352B, fol. 28.

70. *Parl. Hist.*, xi, 380. For the Crown and Anchor meeting see B.L. Loan 29/20 (unsorted) and Foord, *His Majesty's Opposition*, 173–4. Bonamy Dobrée (ed.), *The Letters of Philip Dormer Stanhope, 4th Earl of Chesterfield* (6 vols., 1932), ii, 435. For the British Club, see Velters Cornewall to William Brydges, 25 February 1744, Herefordshire R.O., A 81/32.

71. For the debate on 21 February 1741, see Edward Harley's diary, C.U.L., Add. 6851, ii, fol. 3. Barrymore's career is paradigmatic of the tory tendency to regard Jacobitism only as a last resort. In the late 1720s he had worked loyally for Lord Carteret in the Irish Privy Council; in 1740 he was still out of office and seventy-three years old. For Brett's mission, see Sempill to the Pretender, 28 March and 13 June 1740, and Sempill to Edgar, 18 April 1740, R.A. SP 221/109 and 178 and 223/124. For tory–Jacobite intrigue in this period, see R.A. SP 221–7.

72. *H.M.C. Fourteenth Report*, App., ix, 467.

73. It is impossible to reconstruct a precise list of tory rebels in the division of 13 February 1741; see the slightly different lists in the *Gentleman's Magazine*, xi (1741), 232, and Coxe, *Memoirs of Sir Robert Walpole*, iii, 563, and the

estimate by I. G. Doolittle, 'A First-Hand Account of the Commons Debate on the Removal of Sir Robert Walpole, 13 February 1741', *B.I.H.R.*, LIII (1980), 139–40. My own research would suggest that the tories who voted against the motion were J. Bankes, T. Cartwright, the Hon. G. Compton, Lord Cornbury, C. Cotes, C. Gore, T. Gore, H. Mackworth, W. Mackworth Praed, the Hon. B. Mansel, H. Marshall, the Hon. J. Noel, W. H. Packer, Sir H. P. Pakington, C. Sibthorp, and E. Southwell. The tories who withdrew were Lord Andover, Sir E. Bacon, J. Basset, the Hon. B. Bathurst, P. Bathurst, J. Browne, T. Carew, G. Chaffin, Sir W. Courtenay, J. Crewe, Sir N. Curzon, Sir J. Dashwood, the Hon. E. Digby, Lord Guernsey, E. Harley, R. Harley, J. Houblon, J. Hylton, E. Lechmere, W. Levinz, Sir C. Mordaunt, Sir J. Morgan, W. Noel, Sir H. Northcote, C. Pelham, J. Proby, T. Prowse, Lord Quarendon, T. Rowney, W. Shippen, E. Smith, Sir H. Smithson, W. Taylor, Sir C. Vernon, J. Wigley, A. Wodehouse, and G. Wrighte. I have included Rowney among the abstainers on the evidence of Edward Southwell to Robert Smith, 15 February 1741, Bristol City Reference Library, Southwell Papers, VI. I have excluded Henry Rolle, M.P. for Devon, from the tory opponents of the motion because he had gone over to the administration in 1739.

74. Velters Cornewall to William Brydges, 20 February 1741, Herefordshire R.O., A81/31; cf. Edward Harley's account of his abstention from the division, C.U.L., Add. 6851, II, fols. 24–5. For Jacobite support of the motion, see Lord Barrymore to Dr Francis Price, 17 February 1741, N.L.W., Puleston MS. 22, fol. 62.

75. Beaufort to Lord Gower, 27 August 1740, and Joseph Damer to the duke of Bedford, 7 October 1740, Bedford Estates Office, Bedford Correspondence, VIII, fols. 107, 111. *The Conduct of the Late and Present Ministry Compared* (1742), 5. In June 1741 Dodington wrote of a committee 'instituted to watch over and defend elections', Coxe, *Memoirs of Sir Robert Walpole*, III, 573.

76. Gower to Bruce, 5 September 1741 (my italics), and Pulteney to Bruce, 2 January 1741, Wiltshire R.O., Savernake MS. 3533. On 9 November 1740 Thomas Prowse had advised Thomas Carew that it would be better for the tory candidate at Wells to join with a ministerialist than with Dodington; 'a Man with such Principles, who has so strongly intimated that Sir Robert has it in his Power to make him his friend again' (Somerset R.O., DD/TB/ Box 15 FT 8). For the 1741 Bridgwater contest, see Sedgwick, I, 314.

77. Lord Thanet to Viscount Perceval, 19 November 1741, B.L. Add. MS. 47012B, fol. 55. Perceval's subscription list is in B.L. Add. MS. 47159, fol. 4. Charles Wyndham to Lord Gower, 28 May 1741, P.R.O., 30/29/1/11.

78. This list is in Bodleian Library, MS. Eng. Misc. b. 48. For other post-election calculations see H.L.R.O., Phillipps MSS., Lot 1633; B.L. Add. MSS. 35876, fols. 138–9, 33002, fols. 454–6.

79. For an excellent account of the final instalment of the opposition's campaign against Walpole, see Owen, *Rise of the Pelhams*, 1–40. ? to Peter Legh, 17 December 1741 (franked by Shippen, but not in his handwriting), John Rylands Library, Manchester, Bromley-Davenport MSS.

80. Cruickshanks in Sedgwick, I, 70–1.

81. For the Denbighshire meeting, see Thomas Price to John Myddelton, 29 October 1741, N.L.W., Chirk Castle MS. E4832; for the Liverpool meeting, see Baskerville, 'Tory Interest', 245. Dodington cited in Coxe, *Memoirs of Sir Robert Walpole*, III, 569–73.

82. George Bubb Dodington to ?, 4 February 1742, Bodleian Library, MS. Eng. Letters c. 144.

83. Pulteney to Jonathan Swift, 22 November 1735, Harold Williams (ed.), *Correspondence of Jonathan Swift* (5 vols., Oxford, 1963–5), IV, 436–7. For Rockinghamite interest in the secession, see Frank O'Gormon, *The Rise of Party in England: the Rockinghamite Whigs 1760–82* (1975), 291–2, 347–54.

84. Owen, *Rise of the Pelhams*, 42; Peter D. G. Thomas, *The House of Commons in the Eighteenth Century* (Oxford, 1971), 124–6.

85. For placemen in the Convention division, see the *Gentleman's Magazine*, IX (1739), 304–10. Owen, *Rise of the Pelhams*, 24, 56. On Oughton, see Sedgwick, II, 316.

86. This estimate is based on 'A Compleat List of Members', H.L.R.O., Phillipps MSS. Lot 1633 (Historical Collections 82), correlated with information on M.P.s in Sedgwick, I, II, *passim*.

87. 'Calculations of majorities', C.U.L., C(H) MS. 66/8. On Scrope, see Sedgwick, II, 413–14.

88. Sedgwick, I, 571. Burke's comment on Walpole is from *An Appeal from the New to the Old Whigs* (1791), printed in Kramnick, *Bolingbroke and his Circle*, 121.

89. Gray to Lord Egmont, 5 June 1749, A. N. Newman, 'Leicester House Politics, 1750–60', *Camden Miscellany*, XXIII (1969), 181.

CHAPTER 9

1. [James Oglethorpe], *The Naked Truth* (1755), 9. John Owen, *The Rise of the Pelhams* (1957), 88, 90, 97–8. Owen's account is crucial to an understanding of high politics between 1741 and 1747.

2. Archibald S. Foord, *His Majesty's Opposition 1714–1830* (Oxford, 1964), 256.

3. H.M.C. *Egmont Diary*, III, 252. William Parry to Thomas Rawlins, 13 March 1742, Bodleian Library, MS. Ballard 29, fol. 74. For Carteret's approach to the tories in 1743, see Owen, *Rise of the Pelhams*, 188–90.

4. Undated memorandum by Perceval, B.L. Add. MS. 47096 (unfol.). William Parry to Thomas Rawlins, 7 January 1742, Bodleian Library, MS. Ballard 29, fol. 73.

5. *Parl. Hist.*, XII, 434–5. Arthur Jessop's diary for 14 February 1742, in E. Whiting (ed.), *Two Yorkshire Diaries*, Yorkshire Archaeological Society Record Series, CXVII (1952), 70.

6. Sir John St Aubyn to William Borlase, 22 June 1742, Penzance Private Library, Borlase Letter Book, OL 47. Brickdale to Southwell, 10 February 1742, Bristol City Reference Library, Southwell Papers, VI. Moritt to Godfrey Wentworth, 2 February 1742, Brotherton Library, Special Collections, Wentworth of Woolley Papers, 15/3: I am grateful to John Styles for this reference.

7. Fox quoted in Betty Kemp, *Sir Francis Dashwood: an Eighteenth-Century Independent* (1967), 3.

8. Orford to Pelham, 31 October 1742, printed in William Coxe, *Memoirs of the Administration of the Rt. Hon. Henry Pelham* (2 vols., 1829), I, 35.

9. For Master, see Stephen W. Baskerville, 'The Management of the Tory Interest in Lancashire and Cheshire, 1714–47' (unpub. D.Phil. dissertation, Oxford University, 1976), 315–16; for Isham, *Weekly Worcester Journal*, No. 1708, 19/26 March 1742, and Charles to Sir Edmund Isham, 5 April 1742, Northamptonshire R.O., IC 2506. For Cotton in 1742, see H.M.C. *Egmont Diary*, III, 260.

10. Gower's apostasy has been pre-dated to 1742 by historians as varied as Tindal

and J. C. D. Clark, 'The Decline of Party, 1740–60', *E.H.R.*, xciii (1978), 515n. Cf. Thomas Carte to O'Brien, 22 December 1742, R.A. SP 246/72.

11. *Parl. Hist.*, xii, 1053–8, 1068.
12. Hay's Journal, iv. Since both the Newcastle and Hardwicke papers are sparse for the beginning of 1742, the Seaford M.P.'s account is invaluable for a ministerial perspective at this stage. For Wilmington, see Edward Bayntun Rolt's diary for 28 May 1749, Bristol University Library (microfilm). The Prince's subsidies to 'some tories' are noted in B.L. Add. MS. 51437, fols. 2, 8.
13. Pulteney's interview with the King is described by Thomas Newton in *The Lives of Dr. Edward Pocock by Leonard Twells; of Dr. Zachary Pearce and of Dr. Thomas Newton by Themselves and of the Rev. Philip Skelton by Mr. Burdy* (2 vols., 1816), ii, 60–2.
14. Sir Richard Lodge (ed.), *Private Correspondence of Chesterfield and Newcastle 1744–46*, Camden Society, xliv (1930), 20. Chesterfield to Gower, 2 October 1743, P.R.O., 30/29/1/11, fols. 285–6.
15. The tories' moderation at the Fountain Tavern meeting is noted by Archbishop Secker, B.L. Add. MS. 6043, fol. 110. Hay's Journal, iv, quotes Sandys' speech at the meeting. Beaufort to Paston, 18 February 1742, Bodleian Library, MS. Ballard 29, fol. 75; I am grateful to Dr Stephen Baskerville for drawing my attention to this letter.
16. Sedgwick, i, 72.
17. This paragraph is based on Hay's Journal, iv. Beaufort to Paston, 18 February 1742, Bodleian Library, MS. Ballard 29, fol. 75.
18. Egmont's political notes for 4 October 1742, B.L. Add. MS. 47089, fol. 5 (numbered from back of volume).
19. Oxford's journal, 6 April 1742, C.U.L., Add. 6851, fol. 47.
20. *Parl. Hist.*, xii, 543, 649, 723; Hay's Journal, iv.
21. Most of these Instructions and, in some cases, the signatories, were published in *The Second Part of Great Britain's Memorial* (1742).
22. For an extended description of these tory tracts, see Foord, *His Majesty's Opposition*, 234–5.
23. For Newcastle's calculations, see B.L. Add. MS. 32699, fols. 467–8. Sedgwick, i, 103–4, lists eighty-one whig M.P.s still in opposition at the end of 1742: I would omit Ongley, Philipps, and Southwell from this total, as being at this stage tory M.P.s.
24. Sedgwick, i, 55. 'The Younger Grenville wished the Electorate under the Sea', William Hay reported in January 1744, 'and Pitt wished to see it given ... to a younger Branch' (*Hay's Journal*, iv). As well as the Patriot defectors, five tory M.P.s went over to the administration in 1742: the Hon. Henry Bathurst, the Hon. George Compton (who reverted to opposition in co-operation with the tories in the 1750s), Charles Cotes, William Noel, and Sir Charles Wyndham. They all voted for the Hanoverians in December 1742, see *Parl. Hist.*, xii, 1053–8.
25. These are my own calculations based on *C.J.*, xxiv, 337–688.
26. For the 1743 opposition committee, see Owen, *Rise of the Pelhams*, 199 and n.
27. The opposition's negotiations with Pelham and Carteret in 1743–4 can be traced in Lord Oxford's journal, C.U.L., Add. 6851, and *The Case Fairly Stated* (1745), a pamphlet which Oxford judged supplied a 'full and clear' (tory) account. See also H. T. Dickinson, *Bolingbroke* (1970), 282–5; Owen, *Rise of the Pelhams*, 159–238; G. H. Rose (ed.), *A Selection from the Papers of the Earls of Marchmont illustrative of Events from 1685–1750* (3 vols., 1831), i, 10–93.

28. Undated memorandum by Perceval, B.L. Add. MS. 47096 (unfol.); *The Case Fairly Stated*, 6.

29. For reports of tory promotions, see John Campbell to Pryse Campbell, 20 December 1744, N.L.W., MS. 1352B, fols. 247–8; Owen, *Rise of the Pelhams*, 72; Sir Dudley Ryder's political notes, December 1744, *History of Parliament Trust*, Ryder transcripts, 21.R. 145. For Fazakerley and the Lord Chancellorship in the 1730s, see George Harris, *The Life of Lord Chancellor Hardwicke* (3 vols., 1847), I, 363n.

30. Owen, *Rise of the Pelhams*, 240–1; Sir Dudley Ryder's political notes, December 1744, History of Parliament Trust, Ryder transcripts, 21.R. 144.

31. Countess of Cork and Orrery (ed.), *The Orrery Papers* (2 vols., 1903), II, 194. Barrymore to Dr Francis Price, 5 December 1744, N.L.W., Puleston MS. 22, fol. 84.

32. [R. Glover], *Memoirs by a Celebrated Literary and Political Character* (2nd edn, 1814), 35. For Prowse's scepticism about the coalition, see his letter to Sir Charles Kemys Tynte, 1 December 1744, Glamorgan R.O., D/DKT/4.

33. Glover, *Memoirs*, 34. For conflicting interpretations of Gower's conduct, see Dr William King to Lord Orrery, 24 June 1745, Bodleian Library, MS. Eng. Hist. d. 103, fol. 90; Sir Dudley Ryder's political notes, December 1744, History of Parliament Trust, Ryder transcripts, 21.R. 144. For the 1742 re-election riots, see Hay's Journal, IV.

34. Ryder's notes for March 1745, History of Parliament Trust, Ryder transcripts, 21.R. 162: the pamphlet was *An Expostulatory Epistle to the Welch Knight* (1745). *Old English Journal* cited in the *Gentleman's Magazine*, XV (1745), 90; *Christmas Chat: or, Observations on the Late Change at Court* (1745), 6–7.

35. *Parl. Hist.*, XIII, 1057, 1090–1107.

36. Andrew Stone's report to Newcastle, 16 February 1745, B.L. Add. MS. 32704, fols. 72–5; for the debate on the City Election Act, see *Parl. Hist.*, XIII, 1129–30.

37. *The Case Fairly Stated*, 9–10, and cf. Oxford's account of this transaction, C.U.L., Add. 6851, fols. 91–3. For Gower's misinformation, see Chesterfield's letter to him on 13 April N.S. 1745, P.R.O., 30/29/1/11, fol. 290.

38. Both Oxford's journal and *The Case Fairly Stated* give this same nine-point programme. The scabrous *An Address of Thanks to the Broad Bottoms* (1745), 33–5, claimed that Wynn and Somerset also demanded repeal of the Septennial Act and inquiries into the war and the Civil List. It is not clear whether these extra proposals were genuinely believed, or whether a hostile author wished to seduce tory opinion out-of-doors into expecting more than could be obtained.

39. L. K. J. Glassey and Norma Landau, 'The Commission of the Peace in the Eighteenth Century: a New Source', *B.I.H.R.*, XLV (1972), 247–65. Yorke's parliamentary journal as printed in *Parl. Hist.*, XIII, 1244.

40. Sir John Dutton to the earl of Berkeley's secretary, 18 September 1742, Gloucestershire R.O., D678 57D. Hertford to Hardwicke, 12 April 1742, B.L. Add. MS. 35601, fol. 43.

41. *Parl. Hist.*, XIII, 1051–1244.

42. Lord Herbert to Hardwicke, 2 February 1745, B.L. Add. MS. 35602, fol. 34; Owen, *Rise of the Pelhams*, 261–2.

43. For these 1745 fiats and the improvement they represented on the tories' previous county status, see P.R.O., C234/1 (Bedfordshire, 12 July); C234/4 (Cambridgeshire, 28 October); C234/14 (Hampshire, 10 September); C234/15 (Herefordshire, 9 August); C234/21 (Lincolnshire, 30 July); C234/30 (Oxfordshire, 21 September); C234/43 (Yorkshire, North Riding, 21 June). Owen, *Rise of the Pelhams*, 262–3.

44. Robert Tracy to Hardwicke, 25 April 1745, B.L. Add. MS. 35601, fol. 317; for Doneraile, see Owen, *Rise of the Pelhams*, 261.
45. Chesterfield to Newcastle, 27 February 1746, and Newcastle's reply on 5 March, in Lodge (ed.), *Private Correspondence of Chesterfield and Newcastle*, 114, 118.
46. See B.L. Add. MS. 35602, fols. 38, 40, 42, 44, 120, for tory applications for new Commissions for Carmarthenshire, Denbighshire, Montgomeryshire, Pembroke-shire, and Suffolk.
47. Lord Montfort to Hardwicke, 21 June 1745; Lord Malton to Hardwicke, 11 May and 8 June 1745; Lord Oxford to Hardwicke, 13 August 1745, B.L. Add. MS. 35602, fols. 66, 69–70, 85, 114.
48. Dr William King to Lord Orrery, 24 June 1745, Bodleian Library, MS. Eng. Hist. d. 103, fol. 90. For Gower's panic response to the '45, see B.L. Add. MS. 47098B, fol. 10.
49. Notes of Sir Edmund Isham, n.d., Northamptonshire R.O., IL 3953; *Remembrancer*, 18/26 December 1747.
50. Lodge (ed.), *Private Correspondence of Chesterfield and Newcastle*, 108. For Pitt's 1743 asseveration, see John Campbell to Pryse Campbell, 22 January 1743, N.L.W., MS. 1352B, fol. 109.
51. Lord Ilchester, *Henry Fox, First Lord Holland, his Family and Relations* (2 vols., 1920), 1, 131. Of these politicians, Pitt, Barrington, and Legge became Paymaster General, Lord of the Admiralty, and Lord of the Treasury in 1746; George Grenville and Lyttelton had been Lord of the Admiralty and Lord of the Treasury since 1744.
52. Historians who have argued that 1746 completed tory disjunction include Dickinson, *Bolingbroke*, 286; Keith Feiling, *The Second Tory Party 1714–1832* (1938), 44; Foord, *His Majesty's Opposition*, 264n; and Owen, *Rise of the Pelhams*, 257–8. The 1747 estimate – possibly by Lord Sandys – is in Bodleian Library, Dashwood MS. D1/3/13.
53. Wynn to Sir John Hynde Cotton, 16 November 1746 (copy), P.R.O., SP 36/89/267. For the 1746 Hanoverian division, see B.L. Add. MS. 33034, fols. 110–11, and Bodleian Library, MS. D. D. Dashwood, c.12. The Lords Protest is printed in *Parl. Hist.*, XIII, 1412.
54. For post-coalition tory accidie, see James Bonnell to Thomas Hill, 18 July 1745 and 22 October 1747, Salop R.O., Attingham MSS., Box 24. Wynn to Cotton, 16 November 1746, P.R.O., SP 36/89/267.
55. Carew to Lord Orrery, n.d., Somerset R.O., DD/TB/FT 18. This estimate of the tory performance in 1747 is my own, based on Sedgwick, 1, 189–381.
56. Carew to Orrery, n.d., Somerset R.O., DD/TB/FT 18; Newdigate's canvassing diary for 30 April 1747, Greater London R.O., Acc/1085/FP/2 (unfol.).
57. For metropolitan reaction in 1747, see Nicholas Rogers, 'Resistance to Oligarchy: the City Oppositon to Walpole and his Successors, 1725–47', in John Stevenson (ed.), *London in the Age of Reform* (Oxford, 1977), 20–3; Baskerville, 'Tory Interest', 281–6. Ryder's comment is quoted in Sedgwick, 1, 57.
58. Philip to Joseph Yorke, 24 July 1747, B.L. Add. MS. 35363, fol. 179; Sedgwick, 1, 192, 217, 318–21.
59. The declaration is printed in E. N. Williams, *The Eighteenth-Century Constitution 1688–1815* (Cambridge, 1960), 180–1.
60. Kemp, *Sir Francis Dashwood*, 29n. For the Hereford contest, see Cornewall to the Prince, 24 June and 8 July 1747, Buckinghamshire R.O., D/LE/K1/2–3.
61. Frederick to Dr George Lee, n.d., R.A. Georgian MS. 73969; Oxford's journal,

C.U.L., Add. 6851, fol. 122; Yorke's notes on the Carlton House declaration, B.L. Add. MS. 35337, fol. 116.

62. This account of the 1747–8 negotiations is based on the coded correspondence between Richard Powney and Theophilus Leigh. Some of these papers are in Balliol College, Oxford, MS. 403; others are in the possession of Mrs Gwen Beachcroft of Bristol, who kindly gave me access to them. For the tory reply to the Prince, see B.L. Add. MS. 35870, fol. 130.

63. Bayntun Rolt diary, Bristol University Library (microfilm); Reed Browning, *The Duke of Newcastle* (1975), 171–2. I am grateful to Dr W. A. Speck for information on Cumberland's response to the coup of February 1746.

64. These are my own calculations based on *C.J.*, xxv, 481–1103. For estimates of the size of the opposition, see B.L. Add. MS. 35363, fol. 186, and Bayntun Rolt's diary, 28 October 1748, Bristol University Library (microfilm).

65. *H.M.C. Eighth Report*, App., 572, and cf. J. Carswell and L. A. Dralle (eds.), *The Political Journal of George Bubb Dodington* (Oxford, 1965), 45.

66. A. N. Newman, 'Leicester House Politics, 1748–51', *E.H.R.*, LXXVI (1961), 578; Philip C. Yorke, *The Life and Correspondence of Philip Yorke, Earl of Hardwicke* (3 vols., Cambridge, 1913), II, 132. Ross McKibbin's description of many twentieth-century high-political archives may aptly be applied to some of Newcastle's copious remains: 'A sort of elevated gossip which rarely intersected with reality' (*The Evolution of the Labour Party, 1910–24* (1974), 112).

67. Carswell and Dralle (eds.), *Dodington's Journal*, 42; Browning, *The Duke of Newcastle*, 148–93.

68. W. R. Ward, *Georgian Oxford: University Politics in the Eighteenth Century* (Oxford, 1958), 184–5; Paget Toynbee, 'Horace Walpole's "Delenda est Oxonia" ', *E.H.R.*, XLII (1927), 95–108; Sedgwick, II, 511.

69. For accounts of this oration, see David Greenwood, *William King: Tory and Jacobite* (Oxford, 1969), 197–203, and 'The Opening of the Radcliffe Library in 1749', *Bodleian Library Quarterly Record*, I (1915), 165–72.

70. For Frederick's attempts to conciliate tory opinion, see Carswell and Dralle (eds.), *Dodington's Journal*, xix; George Heathcote to Dr Lee, 12 October 1750, Buckinghamshire R.O., D/LE/C3/13. For tory–Jacobite disillusionment with Charles Edward, see William King, *Political and Literary Anecdotes of his own Times* (2nd edn, 1819), 196–209.

71. Theophilus Leigh to the dowager duchess of Chandos, 5 May 1749, Balliol College, Oxford, MS. 403.

72. *Ibid.* Cf. the Jacobite Carte's deliberate underestimate of the significance of the St Albans meeting, Sedgwick, I, 76.

73. For Egmont's comments on Berkeley, Pitt, and Chaffin, see A. N. Newman (ed.), 'Leicester House Politics, 1750–60', *Camden Miscellany*, XXIII (1969), 132, 137; for Shaftesbury's club, P.R.O., 30/24/28, Pt I, fol. 64. Bayntun Rolt got Egmont exactly right: 'Excessive vanity', he noted in his diary in September 1750, 'no knowledge of men – thinks he shall be prime minister etc.', Bristol University Library (microfilm). For Frederick's contacts with metropolitan politics, see Newman (ed.), 'Leicester House Politics, 1750–60', 188–9; B.L. Add. MS. 47012A, fol. 20; and Carswell and Dralle (eds.), *Dodington's Journal*, 60–1.

74. *C.J.*, xxv, 1030; *Gentleman's Magazine*, xx (1750), 425. For the King's Arms Club, see David Erskine (ed.), *Augustus Hervey's Journal, 1746–59* (1953), 80.

75. *C.J.*, xxv, 769, 773–7, 839, 937, 968. For Morton, see Lionel Cust (ed.), *Records of the Cust Family*, Series III (1927), 137–8, and for Gray, Newman (ed.), 'Leicester House Politics, 1750–60', 180–2.

76. Cited in Williams, *Eighteenth-Century Constitution*, 181–2.
77. See Newman (ed.), 'Leicester House Politics, 1750–60', 115–16, and B.L. Add. MS. 47012A, fols. 72–6, for Egmont's schemes for tory advancement. Some Leicester House men objected: see Bayntun Rolt's diary account of a conversation with Dodington's friend, Robert Henley, in October 1750, Bristol University Library (microfilm).
78. Newman (ed.), 'Leicester House Politics, 1750–60', 116, 142; Fazakerley to Thomas Prowse, 11 January 1748, Walton Hall, Prowse Memoranda, fol. 55.
79. For the tories' early hopes from the Princess Dowager's dislike of the Pelhams, see *H.M.C. Eighth Report*, App., 572. Pitt's approach to the opposition and his re-entry into polite tory society after 1749 can be traced in Sedgwick, I, 60, and the London diary of the tory debutante Ireland Greene, printed in R. Stewart-Brown, *Isaac Greene, a Lancashire Lawyer of the Eighteenth Century* (Liverpool, 1921). I am indebted to Dr Stephen Baskerville for this latter reference.
80. James Ralph to the earl of Harley [sic], 10 May 1751 (copy), Bodleian Library, MS. D.D.Dashwood (Bucks), I, 1/2/3. See also Carswell and Dralle (eds.), *Dodington's Journal*, 110–11, for tory attempts to prolong the Leicester House connection.
81. Kemp, *Sir Francis Dashwood*, 164; Carswell and Dralle (eds.), *Dodington's Journal*, 114.
82. John Dobson to John Mordaunt, 15 November 1753, Warwickshire R.O., CR 1368, Box 5, fol. 7. For Beckford's association with the duke of Bedford in 1753–4, see Lord John Russell (ed.), *Correspondence of John Fourth Duke of Bedford* (3 vols., 1842–6), II, 150, and Carswell and Dralle (eds.), *Dodington's Journal*, 218.
83. Carswell and Dralle (eds.), *Dodington's Journal*, 184–5, 278–9. Anglo-French tensions in America 1748–56 are analysed by P. Higonnet, 'The Origins of the Seven Years War', *Journal of Modern History*, XL (1968), 57–90, and by T. R. Clayton, 'The Duke of Newcastle, the Earl of Halifax, and the American Origins of the Seven Years War', forthcoming.
84. Horatio Walpole to Lord Hartington, 10 October 1754, Chatsworth House, Devonshire MSS., Box 7, and cf. his opinion in July 1753; 'The Tories are not inconsiderable in numbers, but for want of heads and hearts, and *the plausible pretext of patriotism*, they are loose, disconcerted, and a band incapable of acting' cited in William Coxe, *Memoirs of Horatio, Lord Walpole* (1802), 431–2 (my italics). [J. Butler], *An Address to the Cocoa-Tree, from a Whig* (3rd edn, 1762), 6.

CHAPTER 10

1. John Almon, *A Review of the Reign of George II* (2nd edn, 1762), 258; Horace Walpole, *Memoirs of the Reign of King George III*, ed. Sir Denis Le Marchant (4 vols., 1845), I, 5; Derek Jarrett, 'The Regency Crisis of 1765', *E.H.R.*, LXXXV (1970), 282. The description of Pelham's ministry is Keith Feiling's, *The Second Tory Party 1714–1832* (1938), 48.
2. J. C. D. Clark, 'The Decline of Party, 1740–60', *E.H.R.*, XCIII (1978), 499–527, *passim*.
3. *Ibid.* 514, 516–17; for the use and validity of 'New Toryism' accusations after 1760, see I. R. Christie, *Myth and Reality in Late-Eighteenth-Century British Politics* (1970), 196–213.
4. Clark, 'The Decline of Party', 523, 526. It is not clear how the tories could at

one and the same time derive their identity from Jacobitism *and* have their 'distinctive Patriot platform' pre-empted by Pitt.

5. Quoted in L. S. Sutherland, 'The City of London and the Devonshire–Pitt Administration, 1756–7', *Proceedings of the British Academy*, XLVI (1960), 160n. Prince George to Bute, November 1760, History of Parliament Trust, Bute transcripts. For the vexed question of George III and his ministers, see John Brewer, *Party Ideology and Popular Politics at the Accession of George III* (Cambridge, 1976), 112–36.

6. Sedgwick, II, 286. Richard Pares, *George III and the Politicians* (Oxford, 1953), 71n.

7. Clark, 'The Decline of Party', 508, 514. For the 1762 fiasco, see Lewis Namier, *England in the Age of the American Revolution* (2nd edn, 1974), 403–15.

8. Namier, *England in the Age of the American Revolution*, 62.

9. Chase Price to the duke of Portland, 'Ye state of ye parties 1 Sept. 1762', from a transcript of one of the Chase Price MSS. at Hatfield House kindly lent me by Professor John Brewer. It was the tory courtiers' separate advancement which worried moderate whigs like the fourth duke of Devonshire, see his political journal for 5 December 1760, Chatsworth House, Devonshire MSS., fol. 90.

10. For this contest and its aftermath, see R. J. Robson, *The Oxfordshire Election of 1754* (Oxford, 1949), *passim*. John Dobson to John Mordaunt, 19 November 1754, Warwickshire R.O., CR 1368 Box 6 V/9; Peregrine Palmer to ?, 27 November 1754, Bodleian Library, Top. Oxon. c. 209, fols. 25–8.

11. Samuel Martin's memoranda, 6 and 4 December 1754, B.L. Add. MS. 41355, fol. 28 (my italics), and see fol. 23 for his analysis of Pitt's current tactics. For Lee and the tories, see James, Earl Waldegrave, *Memoirs from 1754 to 1758* (1821), 153, and Fox to Hartington, 8 November 1754, Chatsworth House, Devonshire MSS., 330.28.

12. Lewis Namier, *The Structure of Politics at the Accession of George III* (2nd edn, 1970), 200, 203.

13. Gordon to Newcastle, 17 December 1754, B.L. Add. MS. 32737, fol. 454.

14. See Dupplin's list of the new Parliament, c. May 1754, B.L. Add. MS. 33034, fols. 173–81. For a detailed account of the Mitchell dispute and the final division list, see Linda Colley, 'The Mitchell Election Division, 24 March 1755', *B.I.H.R.*, XLIX (1976), 80–107.

15. Edward Bayntun Rolt's diary for 10 March 1755, Bristol University Library (microfilm). Richard Blacow to Thomas Bray, 8 March 1755, Exeter College, Oxford, Bray MSS. Horace Walpole, *Memoirs of the Last Ten Years of the Reign of George the Second* (2 vols., 1822), I, 376–7.

16. Boscawen to Newcastle, 20 March 1755, B.L. Add. MS. 32853, fol. 395. For Henley Ongley's independence, see Namier & Brooke, II, 606.

17. Digby to Lord Ilchester, [25] March 1755, B.L. Add. MS. 51340, fol. 110. In 'The Decline of Party', 506n, Clark comments 'Mitchell was not an example of "duplicity", as Miss Colley suggests, but a belated adherence to a generalized commitment to Newcastle.' But from a Foxite viewpoint, the behaviour of some tories was indeed treacherous, while Sir Roger Newdigate argued that there was no widespread tory commitment to Newcastle, however 'generalised'; see his journal for 24 March 1755, Warwickshire R.O., CR 136/A (585).

18. *C.J.*, XXVIII, 291.

19. *A Third Letter to the People of England* (3rd edn, 1756), 60. For an account of these foreign policy developments, see Reed Browning, *The Duke of Newcastle* (1975), 206–30.

20. J. Carswell and L. A. Dralle (eds.), *The Political Journal of George Bubb Dodington* (Oxford, 1965), 326.

21. I estimate that the average age of tory M.P.s in 1755 was between forty-four and forty-five.

22. L. S. Sutherland and J. Binney, 'Henry Fox as Paymaster General of the Forces', *E.H.R.*, LXX (1955), 254.

23. Carswell and Dralle (eds.), *Dodington's Journal*, 310. For the Pitt–Leicester House negotiations, see W. H. Smyth, *Aedes Hartwellianae* (2 vols., 1864), II, 146–7.

24. Thomas Prowse to Pitt, 29 September 1755, P.R.O., 30/8/53, Pt II, fol. 337. For a list of the thirty whigs who voted against the Address in November 1755, see B.L. Add. MS. 33034, fol. 208: it also includes John Morton, whom I would count as a tory M.P. For the 1755 pre-sessional meetings, see Browning, *The Duke of Newcastle*, 227.

25. See J. R. Western, *The English Militia in the Eighteenth Century: the Story of a Political Issue 1660–1802* (1965), esp. 77–205; E. N. Williams, *The Eighteenth-Century Constitution 1688–1815* (Cambridge, 1960), 180; and for the 1752 initiative, *Parl. Hist.*, XIV, 1204.

26. Townshend's original bill is printed in Sheila Lambert (ed.), *House of Commons Sessional Papers of the Eighteenth Century* (147 vols., Wilmington, Del., 1975–76), X, 69–123.

27. Newcastle to White, 17 August 1758, B.L. Add. MS. 32882, fol. 398; *C.J.*, XXVIII, 913, 919.

28. *A Second Letter to the People of England* (1755), 22–3. C. Kirby, 'The English Game Law System', *American Historical Review*, XXXVIII (1932–3), 253–4, and see F. G. Stephens and E. Hawkins, *Catalogue of Prints and Drawings in the British Museum* (5 vols., 1870–1935), III.ii, 980–1.

29. See E. P. Thompson's remarks on the Wilkites and republicanism, 'Eighteenth-Century English Society: Class Struggle without Class?', *Social History*, III (1978), 160–1.

30. *An Alarm to the People of England* (1757), 26. For the *Monitor*'s support of a militia, see Nicholas Rogers, 'London Politics from Walpole to Pitt: Patriotism and Independency in an Era of Commercial Imperialism, 1738–63' (unpub. D.Phil. dissertation, Toronto University, 1974), 185, and see *A Letter from a Country Gentleman, to his Neighbour in Gloucestershire* (Bristol, 1758). *Universal Magazine* cited in Kirby, 'English Game Law System', 261. For contemporary claims that the militia would lead to social insubordination, see Western, *The English Militia*, 109, 286.

31. Bayntun Rolt's diary entry on Kynaston and Guernsey, 5 May 1756, Bristol University Library (microfilm); *C.J.*, XXVIII, 395, 627, 898.

32. W. Percy Hedley, 'An Episode of the Hexham Riots, 9 March 1761', *Proceedings of the Society of Antiquaries, Newcastle-upon-Tyne*, X (1942–6), 233–4; Tony Hayter, *The Army & the Crowd in Mid-Georgian England* (1978), 100, 207 n. 91.

33. For the Minorcan crisis see Browning, *The Duke of Newcastle*, 234–45, and see Marie Peters, *Pitt and Popularity* (Oxford, 1981), 32–58.

34. Most of these protests are printed in *The Voice of the People* (1756); for the campaign and its high-political context, see Sutherland, 'London and the Devonshire–Pitt Administration', 152–9. Robert Phillimore (ed.), *Memoirs and Correspondence of George, Lord Lyttelton* (2 vols., 1845), II, 536.

35. Lord Royston to Hardwicke, 24 August 1756, B.L. Add. MS. 35351, fol. 343. The tory-represented constituencies which submitted Instructions or Addresses

were Buckinghamshire, Cheshire, Devon, Dorset, Essex, Herefordshire, Lancashire, Norfolk, Salop, Somerset, Staffordshire, Suffolk; Boston, Bristol, Chester, Coventry, Exeter, Leominster, London, Maidstone, Nottingham, Oxford, Salisbury, and York.

36. G. B. Hill and L. F. Powell (eds.), *Boswell's Life of Johnson* (6 vols., Oxford, 1934–50), II, 196.

37. Barrington to Newcastle, 7 December 1756, B.L. Add. MS. 32869, fol. 266; Sutherland, 'London and the Devonshire–Pitt Administration', 155.

38. Lord Ilchester, *Henry Fox, First Lord Holland, his Family and Relations* (2 vols., 1920), II, 19. A copy of this whip is amongst Sir Edmund Isham's papers, Northamptonshire R.O., IC. 2918.

39. For Bayntun Rolt's exchange with Sir Edmund Thomas, see his diary for 20 December 1756, Bristol University Library (microfilm); Lichfield to Brudenell Rooke, 13 November 1756, Gloucestershire R.O., D1833 F1/24. Philip C. Yorke, *The Life and Correspondence of Philip Yorke, Earl of Hardwicke* (3 vols., Cambridge, 1913), II, 377.

40. *C.J.*, XXVII, 724, 754, 768.

41. For a tory reaction to the 1756 speech, see E. Hamilton, *The Mordaunts, an Eighteenth-Century Family* (1965), 194; *C.J.*, XXVII, 621–2 and cf. the tory response to the 1754 royal speech, *ibid.* 15. For Philipps' approval of the Address, see W. J. Smith (ed.), *The Grenville Papers: being the Correspondence of Richard Grenville Earl Temple K.G., and the Right Hon. George Grenville* (4 vols., 1852), I, 184.

42. *Parl. Hist.*, XV, 805; *C.J.*, XXVII, 715, 723, 740, 759. For the wine licensing proposals, see Walpole, *Memoirs of the Reign of George II*, II, 194.

43. Newdigate's diary for 14 January and 1 February 1757, Warwickshire R.O., CR 136/A (588); *C.J.*, XXVII, 872. Newcastle's estimate of February 1757 is in B.L. Add. MS. 32997, fols. 101–11. On Legge's disrelish of the tory–Pittite entente, see Sir John Barrow, *The Life of Lord Anson* (1839), 283–4.

44. Josiah Tucker to Forster, 22 December 1756, B.L. Add. MS. 11275, fol. 174; the *Test*, 22 January and 16 April 1757; Browning, *The Duke of Newcastle*, 255.

45. For tory participation in the June 1757 negotiations see Henry Fox to the duke of Cumberland, 10 June 1757, B.L. Add. MS. 51375, fol. 116, and Lord Digby to Sir Charles Hanbury Williams, 12 June 1757, B.L. Add. MS. 9196, fol. 132.

46. Paul Langford, 'William Pitt and Public Opinion, 1757', *E.H.R.*, LXXXVIII (1973), 54–80.

47. These verses were originally published separately as *The Simile* (1759). Langford, 'William Pitt and Public Opinion', 72–7; extract from the *Monitor* printed in Sutherland, 'London and the Devonshire–Pitt Administration', 158.

48. William Beckford to Pitt, 6 November 1756, W. S. Taylor and J. H. Pringle (eds.), *The Correspondence of William Pitt, Earl of Chatham* (4 vols., 1838–40), I, 185; Beckford's December letter is quoted in Rogers, 'London Politics from Walpole to Pitt', 195.

49. Walpole to the Hon. Henry Conway, 19 January 1759, as printed in *Parl. Hist.*, XV, 938; for Northey's reaction to the Pitt–Newcastle agreement, see Bayntun Rolt's diary for 23 June 1757, Bristol University Library (microfilm).

50. Chase Price to the duke of Portland, 1 September 1762 (transcript see above, n.9). The most detailed, if now dated, account of British strategy is J. S. Corbett, *England in the Seven Years' War* (2 vols., 1907).

51. Thomas Potter to William Pitt, n.d. but April 1758, P.R.O., 30/8/53, Pt 1, fol. 98.

52. For tory adulation of Frederick, see *ibid.* and John Shebbeare, *A Letter to the People of England* (1755), 6–7. *C.J.*, xxviii, 318.

53. Bayntun Rolt diary, 4 July 1758, Bristol University Library (microfilm); for Northey's reported disillusionment with Pitt, see Charles Townshend to George Townshend, 13 March 1759, Bodleian Library, MS. Eng. Hist. d. 211, fol. 5. In November 1759 only four tory M.P.s ratified the Royal Speech, *C.J.*, xxviii, 630.

54. William Blackstone to Newdigate, 27 February 1758, Warwickshire R.O., CR 136 B1494. The increasing use of the term 'Country Gentlemen' in this decade is marked, but like 'the Country Party' (above, 283), it is normally used at this stage as a synonym for the tories, *not* for parliamentary 'independents'.

55. Duke of Devonshire's political journal, 30 January 1760, Chatsworth House, Devonshire MSS., fol. 34; *C.J.*, xxviii, 120; for the trained bands, see Rogers, 'London Politics from Walpole to Pitt', 240.

56. Blackstone's promotion was announced in October 1758, *Gentleman's Magazine*, xxviii (1758), 397; for Glynne, see Pitt to Sir Richard Grosvenor, 7 August 1759, Chester City R.O., Grosvenor MSS.

57. Sir John Philipps' letter book, N.L.W., Picton Castle MS. 572, fols. 82, 120.

58. Poulet to Pitt, 29 January 1759 and 'Sunday Evening', June 1758, P.R.O., 30/8/53, Pt 1, fols. 115–16; Western, *The English Militia*, 146–53. Discrimination against tories at J.P. level continued in some counties until the 1760s; see Devonshire's journal entry on the Radnorshire Commission, 5 April 1762, Chatsworth House, Devonshire MSS., fol. 253.

59. *A Letter to the Whigs with some Remarks on a Letter to the Tories* (1762), 16; Paget Toynbee and Leonard Whibley (eds.), *Correspondence of Thomas Gray* (3 vols., Oxford, 1971), ii, 719.

60. There is some disagreement as to which politician was chiefly responsible for advising these tory appointments. Edmund Pyle believed that it was Pitt's doing '& Scotch Bute bears the blame, with the vulgar', while Egmont noted on 16 November 1760 that 'the Duke of Newcastle declared he knew nothing of it, not so much as acquainted with it... At length Bute avowed it to be his measure as he did to me some time after.' Pitt told Devonshire that he had desired a peerage for Grosvenor, but apart from this 'had advis'd ye measure not the men'. Bute himself admitted on 9 December that he had suggested Norborne Berkeley for an appointment; and it seems strange that George Pitt should write to Bute 'entreating yt my services may be offer'd to the King' on 30 November 1760, and that four days later he should be appointed a groom of the bedchamber. A. Hartshorne (ed.), *Memoirs of a Royal Chaplain, 1729–63* (1905), 334; A. N. Newman (ed.), 'Leicester House Politics, 1750–60', *Camden Miscellany*, xxiii (1969), 226; duke of Devonshire's political journal for 12 November and 5 and 9 December 1760, Chatsworth House, Devonshire MSS., fols. 80, 89–95; George Pitt to Bute, 30 November 1760, History of Parliament Trust, Bute transcripts.

61. This estimate is based on a MS. division list, 'An Alphabetical List of the House of Commons... 1 March 1764', Cumbria R.O., D/Lons/L/Acc. 629.

62. Namier, *England in the Age of the American Revolution*, 419–21. I have benefited in my assessment of post-1760 toryism from a seminar paper by Derek Jarrett on the tories 1760–8, delivered at the Institute of Historical Research.

63. For reports of George III's rectitude, see Toynbee and Whibley (eds.), *Gray's Correspondence*, ii, 715; for Lord Bruce, see Lady Anne Egerton to Count

Bentinck, 5 December 1760, B.L. Egerton MS. 1719, fol. 171; for Wodehouse, see Namier & Brooke, III, 652.

64. Lady Anson to Lord Anson, letter begun 2 May 1758, Staffordshire R.O., D615/P(S) 1/2. It is also likely that Leicester House disapproved of the bill; see James Lee McKelvey, *George III and Lord Bute: the Leicester House Years* (Durham, N.C., 1973), 75.

65. Namier & Brooke, III, 336. This calculation is based on 'An Alphabetical List', Cumbria R.O., D/Lons/L/Acc. 629.

66. Paul Langford, 'Old Whigs, Old Tories, and the American Revolution', *Journal of Imperial and Commonwealth History*, VIII (1980), 106–30. For Mackworth, see Namier & Brooke, III, 91. The 1770s assault on the Established Church is well described in W. R. Ward, *Georgian Oxford: University Politics in the Eighteenth Century* (Oxford, 1958), 239–68.

67. Professor Ian Christie has informed me that of the forty-nine M.P.s listed by Namier as tory in 1761 and returned to the 1768–74 Parliament, eight became regular supporters of the Rockingham party. Macaulay's description is quoted in Brewer, *Party Ideology*, 42.

68. Namier & Brooke, II, 328–9.

69. Quoted in Langford, 'Old Whigs, Old Tories, and the American Revolution', 126; Norman Ravitch, 'The Social Origins of French and English Bishops in the Eighteenth Century', *H.J.*, VIII (1965), 319.

CONCLUSION

1. A. P. S. Stanley, *The Life and Correspondence of Thomas Arnold, D.D.* (2 vols., 1844), II, 62.

2. G. R. Elton, *Studies in Tudor and Stuart Politics and Government* (2 vols., Cambridge, 1974), II, 187.

3. M. M. Reese (ed.), *Gibbon's Autobiography* (1970), 16.

4. Iain Bain (ed.), *Memoirs of Thomas Bewick, Written by Himself* (Oxford, 1979), 53. For a development of this argument, see my 'Eighteenth-Century English Radicalism before Wilkes', *T.R.H.S.*, 5th ser., XXXI (1981), 1–19.

5. Benjamin Disraeli, *Sybil; or, The Two Nations* (3 vols., 1845), I, 30. B. W. Hill (ed.), *Edmund Burke on Government, Politics and Society* (1975), 114, and see John Brewer, *Party Ideology and Popular Politics at the Accession of George III* (Cambridge, 1976), 77–95.

APPENDIX, TABLE I

1. *An Exact and Correct List of the Members . . . who Voted for and against the Bill for Repealing the Triennial Act* (1716).

2. Chandler, VIII, App.

3. *Parl. Hist.*, VII, 624–7.

4. *Parl. Hist.*, VIII, 703.

5. *A True List of such Gentlemen of the House of Commons, as Voted for and against . . . the Expense of Twelve Thousand Hessian Troops* (1730).

6. *Supplement to the Protests of the Lords . . .* (1732).

7. *Gentleman's Magazine*, III (1733), 575–80.

8. *A Compleat List of the Members who Voted for and against the bill for Repealing the Septennial Act* (1734).

9. *Gentleman's Magazine*, IX (1739), 304–10.

10. 'List of Members Absent', C.U.L., C(H) MSS., P. 66/10.

11. Chandler, xii, App.

12. 'List of Members Absent', C.U.L., C(H) MSS., P. 66/11.

13. Chandler, xiii, 55–60.

14. *A List of the Members . . . who Voted for and against Taking the Hanover Troops into British Pay* (1742).

15. *A List of the Members . . . 18 January 1743–4*, B.L. 112.f.43.30.

16. Bodleian Library, MS. D.D.Dashwood (Bucks) B6/1/5.

17. See Linda Colley, 'The Mitchell Election Division, 24 March 1755', *B.I.H.R.*, xlix (1976), 80–107.

Index

84130

DATE DUE